Reading for History in the
Damascus Document

Studies on the Texts of the Desert of Judah

VOLUME XLV

EDITED BY
F. Garcia Martínez

ASSOCIATE EDITOR
P. W. Flint

READING FOR HISTORY IN THE
DAMASCUS DOCUMENT

Reading for History in the Damascus Document
A Methodological Study

Maxine L. Grossman

Society of Biblical Literature
Atlanta

READING FOR HISTORY IN THE DAMASCUS DOCUMENT

Copyright © 2002 by Koninklijke Brill NV, Leiden,
The Netherlands

This edition published under license from Koninklijke Brill NV, Leiden, The Netherlands by the Society of Biblical Literature.

All rights reserved. No part of this work may be reproduced or transmitted in any form or by any means, electronic or mechanical, including photocopying and recording, or by any means of any information storage or retrieval system, except as may be expressly permitted by the 1976 Copyright Act or in writing from the Publisher. Requests for permission should be addressed in writing to the Rights and Permissions Department, Koninklijke Brill NV, Leiden, The Netherlands.

Authorization to photocopy items for internal or personal use is granted by Brill provided that the appropriate fees are paid directly to The Copyright Clearance Center, 222 Rosewood Drive, Suite 910, Danvers, MA 01923, USA. Fees are subject to change.

Library of Congress Cataloging-in-Publication Data

Grossman, Maxine L.
   Reading for history in the Damascus document: a methodological study / by Maxine L. Grossman
       p. cm. – (Studies on the texts of the desert of Judah ; v. 45)
   Originally published: Leiden ; Boston : Brill, 2002.
   Includes bibliographical references and index.
   ISBN: 978-1-58983-427-9 (paper binding : alk. paper)
   1. Damascus document. 2. Judaism—History—Post-exilic period, 586 B.C.–210 A.D.—Historiography. I. Title.

BM175.Z3G76   2009
296.1'55—dc22   2009011933

Printed in the United States of America
on acid-free paper

To Hayim

CONTENTS

Preface	ix
List of Abbreviations	xiii

I. Methodology: Toward a Literary-Critical Historiography	1
Reading the Damascus Document	6
Contemporary literary criticism and the Damascus Document	12
Textual meaning, foundation documents and sectarian discourse	24
Toward a 'New Historiography'	37
II. Two Test Cases	42
Case one: querying gender in the Damascus Document	43
Reading for community in the text	52
Case two: history and communal identity in 4QMMT	57
MMT, text and content	61
Reading for history in MMT	65
MMT and the construction of communal history	73
MMT, Torah-truth, and sectarian readings	78
Contextualizing the MMT calendar	85
III. History and Time in the Damascus Document	88
Constructions of history and the second admonition	92
Scriptural parallels for primordial language	98
Concluding the second admonition	101
Narrative history and the first admonition	107
Narrative history in the third admonition	118
History and ideology in the Damascus Document	124
IV. Reading for History and Time in the Damascus Document	127
Focus on covenant formation	129
Sectarian schism as historical marker	132
Endtime expectations and textual development	136
Textual redaction and communal foundations	144

Beyond the first generations 153
Reading for history 160

V. Reading for Identity in the Damascus Document 162
   Priestly imagery in the Damascus Document 167
   Exile, return, and the status of the righteous remnant 177
   Reading for Zadokite identity 185
   History and Zadokite priestly identity 188
   Foregrounding exilic origins 196
   'Zadokite' status in later interpretations 201
   Reading for identity 209

VI. Conclusions and Challenges 210
   The challenge of the medieval manuscripts 212
   History, origins, and covenant-formation 218
   Zadokites, Sadducees, and priestly status 221
   Endtimes expectations and messianic claims 223
   Conclusions and challenges 225

Bibliography 229
Modern Authors 243
Index of Ancient Sources 246
Selected Subject Index 254

PREFACE

In his Introduction to *Behind the Essenes: History and Ideology in the Dead Sea Scrolls*, Philip Davies argues for a critical approach to the reconstruction of the history of the scrolls community. His approach, he asserts, "is not structuralism, nor any variety of 'reader-response' criticism," not because he necessarily disagrees with the use of such methods, but simply because these approaches "do not produce history."[1]

Readers of the present volume will see the influence of Davies' scholarship throughout. I share with him a number of key assumptions: that Qumran pesher cannot be taken only at 'face value,' that the historical claims of the Damascus Document must be read in their larger ideological context, and that individual texts (and even manuscripts) must be read in light of their contradictions and not only their points of harmony. It is ironic, then, that the primary line of analysis in my project should stand in opposition to this claim of Davies'. In fact, I think it *is* possible to 'produce history' while working from a literary critical perspective. A history of this sort may look unfamiliar, but its very difference will provide insights that are not revealed by a more standard historical analysis of the scrolls.

The goal of this book is to introduce an 'alternative' approach to historiography, taking into account some key observations of contemporary literary criticism: that texts are not fixed entities, and that their meanings depend on how they are interpreted; that interpretations of even the most authoritative texts can change over time, depending on audiences' expectations and agendas; and that competing interpretations of a text may arise even in a single interpretive community. Rather than emphasizing the original meaning of the text, associated with its author's 'intention' (a term that will be discussed in the chapters that follow), this approach shifts the historiographical focus. 'History' no longer refers predominantly to the events that led up to the writing of the text (i.e., what lies 'behind' it), but rather to the whole range of events associated with its composition, transmission, and reception. The historical significance of

---

[1] Philip Davies, *Behind the Essenes: History and Ideology in the Dead Sea Scrolls* (Atlanta: Scholars Press, 1987), 11.

the text is considered in dynamic terms, reflected in a shifting analytical focus that takes into account the varying contexts in which the text was read and the varying interpretations of its authoritative claims.

I suggest in my methodological discussion (chapter one) that we might think of such an approach as a 'New Historiography.' Here, I mean less to lay claim to a novelty of practice than to play off the insights of the literary critical approach labeled New Historicism. In their response to New Criticism, the New Historicists swing the pendulum of literary theory away from a focus on 'the text in isolation' and toward a reading of texts in light of their social and historical contexts. My own suggestion is that our historical approach to the Dead Sea Scrolls needs to move away from a view of the scrolls only as 'historical evidence' and toward a recognition that they are, themselves, literary texts presenting ideological constructions of history and not simple statements of fact.

The approach that I advocate involves a multi-stage process. We begin by reading individual texts (or even individual manuscripts) in isolation, attempting to sort out their individual ideological claims. While the ideology of a text may not be transparent, hints of its content are found in the text's selective use of scripture, choice of words and images, constructions of history, and so on. A second stage of analysis asks how the ideology of a given text might have been interpreted (or 'mobilized'), by its original audience and by other readers as well. The competing or contradictory interpretations generated by such a reading can then be assessed—in light of other literary works, material and archaeological evidence, and theoretical reconstructions of historical events—to identify the range of historical accounts that a given text might support.

The 'history' generated by this approach will be neither unitary nor definitive, and readers may be uncomfortable with the tentativeness of my conclusions. But it is hoped that these conclusions will have a salutary (if negative) effect, in showing that *no* single historical reading of the scrolls can be both unitary and definitive. In place of a historical account that is comprehensive and definitive, thinking in terms of 'ranges' of historical probability allows for a new focus of attention. Such a view allows us to recognize the potential for contradiction, fragmentation, and contestation, in the texts that we study and in the communities for whom these texts were foundational. It allows us to think in terms of changes over time and diversity within a single community. And it allows us to recognize our own agendas and ideologies, even as we attempt to sort out those of our ancient sources.

I suggest in the pages that follow that 'texts' are never complete or bounded, but rather that they are always 'multiple.' As a revised dissertation, this book is the product of multiple stages of work, and at each stage I have owed multiple, substantial debts of gratitude. First and foremost, I must thank Robert A. Kraft, Ross S. Kraemer, E. Ann Matter, and David Stern. As a dissertation committee, they proved invaluable, and their guidance and engagement kept me going through the many stages of 'completion' of my dissertation process. My classmates at the University of Pennsylvania and colleagues in the Philadelphia Seminar on Christian Origins asked provocative questions and were willing partners in my effort to think about literary criticism and the ancient world at the same time. Kim Haines-Eitzen and Jonathan Klawans provided the best of 'dissertation conversation' during crucial thinking and writing stages.

The final drafts of the dissertation were completed while I was on the faculty of the Department of Religious Studies at the University of North Carolina at Greensboro. I cannot say enough in praise of my experience at UNCG. The support and encouragement of my colleagues gave me the energy to finish, and the excitement of my students (especially in my spring 1999 Dead Sea Scrolls seminar) reminded me of the joy in the endeavor. Derek Krueger and Pat Bowden deserve an extra thank you, for going above and beyond the call at every turn.

In revising this manuscript, I have benefited from the comments and critiques of a number of generous readers. Robert Kugler, Moshe Bernstein, Cecilia Wassen, John J. Collins, and especially Florentino García Martínez read all or part of the dissertation and provided important advice and correctives. Ross Kraemer, Ann Matter, Susan Marks, and Kim Haines-Eitzen contributed additional insights into the revised gender discussion. Steven Fraade was most generous in sharing his work on MMT, and I am grateful for his many insights.

A number of research grants provided material support for this project. I began my research with the aid of a Mellon Dissertation Award. Early drafts of the dissertation were written under the auspices of the Jewish Studies Program at the University of Washington, thanks to their Hazel D. Cole Fellowship in Jewish Studies. The

Joseph and Rebecca Meyerhoff Center for Jewish Studies at the University of Maryland provided support through a graduate research fellowship in the fall of 1997 and then, in 2000–2001, provided the post-doctoral fellowship that allowed me to revise the dissertation into a book.

In the fall of 2001, I began a longterm position as a Visiting Assistant Professor at the Meyerhoff Center for Jewish Studies at the University of Maryland. I am grateful for the warm welcome that I have received at the center and for the new opportunities for research, teaching, and community that come with this new position.

For all that life in the postmodern world is a fragmentary experience of multiplicity, there are occasional (if ideologically indefensible) moments of wholeness to be found. With that thought in mind, I give my thanks and dedicate this volume to Hayim Lapin. Friend, colleague, and spouse, his confidence in me has given me confidence in myself. I look forward to a future of great adventures together.

LIST OF ABBREVIATIONS

ABD	David Noel Freedman, et al., eds., *Anchor Bible Dictionary* (New York: Doubleday, 1992)
b.	Babylonian Talmud
BA	*Biblical Archaeologist* (now, *Near Eastern Archaeology*)
BAR	*Biblical Archaeology Review*
BDB	Francis Brown, S. R. Driver, and Charles Briggs, eds., *A Hebrew and English Lexicon of the Old Testament* (Oxford: Clarendon Press, 1906)
DJD	Discoveries in the Judaean Desert series
DSD	*Dead Sea Discoveries*
GKC	E. Kautzsch, ed., *Gesenius' Hebrew Grammar* (trans. A. E. Cowley; Oxford: Clarendon Press, 1910)
HTR	*Harvard Theological Review*
HUCA	*Hebrew Union College Annual*
Ioud. Rev.	*Ioudaios Review*
JAAR	*Journal of the American Academy of Religion*
JBL	*Journal of Biblical Literature*
JJS	*Journal of Jewish Studies*
JNES	*Journal of Near Eastern Studies*
JQR	*Jewish Quarterly Review*
JSOT	*Journal for the Study of the Old Testament*
JSSR	*Journal for the Scientific Study of Religion*
m.	Mishnah
JTS	*Journal of Theological Studies*
NTS	*New Testament Studies*
OTP	James H. Charlesworth, ed., *The Old Testament Pseudepigrapha* (2 vol.; Garden City, N.Y.: Doubleday, 1983, 1985)
RB	*Revue Biblique*
RevQ	*Revue de Qumran*
VT	*Vetus Testamentum*
ZAW	*Zeitschrift für die alttestamentliche Wissenschaft*

CHAPTER ONE

METHODOLOGY: TOWARD A LITERARY-CRITICAL HISTORIOGRAPHY

In the last hundred years, since its discovery in the Cairo Genizah,[1] and especially in the fifty years since the discovery of the Dead Sea Scrolls,[2] the Damascus Document has been read by scholars as an important window into the history of ancient Judaism and ancient Jewish sectarian movements. In its most complete witness, the text

---

[1] The first known witnesses to the Damascus Document (CD) were discovered in the Cairo Genizah in the late nineteenth century and were brought to Cambridge by Solomon Schechter in 1896. Although recognized as pages from two different codices, the two manuscripts (labeled MSS A and B) were numbered sequentially. Thus, MS A, dated to the 10th century, is said to contain CD 1–16, while MS B, dated to the 12th century, is said to contain CD 19–20 (pages 17 and 18 are missing from the numbering of the texts). Scholars have since concluded that CD 15–16 appropriately is placed between CD 8 and CD 9. The overlaps of MSS A and B (including partial duplications, as well as significant variants) are discussed at length below. The original publication of the two manuscripts was in Solomon Schechter, *Fragments of a Zadokite Work* (Cambridge: Cambridge University Press, 1910), reprinted with a 'Prolegomenon' in Joseph Fitzmyer, ed., *Documents of Jewish Sectaries* (New York: Ktav, 1970). The text assumed by this study is that of Joseph Baumgarten and Daniel Schwartz, 'Damascus Document (CD),' in *Damascus Document, War Scroll, and Related Documents* (ed. James H. Charlesworth; vol. 2 of *The Dead Sea Scrolls: Hebrew, Aramaic, and Greek Texts with English Translations*; Louisville: Westminster John Knox Press, 1995), 4–57. Other important recent publications of the text include Florentino García Martínez and Eibert J. C. Tigchelaar, eds., *The Dead Sea Scrolls Study Edition* (Boston: Brill and Grand Rapids, Mich.: Eerdmans, 2000), 1.550–81 (Hebrew text with translation); and Magen Broshi, ed., *The Damascus Document Reconsidered* (Jerusalem: Israel Exploration Society, 1992), a facsimile edition with transcription and notes. A history of the publication of the Damascus Document and a concise but thorough discussion of its primary witnesses, character, and content can now be found in Charlotte Hempel, *The Damascus Texts* (Sheffield: Sheffield Academic Press, 2000); for additional bibliography, see Fitzmyer, *Documents*, 25–34; Florentino García Martínez, 'Damascus Document: A Bibliography of Studies 1970–89,' in Broshi, *Damascus Document Reconsidered*, 63–83; and Baumgarten and Schwartz, 'CD,' 8–9. See also the recent discussions in Joseph Baumgarten, Esther Chazon, and Avital Pinnick, eds., *The Damascus Document, A Centennial of Discovery: Proceedings of the Third International Symposium of the Orion Center for the Study of the Dead Sea Scrolls and Associated Literature, 4–8 February, 1998* (Boston: Brill, 2000).

[2] Among the Dead Sea Scrolls, scholars have identified fragments of ten Damascus Document manuscripts: 4Q266–273, 5Q12, and 6Q15. For the cave four texts, see Joseph Baumgarten, ed., *Qumran Cave 4.XIII: The Damascus Document (4Q266–273)* (DJD XVIII; Oxford: Clarendon Press, 1996), and now García Martínez and

contains a collection of sermons, scriptural exegeses, and legal pronouncements, which articulate the specifics of a covenant between God and the righteous remnant of the people of Israel. This remnant, who have gathered together on the eve of the endtimes, look backward over their shoulders to a scriptural heritage while also looking forward to the end of the time of wickedness and the beginning of (or return to) a sacred time in which they will live in the eternal presence of God.

In presenting their accounts of communal history, the sermons and laws of the Damascus Document tap into scriptural language, as well as a number of primary scriptural motifs: the power and responsibility of God's loyal priesthood; the importance of covenant, as a part of both the ancient and the more recent past; the notion of exile, as a communal experience and possibly a place of origin; and especially the identity of the true Israel. These motifs contribute to the construction of various identities for the members of the community, who are imagined collectively as participants in a new covenant, established in the land of Damascus by the penitents of Israel, who have departed from the land of Judah.

Much can be said about this covenant community. They are assumed to be well-versed in scripture and conscious of the immediate and practical implications of ancient prophecies. They have a conflict with certain other Jewish groups, who fail to understand scripture appropriately, and whose standing in God's world is problematic. And they are in expectation of a significant and immediate change in the state of the world.

At the same time, there are some details we do not know about this group. Their names, locations, and family lineages are, for example, quite absent from the text, although a line in one of the admonitions implies that such material once appeared there.[3] The names

---

Tigchelaar, *Study Edition*, 1.580–627. For the materials from caves five and six (as well as preliminary publications of some cave four material), see Joseph Baumgarten and Michael Davis, 'Cave IV, V, VI Fragments,' in Charlesworth, *Damascus Document, War Rule, and Related Documents*, 59–79; García Martínez and Tigchelaar, *Study Edition*, 2.1134–35, 1152–55. Of additional interest is 4Q265 (4QSD), a text that shows affinity to both the Community Rule and the Damascus Document. See Joseph Baumgarten, 'C. Miscellaneous Rules,' in *Qumran Cave 4.XXV: Halakhic Texts* (ed. Joseph Baumgarten, et al.; DJD XXXV; Oxford: Clarendon Press, 1999), 57–78. For a discussion of 4Q265 and it relevant publications, see Hempel, *Damascus Texts*, 90–104.

[3] CD 4.4–6, following translation by Schwartz: "Here are the detail(s) of their

of the group's founders, leaders, and opponents also are missing from the text, although we know of some of these figures from their coded nicknames: the 'Teacher of Righteousness,' the 'Spouter of Lies,' and the 'Builders of the Barrier,' among others.[4] And, for all that the text mentions a series of historical periods (including 390 years from the Babylonian conquest of Judah to the founding of the group, and another 20 years between that time and the arrival of their teacher),[5] we have little transparent information with regard to when and where the covenant community was founded, and in what sorts of social settings it may have developed and flourished.

The Damascus Document's construction of history presents a conundrum for scholars of ancient Judaism. On the one hand, the text provides important evidence for Jewish religious development and communal conflicts in the last few centuries before the common era. On the other hand, the evidence presented by this text (and others like it) is so allusive and so open to interpretation that it often confuses as much as it clarifies. Attempts to write historical accounts from these narratives stand vulnerable, consequently, to a number of common pitfalls: the danger of taking the accounts of these texts too literally (as transparent fact, rather than as an ideological construction), the danger of taking scriptural allusions as references to historical events, and the danger of harmonizing diverse accounts in an attempt to create a coherent picture.[6]

---

names (פרוש שמותיהם) in their generations and the time(s) of their standing (קץ מעמדם) and the number(s) of their troubles (מספר צרותיהם) and the years of their residence and the detail(s) of their works (פירוש מעשיהם)." See Baumgarten and Schwartz, 'CD,' 19 n. 32.

[4] For "Teacher of Righteousness" (מורה צדק), see CD 1.11; a related expression is "unique teacher" (מורה היחיד), found in CD 20.1, 20.14. Opponents of the righteous include the "man of mockery" (איש הלצון), in CD 1.14, who is associated with the "spouting" or "spitting" (הטיף) of false teachings, in CD 1.14–15; the "builders of the barrier" (בוני החיץ), who are similarly associated with this false "spouting" in CD 4.19–20; and the "man of the lie" (איש הכזב), in CD 20.15. See also CD 8.13, 8.18, 19.24–25, and 19.31.

[5] A remnant of Israel arises some 390 years after the beginning of the Babylonian exile, CD 1.5–6; the remnant wanders without a leader for 20 years, before the teacher arises, CD 1.10; in a very different context, we learn that the time from the 'gathering in' of the teacher until the destruction of the men of war is 40 years, CD 20.15.

[6] I use the word 'scripture' as a generalized term for those texts that had achieved a state of significant importance for members of the covenant community. This approach recognizes that certain texts were held as central and authoritative while allowing for the fact that the boundaries of the 'biblical canon' were still in flux at

The goal of this book is to articulate a reading strategy that addresses some of these interpretive conflicts, providing the basis for an alternative approach to historiography based upon this text and others like it.[7] My reading strategy in this project is two-fold. It begins with the understanding that a scholarly construction of history based on this text must take seriously the text's larger understandings and constructions of history and must contextualize those constructions, rather than merely 'mining' the text for out-of-context readings of significant images. A second, and more radical, aspect of this reading strategy involves a shift of focus, away from the 'original meaning' of the text and toward a discussion of a construction *and reconstruction* of meaning in readings of the text, throughout the history of its use.

This approach can be understood as radical because it brings with it a significant shift in historiographical practice. Instead of writing historical accounts that focus only on the events 'behind' the text (those that inspired its writing or are reflected, however problematically, in its narratives), this approach also emphasizes the historical significance of events that occur after the text is composed: the adaptations and interpretations of it by a variety of audiences, and the development of new understandings of history based on those adaptations. Together, these reading strategies contribute to an alternative approach to the scholarly practice of historiography, understood here not only as the writing of historical accounts based upon these texts, but also as the evaluation of such accounts, in terms of their ability to make sense of the evidence in productive and responsible ways.[8]

In understanding the various readings of the Damascus Document as historical 'moments' or 'events' in themselves, this project makes

---

the time of the Damascus Document's composition. For a brief state-of-the-field discussion of the biblical canon in contemporary scrolls research, see Adam van der Woude, 'Fifty Years of Qumran Research,' in *The Dead Sea Scrolls After Fifty Years: A Comprehensive Assessment* (ed. Peter Flint and James VanderKam; 2 vols.; Boston: Brill, 1998–1999), 1.39–44.

[7] For a discussion of 'textual strategies,' as part of the complex process of meaning-construction, see Josué Harari, 'Critical Factions/Critical Fictions,' in *Textual Strategies: Perspectives in Post-Structuralist Criticism* (ed. Josué Harari; Ithaca: Cornell University Press, 1979), 17–72.

[8] My understanding of historiography and the modern literary production of historical narratives is grounded, to a great extent, in the insights of Hayden White and Michel Foucault. See the discussion and bibliographical references below.

several theoretical claims with regard to texts, reading, and cultural formation. First, the arguments presented in a text that receives ongoing use cannot be understood as static, unitary, or transparent. Although in its original setting a text may be intended to present a specific view, this in no way ensures that the text will be understood in terms of its original claims whenever it is read or interpreted. The more complex and multivalent a text, the greater its potential to be understood in diverse ways, including ways that may contradict the original agenda(s) of its original author(s) or editor(s). Second, in interpreting a text's specific agenda, an audience simultaneously engages in mobilizing the text toward a (potentially new) set of arguments or claims. In this way, a text whose meaning is shaped first by its author(s) or editor(s) and by its initial audience can go on to shape (and repeatedly be shaped by) the communities that read and interpret it in later periods. From this perspective, 'the meaning' of a text is determined not only by its content but also by the assumptions of its audiences and their readings in light of their own knowledge, agendas, needs, and concerns.

Writing history based on this sort of textual reading involves something of a shift of focus, away from the 'original meaning' of a text (which scholars tend to understand as unitary and often associate with its author's original intentions) and toward a foregrounding of the qualities of textual meaning that are incomplete, allusive, and constantly in need of activation by a text's audience or audiences. What is at work in this project, in other words, is an approach to historiography that is grounded in contemporary literary criticism, especially in terms of its insights with regard to the constructions of textual meaning, the roles of audiences in shaping the meanings that are given to texts, and the place of power and authority in such constructions of textual meaning. By turning from a focus on an original textual meaning to an approach that addresses the potential both for *multiple* 'original' meanings and also for ongoing changes in textual meaning over time, this literary critical project lays the groundwork for an alternative approach to history, as well. According to this alternative historiography, an audience's experience of a text (and the ability of the audience members to mobilize such readings toward ends of their own) is as much a subject for historical analysis as are the events or issues of which the author/editor(s) of the text originally claimed to speak.

Reading the Damascus Document

From the time of its initial discovery a century ago, the historical value of the Damascus Document—and the identity of the community with which it is associated—has been a point of discussion among scholars of ancient Judaism. Early in the period of modern scholarship on this text, there was a tendency either to take its historical claims as basically straightforward or to reject them outright as a literary invention. In part, this dichotomy of extremes had to do with the lack of comparative context available to scholars of the text. In the period before the discovery of the Dead Sea Scrolls, grounding the covenantal and historical claims of the Damascus Document required reading the text in light of the known evidence for ancient Judaism: the canonical scriptures, apocrypha, and pseudepigrapha; Josephus' historical accounts and his descriptions of the sectarian Jewish movements of the Second Temple period; and evidence from rabbinic texts and the New Testament.

This contextual evidence defined the primary categories of discussion and provided the potential identifications for the community, so that in the course of scholarly analysis the Damascus covenanters were variously identified by scholars with the Sadducees, Pharisees, or other known groups.[9] Some scholars presented the view that this text was the work of a previously unknown ancient Jewish movement.[10] In addition, scholars noted the potential for theological or historical connections with the Karaite tradition,[11] especially as reported

---

[9] For a discussion of pre-Qumran scholarship on the Damascus Document, see Philip Davies, *The Damascus Covenant: An Interpretation of the "Damascus Document"* (Sheffield: JSOT Press, 1983), 1–14, 205–6; and the fascinating and sometimes scathing literature review in Louis Ginzberg, *An Unknown Jewish Sect* (New York: Jewish Theological Seminary of America, 1976; trans. and revision of *Eine unbekannte jüdische Sekte*, New York, 1922), 304–37. Ginzberg's review discusses the treatments of some 25 different scholars, most from the first few years after Schechter's 1910 publication of the text. In that period, the text was linked (directly or indirectly) with the Hasidim (Charles, Meyer); the Pharisees (Ginzberg, Gressmann); a reforming Sadducean movement (Schechter, Adler, Bacher, Levi, Leszynsky, Charles again); and a Sadducean Christian movement (Margoliouth); among others. Also see Schechter's discussion, reprinted in Fitzmyer, *Documents*, 50–61.

[10] Lagrange, for example, identifies the covenanters as an apocalyptic priestly community without connections to previously-known Jewish sectarian movements. See Davies, *Damascus Covenant*, 10–11; Ginzberg, *Unknown Jewish Sect*, 320–21; as well as M.-J. Lagrange, 'La secte juive de la Nouvelle Alliance au pays de Damas,' *RB* 9 (1912): 358–60.

[11] For a recent summary discussion, see Nathan Schur, 'Dead Sea Scrolls,' in

in the accounts of Qirqisani.¹² For scholars with this perspective, the text was undoubtedly the product of a medieval Jewish authorship, whose use of scriptural language and claims of ancient origins reflected an invention rather than a historical reality.¹³

After the discovery of the Dead Sea Scrolls, some fifty years later, scholarly attention toward the Damascus Document was renewed, this time in the context of significant new evidence and a range of new scholarly theories. In literary terms, the scrolls provided an array of manuscripts with similar outlooks and literary forms, as well as additional manuscript fragments of the Damascus Document itself, including some previously-unknown passages of that text.¹⁴ New scholarly

---

The Karaite Encyclopedia (New York: Peter Lang, 1995). See also Naphtali Wieder, *The Judean Scrolls and Karaism* (London: Horovitz Publishing, 1962); Wieder, 'The Qumran Sectarians and the Karaites,' *JQR* 47 (1956/57): 97–113, 269–92; and S. Szyszman, 'A propos du Karaïsme et des textes de la Mer Morte,' *VT* 2 (1952): 343–48.

¹² See the translation presented in Leon Nemoy, 'Al-Qirqisani's Account of the Jewish Sects and Christianity,' *HUCA* 7 (1930): 326. See chapter six for further discussion of Qirqisani. Wacholder uses this text as an element in his identification of the Teacher of Righteousness as the historical figure Zadok. See Ben Zion Wacholder, *The Dawn of Qumran: The Sectarian Torah and the Teacher of Righteousness* (Cincinnati: Hebrew Union College Press, 1983), 141–69.

¹³ This view is taken by Büchler, Marmorstein, and most vociferously, Zeitlin; the discussion can be followed in the pages of *JQR*. Responses to Schechter's publication of the text include M. H. Segal, 'Additional Notes on "Fragments of a Zadokite Work,"' *JQR* 3 (1912/13): 301–11; Adolph Büchler, 'Schechter's "Jewish Sectaries,"' *JQR* 3 (1912/13): 429–85; and Solomon Schechter, 'Reply to Dr. Büchler's Review of Schechter's "Jewish Sectaries,"' *JQR* 4 (1913/14): 449–74. See also Solomon Zeitlin, 'The Pharisees,' *JQR* 16 (1926): 383–94, where a review of R. Travers Herford, *The Pharisees* (New York: Macmillan, 1924) provides Zeitlin with the opportunity to argue for the medieval origins of the Damascus Document and to discuss the earlier scholarship of Büchler and Ginzberg; see esp. 385. In the period after the discovery of the Dead Sea Scrolls (when he was an editor of *JQR*), Zeitlin's denial of the antiquity of these texts—both CD and the Qumran manuscripts—became increasingly intensive. See especially P. R. Weis, 'The Date of the Habakkuk Scroll,' *JQR* 41 (1950): 125–53, with an editor's note by Zeitlin, 153–54; Solomon Zeitlin, 'The Hebrew Scrolls: A Challenge to Scholarship,' *JQR* 41 (1951): 251–75; Millar Burrows, 'Concerning the Dead Sea Scrolls,' *JQR* 42 (1951): 105–32; and Solomon Zeitlin, 'The Hebrew Scrolls and the Status of Biblical Scholarship,' *JQR* 42 (1951): 133–92. From the same period, see also the literature review and summary discussion in Solomon Zeitlin, 'Introduction,' in *The Zadokite Fragments: Facsimile of the Manuscripts in the Cairo Genizah Collection in the Possession of the University Library, Cambridge, England* (Philadelphia: Dropsie College for Hebrew and Cognate Learning, 1952), 1–32. Additional discussions of these disputes can be found in Davies, *Damascus Covenant*, 14; and Ginzberg, *Unknown Jewish Sect*, 338–408, who offers an extensive refutation of the Karaite hypothesis associated with Büchler.

¹⁴ These include additional introductory and concluding passages, as well as an additional admonition and a significant body of previously unknown legal material.

theories on the history and development of a so-called Qumran community also tended to pay attention to the Damascus Document, if only in order to explain its presence in this collection of texts, and to hypothesize on the place of a Damascus covenant community in the larger narrative of Qumran origins.

A widely-accepted interpretation of this evidence (which is now in a second-generation stage of deconstruction and reconsideration)[15] led to the classical 'Essene Hypothesis,' which constructs an account based on the historical claims of the scrolls (especially the Damascus Document and the pesher texts), understood in light of the literary descriptions of an Essene sectarian movement provided in the writings of Pliny, Josephus, and Philo.[16] In the context of this sort of reading—which draws on Pliny in locating a celibate, all-male 'Essene' community at the site of Khirbet Qumran, and which utilizes Josephus' descriptions of celibate and marrying Essenes to distinguish between groups associated with the Community Rule and the Damascus Document respectively—scholars narrowed the range of possible readings of the Damascus Document, creating a handful of related pictures of the text's covenant community.[17]

For a summary of the significance of these passages to our larger understanding of the Damascus Document, see Baumgarten, DJD XVIII, 1–22, esp. 6–7.

[15] For a reconsideration of the classical Essene hypothesis, see Davies, *Behind the Essenes*, 15–31; more recently, see the collection of essays in Davies, *Sects and Scrolls: Essays on Qumran and Related Topics* (Atlanta: Scholars Press, 1996); and Davies, 'Was there Really a Qumran Community?' in *Currents in Research: Biblical Studies* 3 (1995): 9–35. Examples of influential alternatives to (or revisions of) the classical Essene hypothesis include Florentino García Martínez, 'Qumran Origins and Early History: A Groningen Hypothesis,' *Folia Orientalia* 25 (1988): 113–35; Hartmut Stegemann, 'The Qumran Essenes—Local Members of the Main Jewish Union in Late Second Temple Times,' in Julio Barrera and Luis Montaner, eds., *The Madrid Qumran Congress: Proceedings of the International Congress on the Dead Sea Scrolls; Madrid, 18–21 March, 1991* (New York: Brill, 1992), 83–166, expanded and elaborated in Stegemann, *The Library of Qumran: On the Essenes, Qumran, John the Baptist, and Jesus* (New York: Brill and Grand Rapids, Mich.: Eerdmans, 1998), esp. 139–210; and Lawrence Schiffman, *Reclaiming the Dead Sea Scrolls: The History of Judaism, the Background of Christianity, the Lost Library of Qumran* (Philadelphia: Jewish Publication Society, 1994). A very different reading of the evidence is found in Norman Golb, *Who Wrote the Dead Sea Scrolls? The Search for the Secret of Qumran* (New York: Scribner, 1995).

[16] The relevant ancient passages include Pliny the Elder, *Nat. Hist.*, 5.73; Philo, *Every Good Man is Free*, 75–91, *Hypoth.*, second extract, 8.11.1–18, and *Cont. Life* (which presents the Therapeutae as a foil to the Essenes); Josephus, *War* 2.119–61, and *Ant.*, 13.171–72, 18.11, and 18.18–22. For Josephus' reference to 'marrying Essenes,' see *War* 2.160–61. See also Geza Vermes and Martin Goodman, eds., *The Essenes According to the Classical Sources* (Sheffield: JSOT Press, 1989).

[17] For contemporary presentations of this approach, see Geza Vermes, *The Complete*

Although modern readings of the Damascus Document's historical claims are remarkably wide-ranging, they tend to cluster into several varieties. One approach to these references, which might be termed a 'maximalist' view, takes them as basically historically transparent, suggesting that—in line with the narrative of the text—the community arose some 390 years after the Babylonian conquest of Judah in the early sixth century BCE and departed from Judah and dwelt in Damascus while waiting the time of God's ultimate judgment of humanity.[18] From this perspective, the evidence of the text can be accepted as 'basically reliable' in its historical claims, at least until proven otherwise.[19] This approach allows for the most straightforward historical reconstructions, but it brings with it a number of major methodological pitfalls. First, an out-of-context reading of the text's temporal details may lead scholars to interpretations that fail to correspond with its larger literary structures and primary themes. Second, such a reading runs the risk of being inappropriately credulous, generating an interpretation that is understood as historical but in fact merely restates the text's own ideological claims and constructs (which, themselves, may or may not correspond to a series of real historical events).[20]

Dead Sea Scrolls in English (New York: Penguin Books, 1997), 26–66, esp. 'Appendix: The Essenes and the Qumran Community,' 46–48; James VanderKam, *The Dead Sea Scrolls Today* (Grand Rapids, Mich.: Eerdmans Publishing, 1994), 71–92; Lester Grabbe, *Judaism from Cyrus to Hadrian: Vol. 2, the Roman Period* (Minneapolis: Fortress Press, 1992), 493–97; and Geza Vermes, Fergus Millar, and Matthew Black, eds., *The History of the Jewish People in the Age of Jesus Christ* (vol. 2; revision of Emil Schürer; Edinburgh: T. and T. Clark, Ltd., 1979), 555–90. See also Michael Knibb, *The Qumran Community* (New York: Cambridge University Press, 1987), 14–17.

[18] CD 1.5–7, 4.3, 6.5. References to 'maximalist' and 'minimalist' historiography are grounded in the recent (and at times heated) discussions of the history of ancient Israel. Although there is some disagreement on the precise definitions of these terms, there is a tendency to understand 'maximalist' readings as those that take their textual evidence as largely credible and 'minimalist' readings as particularly critical of the historical veracity of textual evidence. For a range of views on the subject, see John Van Seters, *The Yahwist as Historian in Genesis* (Louisville: Westminster/John Knox Press, 1992); Baruch Halpern, *The First Historians: The Hebrew Bible and History* (San Francisco: Harper and Row, 1988); and the exchange of Iain Provan, 'Ideologies, Literary and Critical: Reflections on Recent Writing on the History of Israel,' *JBL* 114 (1995): 585–606; Thomas Thompson, 'A Neo-Albrightean School in History and Biblical Scholarship?' *JBL* 114 (1995): 683–98; and Philip Davies, 'Method and Madness: Some Remarks on Doing History with the Bible,' *JBL* 114 (1995): 699–705.

[19] See, for example, Phillip Callaway, 'Qumran Origins: From the *Doresh* to the *Moreh*,' *RevQ* 14 (1990): 638.

[20] Davies has been particularly prominent in his critique of literal or harmonizing readings of the historical claims in the Damascus Document and the pesharim.

As an alternative to atomistic or face-value readings of history in the Damascus Document, a number of scholars have recognized the importance of taking into account the scriptural grounding of the text and its larger ideological framing.[21] A primary claim of this sort of reading is that any single detail of the text must be understood in light of the text's larger structures: the types of scriptural passages that are highlighted, how those passages are interpreted, the underlying arguments that shape the text, and the worldview or larger agendas expressed within it. In other words, scholars must understand a text's implicit ideology—its basic assumptions and constructions of reality, and the agendas that arise from those constructions—in order properly to contextualize any single element in the text. Readings in this light may vary widely, depending on what sorts of ideological frameworks and scriptural references are identified in the text, and what sorts of interpretive strategies are brought to bear upon it. Such readings may be composite, taking some expressions at face value and others as metaphorical references, or recognizing that a reference may be grounded in scripture and simultaneously be understandable as historically accurate.[22] The interpretive possibilities for readings of this sort are wide-ranging: the 390 years before the foundation of the covenant community may be read as a literal state-

---

He also points out the hazards of 'mining' the text for its items of historical importance, remarking on a scholarly tendency "to extract passages out of their documentary context and rearrange them into modern reconstruction." See Davies, *Behind the Essenes*, 15–31, esp. 29–30; see also Hempel, *Damascus Texts*, 63–65.

[21] Davies, Brooke, Newsom, and A. Baumgarten stand out as scholars who have addressed these literary and ideological issues. See Davies, *Damascus Covenant*; Davies, *Behind the Essenes*; and the further discussion below. Note the discussion of ideology in Albert Baumgarten, 'The Perception of the Past in the Damascus Document,' in Baumgarten, Chazon, and Pinnick, *Centennial of Discovery*, 1–15. On the use of scripture in CD, see Jonathan Campbell, *The Use of Scripture in the Damascus Document 1–8, 19–20* (New York: Walter de Gruyter, 1995); and Ottilie Schwarz, *Der erste Teil der Damaskusschrift und das Alte Testament* (Lichtland/Diest, 1965). Campbell's approach is discussed at length below.

[22] For readings of these details as both historically-useful and ideologically articulated, see the remarks of Schwartz (who notes, with regard to 390 years, that "the number is canonical (cf. Ezek 4:5); it may, nevertheless, be approximately accurate") and Campbell (who observes that although the 390 years "may well be inextricably linked to the writer's employment of the Scriptures, ... the possibility should not be excluded that there is an element of truth in the assertion"). See Baumgarten and Schwartz, 'CD,' 13 n. 4; Jonathan Campbell, 'Essene-Qumran Origins in the Exile: A Scriptural Basis?' *JJS* 46 (1995): 155. See also H. H. Rowley, 'The 390 Years of the Zadokite Work,' in *Melanges bibliques rediges en l'honneur de Andre Robert* (Paris: Bloud and Gay, 1957), 341–47.

ment or simply an approximate reckoning, and in either case, it may be understood also in terms of the prophecy of Ezekiel. Damascus, in this context, may refer specifically to that city, or it may be a coded reference for Babylon, or Qumran, or some other site in which the community's covenant is thought to have been established. Similarly, the claim that the community has 'departed from Judah' may be taken at face value or as a reference to any of a number of other literal or metaphorical migrations, grounded again in scriptural passages.

The diversity of potential readings of the text's historical details masks a number of basic commonalities. First, and most importantly, although scholars differ in their reconstructions of the actual historical events that the text purports to describe (and also in terms of whether they think we can gain access to those events through the filter of the text's description of them),[23] they tend to share the view that the text does, in fact, reflect a set of actual events, understood as the experiences of the author(s) or editor(s) of the text, or of the community that is described in it.[24] This understanding, in turn, reveals an even more basic view: that the goal of a historiographical project is to read a text in terms of its original meaning, in order to understand how that meaning reflects—and provides insight into—whatever historical events are believed to have occurred 'behind' the text and to be reflected in it. Even for source-critical scholars, who understand the text as the product of a series of redactions, the various stages of textual development tend to be understood as reflective of a matching set of communal developments.[25] The final assumption of this approach is that textual meaning can be understood as singular or unitary. The 'real' meaning of a text is the meaning that its author/editor(s) intended, in the original composition, and it is linked to the events that inspired the writing of the text or are described within it. Although a given passage may be read by different scholars in entirely different ways—and may be understood, variously, as transparently clear, problematically allusive, or entirely ambiguous by those scholars—generally it is understood to have a

---

[23] For a discussion of the view that the text's ideological claims prevent access to the history 'behind' the text, see Campbell, 'Essene-Qumran Origins,' 147–50.

[24] There are, of course, scholars who view the entire text as a fictional account with no relation at all to 'real' history (e.g., Zeitlin, as noted above), but the general tendency is to read this text as somehow historically useful.

[25] Source-critical approaches to the text are addressed, with additional bibliography, in chapter four, as well as in the discussion below.

direct relationship to real historical events, however inaccessible these may be to modern scholarly investigation.

An alternative reading of the Damascus Document, in light of some of the insights of contemporary literary criticism, allows for a shift of attention away from an original, unitary meaning of the text, associated with the historical events that lie 'behind' it. This alternative reading focuses instead on the text's potential for use, interpretation, and re-use by a variety of audiences, whose assumptions, agendas, and understandings may vary as widely as their social setting and textual knowledge. This approach allows us to ask not only what the text 'means' in any given reading, but also how that meaning might have been mobilized by its various audiences, to bolster their own authoritative, communal, and historiographical claims. From unitary and original textual meaning, we turn to a discussion of the 'lifetime' of the text and its mobilization by diverse audiences (with diverse interpretive agendas); in turn, from a unitary historiography focused on the events 'behind' the text, we turn to a historiographical project that considers the range of narratives that might be reflected in—or constructed by—a variety of readings of it.

Contemporary literary criticism and the Damascus Document

The shift away from a focus on original textual meaning and toward a definition of textual history as complex and multivalent is hardly new in contemporary literary critical circles,[26] and it has made a sig-

---

[26] I use 'contemporary literary criticism' and 'contemporary literary critical' here as fairly neutral catch-all expressions, to denote a variety of literary critical approaches that might also be deemed postmodern, poststructuralist, or (in the language of several anthologies of biblical criticism) 'new.' My goal in the use of this language is to avoid the pitfalls implicit in several of the other terms that I might have chosen. 'Critical theory' tends to sound offensive to scholars who do not use it (after all, what scholarship is not critical?), and 'postmodernism' carries with it serious baggage, in that it defines itself, not necessarily usefully, in terms of earlier approaches (modernism) or earlier historical periods (modernity). 'Poststructuralism' is probably the closest cognate to my understanding of 'contemporary literary criticism,' but it too introduces an array of baggage, especially in that it tends to be understood as a synonym for 'deconstruction,' and while my approach takes a deconstructive turn and benefits from the insights of literary critical deconstruction, it does not stand within the scholarly practice of deconstruction as such. For a discussion of the implications of this terminology, see Elizabeth Castelli, Stephen D. Moore, Gary Phillips, Regina Schwartz, et al., eds., *The Postmodern Bible* (New Haven: Yale University Press, 1995), 1–19.

nificant impact on the recent scholarship of canonical biblical texts,[27] but it has received only limited attention from scholars of the Dead Sea Scrolls. Several scholars have presented experimental readings of the scrolls from contemporary literary critical perspectives,[28] or have acknowledged the impact of such approaches on their work,[29] but it is only quite recently that such approaches actually have been incorporated in explicit ways into scholarship on these texts.[30] Where they have been incorporated explicitly, as in Jonathan Campbell's recent study of the Damascus Document,[31] these approaches tend not to be taken to their full interpretive potential, nor to be incorporated into a significant reconsideration of historiographical method.

---

[27] There is a vast bibliography on the use of contemporary literary criticism or critical theory in the study of canonical biblical texts. Particularly enlightening discussions may be found in Castelli, et al., *Postmodern Bible*; Stephen D. Moore, *Literary Criticism and the Gospels: The Theoretical Challenge* (New Haven: Yale University Press, 1989); and A. K. M. Adam, *What is Postmodern Biblical Criticism?* (Minneapolis: Fortress Press, 1995). See also Elizabeth Malbon and Edgar McKnight, eds., *The New Literary Criticism and the New Testament* (Sheffield: JSOT Press and Valley Forge, Penn.: Trinity Press International, 1994); David Seeley, *Deconstructing the New Testament* (New York: Brill, 1994); Cheryl Exum and David Clines, eds., *The New Literary Criticism and the Hebrew Bible* (Sheffield: JSOT Press, 1993); Janice Anderson and Stephen D. Moore, eds., *Mark and Method: New Approaches in Biblical Studies* (Minneapolis: Fortress Press, 1992); David Clines, Stephen Fowl, and Stanley Porter, eds., *The Bible in Three Dimensions: Essays in Celebration of Forty Years of Biblical Studies in the University of Sheffield* (Sheffield: JSOT Press, 1990); and David Clines, David Gunn, and Alan Hauser, eds., *Art and Meaning: Rhetoric in Biblical Literature* (Sheffield: JSOT Press, 1982). A number of volumes of the journal *Semeia* were devoted to related topics; see especially *Semeia* 40 (Charles Winquist, ed., *Text and Textuality*, 1987); *Semeia* 51 (Gary Phillips, ed., *Poststructural Criticism and the Bible: Text/History/Discourse*, 1990), and *Semeia* 54 (David Jobling and Stephen D. Moore, eds., *Poststructuralism as Exegesis*, 1991).

[28] See especially Carol Newsom, 'Apocalyptic and the Discourse of the Qumran Community,' *JNES* 49 (1990): 135–44; Newsom, 'The Case of the Blinking I: Discourse of the Self at Qumran,' in *Discursive Formations, Ascetic Piety and the Interpretation of Early Christian Literature, Part 1* (ed. Vincent Wimbush; *Semeia* 57; 1992): 13–23; and George Brooke, 'Shared Intertextual Interpretations in the Dead Sea Scrolls and the New Testament,' in *Biblical Perspectives: Early Use and Interpretation of the Bible in Light of the Dead Sea Scrolls* (ed. Michael Stone and Esther Chazon; Leiden: Brill, 1998), 35–57.

[29] See Davies, *Behind the Essenes*, 11, for a discussion of the utility of such approaches for historiographical investigation.

[30] An important recent contribution is Robert A. Kugler, 'Hearing 4Q225: A Case Study in Reconstructing the Religious Imagination of the Qumran Community,' *DSD* 9 (2002): forthcoming. Kugler reads 4Q225 (a 'pseudo-Jubilees' text) in light of the oral culture of the scrolls community and H. R. Jauss' reception theory (especially the notion of horizons of expectation) to provide insights into the character of the community and its textual practice.

[31] See Campbell, *The Use of Scripture*, esp. 'Conclusions,' 175–208.

Campbell's study of the use of scripture in the Damascus Document takes steps toward introducing contemporary literary criticism into the world of the Dead Sea Scrolls.[32] Because of the nature of Campbell's project—he includes a discussion of allusion, as well as direct quotation and quotation prefaced by standard citation formulas in the text—he must address the role of readers' experiences in the construction of textual meaning. In this context Campbell has occasion to incorporate several significant points from the realm of contemporary theory, including discussions of authorship, audience, and constructions of textual meaning. Although his use of literary theory is somewhat conservative, it sets the stage in important ways for a more radical reading of textual meaning, as well as a more radical understanding of the historical narratives that can be based on such a construction of meaning.

In the course of his discussions, Campbell makes several important methodological observations. He is aware of the complications implicit in assigning a single 'author' or 'writer' to the text and consequently defines the text's 'author' as whatever group, individual, or redaction history might lie behind the writing of it.[33] He also addresses the complex dynamics associated with the construction of textual meaning, noting that constructions of meaning may occur "in the mind of the writer, in the text as an [artifact], or in the reader's experience of the document."[34] Readers are especially important for Campbell, who notes that his discussion of textual allusion must take into account his own expectations, education, and assumptions, as well as those of the text's authors and ancient audiences. In this regard, he notes that "a holistic reading must guard against imposing literary expectations from a later period onto the products

---

[32] Campbell's primary argument is that the text's admonitional material demonstrates an ideological and stylistic consistency. He does not deny the possibility of a multi-stage redaction of the text, but he notes that its various sections focus on a core set of scriptural passages and periods in the history of ancient Israel, which suggests a consistent editorial agenda throughout the text; see esp. 183. I address Campbell's historiographical claims more extensively in chapter three. See also the review in George Brooke, 'Book Reviews: *The Use of Scripture in the Damascus Document 1–8, 19–20*,' *DSD* 4 (1997): 112–16.

[33] Campbell, *The Use of Scripture*, 45.

[34] Campbell, *The Use of Scripture*, 183. Campbell's use of an audience-oriented approach is especially important in his discussions of allusion (as opposed to direct quotations or quotations with explicit citation formulas). See Campbell, *The Use of Scripture*, 31.

of an earlier one"³⁵ and that an understanding of 'literary competence' on the part of a reader must include not only the reader's facility with grammar and vocabulary, but also an ability to understand the full significance of a text, in its larger cultural and social setting.³⁶

With each of these observations, Campbell's presentation of scriptural quotation and paraphrase in the Damascus Document acknowledges an ongoing literary critical discussion of the construction of textual meaning. This discussion includes controversies over the role of the author (of ancient texts, or of 'texts' more generally) in shaping the meaning of a text, the place of the text itself (as artifact or as 'process') in meaning-construction, and the importance of audience expectations as elements in the reading and interpretive process.

Campbell's discussion of authorship, first, brings to mind two distinct (but not-unrelated) issues, one historical and the other literary-critical. From a historical perspective, sensitivity with regard to authorship reflects the understanding that the writing and redaction of ancient texts was a complicated process, involving multiple stages and multiple or complex authorships.³⁷ For this reason, the notion that ancient texts had single, individual 'authors' has come to be seen as a problematic modern construct, rather than a reflection of real textual origins. For the Damascus Document, this point is especially thorny. On the one hand, a number of scholars have suggested that the text is ideologically consistent and demonstrates a reasonably holistic worldview and use of scripture.³⁸ But on the other hand, scholars also have noticed—since the very earliest modern

---

³⁵ Campbell, *The Use of Scripture*, 44–45.
³⁶ Campbell, *The Use of Scripture*, 44; Campbell's discussion of literary competence is drawn from the work of Barton; see, most recently, the revised and enlarged discussion in John Barton, *Reading the Old Testament: Method in Biblical Study* (Louisville, KY: Westminster/John Knox Press, 1996).
³⁷ For discussions of textual development in the ancient world, see Raymond J. Starr, 'The Circulation of Literary Texts in the Roman World,' *CQ* 37 (1987): 213–23; and Ross S. Kraemer, 'Women's Authorship of Jewish and Christian Literature in the Greco-Roman Period,' in *"Women Like This": New Perspectives on Jewish Women in the Greco-Roman World* (ed. Amy-Jill Levine; Atlanta: Scholars Press, 1991), 221–42.
³⁸ This is the basic thesis of Campbell, *The Use of Scripture*, and it is also a major claim in Davies, *Damascus Covenant*; see also Mark Boyce, 'The Poetry of the *Damascus Document* and its Bearing on the Origin of the Qumran Sect,' *RevQ* 14 (1990): 615–28. An earlier discussion of this issue is found in Schwarz, *Der erste Teil der Damaskusschrift*.

readings of this text—that it has a composite feel, which suggests that it may have developed in a series of redactional stages.[39] The source-critical question is made even more pressing by the form and content of our extant manuscript witnesses: where the medieval witnesses overlap (MS A = CD 7.5–8.21; MS B = CD 19.1–34a), they include significant textual variants; where they do not overlap (in particular, MS B = CD 20.1–34), the text exhibits a fairly distinctive style, with a tone and wording that differs from the other sections of the text in interesting ways. The primary ancient manuscript witnesses (4Q266–273), in turn, provide evidence for a text that is similar in tone and form to the text represented by the medieval manuscripts, but with a significantly greater emphasis on the legal material and no obvious references to the manuscript tradition represented in CD 19.1–34.[40]

Addressing the problem of authorial identity in the face of complex textual development requires making strategic decisions with regard to both terminology and analysis. Campbell acknowledges the problem of authorial identity and makes the decision to read the text in a fairly holistic fashion, while understanding terms like 'author' and 'writer' in a generalized sense, which might include a group consciousness.[41] In a similar fashion, I refer to the 'author/editor(s)' of the text, by which I mean to include its various writer(s), editor(s), and redactor(s), in its original moment(s) of composition.[42] The

---

[39] Murphy-O'Connor has presented the most extensive source-critical reading of this text. See Jerome Murphy-O'Connor, 'An Essene Missionary Document? CD II,14–VI,1,' *RB* 77 (1970): 201–29; 'A Literary Analysis of Damascus Document VI,2–VIII,3,' *RB* 78 (1971): 210–32; 'The Critique of the Princes of Judah (CD VIII,3–19),' *RB* 79 (1972): 200–16; 'A Literary Analysis of Damascus Document XIX,33–XX,34,' *RB* 79 (1972): 544–64; 'The Essenes and their History,' *RB* 81 (1974): 215–44; and the re-evaluation in Murphy-O'Connor, 'The *Damascus Document* Revisited,' *RB* 92 (1985): 223–46. See also Davies, *Damascus Covenant*, 198–204.

[40] For charts that summarize the content of the QD material, see Baumgarten, DJD XVIII, 3–5. Baumgarten notes that ancient manuscript witnesses to a text paralleling CD 20 are found in 4Q266 4 i 1–13 and 4Q267 3 1–7; see his discussion on pages 46–47, 98–99. For notes on Milik's arrangement of these fragments, and his view that an ancient redaction of the text included material that paralleled CD 8.9–21, 19.34–35, and 20.1–4, see page 46, esp. the 'Comments' on lines 7–25.

[41] Campbell, *The Use of Scripture*, 45.

[42] For the formulation of 'author/editor' language, see Robert A. Kraft, *Barnabas and the Didache* (New York: Nelson and Sons, 1965). An alternative, following Neusner, is to speak of the 'authorships' of a text. His use of this expression, however, is part of a larger approach to textuality. See, for example, Jacob Neusner, *Writing*

use of a singular/plural composite expression serves to underscore the complexities of the composition of this text: in its most complete form, it most likely reflects a series of redactions and thus a series of authorships, but even in this composite state it presents a coherent message. Similarly, at any of its earlier redactional moments, the text would have been understood as reflective of a coherent (though perhaps still multivalent) meaning. That these meanings might differ, or that an earlier redaction of the text might be rewritten by a later editor (or the same editor, with new goals in mind) is implied in the composite expression 'author/editor(s).'[43]

In the readings that follow, I attempt to take into account the potential for complex textual composition and the potential for changes in 'authorial intentions,' in terms of either a single author (who, having written a text, later reconsiders and revises it) or a series of authors and redactors (who build upon and reshape each other's work). At times, my readings focus on a single section of the Damascus Document, taking it as a coherent unit, with no attention to redactional change; at other times I read a section of the text in terms of a hypothetical redactional process, asking how the meaning of that section might have changed over the course of a process of editing and re-editing. The practice of toggling between the various parts of the text and the text understood as a (theoretical) 'whole,' and of shifting between synchronic and diachronic readings, allows for a consideration of authorial intention as composite, dynamic, and complex. In any given manifestation, the text might support a number of different (and even conflicting) agendas, overlaid upon one another by a series of author/editors, whose own agendas led them to reconsider and even rewrite the text. In this sense, the lines between the composition of the text and its development over time are blurred, so that 'the authorial voice' of the text becomes a composite layering of authorial intentions, even as its audience in any given moment may continue to understand it in terms that are unitary and coherent.

In addition to the notion of authorship as a historical question, a second debate may underlie the discussion of authorship in Campbell's

---

with Scripture: The Authority and Uses of the Hebrew Bible in the Torah of Formative Judaism (Minneapolis: Fortress Press, 1989), 154–55.

[43] Again, Davies is the scholar who has most extensively addressed the potential for writing, rewriting, and revision of the Damascus Document text, in light of a series of different authorial and editorial agendas. See especially Davies, *Damascus Covenant*, 198–201.

reading of the Damascus Document, and this latter discussion certainly is central to my own readings of the text. This debate is explicitly literary-critical in nature and asks: what is the role of authorial intent in the determination of textual meaning in the first place? The view that once dominated literary critical circles held that an author's agenda should be understood as the sole source of textual meaning, so that readers can be said to understand the meaning of a text only when they have grasped the full scope of its author's intended message.[44] In response to this view, a generation of literary critics has argued for an understanding of textual meaning as separate from—or not necessarily shaped entirely in terms of—the author's own understanding of the meaning of a text. It is not only the case that the author's intended meaning may be unclear or not fully communicated in a text, although this is part of the picture. Even more radically, this approach asserts that the author is no longer the expert on 'the meaning' of the text.[45] Authorial intention remains a central element in the construction of textual meaning according to this view, but it is in fact only *one* of a number of such components. From this perspective, a text may be 'meaningful' in ways other than those anticipated by its author, and even in ways of which an author might not approve. At its most extreme, this rebellion against the authority of the compositional moment has been articulated in terms of 'the death of the author.'[46] A less-dramatic

---

[44] Eagleton provides a helpful introduction to this argument, locating the modern origins of the emphasis on authorial intent in the philosophy of Husserl and Heidegger and the literary criticism of Hirsch; see Terry Eagleton, 'Phenomenology, Hermeneutics, Reception Theory,' in *Literary Theory: An Introduction* (Minneapolis: University of Minnesota Press, 1983), 54–90. Eagleton critiques Hirsch's view "that literary meaning is absolute and immutable, wholly resistant to historical change," and reflective of the author's intention, in his discussion on pages 67–71.

[45] In framing this question in terms of a writer's 'authority' (control over permitted interpretations of a text), this literary critical discussion is more concerned with the question of who is permitted to assign meaning to a text (a matter of power) than with the fundamental problems of communication itself (that texts never perfectly reflect a writer's specific arguments or general worldview; that writers may never fully grasp the extent of their own arguments, etc.). This latter question itself has been subject to significant discussion, especially among scholars of hermeneutics. For a discussion of the hermeneutical questions not pursued here, see Hans-Georg Gadamer, *Truth and Method* (2nd rev. ed.; New York: Crossroad, 1989); for bibliography and a discussion of the Gadamer-Habermas debate (which clarified many of the primary concerns of the hermeneutical school) see Demetrius Teigas, *Knowledge and Hermeneutic Understanding: A Study of the Habermas-Gadamer Debate* (Lewisburg: Bucknell University Press, 1995).

[46] See especially Roland Barthes, 'The Death of the Author,' recently reprinted

pose warns readers of the danger of succumbing to the 'intentional fallacy.'

When authorial intention is not the sole arbiter of textual meaning, a new understanding of the construction of such meaning becomes crucial. Some literary critics have suggested the strategy of locating textual meaning in 'the text' itself, but only after introducing a fundamental redefinition of the notion of 'the text.' According to Roland Barthes, who shaped much of this discussion in its earliest articulations, distinctions must be made between 'the work' (the text as artifact) and 'the text,' whose meaning is accessible only "in an activity, a production." Texts, according to Barthes, should be understood not in terms of their form (what they *are*), but in terms of how they can be understood and interpreted (what they *do*, and what readers do with them).[47] At its extreme, this view implies that a text never offers a full meaning, but instead only "a serial movement of dislocations, overlappings, and variations."[48] Textual meaning, in this context, is always evocative and plural, rather than finite or potentially complete.[49]

This re-presentation of the 'the text' as experience, rather than object, puts a serious responsibility on the audience, as a primary actor in the construction of textual meaning. Campbell notes the importance of audience interpretations, but in our own reading of the Damascus Document it will be useful to provide a more specific introduction to two distinct audience-oriented reading strategies. The

---

in Sean Burke, ed., *Authorship: From Plato to the Postmodern, A Reader* (Edinburgh: Edinburgh University Press, 1995), 125–30; and Michel Foucault, 'What is an Author?' in Harari, *Textual Strategies*, 141–60. Harari notes, with respect to Foucault's claims, that the author represents only one element in the process of assigning meaning to texts and is "but *one* of the dimensions of discourse and not, as the traditional conception would have it, the absolute originator of discourse." See Josué Harari, 'Critical Factions/Critical Fictions,' 42.

[47] For this notion of text as practice, and an understanding of texts not in terms of genre but in terms of how they confound genres, see Roland Barthes, 'From Work to Text,' in Harari, *Textual Strategies*, 75.

[48] Barthes, 'From Work to Text,' 76.

[49] Deconstruction, as a form of literary and cultural criticism, was one of the major developments out of this understanding of the text. See, most notably, Jacques Derrida, *Of Grammatology* (trans. Gayatri Spivak; Baltimore: Johns Hopkins Press, 1974); and, for a more accessible introduction, Jonathan Culler, *On Deconstruction: Theory and Criticism after Structuralism* (Ithaca: Cornell University Press, 1982). In the context of religious studies, see also the sensitive application of this approach to gnostic literature and theology in Patricia Cox Miller, '"Words With an Alien Voice": Gnostics, Scripture, and Canon,' *JAAR* 57 (1989): 459–83.

first is the aptly-named 'audience-oriented' (or 'reader-response') approach to textual meaning, a literary critical practice that has had a significant impact on biblical studies and related fields in the last two decades.[50] The notion that the audience of a text constructs and reconstructs the meaning of the text in each experience of it has been important as an extension of the view that textual meaning is 'multiple' rather than unitary, and that the original meaning of the text (associated with the author's intention for it) is no more than one of a host of relevant interpretations of the text. The recognition of the audience's place in the shaping of textual meaning has, in turn, led to an elaborate (and at times problematic) discussion of just how to define that audience (as ideal readers, real readers, implied

---

[50] For a comprehensive and critical summary of recent reader-response biblical criticism, see 'Reader-Response Criticism,' in Castelli, et al., *Postmodern Bible*, 20–69. See also Moore's excellent chapter, 'Stories of Reading: Doing Gospel Criticism as/with a Reader,' in Moore, *Literary Criticism and the Gospels*, 71–107; *Semeia* 31 (Robert Detweiler, ed., *Reader Response Approaches to Biblical and Secular Texts*, 1985) and *Semeia* 48 (Edgar McKnight, ed., *Reader Perspectives on the New Testament*, 1989); and the volumes mentioned above. Of related interest is E. J. van Wolde, *A Semiotic Analysis of Genesis 2–3* (Assen/Mastricht, The Netherlands: Van Gorcum, 1989). In this volume, the semiotic analysis relies on an understanding of textual meaning as the product of an audience's experience of the text. Among biblical scholars, the most influential reader-response critic is probably Iser; see especially Wolfgang Iser, *The Act of Reading: A Theory of Aesthetic Response* (Baltimore: Johns Hopkins University Press, 1978); and *The Implied Reader: Patterns of Communication in Prose Fiction from Bunyan to Beckett* (Baltimore: Johns Hopkins University Press, 1974). For critiques of his approach, see Eagleton, *Literary Theory*, 78–85; Stanley Fish, 'Why No One's Afraid of Wolfgang Iser,' and other essays in *Doing What Comes Naturally: Change, Rhetoric, and the Practice of Theory in Literary and Legal Studies* (Durham: Duke University Press, 1989); and Castelli, et al., *Postmodern Bible*, 39–41, 44–51. The critique of Iser in Castelli, et al., is that his theory has allowed biblical reader-response critics to maintain a positivistic reading strategy while claiming to use literary critical approaches. A more general introduction to audience-oriented criticism can be found in Jane Tompkins, ed., *Reader-Response Criticism: From Formalism to Post-Structuralism* (Baltimore: Johns Hopkins University Press, 1980); and Susan Suleiman and Inge Crosman, eds., *The Reader in the Text: Essays on Audience and Interpretation* (Princeton: Princeton University Press, 1980). A related approach, used to great advantage by Kugler (see above, n. 30), is that of reception theory, associated with the so-called Konstanz school of literary criticism. See especially Hans Robert Jauss, *Toward an Aesthetic of Reception* (Minneapolis: University of Minnesota, 1982); and Jauss, 'Literary History as a Challenge to Literary Theory,' in *New Directions in Literary History* (ed. Ralph Cohen; Baltimore: Johns Hopkins University Press, 1974), 11–41. In James L. Machor and Philip Goldstein, eds., *Reception Study: From Literary Theory to Cultural Studies* (New York: Routledge, 2001), articles by the greats of reader-response criticism and reception history (including Jauss, Fish, and the like) are juxtaposed with cultural-studies applications of the theories and critical responses to them.

readers, first-time readers, experienced readers, and so on).⁵¹ In addition, the role of a reader's community (and the authority of communal leaders) has been understood as a significant element in shaping the readings of an individual audience.⁵²

If social and communal settings are an important factor in an audience's understanding of a text, so too are the *literary* 'contexts' of reading, by which I mean the textual knowledge and preconceptions that an audience brings to the reading of a given document. Literary-critical approaches associated with 'intertextuality' reflect this interest, in that—although discussion is often framed in terms of the relationships of texts to one another and the reinterpretation of one text in light of readings of others—it is the audience that determines the readings of texts and their interrelationships.⁵³ At its most radical, an intertextual approach can undercut the basic notion of unitary textual meaning. If textual interpretation is the process by which a new textual "system" causes "the absorption and transformation of another," then the meanings of a text will vary directly in terms of the 'system' in which it is read and the purpose to which it is applied.⁵⁴

This approach, which views the construction of textual meaning in terms of context more than text, problematizes the notion of textual authority in useful ways, underlining the extent to which the

---

⁵¹ For an ironic and insightful critique of the "many aliases and roles" of the reader of scriptural texts, see Moore, *Literary Criticism and the Gospels*, 71–73.

⁵² The classic literary critical discussion of interpretive communities is found in Stanley Fish, *Is There a Text in This Class? The Authority of Interpretive Communities* (Cambridge: Harvard University Press, 1980); see especially the section on interpretive communities in 'Interpreting *The Variorum*,' 167–73, and the title essay, 303–21. For a discussion of 'textual communities' (in which the interpretations of a literate leader may shape the understandings of an illiterate community with a shared textual tradition), see Brian Stock, *Listening for the Text: On the Uses of the Past* (Baltimore: Johns Hopkins University Press, 1990), 140–71, esp. 150–51.

⁵³ Here, again, an alternative but compatible approach might follow Jauss' formulation of horizons of expectation. See n. 30 and n. 50, above.

⁵⁴ Julia Kristeva, 'Word, Dialogue, and Novel,' in *Desire in Language: A Semiotic Approach to Literature and Art* (ed. Leon Roudiez; New York: Columbia University Press, 1980), 66. Kristeva's argument stems from a discussion of Bakhtinian literary theory, understood in explicitly revolutionary terms. For guidance and more light on Kristevan terminology, see Roudiez' 'Introduction' to the volume, 1–20. Further discussions and bibliography can be found in Heinrich Plett, ed., *Intertextuality* (New York: Walter de Gruyter, 1991); and Michael Worton and Judith Still, eds., *Intertextuality: Theories and Practices* (New York: Manchester University Press, 1990).

basic authority of an 'authoritative text' is grounded in an audience's acceptance and acknowledgment of it. Scholars of the canonical biblical texts have taken to this approach enthusiastically, finding in it a new language for discussions of the authority and meaning of scriptural texts.[55] In the process, most have tended to tone down the revolutionary qualities of this approach, in the face of their own perceptions of scriptural authority.[56] But toned down in this way, intertextuality quickly becomes a sort of modified source criticism, grounded in the much-repeated assertion that "any text is constructed as a mosaic of quotations" of other texts.[57]

In his discussion of quotation practices in the Damascus Document, Campbell draws occasionally upon contemporary literary criticism, and his references demonstrate the basic usefulness of such an approach: contemporary criticism provides for a more fluid discussion of textual meaning, with an understanding that this meaning is generated in the complex interaction of text, author, and audience. Such an approach has the potential to rewrite basic notions of textual meaning in radical ways. However, as we have seen in this discussion, biblical scholars share the tendency to embrace these insights, if at all, in their least radical forms, which neither push the boundaries of 'the meaning' of the text, nor take full advantage of the potential displacements of such textual meaning.[58]

---

[55] Examples of this extensive literature include *Semeia* 69/70 (George Aichele and Gary Phillips, eds., *Intertextuality and the Bible*, 1995); Danna Fewell, ed., *Reading Between Texts: Intertextuality and the Hebrew Bible* (Louisville: Westminster/John Knox Press, 1992); and Sipke Draisma, ed., *Intertextuality in Biblical Writings: Essays in Honour of Bas van Iersel* (Kampen: Uitgeversmaatschappij J. H. Kok, 1989). See also Gail O'Day, 'Jeremiah 9.22–23 and 1 Corinthians 1.26–31: A Study in Intertextuality,' *JBL* 109 (1990): 259–67; and Willem Vorster, 'The Protevangelium of James and Intertextuality,' in *Text and Testimony: Essays on New Testament and Apocryphal Literature in Honour of A. F. J. Klijn* (ed. T. Baarda, A. Hilhorst, et al.; Kampen: Uitgeversmaatschappij J. H. Kok, 1988), 262–75. See also the influential discussion in Daniel Boyarin, *Intertextuality and the Reading of Midrash* (Bloomington: Indiana University Press, 1990).

[56] See especially the criticism of biblical scholars' conservative use of this theory in Ellen van Wolde, 'Trendy Intertextuality?' in Draisma, *Intertextuality in Biblical Writings*, 43–49.

[57] Kristeva, 'Word, Dialogue, and Novel,' 66.

[58] The scholarly tendency to downplay the radical or revolutionary implications of contemporary literary criticism is discussed and critiqued in Stephen D. Moore, 'The "Post"-Age Stamp: Does It Stick? Biblical Studies and the Postmodern Debate,' *JAAR* 57 (1989): 543–57. Moore's literary criticism stands out among biblical scholars both for its ironic presentation and for its explicit articulation of a political

Campbell's approach to the Damascus Document is located within this slightly more conservative frame. His methodological decision to define textual meaning (for the sake of this particular study, at least) as interchangeable with the intentions of the text's (individual or group) 'author'[59] effectively collapses the useful distinction between author and text (which he further concretizes by understanding 'text' as artifact, rather than process). This approach re-formalizes the understanding of textual meaning as finite, unitary, and the product of the text's origin-moments. Campbell's audience-oriented reading is similarly constrained: if textual meaning is equated with authorial intent, then the primary audiences under consideration are those at the time of the text's composition (its author/editor(s) and their community) and that of the modern scholarly community (whose experience of the text is significantly different). Such an approach does not create space for more complex audience-oriented readings, which might take into account the history of usage of the text and the potential for repeated and dynamic mobilizations of textual meaning.[60]

Starting from Campbell's discussion of the problems of textual meaning, we can envision a more radical interpretive project, based on the insights of contemporary literary criticism, but insisting upon the fundamental distinctions between 'text,' 'author,' and 'audience.' Admittedly, the boundaries between the three categories are fuzzy, and it is often impossible to identify the source of a given interpretation (is it 'in the text' or did the audience 'import' it? would 'any reader' draw this meaning from the text? etc.). However, the benefit of distinguishing among these three loci does not lie in identifying the ultimate and absolute source of a given passage's meaning, but rather in recognizing the constant tensions among—and fundamental

---

agenda. In particular, he addresses the continued survival of master narratives and their potential for oppressiveness ("totalization's announced death rattle has all too often turned out to have been a clearing of the throat," 551) and the differentials of power among cultural critics ("the 'post' of postmodernism must be driven into the silence of the white, Occidental male. That is the real stake in the postmodern debate," 556).

[59] Campbell, *The Use of Scripture*, 45.

[60] Campbell, *The Use of Scripture*, 44. Campbell notes that the cultural gap between ancient and modern readers is illustrated by the fact that theoretical approaches to the text are necessary in the first place, and that in fact they "are not fully satisfactory." For other references to the different experiences of modern and ancient readers, see his discussions on pages 47, 131, and 199–200. Note also his discussion of textual interpretation and the authority attributed to the author or the covenant community, on page 144.

distinctions between—these separate influences on textual meaning-construction.

From this perspective, the text is never a complete 'work' as such, with a clear unitary meaning implicit in its words. Instead, it always requires interpretation, in each individual encounter. Authorial intent may provide one set of meanings for the text, but these meanings—no matter how clearly they may be conveyed—are always susceptible to revision and reinterpretation, either by the author/editor(s) themselves, or by other redactors and interpreters. Audiences, in turn, may reshape and reconsider the potential meanings of the text, in light of their own needs and ideologies, providing interpretations of 'the meaning' of a text that serve their own immediate and pressing concerns at different moments in the history of the text. The result of this sort of literary critical approach is an understanding of textual meaning as something that is fundamentally dynamic, and fundamentally contested, as well.

Textual meaning, foundation documents and sectarian discourse

Understanding textual meaning as fundamentally multiple serves as the first stage in a literary-critical historiographical project. Understanding such meaning as fundamentally *contested* provides the next set of contextualizing questions. To say that the meaning of a text is 'contested' not only implies that the text is susceptible to multiple interpretations but further highlights the social setting(s) in which that text might be read, and the ways in which it might be mobilized by readers with competing agendas. The Damascus Document, in presenting an account of communal history and a halakhic communal framework, is one of a number of Dead Sea Scrolls texts that can be labeled as 'foundation documents,' texts that take on authoritative status for the communities in which they are read and interpreted. But 'the meaning' of a foundation document is never transparent, and competing readings of the text can support (or, in fact, generate) competing constructions of communal authority and covenantal identity. A better understanding of the interpretation of foundation documents thus lays the groundwork for a discussion of historiography in the diverse readings and mobilizations of these texts.

Scholars sometimes refer to the 'sect' or 'sectarian movement' associated with the scrolls, making use of categories drawn from sociology of religion. The language of 'sectarianism' can be problematic, but it ultimately provides a useful framework in which to ground one approach to the historiography of the scrolls.[61] A primary problem with the language is that it may imply a more specific definition than scrolls scholars realize or would accept. Although the term 'sect' appears interchangeably with 'group' or 'community' in discussions of the scrolls, the modern sociological sense of this term reflects a very specific type of religious social movement: the small offshoot of a larger, established religious movement, or 'ecclesia.'[62] According to one contemporary articulation of this model, a sect is defined as a group that has arisen through "the social fragmentation of denominational schism." Such a group includes members who come disproportionately from less-educated and economically-disprivileged classes, and who espouse beliefs and practices that are in line with, but significantly more intense than, those of the mainstream religious community.[63] A related definition stresses the view that sects demonstrate certain shared traits: a separation from (or separatist attitude toward) mainstream culture and institutions; an emphasis on voluntary entry into the group, combined with a transformative or 'conversion'

---

[61] See especially the recent analysis of ancient Jewish sectarianism in Albert Baumgarten, *The Flourishing of Jewish Sects in the Maccabean Era: An Interpretation* (New York: Brill, 1997). Baumgarten's careful sociological analysis includes a comparative discussion of Christian sectarianism in modern Britain. Although they do not ground their discussions in explicit sociological framing, assumptions with regard to the scrolls community's schismatic origins are also central in the Groningen Hypothesis and other revisions of the classical Essene hypothesis. See García Martínez, 'Qumran Origins and Early History'; and Florentino García Martínez and Adam van der Woude, 'A "Groningen" Hypothesis of Qumran Origins and Early History,' *RevQ* 14 (1990): 521–41. See also Gabriele Boccaccini, *Beyond the Essene Hypothesis: The Parting of the Ways Between Qumran and Enochic Judaism* (Grand Rapids, Mich.: Eerdman Publishing Company, 1998), esp. 53–58.

[62] The original formulation of 'church-sect' theory, which distinguished between an established 'ecclesia' and non-mainstream 'sects' and 'cults,' is presented in Ernst Troeltsch, *The Social Teaching of the Christian Churches* (trans. Olive Wyon; New York: Harper, 1960; orig. publ. 1911). For an overview of this approach and a contemporary revision of it, see William Bainbridge, *The Sociology of Religious Movements* (New York: Routledge, 1997), 38–42. Bainbridge adapts the church-sect theory for the analysis of diverse religious communities, in which no one ecclesia dominates; he includes the element of 'tension' as a means of distinguishing between more- and less-mainstream religious groups (high-tension groups are at odds with surrounding culture, while low-tension groups fit more easily into their cultural milieu). For the introduction of tension as an analytical category, see Rodney Stark and William Bainbridge, 'Of Churches, Sects, and Cults,' *JSSR* 18 (1979): 117–33.

[63] Bainbridge, *Sociology of Religious Movements*, 31.

experience; and a sense of exclusiveness, spiritual regeneration, and superiority over outsiders.[64]

Some details of these sociological definitions are problematic for a discussion of a Damascus covenant community or a community associated with the Dead Sea Scrolls more generally,[65] but the insights of this approach are nevertheless useful for this discussion. For this reason, an understanding of sectarian movements that reflects the view of contemporary sociologists of religion does provide a useful framework for our discussion of the Damascus covenant community. According to this contemporary approach, sectarian movements can be defined in terms of their ideology, rather than their specific social location. A 'sect' is a group whose members *understand themselves* as separate from and superior to the potentially hostile mainstream population in which they find themselves.[66] Sectarians may (or may not) be intensely religious, and sects may (or may not) be schismatic in origin, according to this definition; a sectarian sense of alienation need not reflect an absolute social state. Sociologists speak of 'relative deprivation' as a means of explaining the sense of alienation or isolation that the members of a community may feel, even if the members of that community are economically successful and apparently socially integrated into a larger population.[67]

In addressing the complexities of ancient Jewish sectarianism, Albert Baumgarten provides a definition of the word 'sect' that may be useful to keep in mind. A sect, he argues, is:

> a *voluntary association of protest, which utilizes boundary marking mechanisms— the social means of differentiating between insiders and outsiders—to distinguish between its own members and those otherwise normally regarded as belonging to*

---

[64] Thomas O'Dea, *The Sociology of Religion* (Englewood Cliffs, N.J.: Prentice-Hall, 1966); see the chart reproduced in Bainbridge, *Sociology of Religious Movements*, 41.

[65] In particular, the issue of education and socio-economic class is worthy of further study. 'Sects,' at least in modern settings, tend to attract their members from economically disprivileged or less educated sectors of society, while the community or communities associated with the scrolls tends to be understood by scholars as economically privileged and well educated, relative to the general populace.

[66] Bainbridge, *Sociology of Religious Movements*, 22–23.

[67] For an introductory discussion of relative deprivation theory, see Bainbridge, *Sociology of Religious Movements*, 50–53. A classic discussion of this issue with respect to millenarian movements is found in Kenelm Burridge, *New Heaven, New Earth: A Study of Millenarian Activities* (Oxford: Basil Blackwell, 1969); see also Baumgarten, *Flourishing of Jewish Sects*, 156–61; and Jean Duhaime, 'Relative Deprivation in New Religious Movements and the Qumran Community,' *RevQ* 16 (1993): 265–76.

the same national or religious entity. Ancient Jewish sects, accordingly, differentiated *between Jews who were members of their sect and those not.*⁶⁸

By highlighting the voluntary nature of membership in a sectarian group, and by noting that sectarian groups distinguish between insiders and outsiders who otherwise might not appear different to one another, Baumgarten foregrounds a number of issues that will be important to our discussion of the Damascus Document.⁶⁹ For the sake of this discussion, a sectarian worldview is one that stresses the difference between a group or community and the larger community within which it could be associated. The focus on difference and separation—and often superiority, as well—is more important to this definition than the practical boundaries between the group and its larger social setting. That is, a group may demonstrate a sectarian ideology even while it is apparently integrated into a larger community in economic, social, or cultural terms. It is the *purported desire* for separation and the *language* of separation that defines sectarianism, from this perspective, and not necessarily the success that the members of a community have in separating themselves materially from the sinful or inferior mainstream.

Given this sociological discussion, a reading of the Damascus Document does reveal an ideology—if not a historical experience—that can be classified as sectarian. The text distinguishes between members of the covenant community and those who are outside the covenant, ascribing to the covenanters a knowledge and understanding of God's will that is inaccessible to outsiders. Although there is still time to join the group, the text asserts that sometime in the near

---

⁶⁸ Baumgarten, *Flourishing of Jewish Sects*, 7; italics in original.

⁶⁹ Other scrolls scholars have offered equally insightful definitions of 'sectarianism' as it relates to the scrolls. See especially the discussions in Carol Newsom, '"Sectually Explicit" Literature from Qumran,' in *The Hebrew Bible and its Interpreters* (ed. William Propp, Baruch Halpern, and David Noel Freedman; Winona Lake, Ind.: Eisenbrauns, 1990), 167–87; Esther Chazon, 'Is *Divreh Ha-Me'orot* a Sectarian Prayer?' in *The Dead Sea Scrolls: Forty Years of Research* (ed. Devorah Dimant and Uriel Rappaport; Leiden: Brill, 1992), 3–17; and, most recently, the discussion of Newsom and Chazon's definitions in Charlotte Hempel, *The Laws of the Damascus Document: Sources, Tradition and Redaction* (Boston: Brill, 1998), 18–20. On rhetoric and ideological stance, see Newsom, '"Sectually Explicit" Literature,' 178–79; and Hempel, *The Laws*, 18–20. See also Baumgarten, *Flourishing of Jewish Sects*, 7 n. 19, with reference to the definitions of sectarianism provided in Shaye Cohen, *From the Maccabees to the Mishnah* (Philadelphia: Westminster Press, 1987), 125–27; and Schiffman, *Reclaiming*, 72–73.

future (in the rapidly-impending endtimes) the doors will close, and anyone who is left on the outside—even a truly righteous person—will be judged with the wicked of Israel. On several occasions, the text makes reference to schisms within the community, which include intracommunal conflicts over the leadership of the Teacher of Righteousness and the false claims of the Man of the Lie, as well as smaller-scale disputes, which may have provoked the apostasy of individual members. Together, these textual elements suggest that the Damascus Document is reflective of a sectarian ideology, if not also a sectarian covenant community.

At least one scholar has suggested that we should view the community associated with the scrolls as a mainstream and even dominant movement in ancient Judaism. According to Hartmut Stegemann, although the scrolls community practiced "segregation" from the mainstream, and maintained an elitist attitude toward outsiders, it should not be labeled a sectarian group, because "Jews become 'sectarian' only if their halakhot are not accepted any longer by the majority," and this was not the case, at least according to his reconstruction of the place of the scrolls community in ancient Jewish history.[70] Based on his interpretation of the evidence, the practices and standards of the scrolls community actually reflect those of the "main Jewish union in late Second Temple times."[71]

Stegemann's claims with regard to halakhic conflicts remain to be addressed (in that some scholars continue to view 'Qumran halakhah' as a minority opinion in ancient Judaism),[72] but his argument falters more seriously in its definition of sectarianism. To say that the scrolls community is not sectarian because its halakhic views conform to those of the larger mainstream society misses the point of 'sectarianism,' at least as defined sociologically. According to a sociological definition, a sect is a non-mainstream group whose religious con-

---

[70] Stegemann, 'The Qumran Essenes,' 161; Stegemann, *The Library of Qumran*. His analysis includes a reconsideration of the evidence from Pliny and Josephus, which leads him to describe the scrolls community as 'Essene,' in a rather new sense of this term. While recognizing their elitist and separatist tendencies, he asserts that there is "nothing which could be regarded as 'sectarian' in any way" about this group. See Stegemann, 'The Qumran Essenes,' 160 (including n. 173).

[71] Stegemann, 'The Qumran Essenes,' 83.

[72] See, for example, Lawrence Schiffman, 'The Law of Vows and Oaths (*Num.* 30, 3–16) in the *Zadokite Fragments* and the *Temple Scroll*,' *RevQ* 15 (1991): 213; and, more generally, Schiffman, *Sectarian Law in the Dead Sea Scrolls: Courts, Testimony and the Penal Code* (Chico, Calif.: Scholars Press, 1983).

sciousness and practices *conform* to those of the mainstream, but are taken to excessive heights.[73] In this sense, even if the halakhic views of the community can be seen to conform to those of the ancient Jewish mainstream, this in no way prevents our understanding the ideology of some of the scrolls (including the Damascus Document) as sectarian in their outlook. This choice of definition is based on the ideology of isolation and superiority articulated in the scrolls, which suggests that the community sought to distinguish itself from the rest of mainstream Judaism, even when its purported distinctions (in historical and halakhic terms) may have appeared insignificant to those outside the sect.

Among the Dead Sea Scrolls, we can point to sectarian texts that are more isolationist in their ideologies, as well as texts that are more open to people outside the covenant; we might also identify texts that fail to demonstrate any overt sectarian traits at all. In several recent adaptations of the Essene hypothesis, scholars have distinguished among the various scrolls—classifying them as non-sectarian, proto-sectarian, or fully sectarian in their ideologies—and have correlated the composition of the texts with various presumed moments in the history of the sectarian community.[74] In the category of 'non-sectarian' texts, scholars include those that ultimately found their way into the canonical Hebrew scriptures, as well as other texts that are presumed to have been in general usage in ancient Judaism, such as the book of Tobit. The texts that have been designated 'proto-sectarian'—including the Temple Scroll, Enoch, Jubilees, and for some, 4QMMT, the so-called 'Halakhic Letter'—share certain calendrical and halakhic assumptions but do not introduce a rigid sense of separation between a covenant community and its opponents. In contrast, the fully sectarian texts—including the Community Rule and related texts, the War Scroll, the pesharim, and the Hodayot, as well as the Damascus Document—tend to assume a distinction between the covenant community of the texts and a Judaism outside the sect, whose religious practices and interpretations of scripture are

---

[73] See Bainbridge, *Sociology of Religious Movements*, 31.
[74] For example, García Martínez, 'Qumran Origins and Early History,' esp. 116–17; García Martínez and van der Woude, 'A "Groningen" Hypothesis,' 521–41; and Boccaccini, *Beyond the Essene Hypothesis*, esp. 53–58. For a review of the Groningen hypothesis that includes some positive analysis but ultimately dismisses its claims, see Stegemann, 'The Qumran Essenes,' 99–104. See also the critique in Hempel, *The Laws*, esp. 5–8.

intensely problematic. In their degree of alienation, the sectarian texts range from an 'inclusive, for now' perspective (like that of the Damascus Document) to the view that the doors are shut and the barriers between the righteous and the wicked are fully formed.

To contextualize our discussion of sectarian texts, the sociological concept of 'foundation documents' also proves helpful. Sociologists understand foundation documents as the texts upon which communities—including sectarian movements—ground their group identity and understanding of authority. Howard Kee describes foundation documents as the texts that are of primary importance to a community, in that they speak authoritatively on issues such as "requirements for admission, the structures of authority and decision making, [and] the basic pattern of proper performance by the adherents" of a group.[75] Texts of this sort have both past and future orientations, in that they may "trace the origins of the group, the guidelines for the ongoing life of its members, and the shared expectations for the fulfillment of what they see as their divinely given destiny."[76] In line with this definition, foundation documents serve as authoritative texts in a community, providing the basis for its structure and offering insight into its basic ideologies. In addition, these texts hint at the boundaries between the groups they serve and the groups or individuals that they would designate as 'outsiders.'

Scrolls scholars have approached the problem of connecting the sectarian texts to real historical communities in a number of different ways. The classical Essene Hypothesis, for example, has tended to read the various sectarian texts harmonistically, noting their many similarities but paying less attention to their differences in terminology, theology, and assumptions with regard to social order.[77] Recent scholarship, as noted above, introduces a developmental view of sectarianism, in which the diversity of the sectarian documents is reflective of the periods in which they were composed (understanding the more-sectarian texts as generally later in composition and the less-sectarian texts as evidence for earlier periods in the history of the community).[78] Scholars also have noted that the sectarian texts may

---

[75] Howard Kee, 'Membership in the Covenant People at Qumran and in the Teaching of Jesus,' in *Jesus and the Dead Sea Scrolls* (ed. James H. Charlesworth; New York: Doubleday, 1992), 120.

[76] Kee, 'Membership,' 120.

[77] For example, Vermes, *The Complete Dead Sea Scrolls*, 26–66.

[78] For an account of the three-stage textual model (non-sectarian, proto-sectarian,

provide evidence for more than one covenantal community (the common distinction is between the Damascus covenant community and a community associated with the Community Rule), or that they may reflect the existence of several communities that were related to one another, or a single community that underwent significant changes in structure and leadership over the course of its history.[79]

Sarianna Metso, in a recent article on the Damascus Document and the Community Rule, introduces a number of challenges to these attempts to connect the sectarian scrolls with a covenant community or communities.[80] Metso's own work on the history of the Community Rule has shifted the ground of discussion of the sectarian foundation documents, by demonstrating that the Community Rule may never have existed in a single authoritative redaction, but rather that several different versions of the text—with different understandings of communal leadership—may have been in circulation at the same time.[81] From this analysis, Metso concludes that we must understand the sectarian rule scrolls in terms of their ongoing use and development in the communities for which they were authoritative. Rather than understanding texts like the Community Rule as 'handbooks' or 'rule-books,' she suggests viewing them as evidence of the judicial decisions and oral traditions of the community, which

---

sectarian), see Boccaccini, *Beyond the Essene Hypothesis*, 57–58. García Martínez and van der Woude divide the scrolls into five categories, four of which appear as part of a developmental model. In addition to scriptural texts, they refer developmentally to (1) "works belonging to the apocalyptic tradition which gave rise to Essenism and which were considered as part of the common heritage"; (2) works which are demonstrably 'Essene' in character but which display none of the characteristic tendencies of the sectarian texts; (3) "works of the formative period" of the community, in which the beginnings of sectarianism are noticeable as a departure from the 'Essenism' in which the movement developed; and (4) sectarian works that display "the thought or the halakhah of Qumran in its most developed and typical form." See García Martínez and van der Woude, 'A "Groningen" Hypothesis,' 525.

[79] Davies, 'Was there a Community?' 9–35. See esp. 13–14, for his discussion of multiple communities described in the scrolls. Also see 17–23 for his review and critique of the theories of community presented in VanderKam, *Dead Sea Scrolls Today*, 71–98; and Stegemann, 'The Qumran Essenes,' 83–166.

[80] Sarianna Metso, 'Constitutional Rules at Qumran,' in Flint and VanderKam, *Dead Sea Scrolls After Fifty Years*, 1.186–210. Metso ends her overview article with a series of provocative questions about the functions of rule texts in the communities associated with them, the relationships between the rule texts and scriptural law, and the usefulness of the rules for the reconstruction of community history. See 208–9.

[81] Sarianna Metso, *The Textual Development of the Qumran Community Rule* (New York: Brill, 1997), esp. 154–55.

would have been binding in a way that no single manuscript tradition could have been.⁸² Especially significant for our discussion is Metso's sophisticated response to the question of how textual development and communal development relate to one another. As she observes:

> The plurality of the various rule texts found at Qumran, on the one hand, and the fact that older versions of the documents continued to be copied even when new versions were available, on the other hand, warn us against placing an equal-sign between the picture painted by a document and the historical reality behind it. Whereas literary- and redaction-critical analysis of a document can provide some indication about the comparative age of a rule or practice, linking a rule or practice with an actual historical period of time is far more difficult.⁸³

Although we may be able to indicate the origin-period of a text, or of a particular redaction (or subsection) of a text, this does not necessarily allow us to correlate 'the meaning' of the text with a single historical period or set of historical events.

The literary critical approach to sectarian texts taken in this volume is supported by Metso's insights into the construction of 'constitutional rules' and their relationship to specific historical periods. As well as highlighting the complexities of textual composition, even in a single period in the history of the text, Metso also introduces the issue of textual authority and its mobilization in sectarian communities. Based on these insights, we can suggest a further issue for discussion: the potential for changes in the meanings of sectarian texts, even outside the process of revision, through their re-interpretation and in light of new ideological claims or challenges to communal authority. It is not only the case that the *content* of a text may change in the course of its transmission in a sectarian community. More to the point, even in cases where 'the text' itself does not change, 'the meaning' of the text—grounded in audience interpretations of it—may continue to develop in complex and dynamic ways.

---

⁸² Sarianna Metso, 'In Search of the *Sitz im Leben* of the *Community Rule*,' in *The Provo International Conference on the Dead Sea Scrolls: Technological Innovations, New Texts, and Reformulated Issues* (ed. Donald Parry and Eugene Ulrich; Boston: Brill, 1999), 314.

⁸³ Metso, 'Constitutional Rules,' 209. 'Literary-critical analysis' in this case is specifically a reference to source-critical approaches to the sectarian texts; see Metso, 'Constitutional Rules,' 188–89, 194–95, for discussions of source critical approaches to the Community Rule and the Damascus Document.

Communal authority is a major point of concern in our understanding of the relationships between text and community. As we have seen in our earlier discussions, scrolls scholars tend to focus on the origin-moments of a text, and on an author's original intention—grounded in a set of real historical events—which is associated with those origin-moments. The view of communal authority that is constructed in this context tends to be fairly static, and when it is combined with a harmonistic reading of the sectarian scrolls, it allows for a fixed presentation of the origins of communal authority. A common version of this narrative has located communal authority in the figure of the Teacher of Righteousness, who is perceived to be a founder (or early leader) of the covenant community, and who often is presented as the author of the various sectarian and proto-sectarian scrolls (including, especially, the Temple Scroll, the Hodayot, and most recently 4QMMT).[84] The authority of the Teacher, according to this approach, continues after his death in the sectarian texts that his community associates with him or with his authorship. An alternative view, which is significantly more dynamic in its perspective and analysis, understands communal authority as variously "vested in the community's priestly elite, scribal experts, wisdom class, lay 'elders', charismatic figures, or the community as a whole."[85]

From a literary critical perspective, communal authority and textual authority are never simple or absolute. To the extent that a text's 'true meaning' is always a site of interpretation and contestation, the authoritative claims of the text always are subject to the interpretations of the communities who read it, transmit it, and permit it to shape their world.[86] Consequently, authority in the covenant community is not a fixed and eternal status (except to the extent that covenanters attribute final authority to God) but may be conferred upon whichever members or leaders of the community demonstrate a legitimate claim to it, or whichever texts are read in terms

---

[84] One version of this narrative is presented in Vermes, *The Complete Dead Sea Scrolls*, 54–66, although Vermes is careful not to attribute authorship explicitly to the Teacher; see his discussion of the authorship of the Hodayot on page 244. Fraade addresses this question and provides bibliography in Steven Fraade, 'Interpretive Authority in the Studying Community at Qumran,' *JJS* 44 (1993): 49, 51, n. 9, 10, 15.

[85] Fraade, 'Interpretive Authority,' 47.

[86] For an extensive discussion of the complexities of authority, see Bruce Lincoln, *Authority: Construction and Corrosion* (Chicago: University of Chicago Press, 1994).

of such claims. In addition, definitions of 'legitimacy'—which provide the context for appeals to authoritative status—may vary widely. In the Damascus Document, authority often is framed in terms of having a special knowledge of God's will; other texts contain claims that the sectarians have access to the true meanings of scripture and prophecy, including meanings that were not immediately accessible in the past, even to the prophets themselves.[87] Other appeals to authority may vary, depending on the claims of individual leaders and the specific communal conflicts they might face.

Contestation of authority also plays directly into the larger question of the construction of textual meaning. A return to the distinctions between sectarian, proto-sectarian, and non-sectarian texts is a useful frame for this discussion, especially as it points to the dynamic process of authority-construction. For the members of a sectarian community—as for the members of any community with a shared tradition and a shared collection of authoritative texts—a primary tool in the construction of authority would be the mobilization of those shared traditions in support of an interpreter's own more narrowly-drawn ideological claims. That is, in attempting to establish communal authority (whether in terms of halakhic or theological assertions, or in terms of other intracommunal disputes), sectarian leaders would need to demonstrate the authenticity of their specific arguments in the context of the community's shared traditions.

The construction of such intrasectarian claims can be imagined as a series of 'back-readings' of new views onto shared traditions. For Damascus covenanters, this sort of appeal to authority might involve re-reading the original claims of the Damascus Document in support of a new argument or in light of new texts. Or it might involve looking back to earlier and more generalized (i.e., 'nonsectarian') traditions, to demonstrate the extent to which those texts also support the new authoritative claims. The goal of this sort of back-reading is to demonstrate the extent to which the earlier text—whether a sectarian text like the Damascus Document, a proto-sectarian text like the Temple Scroll, or an ostensibly non-sectarian text

---

[87] For example, see CD 2.12, for the claim that God's knowledge is transmitted to the community through the teachings of 'God's anointed.' An even clearer example of this sort of argument is found in 1QpHab 7.1–5, where we learn that Habakkuk received God's prophecy, but that its true message was fully understood only by the Teacher.

like the book of Numbers or the prophecies of Isaiah—*already* assumes the goals or perspectives associated with the new authoritative sectarian claims. The new claims are not new, according to this reasoning; they are merely being exposed for the first time. By 'exposing' the 'true' sectarian meaning of a text whose authority extends far beyond the boundaries of the sect itself, readers tap into a significant source of authority, demonstrating the authenticity and antiquity of arguments that might otherwise—at least to unsympathetic readers—risk appearing problematically 'new' or deviant.

Cycles of reading and interpretation, in this way, contribute to the mobilization of new textual meanings and new authoritative claims, based on texts whose authority is already assumed. That such new interpretations can be understood as 'old' and thereby 'authoritative' demonstrates both the complexity of communal authority and the strength of ideology in constructing historical narratives. This dynamic also works in reverse: just as changes in a community can contribute to changes in textual interpretation or meaning, so can texts, themselves, contribute to the changes in a community, and or at least in its ideological self-understanding. Steven Fraade addresses this point in his larger discussion of interpretive authority. If the main sectarian scrolls were copied in order to be studied and used communally, he proposes:

> we must ask *how* these texts through their very study constructed and confirmed their readers' self-understanding as a socially unitary and separate community, divinely chosen to prepare an exegetical and ruled way through the wilderness to the very end of days.[88]

As Fraade's challenge suggests, textual interpretation can shape a community's self-understanding just as extensively as the community's experiences might shape their understanding of a text. The narratives found in the Damascus Document may begin as 'models of' a community—in the sense that they provide an account of the foundation and early history of the group—but they can serve, in later periods, as 'models for' the order and identity of that community.[89] This process generates a daisy-chain of textual interpretation

---

[88] Fraade, 'Interpretive Authority,' 69; see also Newsom, 'Apocalyptic and Discourse,' 135–44.

[89] The notion that texts (and other cultural formations) can provide both 'models of' a society and 'models for' its ongoing development is presented in Clifford

and identity-construction, in which the dynamic understanding of historical experience (both personal and communal) is shaped by and articulated in terms of the shared ideologies of the community, grounded in the texts they view as authoritative. In looking backward, at the history of their community, sectarian readers find models with which to look forward, to address new challenges and re-shape their community in ways that fit with their inherited traditions.

In the course of the construction of communal authority, and the challenges to it, we might also note the important distinction between acceptable intrasectarian diversity and unacceptable deviation from shared sectarian practices or beliefs. Metso has noted that the complex relationships of the sectarian texts hints at a potential for diversity within the context of a single sectarian movement.[90] At the same time, the basic definition of sectarian movements understands them as arising out of—and being regularly prone to—schismatic conflict.[91] It is possible that the sectarian scrolls are the literary product of a single sectarian movement, but it is also possible that they reflect the presence of a complex network of sectarian movements, divided on issues of halakhah,[92] or on other points of ideological, theological, or social concern. As we lay out a literary critical approach to the history of the Damascus covenant community, this dynamic of sectarian development serves as another reminder of the lack of one-to-one correspondence between any single textual account and a single underlying set of historical events.

Geertz, *The Interpretation of Cultures* (New York: Basic Books, 1973). For a discussion of Geertz' approach to religion as cultural formation, see Brian Morris, *Anthropological Studies of Religion: An Introductory Text* (New York: Cambridge University Press, 1987), 312–19.

[90] Metso, '*Sitz im Leben* of the *Community Rule*,' 306–14.

[91] Here, a particularly useful parallel is the complex development of American Millerite movements in the years following the Great Disappointment of 1843–44. A single charismatic leader inspired the development of scores of religious groups, whose relationships to one another were, at times, quite complex. Some groups grew out of one another, while others developed independently; in the late 19th century, a number of these groups united (or reunited) to form larger and more stable religious organizations. For a brief history of Millerism and the schismatic developments of the Adventist and Jehovah's Witness religious traditions, see Bainbridge, *Sociology of Religious Movements*, 89–118.

[92] See, especially, Stegemann, 'The Qumran Essenes,' 161; for a discussion of the complexities of this issue, see also Baumgarten, *Flourishing of Jewish Sects*, 75–80, esp. n. 126. An influential discussion of the constructions of post-Second Temple (and post-sectarian) Judaism is found in Shaye Cohen, 'The Significance of Yavne: Pharisees, Rabbis, and the End of Jewish Sectarianism,' *HUCA* 55 (1984): 27–53.

Toward a 'New Historiography'

My goal in this book is to present an approach to historiography that takes seriously the challenges of contemporary literary criticism, while still attempting to ask grounded questions about real historical events. As we have seen in the above discussions, contemporary literary criticism underlines the fundamental multiplicity of textual meaning and points to the presence of distinct loci for construction of meaning, in the independent functions of 'author,' 'text,' and 'audience.' A historiographical practice based on these insights must, consequently, take an approach that is similarly 'multiple' and similarly flexible in its focus of attention. In the close readings that follow, I attempt one such practice, by reading and re-reading the Damascus Document (and, in one comparative foil, the text of 4QMMT), in terms of a number of specific ideological and thematic points. Each 'reading' is itself composite, comprising a series of interpretations or constructions of textual meaning, each assuming a different social setting or intertextual reference. With this approach, we are able to generate a variety of distinct, if hypothetical, historical scenarios in which these texts might have been written and read, and in which they might have reflected, but also shaped and had an impact upon, the events that were historically significant for their sectarian audiences.

Each reading begins with a somewhat 'conventional' presentation of textual meaning, asking what the author/editor(s) of the text in question might have intended in a given passage, or in the presentation of a given theme. The ideological constructions of the text—whether of history, group identity, or communal order—are compared, in this context, with the real historical situation in which the text may have been written, redacted, and transmitted. For the Damascus Document, such fundamental themes as righteousness, knowledge, and proper religious practice are highlighted, as is the text's significant interest in notions of exile, redemption, and return. As these readings demonstrate, the text returns repeatedly to several specific periods in Israelite history, which serve as touchstones in a discussion of the history of the community and its place in the larger world order. These readings also identify a number of grammatical or textual strategies that contribute to the text's constructions of history and communal identity.

A second stage of reading turns away from a focus on authorial intent, to focus more directly on audience responses to the text, identifying changes in the potential interpretations of a given passage or theme, when it is read and re-read by audiences in other settings or with different primary concerns. The variables that shape these readings take many forms: changes in the community in which a reading occurs, changes in the approach to interpretation (whether historical, metaphorical, or other), interpretations in light of other authoritative texts, and changes over time (as texts develop authoritative status, or as the endtimes fail to arrive), for example.

Part of the logic behind this approach is related to the common scholarly concern with getting 'behind' the text. A number of scholars have suggested that the historical references in the scrolls (especially the Damascus Document and the pesharim) are hopelessly ambiguous as evidence for real historical events, or that there is no way to get 'behind' the texts, to ask what really happened in the lives of the people who wrote (and read) them.[93] This concern is a valid one, in that it is often hard to know what the author/editor(s) of these texts 'really meant' in their original claims, much less what actual events stand behind them. In fact, it is possible that even in their original settings, these texts were perceived as ambiguous or potentially multivalent. Given this fundamental ambiguity—redefined here as textual multiplicity—an approach to the text that attempts to establish a single coherent, historically-correct narrative is necessarily limited.

This is not to say that the creation of a variety of different interpretations of the same textual passage provides a better chance for writing a single authoritative historical account of the events associated with the scrolls. It is impossible, first of all, for every one of the reconstructions and interpretations in these readings to be historically accurate. In some of the discussions in the following chapters, it may be the case that only a few (or even none) of the readings will provide something like a credible account of 'what really happened' to the community associated with these texts. What this approach underscores, instead, is the extent to which *every* construction of history based on these texts is provisional or partial. Some readings make more sensitive or more responsible use of the evi-

---

[93] See the discussion of the complexities of this issue in Campbell, 'Essene-Qumran Origins,' 143–56.

dence, taking into consideration the potential for complex relationships between texts, interpretations, and communities, but no one reading provides a complete (let alone a verifiable) account of events. Rather, each individual reading creates another layer of potential meaning for the larger interpretation of the text and its history.

We should note that this ambiguity with regard to establishing 'correct' readings does not work in the other direction: it is entirely possible to identify some readings as 'impossible' or 'incorrect,' although there will always be disagreements on what makes a reading possible or not. In some cases, conflicts over definition may lead scholars to conflicting conclusions. For example, in the discussion of sectarianism, above, the definition of the term bears on whether or not it is appropriate to label a Damascus covenant community as a 'sect.' Similarly, conflicts over interpretations of archaeological evidence, manuscript dates, the literary content of texts, and the translations of key phrases or expressions all may contribute to fundamental disagreements among historians of the scrolls.[94] Thus, for historians who date the composition of a majority of the scrolls to the period before the turn of the era, for example, it is possible to eliminate those theories that assign the origins of the community to a Christian setting.[95]

In light of these two observations—that some readings can be judged to be wrong, but no readings can be *proven* right—a literary-critical approach provides a number of methodological tools for writing history. First, a shift away from the focus on the events 'behind' the text allows us to pay more attention to the development of the history and ideology of the covenant community over time, and to recognize the potential for significant changes in the course of that development. Similarly, by turning our attention to ideological constructions rather than historical events, such an approach allows us

---

[94] For technical studies on issues of archaeology, dating of the manuscripts, and other important issues, see such recent volumes as Parry and Ulrich, *Provo International Conference*; Flint and VanderKam, *Dead Sea Scrolls after Fifty Years*; and Michael Wise, Norman Golb, John Collins, and Dennis Pardee, eds., *Methods of Investigation of the Dead Sea Scrolls and the Khirbet Qumran Site: Present Realities and Future Prospects* (New York: The New York Academy of Sciences, 1994).

[95] See, for example, Robert Eisenman, *James the Just in the Habakkuk Pesher* (Leiden: Brill, 1986); Eisenman, *Maccabees, Zadokites, Christians and Qumran* (Leiden: Brill, 1983); Barbara Thiering, *Jesus and the Riddle of the Dead Sea Scrolls* (San Francisco: HarperCollins, 1992); and Thiering, *The Gospels and Qumran: A New Hypothesis* (Sydney: Theological Explorations, 1981).

to ask about a different set of historical topics: what the covenanters thought about their own history, how they understood their role in the world and their own communal identity, how they might have reacted to the events they experienced, and how their understanding of their texts may have changed over time. Together, these approaches allow for a more careful and responsible scholarship, which does not risk identifying as historical an array of evidence that is better understood as an ideological construction.

At the same time, this approach allows for a form of scholarship that can afford to be more radical: in the process of generating a variety of readings of the same text, and speculating on how a text may have been read and re-read, interpreted and re-interpreted, it is appropriate to consider an extreme range of interpretations, which might not be considered in cases where the goal is to generate the single 'most likely' historical account. In this case, even readings that may not make sense as 'original' meanings for a text (such as the various Christian interpretations of the scrolls, to return to that example) can be examined as potential readings, in the context of many potential readings, by hypothetical audiences in situations other than the original setting of the text.

Presenting a 'new historiography' at the intersection of history and literary criticism is not, in itself, a new project: in the last few decades, the work of historians and literary critics has moved—not always unproblematically—toward an overlay of complementary concerns. Scholars have recognized, on the one hand, the 'literariness' of our evidence for the events of history and, on the other, the importance of historically-contextualized readings of the texts known as literature.[96] Assumptions about the cultural construction of discourse and

---

[96] On historiographical narratives as literary texts, see Hayden White, *Tropics of Discourse: Essays in Cultural Criticism* (Baltimore: Johns Hopkins University Press, 1978), esp. 'The Historical Text as Literary Artifact,' 81–100; and White, *Metahistory: The Historical Imagination in Nineteenth-Century Europe* (Baltimore: Johns Hopkins University Press, 1973), esp. 'Introduction: The Poetics of History.' Recent literary critical discussions of 'New Historicism' have reintroduced the importance of historical context into the discussion of literary texts, in marked contrast to the 'New Criticism' of an earlier generation. See H. Aram Veeser, ed., *The New Historicism* (New York: Routledge, 1989) and Veeser, *The New Historicism Reader* (New York: Routledge, 1994). For a historiographical response to New Historicism's literary critical approach, note especially Hayden White, 'New Historicism: A Comment,' in Veeser, *The New Historicism*, 293–302. For discussions in the context of ancient history, see Averil Cameron, ed., *History as Text: The Writing of Ancient History* (London: Duckworth, 1989).

the complex but intimate connections between 'knowledge' and 'power' are equally common in recent historiographical discussions.[97] However, among scholars of the Dead Sea Scrolls, as the discussion above has suggested, such methodological questions remain largely unexplored.

At minimum, the literary-critical historiography of this project highlights several points that might reshape a discussion of ancient Jewish sectarianism: the function of ideology as an element in the construction of textual meaning; the contestation of authority in the course of meaning-construction; and the usefulness of multiple readings and readings in terms of textual multiplicity, in the context of a larger historiographical process. At maximum, this approach goes further, calling into question the conclusiveness of *any* single historical claim, or any historical claim presented as conclusive or comprehensive. To the extent that textual meaning must be understood as complex, dynamic, and constantly a point of tension and contestation, that is, it follows that historical claims based upon readings of such textual evidence can be understood as similarly problematic. In the context of current scrolls scholarship—in which old assumptions have been called into question, and newly-published texts suggest revisions of established historical claims—this experimental approach may contribute to a more fundamental re-evaluation of the methodology and reading strategies that underlie basic Dead Sea Scrolls historiography.

---

[97] The interwoven dynamic of knowledge and power, and the basic understanding of discourse as a practice of cultural construction—both drawn from the scholarship of Michel Foucault—are implicit concerns throughout this study, even if they are not always subject to explicit discussion. See especially the analysis of 'discourse' and the definition of 'statements' in Michel Foucault, *The Archaeology of Knowledge and The Discourse on Language* (trans. A. M. Sheridan Smith; New York: Pantheon Books, 1972). The shorter passages and interviews in Foucault, *Power/Knowledge: Selected Interviews and Other Writings 1972–1977* (New York: Pantheon Books, 1980) provide a particularly accessible introduction to his claims with regard to discourse and its contestation.

CHAPTER TWO

TWO TEST CASES

As an introduction to the methodology of this project, it will be useful to begin with two 'test cases,' which demonstrate in brief the approaches to the Damascus Document that are pursued more extensively in the chapters that follow. The first of these test cases offers a reading of the Damascus Document in terms of a subject that has received very little attention in discussions of ancient Jewish sectarianism: the issue of gender. Foregrounding a discussion of the constructions of masculinity and femininity—and the construction of covenant participation in terms of such gender norms—allows us to raise questions about the Damascus covenant community that are not otherwise possible. This approach highlights the androcentric tendencies of this text, asking how those tendencies might reflect the actual makeup of the covenant community and the actual relationships of real men and real women in that community. By calling into question the text's construction of 'the covenanter' as normatively male, we are able to address a number of important issues that might otherwise remain concealed.

The second reading in this chapter goes further afield, in textual terms, by addressing the text of 4QMMT, Miqsat Ma'ase ha-Torah. This text records a series of halakhic statements, which are presented as the primary points of disagreement between the author/editor of the text and an opposing group within the larger ancient Jewish community. By reading this text in terms of a variety of hypothetical genre constraints (understanding it as an actual letter sent from one leader to another, as a treatise designed for intracommunal use, or as a retrospective account of events remembered or preserved in tradition), we can attempt to locate MMT in its larger historical context. In understanding the text as part of a communal tradition, we are able to ask not only how its interpretations changed over time, but also how readings of the text may have shaped the historical consciousness of its interpreters, throughout the periods of its use. Interpretations of the text will also vary depending on the literary context in which MMT is read, or the specific interpretive strategies that are applied to it.

Case one: querying gender in the Damascus Document

Until quite recently, scholars of the Dead Sea Scrolls have had very little to say about the place of women in the context of an ancient Jewish covenant community,[1] and still less to say about the construction of gender in the scrolls. In part, this is a response to the content of the scrolls themselves: like the Hebrew scriptures, the scrolls tend to be androcentric texts, written by men, for men, and with a marked tendency to focus on men's experiences and men's responsibilities. As such, they manage to erase women from all but the most passive of roles. For this reason, a discussion of the Damascus Document in terms of its construction of gender—understood here as the culturally specific "knowledge of sexual difference"[2]—requires recognizing the ideological basis of that construction, and asking how the understanding of gender articulated in the text may have related to the experiences of a real covenant community, whether it recorded their past experiences, helped to shape their communal norms, or served both of these roles.

---

[1] An increased interest in this topic is reflected by the Qumran Section's decision to devote a full session at the 2000 Annual Meeting of the Society of Biblical Literature to the topic of 'Women and Children at Qumran.' Eileen Schuller has done the landmark work in the field; see Schuller, 'Women in the Dead Sea Scrolls,' in Wise, et al., *Methods of Investigation*, 115–31; Schuller, 'Women in the Dead Sea Scrolls,' in Flint and VanderKam, *Dead Sea Scrolls After Fifty Years*, 2.117–44; and Eileen Schuller and Cecilia Wassen, 'Women: Daily Life,' in *Encyclopedia of the Dead Sea Scrolls* (ed. Lawrence Schiffman and James VanderKam; Oxford: Oxford University Press, 2000), 981–84. Other recent discussions of women in the scrolls include Hannah Cotton, 'Women: The Texts,' in Schiffman and VanderKam, *Encyclopedia*, 984–87; Lawrence Schiffman, 'Laws Pertaining to Women in the *Temple Scroll*,' in *The Dead Sea Scrolls: Forty Years of Research* (ed. Devorah Dimant and Uriel Rappaport; New York: Brill, 1992), 210–28; Schiffman, 'Women in the Scrolls,' in *Reclaiming*, 127–43; Linda Bennett Elder, 'The Woman Question and Female Ascetics Among Essenes,' *BA* 57 (1994): 220–34; Philip Davies and Joan Taylor, 'On the Testimony of Women in 1QSa,' *DSD* 3 (1996): 223–35; Sigrid Peterson, 'Caves, Documents, Women: Archives and Archivists,' in *The Dead Sea Scrolls: Fifty Years After Their Discovery; Proceedings of the Jerusalem Congress, July 20–25, 1997* (ed. Lawrence Schiffman, Emanuel Tov, and James VanderKam; Jerusalem: Israel Exploration Society, 2000), 761–72; and Lena Cansdale, 'Status of Women Members of the Scroll Community,' in *Qumran and the Essenes: A Re-evaluation of the Evidence* (Tübingen: Mohr (Siebeck), 1997), 49–57.

[2] For gender as the "knowledge of sexual difference" (understanding 'knowledge' in the Foucauldian sense, with a recognition of 'power' as a related dynamic), see Joan Scott, *Gender and the Politics of History* (New York: Columbia University Press, 1988).

References to gender in modern scrolls scholarship tend to arise most often—if at all—in a discussion of whether the community associated with the scrolls was celibate or marrying.³ According to the classical Essene hypothesis, the 'Essenes of Qumran' were a community of celibate males, who had gathered together in the Judaean wilderness ("with only the palm trees for company," according to Pliny's account), to await the endtimes, which were rapidly approaching. A corollary to this view recognizes an offshoot community of marrying Essenes, represented by the Damascus Document and mentioned by Josephus in one of his accounts of the Essene lifestyle.⁴

Currently, the Essene hypothesis is receiving a thorough reconsideration. Scholars have become aware of the dangers of equating the Essenes unproblematically with the scrolls community (or communities).⁵ The origins of the group are being re-evaluated, as is the dating of the habitation site at Khirbet Qumran,⁶ and of the manuscripts found in the caves nearby.⁷ Most recently, new attention has

---

³ On this topic see, for example, Elisha Qimron, 'Celibacy in the Dead Sea Scrolls and the Two Kinds of Sectarians,' in *The Madrid Qumran Congress: Proceedings of the International Congress on the Dead Sea Scrolls; Madrid, 18–21 March, 1991* (ed. Julio Barrera and Luis Montaner; New York: Brill, 1992), 287–94; Sara Japhet, 'The Prohibition of the Habitation of Women: The Temple Scroll's Attitude Toward Sexual Impurity and its Biblical Precedents,' *JANES* 22 (1993): 69–87; John Strugnell, 'More on Wives and Marriage in the Dead Sea Scrolls: (*4Q416* 2 ii 21 [Cf. *1 Thess* 4:4] and *4QMMT* B),' *RevQ* 17 (1996): 537–47; and Charlotte Hempel, 'Community Structures in the Dead Sea Scrolls: Admissions, Organization, Disciplinary Procedures,' in Flint and VanderKam, *Dead Sea Scrolls After Fifty Years*, 2.86–87 and n. 71.

⁴ For Josephus' reference to 'marrying Essenes,' see *War* 2.160–61. See chapter one, above, for further discussion of the Essene hypothesis, reinterpretations of it, and relevant bibliography.

⁵ Scholars note that the references to the Essenes in Josephus, Philo, and Pliny may be incomplete, inaccurate, or ideologically-framed; there is also an awareness that these descriptions confirm each other, but not as fully as earlier scholarly readings might have claimed. See Philip Davies, 'The Birthplace of the Essenes: Where is "Damascus"?' *RevQ* 14 (1990): 507–8; Davies, *Behind the Essenes*, 15–31, esp. 23. Many scholars continue to refer to the covenant community as 'Essenes,' noting that this is the most likely (and therefore the most appropriate) designation for the group; see Vermes, *The Complete Dead Sea Scrolls*; VanderKam, *Dead Sea Scrolls Today*. Others make a point of distinguishing between 'Essenes' and the 'Dead Sea sectarians'; see Baumgarten, *Flourishing of Jewish Sects*, 1–2 n. 1, for a discussion of this approach. Of related interest is Joan Taylor and Philip Davies, 'The So-Called Therapeutae of *De Vita Contemplativa*: Identity and Character,' *HTR* 91 (1998): 3–24.

⁶ See Jodi Magness, 'Qumran Archaeology: Past Perspectives and Future Prospects,' in Flint and VanderKam, *Dead Sea Scrolls After Fifty Years*, 1.47–77. See also the series of archaeological articles in Wise, et al., *Methods of Investigation*, 1–113.

⁷ On the paleographic dating of the scrolls, see Frank Moore Cross, 'Paleography and the Dead Sea Scrolls,' in Flint and VanderKam, *Dead Sea Scrolls After Fifty Years*,

been paid to the cemeteries at Qumran and to the gender of the bodies buried in them.[8] It should be no surprise, in the context of these scholarly developments, that the question of marital status among members of the covenant community also has come under recent reconsideration, by scholars who vary in their perceptions of the community as comprising families, married men, celibate men, or some combination thereof.[9]

If this question of marriage-versus-celibacy has been a point of some interest for scrolls scholars, it has been—as Eileen Schuller notes in a recent discussion of women in the Dead Sea Scrolls—almost the *only* point that scholars have raised with regard to women and the scrolls.[10] Schuller's several discussions of women and the scrolls community provide a significant response to this state of affairs, introducing a feminist critical analysis and assessing the possible roles of women in the communities represented by the scrolls. She concludes that women were certainly part of a community associated with the Damascus Document and has suggested that women might

---

1.379–402; this article is an update of Cross, 'The Development of the Jewish Scripts,' in *The Bible and The Ancient Near East: Essays in Honor of William Foxwell Albright* (ed. G. Ernest Wright; Winona Lake, Ind: Eisenbrauns, 1979), 133–202. A chart of standard paleographic dates for the 'sectarian' scrolls can be found in Michael Wise, *The First Messiah: Investigating the Savior Before Jesus* (San Francisco: HarperSanFrancisco, 1999), 330–33 n. 34. On radiocarbon dating of the scrolls, see Greg Doudna, 'Dating the Scrolls on the Basis of Radiocarbon Analysis,' in Flint and VanderKam, *Dead Sea Scrolls After Fifty Years*, 1.430–71; as well as Doudna, 'Paleography and the dating of individual Qumran texts,' posted to http://orion.mscc.huji.ac.il/orion/programs/Doudna.html on Aug. 17, 1999. Doudna argues for a 'single-generation' hypothesis with respect to scrolls composition; his argument has been challenged and discussed at some length on the Orion discussion list; see http://orion.mscc.huji.ac.il/orion/archives (Aug. 15–Sept. 1, 1999), for posts by Doudna, Timothy Jull, and David Suter.

[8] The presence or absence of female skeletons in the main cemetery at Qumran (and the dating of female skeletons in the auxiliary cemeteries) remains an open question, in my opinion. See Olav Röhrer-Ertl, Ferdinand Rohrhirsch, and Dietbert Hahn, 'Über die Gräberfelder von Khirbet Qumran, insbesondere die Funde der Campagne 1956. I: Anthropologische Datenvorlage und Erstauswertung aufgrund der Collectio Kurth,' *RevQ* 19 (1999): 3–46; Joan Taylor, 'The Cemeteries of Khirbet Qumran and Women's Presence at the Site,' *DSD* 6 (1999): 285–323; Joseph Zias, 'The Cemeteries of Qumran and Celibacy: Confusion Laid to Rest?' *DSD* 7 (2000): 220–53; and Jodi Magness, 'Women at Qumran?' forthcoming.

[9] For a variety of developed views, compare Schiffman, *Reclaiming*; Stegemann, 'The Qumran Essenes' and *The Library of Qumran*; and Vermes, *The Complete Dead Sea Scrolls*, 46–48. See also E. Cook, 'What was Qumran? A Ritual Purification Center,' *BAR* 22.6 (1996): 39, 48–51, 73–75.

[10] Schuller, 'Women in the Dead Sea Scrolls,' in Wise, et al., *Methods of Investigation*, 117.

have been able to become full members of such a group.¹¹ She notes that one of the ancient witnesses to the Damascus Document includes a reference to "the mothers" (האמות) and "the fathers" (האבות) of the community, terms that may have referred to positions of authority ('elders') in the group.¹² Although the punishment for an offense against the mothers is minimal compared to the punishment for a similar offense against the fathers (a 10-day penalty as opposed to permanent banishment), Schuller notes that "the obvious discrepancy and apparently lesser honor accorded to the 'mothers' should not blind us to the fact that men and women are given parallel titles."¹³

Schuller's analysis of the descriptions of women in the Damascus Document offers an important corrective to scholarship on the scrolls community. She points to the complex social reality 'behind' the text and is careful to note that androcentric texts (including "legal prescriptions written by men and from a male perspective") are unlikely to have "mirrored totally or accurately the lived situation or status of women within their communities."¹⁴ This observation is an important one, and to it we can add several others, based on the discussions of the previous chapter. First, if the Damascus Document presents an image of women that does not provide a transparent view of real women, it is also the case that its presentation of *men* works in this way. Understandings of proper male and female roles are constructed in the text in ways that reflect the larger goals and ideals of its author/editor(s) but may not reflect a total social reality. It follows, from this observation, that gender in the text is not

---

¹¹ Schuller, 'Women in the Dead Sea Scrolls,' in Wise, et al., *Methods of Investigation*, 121–24. In her later discussion of the subject, Schuller argues for a shift away from language of 'full membership' and toward a discussion of women's 'independent' participation in the community; see Schuller, 'Women in the Dead Sea Scrolls,' in Flint and VanderKam, *Dead Sea Scrolls After Fifty Years*, 2.129–31. Elder argues that women would have lived at Qumran and that, although they may not have been full members of a Qumran community, their self-understanding would have been shaped by the "theological perspectives, ascetic praxis, and doctrinal proscriptions" of the scrolls. See Elder, 'The Woman Question,' 232. Schiffman and Stegemann both hold the view that women could not become full members of the covenant community. See Schiffman, *Sectarian Law*, 57, for the view that women became part of the community only as adjuncts to their fathers or husbands; similarly, see Stegemann, 'The Qumran Essenes,' 129.

¹² 4Q270 7 i 13–15; see Baumgarten, DJD XVIII, 162–66.

¹³ Schuller, 'Women in the Dead Sea Scrolls,' in Wise, et al., *Methods of Investigation*, 122.

¹⁴ Schuller, 'Women in the Dead Sea Scrolls,' in Wise, et al., *Methods of Investigation*, 125.

unitary or absolute. Rather, like the interpretations of scripture or the understandings of history, constructions of gender may develop and change, as part of an ongoing and always-contested interpretive process.[15] The gender constructions in the Damascus Document certainly reflected the beliefs of the author/editor(s) of the text, but they went on to be understood in new ways by the various audiences of the text, who would in turn allow their understandings of those norms to shape their own experiences.[16]

Beginning with these observations, we can address a number of important interpretive questions: how did the author/editor(s) of the Damascus Document understand the roles of women—*and men*—in their covenant community, and to what extent (and in what ways) did that ideological understanding reflect a set of real historical events or structures in the community? Is it possible to get 'behind' the text to those events? Given the ideological claims of the text, how might later covenanters have understood the roles of women and men, as participants in their larger covenant community? Can we imagine a situation in which new interpretations of the Damascus Document might have led to changes in the gendered order of the covenant community, in later periods or in the face of new social circumstances?

A useful place to begin is with a reading of the Damascus Document in terms of its 'original' construction of gender, in the sense of its author/editor(s)' original intentions, understood for the moment as equated with the unitary sense of the text itself. In this context, the textual presentation is explicitly androcentric. Written by, for, and

---

[15] Notions of contestation, in textual meaning and also in social settings, are addressed especially by poststructuralist feminist criticism. See, for example, Linda Nicholson, ed., *Feminism/Postmodernism* (New York: Routledge, 1990); Teresa de Lauretis, ed., *Feminist Studies/Critical Studies* (Bloomington: Indiana University Press, 1986); Michele Barrett, 'Words and Things: Materialism and Method in Contemporary Feminist Analysis,' in *Destabilizing Theory: Contemporary Feminist Debates* (ed. Michele Barrett and Anne Phillips; Cambridge: Polity Press, 1992), 201–19; and Joan Scott, 'Deconstructing Equality-versus-Difference: Or, the Uses of Poststructuralist Theory for Feminism,' *Feminist Studies* 14 (1988): 33–50.

[16] Scott addresses the issue of contestation in constructions of gender, noting the importance of asking "questions about *how* hierarchies such as those of gender are constructed or legitimized. The emphasis on 'how' suggests a study of processes, not of origins, of multiple rather than single causes." See Scott, 'Deconstructing,' 4. For a particularly insightful discussion of the 'how' questions in the context of the gendered study of Judaism, see Miriam Peskowitz, 'Engendering Jewish Religious History,' in *Judaism Since Gender* (ed. Miriam Peskowitz and Laura Levitt; New York: Routledge, 1997), 20–21.

about men, this text assumes that masculinity is the 'normal' or unmarked state of human experience. Women in androcentric texts tend to be invisible, unnamed, and silent adjuncts, who appear when necessary to a storyline or discussion and then, when they are no longer immediately relevant, fade once more into the background.[17] In modeling its accounts of communal history and identity on scriptural accounts of the history of Israel, the Damascus Document adopts androcentric tendencies from the scriptural texts and then develops them in an even more androcentric direction.

The Damascus covenanter is arguably a masculine figure. In part, language contributes to this phenomenon: references to the covenant community consistently appear in the masculine plural (which can, but need not, include a female presence), with some in the masculine singular. The covenanters are those who "know righteousness" (יודעי צדק, CD 1.1). In that they are those who "enter the covenant" (באי ברית, CD 2.2), "each man" is responsible to behave properly with respect to "his brother" (איש ... את אחיהו, CD 6.20, etc.). And a distinction is made between covenanters "who walk [in the ways of the community] in perfect holiness" (המתהלכים ... בתמים קדש, CD 7.4–5) and those who "live (in) camps ... and take wives and beget sons" (מחנות ישבו ... ולקחו נשים והולידו בנים, CD 7.6–7; parallel in CD 19.3).[18] These sons, in turn, are to take an oath and to be initiated into the covenant when they reach the appropriate age (CD 15.5–6). The masculine language in this case masks a certain ambiguity: the covenanters are to initiate "their sons" (בניהם) into the covenant, but the text fails to specify whether this potentially-inclusive term refers to daughters also, or only to male offspring. In this way, the language of the text constructs the covenanter as normatively male but also permits for specifically gendered references should they become necessary.

---

[17] For discussions of these issues in the context of Judaism in antiquity, see especially Ross S. Kraemer, *Her Share of the Blessings: Women's Religions Among Pagans, Jews, and Christians in the Greco-Roman World* (New York: Oxford University Press, 1992); Kraemer, 'Monastic Jewish Women in Greco-Roman Egypt: Philo Judaeus on the Therapeutrides,' *Signs* 14 (1989): 342–70; Levine, *"Women Like This"*; and Miriam Peskowitz, *Spinning Fantasies: Rabbis, Gender, and History* (Berkeley: University of California Press, 1997). For additional bibliography, see Schuller, 'Women in the Dead Sea Scrolls,' in Wise, et al., *Methods of Investigation*, 115 n. 3; Kraemer, 'Monastic Jewish Women,' 343 n. 4.

[18] The ambiguities of gender implicit in this masculine-plural construction are discussed at length below.

Although the text constructs the normal participant in the covenant as a man, it does not erase women entirely. In fact, to the extent that the text imagines the community as a microcosm of the people of Israel,[19] the text's very ideology requires that women be included as part of that population. The references to men's and women's actions in the text, however, are telling. General references take a masculine form: "a man" takes upon himself the oath to return to the covenant (האיש, CD 16.1; איש, CD 16.7, 9), and he is thereupon responsible for his own actions, as well as those of the women in his household (daughters and wives, CD 16.10–12). References to men's actions range widely, addressing everything from theft to sabbath practices to public decency. In contrast, legal references to women almost invariably cluster around a set of related issues: marriage and divorce;[20] the ordeal of the sotah and the reputation of a new bride;[21] menstruation, birth, and post-partum purity;[22] and proper sexual practices within marriage.[23] A few explicit mentions of women (as maidservants, in reference to oaths) are not overtly sexualized,[24] but these are the exceptions to the text's implicit rule: women are of direct interest only in relation to their sexual and reproductive capacities, or to the extent that they may prove disruptive to the normative male order. Women may be "brought into a holy covenant," by marriage to a male covenanter,[25] but this in no way requires the

---

[19] Discussed at greater length in chapter five.

[20] CD 13.17; 4Q266 9 iii 4–5, 4Q266 14 a, and 4Q269 9 1–2 in Baumgarten, DJD XVIII, 70–71, 80, 132–33.

[21] 4Q269 9 4–8, 4Q270 2 i 16–19, 4Q270 4 1–9, and 4Q271 3 15, in Baumgarten, DJD XVIII, 132–33, 142–44, 152–54, 175–77.

[22] 4Q266 6 ii 1–13, 4Q272 1 ii 1–10, and 4Q273 5 4–5, in Baumgarten, DJD XVIII, 55–57, 189–91, 197.

[23] 4Q267 9 vi 4–5, in Baumgarten, DJD XVIII, 110–11. Other laws regarding sexual practices can be found in CD 12.1, and 4Q270 2 ii 15–17, in Baumgarten, DJD XVIII, 144–46.

[24] For nurses dealing with babies on the Sabbath, see CD 11.11; for other references to female slaves and servants, see CD 11.12, 12.10–11; on sex with bondwomen, see 4Q266 12 and 4Q270 4 13–16 in Baumgarten, DJD XVIII, 78–79, 152–54.

[25] Several of the ancient manuscripts contain an injunction against bringing a woman with a bad sexual reputation into 'holy covenant' and assert that such a woman should be examined by a reliable woman before being accepted. See 4Q269 9 4–8, with parallels in 4Q270 5 17, and 4Q271 3 11, in Baumgarten, DJD XVIII, 132–33, 154–55, 175–77. Baumgarten understands this passage only as a reference to marriage and not as a reference to full membership in the covenant community; see Baumgarten, DJD XVIII, 177, esp. the note to line 11. For references to slaves and maidservants as members of the 'covenant of Abraham,' see also CD 12.10–11.

text to present them as full or active participants in the covenant community.

In its historical accounts, the Damascus Document demonstrates an even more pervasive androcentrism, erasing women almost entirely, even from narratives in which their presence might be expected. An account of cosmic history (CD 2.14–3.12) presents mostly generalized references, to groups like the Watchers, the sons of Noah, the patriarchs, and the people of Israel. The patriarchs—Abraham, Isaac, and Jacob—are the only individuals to be named in this narrative. A more specific description of Israelite history (CD 4.12–5.14) includes references to a variety of figures, including prophets (Isaiah), ancestors of priestly lines (Levi, Eleazar, Zadok), and national leaders and kings (Joshua, the elders, Moses, and David). Neither of these large-scale narratives makes reference to specific women, or to women as a part of the greater Israelite population. Even in situations in which we might expect to find mention of women—the account of the Watchers, for example, which might have mentioned the "daughters of man" (CD 2.18)—the framing of the story is entirely in masculine terms.

The text's only real specific discussion of gender norms is in its presentation of the distinctions between the covenant community and its unrighteous opponents. In these passages, the construction of a covenanter's gender is linked intimately with assumptions about sexuality and righteousness. We learn in the text that the sins of the people include unchastity, arrogance, and defilement of the sanctuary (CD 4.17–18), which are associated, in a complex interpretation, with a variety of sexual transgressions: taking two wives in one lifetime,[26] having sex with menstruating women, and permitting marriages between uncles and nieces (CD 4.20–5.11). Again, this approach is wholly androcentric—the sinful actors, in each case, are men—but at times the presentation of arguments is a bit more complex. The discussion of sex with menstruants is the simplest of the three; it includes only a basic statement of the designated transgression (CD 5.7). The reference to polygyny (or marriage after divorce) is more

---

[26] Scholars differ in their interpretations of the text's remark with regard to men who transgress by "taking two wives in their lives" (לקחת שתי נשים בחייהם, CD 4.20–21). The expression may refer either to polygyny or to marriage after divorce. For discussion and bibliography, see Schuller, 'Women in the Dead Sea Scrolls,' in Wise, et al., *Methods of Investigation*, 119–20.

complex but still entirely androcentric in focus. This accusation is grounded in a range of prooftexts—from creation and the flood, as well as the problematic practices of David, which must be explained away in the text—in order to demonstrate the ideological claim that the proper standard of marriage is "male and female" (זכר ונקבה, CD 4.21) and "two by two" (שנים שנים, CD 5.1). This marital arrangement requires partners of two sexes, but the active partner is the male of the pair (men are the ones who "take two wives," CD 4.20–21; "the prince" must not multiply wives for himself, CD 5.1–2, reading Deut 17.17).

In the third example, the case of uncle-niece marriages (CD 5.7–11), the text introduces what may be its first (and perhaps only?) explicit reference to women as actors with volition. A close reading of this passage demonstrates, however, that this is an exegetical discussion whose androcentric quality is not lost, even if an image of women in a not-entirely-passive role is necessary to the text's larger interpretive claims. In this passage, uncle-niece marriages are forbidden, with the assertion that the scriptural ban on marriages between aunts and nephews ("you shall not uncover the nakedness of your mother's sister, for she is your mother's near relation," Lev 18.13, quoted in CD 5.8–9),

> is written from the point of view of males (לזכרים), and like them is it (for) women (וכהם הנשים), so if a brother's daughter uncovers the nakedness of a brother of her father, she is a (forbidden) close relationship (והיא שאר).[27]

This passage stands out in the text for its presentation of a woman as a sexual actor (one who "uncovers nakedness" in a sexual relationship), which is a role normally attributed only to men. However, the inversion of action and passivity is not complete here. The woman "uncovers nakedness," but it is she, and not the man, who is the forbidden close relation. As such, she is the one who is presented as sexually unavailable and unacceptable for marriage, in the larger androcentric context of the text's scriptural sources. In addition, it is interesting to note that this semi-actor is nowhere a "woman" (except in the text's explanation of its exegetical process); instead, she is "a brother's daughter" or, in the case of the quotation of Leviticus, "a mother's sister." Rather than focusing on women as

---

[27] CD 5.9–11, following Baumgarten and Schwartz, 'CD,' 20–21.

actors, this text utilizes a slight alteration of its normal gender construction as an exegetical tactic that ultimately confirms the passive and secondary role of women with respect to the normative male covenanter.

Given the descriptions of the sins of the majority, the Damascus Document appears often to distinguish between righteous covenanters and the unrighteous masses in gendered and sexualized terms. A covenanter is *a righteous man* who is *in control of his sexuality*—and the sexuality of his female partner and his female offspring—while a sinful outsider is someone who is willing to engage in inappropriate sexual or marital behavior, even though scripture clearly shows that such actions are forbidden. Images of the righteous male covenanter appear regularly in the text: he is the audience to whom its admonitions and scriptural interpretations are directed, and he is the recipient of its important halakhic teachings. Alongside this covenanter, it is possible to identify his silent, generally invisible, and usually passive female adjunct or adjuncts, who receive explicit attention when their presence is required, and who otherwise slip to the background of the text.

Reading for community in the text

Given this understanding of the text's construction of gender, the next stage of our literary critical historiography requires asking how—or to what extent—we can understand such a construction as reflective of an actual community 'behind' the text. A reading of the text at face value provides one possible construction of that covenant community. Its members are married men with families. They draft new members both from outside the community and also from the sons of current members, who are sworn into the covenant when they reach the appropriate age. Wives and daughters are a presence in the community, although they are not full members or active participants in the covenant itself.

Of course, the 'face value' reading of the text is not the only one that provides a reasonable historical model of the community 'behind' it. Following Schuller's lead, we can imagine another reading entirely. The masculine-plural language of the text—its references to those who "know righteousness" (יודעי צדק), those who "enter into the covenant" (באי ברית), and their various "children" (בניהם)—need not reflect a male-only community structure. In fact, each of these plural expressions may refer to a group including both male and female actors. Similarly, the term איש may serve, as it does in some scriptural passages, as a gender-neutral collective singular expression, "each one."[28] Like the ancient Israelite covenant at Sinai (to which this text makes at least veiled reference, and which serves as a point of comparison in the text),[29] the new covenant of the Damascus community may be directed to male and female covenanters both. And to the extent that the text imagines the community as a microcosm of the people of Israel, it may make *better* sense to see this covenant community, like the people of Israel more generally, as a group including both male and female actors. Although textually invisible, the female members of the covenant community, according to this reading, are real participants in the social order of the group.

We might note, additionally and quite provisionally, the potential relationship of this text to a community of non-marrying covenanters. Given that the text appears to distinguish between covenanters who marry and those who do not (CD 7.4–5), we can imagine a historical reality behind the text in which some portion of its audience is made up of men who live in a community without women, or with very few women present. In this case, the disjunction between text and history reverses that of our second model. Where that model suggests that women might be active members of the community whose presence is ignored in the text, this model imagines a male-only community, whose text includes the mention of women who are not really there. Such a model is not as far-fetched as it initially may sound. Once again, if this text was the property of sectarians who understood themselves as a microcosm of Israel, their ideology might force them to pay attention to all aspects of their scriptural heritage, or perhaps to the vestiges of older traditions—including laws of marriage and family structure—and not only those that were immediately relevant to their own lives.[30] As a sidenote to this model, we can imagine a Damascus covenant community with both marrying and celibate members. In this case, the celibate members would

---

[28] See, for example, 2 Sam 6.19, where food distribution to all the people (men, women, and children) is framed in terms of the portion that "each one" (איש) receives.

[29] See esp. CD 3.6–10 for the theme of Wilderness experience and the founding of the Israelite covenant.

[30] The extensive rabbinic discussions of Temple practice and ritual purity fall into just this sort of category; the Temple may be gone, but the traditions related to it retain their authority and continue to require attention.

understand their covenantal identity in solidarity with their marrying colleagues' interpretations of the laws of marriage and sexuality, without necessarily applying these laws to themselves.

This brief discussion suggests an important observation. Even at the level of original meaning, when we speak in terms of the ideological claims of the text's original author/editor(s), we can point to a fairly diverse array of potential historical scenarios for the community behind the text: a marrying sectarian group, in which males alone were permitted to join the covenant; a marrying group in which whole families could join; a celibate group that imagined itself as heir to the Sinai covenant and consequently felt responsible for understanding the details of family law; or a diverse group with some celibate and some marrying participants. Some of these models are more likely than others (and the first and last strike me as the most reasonable of the four), but none is entirely impossible, given the details of the text and our evidence from other literary and material sources.[31]

A third stage in the project requires a shift of attention away from the original meaning of the text. Here, we turn to a discussion of how the ideological constructions of gender in this text might have been read, interpreted, and mobilized by members of the covenant in social settings—and with agendas or interpretive concerns—that were not necessarily identical to those of the text's original author/editor(s). The simplest example of this sort of reading focuses on the interpretation that a later covenantal audience might make if that audience shared the ideological assumptions of the text's original author/editor(s). In this context, the text might be mobilized to maintain whatever traditions already were fixed in the community. The interpretations of the masculine-plural forms—whether they are understood as inclusive of women or exclusively male in their meaning—would be viewed as always and eternally reflective of the interpretations that this later-generation covenant community gave them. In other words, for a (celibate or marrying) community in which only men

---

[31] A more extensive historical discussion of this question would take into account the archaeological evidence from Khirbet Qumran, especially the cemeteries; as well as the connections of this text to descriptions of celibate and marrying 'Essenes' in Pliny, Josephus, and Philo; and the gendered references in other scrolls texts (including, but not limited to, 1QSa, 4Q502, and 4Q184). See Schuller, 'Women in the Dead Sea Scrolls,' in Wise, et al., *Methods of Investigation*, 124–27, for a discussion of some directions for further analysis.

were members, a reading of the text would support the view that the community had *always* included men only. For a community in which women and men were active participants in the covenant, the same text might support the eternity of *this* view. In either case, it is interesting to note, as long as gender is not a point of explicit concern, notions of masculinity and femininity would remain in the subtext, assumed as absolutes.

A more complicated interpretation of the text arises in the case of a reading by later-generation covenanters whose ideology was not identical with that of the text's author/editor(s). For example, although the text is written from a basically androcentric perspective, it is possible that, over time, the members of the covenant community might have become more—or less—open to participation by women covenanters. The argument that the community could develop a more egalitarian leaning strikes me as less likely (there is little external evidence to support this view),[32] but it is important to recognize that *there is nothing in the text itself* that would prevent a community from reading it as supportive of the full participation of both male and female covenanters. In fact, because large portions of the text erase gender altogether—focusing instead on the (generic) covenanter's need to be righteous, to seek and follow God's will, to accept the authority of inspired leadership, and to live in harmony with fellow members—a reading in terms of female covenant participation can be made to fit with the basic framing of the text. What labels this interpretation 'unlikely' is not the text itself but the interpretive tradition and social setting in which we imagine that it was read.

At the other end of the spectrum, we can imagine a reading of this text by an audience in which collective androcentrism had given way to a full-scale misogyny. In such a setting, this text's selective erasure of women and selective description of men might have provided support for a full-scale attack on all things feminine.[33] Again,

---

[32] I can think of no scrolls texts that demonstrate an egalitarian view of gender; I present this reading only as an example of the extent to which 'the meaning' of the text can be determined by its covenantal audience, rather than being locked securely into the text or the author/editor(s)' understanding of it.

[33] Feminist scholarship has traced the development of ancient Jewish and early Christian traditions from the androcentrism of the Hebrew scriptures to a variety of misogynist perspectives associated with the rabbis and church fathers. For the Hebrew Bible as an androcentric text, see Carol Meyers, *Discovering Eve: Ancient Israelite Women in Context* (New York: Oxford University Press, 1988); for the complexities of gender in rabbinic texts, see Daniel Boyarin, *Carnal Israel: Reading Sex in*

the ambiguities of this text lend themselves to a variety of interpretations, beginning with the obvious claim that only men could be real members of the covenant. The fact that, with very few exceptions, the text mentions women *only* in discussions of sexuality creates a potential for readers of this text to assign the role of 'sexual being' to women only, and not to men. In this context, a misogynist reading of the text might construct masculinity as a state of righteousness, piety, and obedience to God, while 'the feminine' would be defined as that which is sexually threatening and requires control and containment.[34] The sinfulness of people outside the covenant—including multiple marriages, sex with menstruants, and uncle-niece unions—might be attributed, in this context, to the sexual nature of the women who were involved in those relationships. Given this interpretation, a reader could mobilize the androcentric tendencies of the Damascus Document in support of explicitly misogynist claims, while further arguing not only that the text supported such claims, but that it always had, and that the reader was merely exposing the text's original and eternal explanation of social realities.

In addition to readings of this text in light of changing ideological frames, we can imagine at least one reading in light of a changing social order. If we assume that the Damascus Document was a text of importance or authority for its covenantal audiences, then it is likely that later members of the covenant community would mobilize the authority of the text to support whatever social innovations they might institute. A subgroup of celibate covenanters, in this light, might look to the text for support of their own social order, perhaps suggesting (as in the above example) that their choice of celibacy

---

Talmudic Culture (Berkeley: University of California Press, 1993); and Peskowitz, *Spinning Fantasies*; for a contextualized discussion grounded in the Greco-Roman world, see Kraemer, *Her Share*, esp. 199–208. Feminist theological study of early Christianity has been a contested field in recent years, not least for the claims that feminist interpretations of Christian origins have demonized Judaism as the source of any misogynist tendencies in early Christianity. See the discussion and extensive bibliography in Katharina von Kellenbach, *Anti-Judaism in Feminist Religious Writings* (Atlanta: Scholars Press, 1994). Also now see Ross S. Kraemer and Mary Rose D'Angelo, eds., *Women and Christian Origins* (New York: Oxford University Press, 1999).

[34] This sort of construction of gender-as-sexuality is articulated especially clearly in Ben Sira, which includes diatribes on the sexual untrustworthiness of daughters, wives, and other women. See Claudia Camp, 'Understanding a Patriarchy: Women in Second Century Jerusalem Through the Eyes of Ben Sira,' in Levine, "*Women Like This*," 1–39.

was already implicit in the text, just waiting for interpretation by a reader who understood its true meaning. Again, the sexual nature of the various sins of Israel that the text describes might contribute support to this reading. If sexual sins lie at the base of Israel's primary transgression of the covenant, as the text appears to imply (CD 4.20–5.11), then it is reasonable to assume that any sexuality is a step in the direction of Belial (CD 4.14–17). Although the text never states explicitly that celibacy is synonymous with "perfect holiness" (CD 7.5), it certainly leaves room for an interested covenanter to make that claim.

This brief reading of gender in the Damascus Document is suggestive of the most fundamental claims of my larger project. First, the construction of historical narratives based largely on the claims of an ideological text requires reading the text in terms of its ideology, and asking how that ideology relates (or fails to relate) to a set of real historical events outside the text. Second, the meaning of texts is always the product of how they are read—by diverse audiences, in their diverse social and textual settings, and with diverse agendas—which means that textual interpretation is always multiple. Textual evidence, too, is fragmentary, allusive, ideological, and fundamentally multivalent. Consequently, historical narratives based on those texts cannot function as complete, coherent, or confirmable accounts of the events of the past. Instead, beginning with these observations we may work from the weaknesses of the evidence to the strengths of an alternative methodology. This methodology, by generating multiple narratives and evaluating them in terms of their possibility and likelihood, offers a middle ground between two problematic extremes: the construction of inappropriately definitive histories, on the one hand, and the refusal to engage in historical speculation at all, on the other.

Case two: history and communal identity in 4QMMT

For a discussion of historiography grounded in literary critical understandings of textual multiplicity, the text of 4QMMT, *Miqsat Ma'aseh ha-Torah*, offers another useful test case. This text, which articulates 'Some of the Precepts of the Torah,'[35] has been identified by scholars

---

[35] 4QMMT C 27; see Elisha Qimron and John Strugnell, eds., *Qumran Cave 4.V:*

as a halakhic letter,[36] either an actual epistle or else a treatise written in that literary form, which distinguishes between the community of its author/editor(s) and that of a group or groups somewhere on the edges of the community. While the insider-community of the text (mentioned in the first-person plural) has a proper understanding of scriptural interpretation and religious praxis, there are other actors or groups (labeled 'you' and 'they' in the text) who lack such an understanding.

The purpose of the text—as articulated in its concluding section—is to rectify this misunderstanding and provide a source of proper edification for people outside the community who might be willing to reconsider their errors. Thus, according to the text, 'we' have written to 'you,' to tell 'you' of our rulings on certain important issues, because 'you' seem more open to the truth of our claims than 'they' (the leadership of a second outside party) have proven to be. The main body of the text explains the content of these misunderstandings, presenting a series of rulings on matters of religious praxis and communal standards, including issues of purity, sacrifice, and marriage. The tone of 4QMMT appears to be one of reasoned assuredness; the goal of the text is to clarify and rectify a misconception, to open the door to improved understanding for those who are wise enough to recognize their own errors.

Modern scholarship on 4QMMT has entered a new phase of activity in the last decade. After a period in which discussions of the text focused on controversies related to its publication,[37] attention has

---

Miqsat Ma'ase Ha-Torah (DJD X; Oxford: Clarendon Press, 1994), 63. For the selection of this phrase as a working title for the text, see Qimron and Strugnell, DJD X, 1.

[36] As in Elisha Qimron and John Strugnell, 'An Unpublished Halakhic Letter from Qumran,' *Biblical Archaeology Today* (Jerusalem: Israel Exploration Society, 1984), 400–7.

[37] Delays in the publication of 4QMMT led to a significant "scholarly hullabaloo," as described in John Kampen and Moshe Bernstein, 'Introduction,' in *Reading 4QMMT: New Perspectives on Qumran Law and History* (ed. John Kampen and Moshe Bernstein; Atlanta: Scholars Press, 1996), 1. 'Bootleg' copies of a partial transcription of the text became available to the scholarly public as early as 1984 (I first encountered a transcription of the text in the fall of 1989), although the text itself was not published officially until ten years later. For the original editor's description of the publication delays, see John Strugnell, 'Foreword,' in Qimron and Strugnell, DJD X, vii–ix. Note also the 'opposition' account (with copies of all major correspondence) in Hershel Shanks, 'Publisher's Foreword,' in *A Facsimile Edition of the Dead Sea Scrolls* (ed. Robert Eisenman and James Robinson; Washington: Biblical Archaeology Society, 1991), xii–xlv. This volume originally included a "preliminary

turned to a substantive analysis of the text's literary and historical significance,[38] especially in terms of its contributions to an understanding of the rise of ancient Jewish sectarianism and the development of halakhah.[39] Scholarly interpretations of the text suggest that it preserves traces of a series of historic events: a split between different Jewish groups, based on their distinct religious interpretations and practices; an attempt to reconcile that split, on the part of the leadership of one such group; and (this last grounds a reading of the text in a particular understanding of the history of the scrolls) the ultimate failure of that attempt at reconciliation, which led to the establishment of rigid sectarian boundaries between certain distinct communities. From this perspective, MMT is not a sectarian text but can be understood as proto-sectarian. That is, it anticipates the establishment of major communal boundaries but reflects a period prior to, or early in the history of, such communal division.

From a literary critical perspective in which 'the meaning' of texts

---

text of MMT" ("Figure 8" on xxxi), but this page was removed from each copy of the book following a copyright lawsuit in the Israeli court system. For a comment on editorial conflict with respect to 4QMMT, see Florentino García Martínez, '4QMMT in a Qumran Context,' in Kampen and Bernstein, *Reading 4QMMT*, 15 (he notes that Qimron alone—and not jointly with Strugnell—holds the rights to the 1994 publication); see also Schiffman, *Reclaiming*, xvii–xviii, 21–31.

[38] Such studies have taken a variety of approaches. Most relevant for this discussion are Steven Fraade, 'To Whom It May Concern: *4QMMT* and Its Addressee(s),' *RevQ* 19 (2000): 507–26; and Maxine L. Grossman, 'Reading *4QMMT*: Genre and History,' *RevQ* 20 (2001): 3–22; but note also the approaches of Miguel Pérez Fernández, '*4QMMT*: Redactional Study,' *RevQ* 18 (1997): 191–205; and Carolyn Sharp, 'Phinehan Zeal and Rhetorical Strategy in *4QMMT*,' *RevQ* 18 (1997): 207–22. Other relevant discussions of history, law, and the content of MMT can be found in Charlotte Hempel, 'The Laws of the Damascus Document and 4QMMT,' in *Centennial of Discovery*, 69–84; Israel Knohl, 'Reconsidering the Dating and Recipient of MMT,' *Hebrew Studies* 37 (1996): 119–25; Menahem Kister, 'Studies in 4QMiqsat Ma'ase Ha-Torah and Related Texts: Law, Theology, Language and Calendar,' *Tarbiz* 68 (1999): 317–71; the articles in Kampen and Bernstein, *Reading 4QMMT*; and articles by Brooke, Grabbe, Harrington, and VanderKam in *Legal Texts and Legal Issues: Proceedings of the Second Meeting of the International Organization for Qumran Studies: Cambridge 1995* (ed. Moshe Bernstein, Florentino García Martínez, and John Kampen; New York: Brill, 1997). See also the following note.

[39] On the subject of halakhah in particular, see Elisha Qimron, 'The Halakha,' in Qimron and Strugnell, DJD X, 123–77, esp. 123–30 for an extensive bibliography on halakhah at Qumran; Yaakov Sussman, 'Appendix 1: The History of the Halakha and the Dead Sea Scrolls,' in Qimron and Strugnell, DJD X, 179–200; Yaakov Elman, 'Some Remarks on 4QMMT and the Rabbinic Tradition, Or, When is a Parallel Not a Parallel?' in Kampen and Bernstein, *Reading 4QMMT*, 99–128; and Schiffman, *Reclaiming*, 86–87 and 257–312, esp. 261.

is understood to be constructed not only by their authors or editors, but also in the experiences of their diverse audiences, the historical significance of a text like MMT is particularly interesting. On the one hand, there is much to support a historical hypothesis that finds in the text the roots of a major sectarian schism and understands it as a letter or treatise written by the leader of the 'we' group and directed toward the 'you' group mentioned in the text itself. On the other hand, this is far from the only reasonable reading of the text. Depending on how we understand the genre of this letter, how we define its intended or actual audience, and how we ground it in a specific cultural setting, this text can be read in support of a number of different—and at times radically contradictory—constructions of the historical events that occurred 'behind' it. In addition to providing evidence for the history 'behind' the text, MMT can be read as a source for the construction of communal understandings of history after the fact, and perhaps at some remove from the original setting of the text. In this way, a text like MMT can provide not only a model of past historical events but also a model for future constructions of historical experiences.

For a text like MMT, we can envision a variety of ancient audiences, whose readings would vary in accord with their diverse literary assumptions, social concerns, or reading strategies. The earliest readers who would have given meaning to the text were its own authors or editors, whose own understandings of their text may have changed over time, from the occasion in which they first composed it, through their later interpretations of it. Another hypothetical audience, which is implied in the text, is that of the 'you' group, who are the purported recipients of its communal message. In addition, the community associated with the text's original author/editor(s) can be added to the list: the evidence of multiple manuscript witnesses of MMT suggests that this community (or some descendants of it) continued to copy and transmit this text, for a significant period after its original composition.[40] Their own understanding of its historical significance—both in the first generations after its composition, and in later generations, on the part of audiences with no personal connection to that period of origin—can be viewed as important places for meaning-construction, as well.

---

[40] The six manuscript witnesses of 4QMMT have been dated paleographically to the period between 75 BCE and 50 CE; see Qimron and Strugnell, DJD X, 109.

MMT, text and content

A brief discussion of the content and primary arguments of MMT will help set the scene for the readings of the text that follow. In the composite form that scholars have reconstructed, based on the extant manuscript witnesses,[41] MMT comprises three parts: a short calendrical passage (section A), a series of halakhic disputes (section B), and a 'hortatory epilogue' (section C).[42] This reading begins with a brief overview of the main body of the text, before turning to a discussion of the exhortation. The calendar is discussed separately, below.[43]

The main body of MMT begins with a series of halakhic statements, prefaced by the Deuteronomic introduction, "these are some of our statements" (אלה מקצת דברינו).[44] The rulings that follow take several forms. Some are bare assertions of halakhic points, while others are supported by scriptural references,[45] or prefaced by introductory phrases ("we are of the opinion that...").[46] In addition,

---

[41] Readings of the text of MMT in this chapter are based on Qimron and Strugnell's composite text, although individual manuscript variations are noted. The most significant variant concerns the placement of seven lines of text from fragments 11–13 of 4Q398. For transcriptions of the individual manuscripts, see Qimron and Strugnell, DJD X, 3–42; for the composite text, with translation, see 44–63.

[42] The calendar (4QMMT A) is preserved only minimally, and only in 4Q394; each of the other sections of the text is witnessed in at least two manuscripts. For a discussion of the structure of the text, see especially John Strugnell, 'Appendix 3: Additional Observations on 4QMMT,' in Qimron and Strugnell, DJD X, 204–5. The editors suggest (on page 1) that the text originally included an "opening formula," in addition to the three textual sections that have survived.

[43] The calendrical material may not be original to the text. Although 4Q394 begins with a calendar, a second manuscript (4Q395) preserves the opening of MMT without any calendrical material; see Qimron and Strugnell, DJD X, 14. Note also the text critical problem associated with 4Q394: the majority of the calendar formerly associated with the text has been identified, instead, as belonging to 4Q327. See James VanderKam, 'The Calendar, 4Q327, and 4Q394,' in Baumgarten, García Martínez, and Kampen, *Legal Texts and Legal Issues*, 179–94. More generally, see VanderKam, *Calendars in the Dead Sea Scrolls* (New York: Routledge, 1998).

[44] The editors note that MMT begins and ends in a Deuteronomic fashion (the last word of MMT, as in Deuteronomy, is ישראל). See Qimron and Strugnell, DJD X, 46 n. 1.

[45] In section B: for "it is written" (כתוב), see lines 10, 27, 66, 70, 76, and 77 (twice), noting that line 70 is partially emended, and that line 10 and one of the cases in line 77 are fully supplied by the editors.

[46] In section B: for "we are of the opinion that" (אנחנו חושבים ש-), see lines 8, 29, 36, 37, and 42, noting that line 36 is partially emended, and line 8 fully supplied by the editors; for "we say that" (אנחנו אמרים ש-), see lines 55, 65, and 73,

some rulings are presented as explicit responses to inappropriate actions, which are described and attributed to one of several opposing camps.

A variety of parties appear in the text. Most prominent are the 'we' party, who are presented as the community of the text's own author/editor(s) and a 'they' faction whose practices, especially with regard to sacrifice, are viewed as inappropriate by the author/editor(s) of the text.[47] Other groups mentioned in the text include the gentiles, whose wheat is suspect or prohibited for sacrifice;[48] the priests, whose improper use of sacrificial food may bring punishment on the people;[49] and, more generally, the people themselves.[50] From the descriptive language of the text, it appears that the 'they' party and 'the priests' share some common traits (if not a common identity): each is accused of behaving in ways that are lazy, misguided, or ignorant with respect to proper Temple and halakhic practice. And perhaps most important is the group that falls outside this 'us and them' division, the audience to whom the text is addressed, who appear on occasion as a plural 'you' party (אתם)[51] but also, at times, in the singular.[52]

In terms of its content, the halakhic section of MMT covers such

---

again noting that line 65 is partially emended. Qimron notes that the former expression is unusual, and the latter is more common in this type of context. See Qimron and Strugnell, DJD X, 49 n. 29, 99.

[47] 4QMMT B 6 contains the first unambiguous reference to this group, but it is reasonable to suppose that most or all of the objectionable practices described in the text are to be associated with them.

[48] 4QMMT B 3, 5, 8.

[49] 4QMMT B 11–12. The editors emend the text to refer to "the sons of the priests" (בני הכוהנים), an expression that recurs in lines 25–26; other priestly titles include "sons of Aaron" (בני אהרן) in 4QMMT B 16–17, 79; and "priests" (כוהנים) in 4QMMT B 63, 64, 80. Most of these examples are at least partly emended by the modern editors. No single manuscript retains the full expression בני הכוהנים, although the reference to בני אהרן in line 79 is complete.

[50] 4QMMT B 13. The notion of causing the people to bear punishment also appears in 4QMMT B 27.

[51] 4QMMT B 38, 68, and 80, noting that line 80 is partially emended and line 38 is fully supplied by the editors. See also 4QMMT C 7 and 8; the reference in line 8 is partially emended and the reference in line 7 is fully supplied by the editors.

[52] 4QMMT C 10, 26–30; each of these lines includes at least one explicit use of the second person singular. The intervening lines, which are written in a Deuteronomic style, also focus on a second-person singular reader, although less explicitly.

ground as proper sacrificial practices (lines 1–13), procedures relating to the red heifer (13–16), the purity of hides and bones (18–26), the proper location for slaughtering clean animals (27–34), and the issue of slaughtering a pregnant animal (36–38). A slight shift of focus leads to a discussion of *people*, in terms of proper and improper marriages (39–47) and of the blind and deaf (49–54), but these discussions ultimately point back to a concern for basic purity issues, and in particular the purity of the Temple. Additional discussions address the purity of liquid streams (55–58), the importance of keeping dogs out of the sacred city (58–62), tithing (62–64), the cleansing of lepers and purification offerings (64–72), the impurity of human corpses and bones (72–74), and the issue of improper mixings, including inappropriately 'mixed' marriages (75–82).[53] In these halakhic discussions, the text addresses issues (and uses literary expressions) that also are familiar from other ancient Jewish texts and contexts.[54]

Following the halakhic discussion that makes up the main portion of this text, MMT includes a short exhortation that is conciliatory in tone and apparently directed toward the leader of a community that is separate from that of the text's author/editor(s). This section begins with a now-fragmentary halakhic discussion (a continuation of section B), before proceeding to a full-scale exhortation:

> [And you know (ואתם יודעים) that] we have separated ourselves from the majority of the peo[ple and from all of their impurity] and from being involved with these things and from going [with them] in these things. And you [know (ואתם יודעים) that] treachery and evil and deceit

---

[53] The editors understand this halakhah to be a reference to marriages of priests with Israelites, but they note Joseph Baumgarten's alternative reading of this text as referring to the marriage of Israelites and outsiders. See Qimron and Strugnell, DJD X, 55 n. 75.

[54] Parallels can be made to rabbinic and early Christian texts, as well as to other Dead Sea Scrolls texts. References to Jerusalem as "the camp" of Israel parallel the use of 'camp' language in the Damascus Document and the Temple Scroll (see 4QMMT B 27–34, for a reference to proper locations for slaughtering animals; see 4QMMT B 60–62, for the mention of dogs in Jerusalem). A number of halakhic references, most notably the discussions of the purity of liquid streams, have been associated with questions of Sadducean halakhah, as reflected in later rabbinic texts. See the halakhic discussions noted above, especially Elman's extensive assessment (and, in some ways, rejection) of the textual parallels. The repeated use of "you have heard... but I say" is reminiscent, as well, of the Matthean Sermon on the Mount. See the discussion in John Kampen, '4QMMT and New Testament Studies,' in Kampen and Bernstein, *Reading 4QMMT*, 129–35.

are [not] to be found in our hand, for [on these things] we give
[...And] we have [written] to you (אליכה), that you may study the
book of Moses, and the books of the Prophets, and David [and the
deeds] of ages past ([מעשי] דור ודור).⁵⁵

The text then continues with a discussion that uses Deuteronomic
language in making reference to the waywardness of the people, their
turning away from Torah, their punishment, and the blessings and
curses associated with the endtimes (4QMMT C 11–16). In the composite text, this discussion is followed⁵⁶ by the observation that by
the time of the Israelite monarchy, many of the blessings and curses
of Deuteronomy already had taken place. The blessings, according
to the text, occurred during the reign of Solomon, and the curses
arose during the reign of the kings after him, from Jeroboam to
Zedekiah (4QMMT C 17–21). A reference to the end of days
(4QMMT C 21) is followed in the text by an exhortation to remember the kings of Israel and the fact that those who were "seekers of
Torah" (מב[ק]שי תורה) prospered (4QMMT C 23–25), especially
David, who was forgiven and delivered from his troubles because he
was a man who behaved piously (איש חסדים, 4QMMT C 25–26).
The text then continues with the reminder that:

> We have written to you (אנחנו כתבנו אליך) some precepts of the Torah
> (מקצת מעשה התורה) that we believe [will be] good for you (לך) and for
> your people, for we have seen that you have wisdom (עמך ערמה) and

---

⁵⁵ 4QMMT C 7–11; after Qimron and Strugnell, DJD X, 58–59.
⁵⁶ The placement of these lines (4Q398 11–13) is a matter of dispute between
the editors of the text. Strugnell thinks the passage fits in the composite text immediately after line C 12; Qimron prefers to place it after line C 17. Either choice
may be correct, since the fragment in question contains a rather decontextualized
discussion of Israelite history, and in either case this discussion would be put in a
Deuteronomic context. Strugnell, with reference to the "material shape of the manuscript" and backed by Hartmut Stegemann, places these fragments before fragments 14–17 of 4Q398. Qimron, relying on the literary content of the fragments
and backed by Menahem Kister and Bezalel Porten, says that fragments 11–13 fall
between column one and column two of the text found in fragments 14–17. For
the former discussion, see Strugnell, DJD X, 205–6; see also Strugnell, 'MMT:
Second Thoughts on a Forthcoming Edition,' in *The Community of the Renewed Covenant:
The Notre Dame Symposium on the Dead Sea Scrolls* (ed. Eugene Ulrich and James
VanderKam; Notre Dame: University of Notre Dame Press, 1994), 57–73. For the
latter view, see Elisha Qimron, 'Appendix 2: Additional Textual Observations on
4QMMT,' in Qimron and Strugnell, DJD X, 201–2; see also Qimron, 'The Nature
of the Reconstructed Composite Text of 4QMMT,' in Kampen and Bernstein,
Reading 4QMMT, 12–13. Both Qimron and Strugnell note that either reading is
possible, given the non-specific content of the fragment in question and the fact
that there are no manuscript parallels with which to compare it.

knowledge of the Torah. Consider (הבן) all these things and seek him (בקש מלפנו) that he strengthen your will and remove from you evil thoughts and the counsel of Belial, so that you may rejoice at the end of time, finding that some of our statements are correct.[57]

The text concludes with the assertion that such a response on the part of the recipient will be counted as righteousness (לצדקה) before God, and will serve for both his own welfare and that of all Israel (לטוב לך ולישראל, 4QMMT C 31–32).

Reading for history in MMT

We can imagine a wide variety of readings of the text of MMT: readings grounded in the text's original setting, and readings of the text by covenanters in later generations; readings that interpret the text in isolation, or in comparison with other halakhic claims, or in the context of other literary texts. From a historical perspective, we can imagine readings of this text that understand it as the basis of a coherent narrative of communal development, as well as readings that call such historiographical efforts into question. In the discussion that follows, the first round of readings highlights the text's original setting, asking how genre assumptions help to shape a historical understanding of the text. Additional readings consider 4QMMT in specific literary and social contexts, foregrounding several distinct questions about the text and its relationship to the development of ancient sectarian Judaism.

The matter of genre is actually a point of some interest for a reading of MMT in its original historical setting. MMT has been called a "halakhic letter," but its editors note that this genre description is a bit problematic, in that the text fails to make use of standard epistolary forms that might be expected in a personal letter.[58] Noting the text's "public" tone (it is written with an individual authoritative voice but speaks at times to an individual and at times to a group), they instead suggest that it be "classed with corporate or public letters sent from one group to another, or even with treatises."[59]

---

[57] 4QMMT C 26–30, after Qimron and Strugnell, DJD X, 62–63.
[58] Qimron and Strugnell, DJD X, 113–14 (and more generally, the entire section 'The Literary Character of MMT and its Historical Setting,' in Qimron and Strugnell, DJD X, 109–21).
[59] Qimron and Strugnell, DJD X, 114; see also Dennis Pardee et al., *Handbook*

Given this classification, they understand the text more generally as "a sectarian polemical document."[60] Making a distinction between a reading of MMT as an actual epistle and a view of the text as a treatise-in-epistolary-form is not mere pedantry on the part of scholars. In fact, these genre distinctions allow for the construction of significantly different accounts of the historical events 'behind' the text.

In its original setting, MMT may have been an actual letter, either public or private, written by the leader(s) of one community (the 'we' group) and sent to the leader(s) of another community, with the intention of explaining the sources of conflict between them, in hopes that the recipient(s) might see the error of their ways. In the context of this sort of reading, MMT serves as a historical artifact. Its presence (in the form of copies, if not an actual autograph) bears witness to a set of events surrounding the original draft of the text: its composition by a communal leader, its transmission to an audience outside the community, and whatever repercussions this transmission may have caused. In addition, this understanding of the text foregrounds the presence of a number of real (if anonymous) historical figures: the sender of the text, who is the representative of a specific ancient Jewish constituency; the recipient, who is also a public figure in the community; and the erring priests, whose actions are the cause of concern in the first place. Ultimately, this reading provides grounds for the explanation of the text's own composition: it was written to provide an account of differences of opinion, in order to sway opposing views and heal (or prevent) a potential rift between communities. In this context, the focus on the practices of the Temple priesthood, issues of purity, and the proper behavior for the leaders of Israel suggest an identity for the communities in which this text was first written and then received.[61]

But if MMT is not an actual epistle, and if it was not actually transmitted from one community to another, then this understanding of the history 'behind' the text must be re-evaluated. Imagining

---

of Ancient Hebrew Letters: A Study Edition (Chico, Calif.: Scholars Press, 1982), noted in Qimron and Strugnell.

[60] Qimron and Strugnell, DJD X, 1.

[61] For this construction of the history associated with MMT, see Qimron and Strugnell, DJD X, 109–21; Hanan Eshel, '4QMMT and the History of the Hasmonean Period,' in Kampen and Bernstein, *Reading 4QMMT*, 53–65.

the text as a treatise—an intra-communal text written in the *conceit* of a letter to outsiders—allows us to view the text in several very different ways. On the one hand, if the text does date from the early stages (or pre-history) of the community, then it may in fact reflect the events described in the previous model. But, as an intracommunal record of those events, it would need to be understood as a one-sided explanation of differences, and not an artifact of the conflict itself. In laying out those differences, it would have been directed only to the members of the author/editor(s)' own community, and not actually to the community of their opponents.

Alternatively, if MMT was an intracommunal treatise, it may have been written as a retrospective document. Rather than recording the events of the current moment (or the disagreements that were current at the time of its composition), the text may have been written sometime after the fact, to provide a record of the details of the community's founding argument. In this case, we must distinguish between actors within the text, who are the subjects of it (the implied author and implied recipient of the text, whose moods and motivations may be imagined from a reading of the text), and the actual composer(s) of the text, who are responsible for constructing the image of those subjects. The text, in this case, conveys the memory of an authoritative figure, whom the author(s) may have known, known about, or learned of only from a received tradition. Similarly, the arguments recorded in the text may be those that its composer(s) remembered hearing from the leader, or those that the leader *would have made* or even *should have made*, in the context of the remembered dispute.

Understood in this way, MMT is not an artifact of a past event but a record of it, written after the fact to preserve the memory of an important period in communal development. To what extent it provides an accurate account of those experiences, and in what way it interprets or filters them, is not a question that can be answered easily. A useful parallel here might be found in the pseudo-Pauline letters, texts which are designed both to preserve the memory of an important group leader and also to shape the discourse of the group that he left behind. If this is the case, then both the choice of subject matter and the mode of presentation in MMT can be understood as rhetorical or textual strategies, rather than as neutral markers of historical events.

A third perspective goes one step further in distancing MMT from the real historical events 'behind' it. In this case, we can envision MMT as a literary fiction, constructed as the sort of ideal accounting of how a wise leader might address the ignorance and misdeeds of the Jewish community around him, but not based on any particular discussion or remembered exchange of views. In this case, the author/editor(s) of the text may be constructing their argument in the voice of an actual community leader (past or present), or they simply may be generating a treatise on their own beliefs and standards (or those of their community), articulated in a style that is designed to be authoritative and convincing. Given this scenario, MMT bears no relation at all to an actual set of events, or an actual conflict between communal leaders. If its statements on issues of purity, Temple practice, and communal order reflect a divergence from standard communal practice, they do so in a way that may have had little real impact on public discourse or communal order in the larger ancient Jewish community. In this sense, MMT is not only an intracommunal text, but in fact a text that might have had no impact outside the community at all.[62]

Given these observations with regard to genre—which indicate that MMT may represent the 'artifact' of an actual dispute between communities or only a remembered (or invented) account of such a dispute—it is useful to consider the sorts of historical accounts that scholars might construct, based on readings of this text. For some readers of this text, the process of constructing a historical account of the events 'behind' it is supported by readings of two significant passages from other Dead Sea Scroll texts.[63] The first passage is found in an interpretation of the Book of Psalms (4Q171, the Psalms pesher) and introduces the figures of the Teacher of Righteousness (the inspired leader of a covenant community, who is mentioned in several of the scrolls)[64] and the Wicked Priest (opponent

---

[62] A similar view is presented by Phillip Callaway, who notes that the "rather friendly and informative" tone of 4QMMT suggests that it was written "in all likelihood [to] potential adherents of the writer's legal perspective" and not to an opposition audience. He suggests that it may have been brought or sent to a community housed at Qumran, rather than being sent out from there to an opposing group. See Callaway, 'Qumran Origins,' 649.

[63] See n. 61 above.

[64] The Damascus Document views the Teacher as an important early leader of the covenant community (CD 1.5–11), whose death is a precursor to the endtimes (CD 20.1, 13–17). This text also may anticipate an endtimes Teacher of Righteousness (יורה הצדק, CD 6.11). Other references to the Teacher are found in the Habakkuk

of the Teacher, who is described at length in the pesharim).[65] This pesher records the account of a clash between the Teacher and the Wicked Priest, in which the Wicked Priest "spied on the Teacher of Righteousness and tried to put him to death because of the precept and the law (החוק והתורה) he sent to him."[66] The second passage, from the Community Rule, addresses the issue of disputations between community members and outsiders, stating explicitly that the Master (משכיל) of the community must not dispute with members of any opposing camp or share "Torah-counsel" (עצת התורה) with such people.[67]

We have seen that MMT can be understood as an actual halakhic letter, composed and sent by one leader to another, in hopes of resolving intergroup conflict. In this context, the additional scrolls evidence allows for the construction of a fairly specific historical account. MMT, according to this reading, *is* "the precept and the law" (החוק והתורה), which the Teacher of Righteousness sent to the Wicked Priest. The tone of this letter—which is conciliatory and well-reasoned—suggests that the Priest is viewed as a worthy (if misguided)

---

pesher (1QpHab) and the Psalms pesher (4Q171, 4Q173). The identification of the Teacher as a priest (see 1QpHab 2.7–10; 4Q171 2.15, 3.15) has led to the view that he may have been High Priest in Jerusalem, possibly in the years before 152 BCE (the 'intersacerdotium'). This view was originated by Stegemann; responses to his theory include Murphy-O'Connor, 'Essenes and their History,' 215–44, and, more critically, Michael Wise, 'The Teacher of Righteousness and the High Priest of the Intersacerdotium,' *RevQ* 14 (1990): 587–613.

[65] In addition to passages mentioned in this discussion, references to the Wicked Priest are found in the Habakkuk pesher (esp. 1QpHab 8–12) and the Psalms pesher (4Q171 4.8). Some scholars also equate this figure with other opponents described in the scrolls, such as the Scoffer or the Liar. See Vermes, *The Complete Dead Sea Scrolls*, 60. An important hypothesis suggests that the Habakkuk pesher's references indicate not one Wicked Priest but a series of priests, each described in turn. See A. S. van der Woude, 'Wicked Priest or Wicked Priests? Reflections on the Identification of the Wicked Priest in the Habakkuk Commentary,' *JJS* 33 (1982): 349–59; García Martínez, 'Qumran Origins and Early History,' 136 n. 66.

[66] 4Q171 4.5–9. Scholars read the two pronouns in this passage to refer to a Torah from the Teacher and to the Priest, rather than vice versa.

[67] 1QS 9.16–17. See Qimron and Strugnell, DJD X, 115, for the argument that such disputations would have taken place only during the lifetime of the Teacher. Charlesworth reads this line as indicating that no member of the community is permitted to engage in such disputation: "one must not argue or quarrel with the men of the pit." See Elisha Qimron and James H. Charlesworth, 'Rule of the Community (1QS),' in *Rule of the Community and Related Documents* (ed. James H. Charlesworth; vol. 1 of *The Dead Sea Scrolls: Hebrew Aramaic, and Greek Texts with English Translations*; Louisville: Westminster John Knox Press, 1994), 40–41. Qimron is responsible for the text in this edition, and Charlesworth the translation, according to Charlesworth, *Rule of the Community*, 1 n. 1.

colleague, and not an out-and-out enemy at this point. In support of this suggestion, another scrolls text, the Habakkuk pesher, identifies a Wicked Priest "who was called by the name of truth when he first arose" (1QpHab 8.9–10). The textual evidence suggests that the result of this exchange was disastrous: the Priest took offense at the Teacher's actions and sought revenge against him and his community. The community responded by forbidding any future disputations of this sort. Such withdrawal from dispute can be understood as a hardening of communal boundaries, the confirmation of a sectarian tendency whose beginnings are implicit in the text of MMT itself.

For scholarly readers who take this approach to the evidence, reading MMT as an actual halakhic letter permits a highly specific discussion of its dating and context. If the text was composed by the Teacher (or by one of his associates) and sent to the Wicked Priest, then it must have been written during the lifetime of these two figures. A date for the composition of the text can be determined, based on the identification and dating of the Teacher and, more importantly, his opponent (since the text may have been written by an associate of the Teacher, but was directed, in particular, to the Wicked Priest himself).[68] The official editors of MMT provide an example of this sort of reading, suggesting that the text may have been composed during the period 159–152 BCE, in the time before the firming of hostilities between Hasmonean usurpers of the High Priesthood and a Zadokite opposition to that priesthood.[69] They refrain from suggesting that the text was written by the Teacher himself, noting instead that it "was written in the Teacher's community and reflects the earlier phases of its development."[70]

The historiographical payoff here is remarkable: beginning with an anonymous halakhic treatise, and reading it in the context of the Community Rule, the pesharim, and the historical constructs of a

---

[68] Speculation on the identity of the Teacher and the Priest has been extensive. For a summary of the basic scholarly positions, see Vermes, *The Complete Dead Sea Scrolls*, 60–66; see also Fraade, 'Interpretive Authority,' 51 n. 15; and Paul Rainbow, 'The Last Oniad and the Teacher of Righteousness,' *JJS* 48 (1997): 30 n. 1 for comprehensive bibliography.

[69] Qimron and Strugnell view Jonathan Maccabaeus as the most likely candidate for the role of Wicked Priest, although they also consider Alkimus, Simon Maccabaeus, and John Hyrcanus. See Qimron and Strugnell, DJD X, 117–21.

[70] Qimron and Strugnell, DJD X, 120–21.

Teacher of Righteousness and a Wicked Priest (who are, themselves, known only from the pesharim and the Damascus Document), we can generate a highly specific historical scenario 'behind' the text. This approach not only identifies the authorship and primary audience of this text (the Teacher, or his group, and the Wicked Priest), it also locates them in the context of specific communities and grounds their interaction in a fairly detailed account of communal conflict and sectarian development.

Readings that begin with other assumptions, however, may not contribute to as full an account of the events reflected in the text.[71] At this point it is worth remembering the literary critical distinction between the writer of a text and its 'implied author.'[72] Although we can assume that an actual person (or group of people) wrote the text of MMT, there is no reason to assume a one-to-one correspondence between the experiences or worldview of the writer(s) of the text and the authoritative voice of the 'author' that is 'implied' in its literary tone and form. If we shift to reading MMT as a treatise, rather than an actual epistle, then it becomes clear that the authorial voice of the text may be a construct, adopted by the original author/editor(s) as appropriate to their textual agenda. In other words, MMT *may* provide a transparent reflection of the experiences of its authorship, but we must not assume that it *does*.

Given this caveat with regard to authorial voice, the scholarly practice of viewing the Teacher of Righteousness as the author of specific scrolls texts (not only MMT, but also the Hodayot, and

---

[71] For a discussion of other readings of MMT, with attention to the way that scholarly assumptions shape interpretations and conclusions, see Robert Kugler, 'Review of John Kampen and Moshe J. Bernstein, eds., *Reading 4QMMT: New Perspectives on Qumran Law and History*,' *Ioud. Rev.* 9.001 (April 1999), ftp.lehigh.edu/pub/listserv/ioudaiosreview/9.1999/kampen.kugler.001. Kugler notes that the scholarly readings in this volume tend to reflect their "authors' particular predisposition regarding the Scrolls in general or their typical approach to ancient texts. Among those who venture historical-critical comments, it is not surprising that Schiffman finds 'Sadducean' law in 4QMMT, nor does it come as a surprise that García Martínez assigns it to a pre-community stage in a movement's life (see his Groningen Hypothesis)."

[72] For two contrasting perspectives on distinctions between the actual writers and implied authors in scriptural settings, see Robert Fowler, 'Who is "the Reader," in Reader Response Criticism?' in Detweiler, *Reader Response Approaches*, 5–23; and Bernard Lategan, 'Introduction: Coming to Grips with the Reader,' in McKnight, *Reader Perspectives on the New Testament*, 3–17. See chapter one for additional discussion and bibliography.

sometimes other texts, as well)[73] becomes increasingly problematic. This practice originates in the view that texts which speak of communal leadership or demonstrate a sense of responsibility toward a covenant community must have been written by the leader of that community, who is equated with the Teacher of Righteousness of the Damascus Document and the pesharim. However, it is equally possible that these texts were written by someone attempting to speak in the voice of the Teacher, or by someone writing in memory of (or in the context of a tradition that teaches about) that Teacher. It is possible, too, that the original writer(s) of these texts had authority of their own, as Master (משכיל)[74] or Overseer (מבקר)[75] in a community in which the authority of such positions was taken seriously, or simply as an articulate and insightful member of the community, whose authority might lie not in an official leadership role but in a personal store of halakhic knowledge or interpretive ability.[76]

If we understand MMT as a treatise written in the form of a letter, by a writer who has taken on the responsibility of speaking for a whole community (literally, but not necessarily in the capacity of day-to-day leadership), then it follows that the other historical conclusions of the previous reading lose their historical grounding and, similarly, become products of literary development. If the intended audience of the text is someone other than a historical Wicked Priest—the community of the text's author/editor(s), for example, or an actual community of outsiders that is not connected with the hypothetical priest—then the dating of the text to a time during the leadership of the Priest becomes a moot point. In this case, the composition of the text might date to anytime prior to the dating of our oldest manuscript witness, in the mid-first century BCE.[77]

---

[73] See, for example, Charlesworth's claim that 1QS 3.13ff. may be the work of the Teacher, or "at least contains his teachings," in Charlesworth, *Rule of the Community*, 15 n. 56. See also the critical discussion of this issue in Philip Davies, 'Chapter Six: History and Hagiography; The Life of the 'Teacher' in Hymn and *Pesher*,' in *Behind the Essenes*, 87–105, esp. 89–91.

[74] See 1QS 9.21 for the "rules" for the Master; see 4Q298 for a sermon of the Master to a group called the "sons of dawn." See also the discussions in Vermes, *The Complete Dead Sea Scrolls*, 29, 235.

[75] See 1QS 6.12 and CD 13.6ff. for references to the Overseer, as well as the extensive discussion in Vermes, *The Complete Dead Sea Scrolls*, 28–33, 36–38.

[76] See Fraade, 'Interpretive Authority,' 47, for a discussion of institutional and non-institutional leadership in such a covenant community.

[77] For the dating of the 4QMMT manuscripts, see Qimron and Strugnell, DJD X, 3, 14, 18, 21, 25, 29, 34, and 39. Extensive paleographical analysis, with an

MMT and the construction of communal history

In deconstructing a reading of MMT that locates it in a highly-specific historical context, we demonstrate the fragility of that historiographical structure. However, we have not taken into consideration the additional textual evidence that supports this historical account. If the Teacher of Righteousness did not write MMT, and if he did not send it to the Wicked Priest, then why does the Psalms pesher record an account of just such an event? And why would the author/editor(s) of the Community Rule feel a need to prohibit just such disputation on the part of leaders, or members, of their covenant community?

A useful way to answer these questions is with a hypothetical re-reading of MMT in the context of a sectarian community associated with the Community Rule (which may be at some remove, ideologically or temporally, from the setting of the text's original composition). The specific relationship of the community of MMT and the community of the Community Rule is not clear: the latter may have developed out of the former, the two may be identical, or they may relate in some more complicated way.[78] It is apparent that sections of the Community Rule (especially the Doctrine of the Two Spirits, in 1QS 3.15–4.26) reflect a much more dualistic perspective than that expressed in the arguments of MMT. Although the text of MMT distinguishes between right and wrong halakhic practice, the terms of its arguments suggest that it is still possible to change one's ways, and to refrain from wrong action, by following the standards presented in the text. In contrast, the Community Rule, at least in its more dualistic sections, argues for a fairly rigid distinction between righteousness and wickedness, and also between the righteous and the wicked.

Given this background, we can imagine a reading of MMT in which the question of genre no longer requires foregrounding. Rather

---

indication of relative dating, is provided by Ada Yardeni in Qimron and Strugnell, DJD X, 21–25, 29–34.

[78] Metso addresses some of the complications of textual development and its relationship to communal development, in 'Constitutional Rules,' in Flint and VanderKam, *Dead Sea Scrolls After Fifty Years*, 1.186–210. Her focus is on the development of the Community Rule and the Damascus Document, but many of her observations are equally salient for a discussion of the relationship of MMT and the Community Rule.

than asking whether the text began as an actual letter or only a literary treatise, a later covenantal audience may be more interested in understanding this text in light of its impact on their own community's history and collective identity. A reader in this context may choose, consequently, to background those elements in MMT that appear to take a conciliatory tone, while foregrounding the text's construction of communal boundaries (between right and wrong behavior, if not between the righteous and the wicked per se). Such a reading also may explain how the Community Rule, the Psalms pesher, and MMT together provide evidence for a set of events whose basic historicity we have called into question.

For a member of this covenant community, any reading of MMT must take place in the context of a larger communal tradition. Included within that tradition will be an account of the founding of the community (which may be more or less partisan, as well as more or less historically accurate), as well as accounts of the experiences of the group's founders, its leaders, and its membership. Certain texts and textual interpretations will be valued, and certain kinds of knowledge (of scripture, of interpretation, of God's will) will be viewed as authoritative in communal circles. In the context of such a setting, it is possible to imagine MMT as an element within the shared tradition. Whether written by the community's founder, by a later leader, or by a covenanter attempting to confirm the validity of the community's tradition, the text of MMT might be *understood*, by its covenantal audience, as a historical record of the events and experiences of the community in its pre-history.

We have suggested that one of the basic qualities of this hypothetical covenantal reader is a concern to maintain proper boundaries between the righteous and the wicked. Given this primary concern, we can imagine a reading of MMT that understands it as evidence for an important but troubling period in the group's foundation. Consider the text's statement that:

> We have written to you some precepts of the Torah that we believe [will be] good for you and for your people, for we have seen that you have wisdom and knowledge of the Torah (4QMMT C 26–28).

For a covenanter looking back on a history of conflict with 'outsiders,' such a text may be read as the product of a gentler time, when a covenanter still could hope to educate the misguided masses. The text's further assertion, that its recipient must seek God's will, in order to "remove from you evil thoughts and the counsel of Belial"

(4QMMT C 29), can be interpreted in a similar light. Although this text was designed to turn the wicked from their misguided ways, it was unsuccessful in its attempts, so that the wicked continue to live under the power of Belial. The final hope, that the audience of the text might "rejoice at the end of time, finding that some of our statements are correct" (4QMMT C 30) is similarly a reflection of historical perspective rather than present-time reality. As this covenantal reader knows, there is no hope for the wicked, and they will not rejoice in the endtimes, because they have failed to recognize God's true commandments and the righteous path they require.

We might note that this reading of the text constructs a historical account from the sources of a shared communal tradition. A covenanter who reads this text 'knows' that it reflects a real event, because the traditions of the community have informed him of this event. They may have described it in details that are lost to modern scholarship, or they may have provided rough outlines, which each covenanter could fill in with interpretations of his own. The Community Rule, as another element in this tradition, fills in an important piece of the historical picture. The time of disputation is now past, and the members of the community have moved beyond the need to argue with the wicked. There is no benefit in such disputation, and consequently, the text forbids it (1QS 9.16–17).

For such a covenanter, the history of the community will contain records of its great leaders, opponents, and apostates. Such figures as the Teacher of Righteousness, the Wicked Priest, the Liar, the Spouter, and so on, all contribute to that history, and their experiences and actions would be recorded in the oral, and written, traditions of the community. One such record is the account, described above, of the conflict between the Teacher and the Wicked Priest, over an exchange of Torah. According to this text's interpretation of Ps 37.32–33:

> *The wicked watches out for the righteous and seeks [to put him to death. The Lord will not abandon him into his hand or] let him be condemned when he is tried.*
>
> Interpreted, this concerns the Wicked [Pr]iest who [watched the Tea]cher of Right[eousness] and sought to put him to death [because of the ordi]nance (החוק) and the law (והתורה) which he sent to him.[79]

---

[79] 4Q171 4.5–9. For additional discussion of this passage, see Qimron and Strugnell, DJD X, 120.

It is worth reading this pesher text in several modes, asking first how its original author/editor(s) may have understood it, and also how it may have been interpreted by other covenanters, in other situations. We may note that pesher readings tend to stay very close to the language of the scriptural passages they interpret,[80] and also to make use of a number of 'standard' readings.[81] The text's observations that 'the wicked' of the Psalm is the Wicked Priest, for example, and that 'the righteous' is the Teacher are not unexpected interpretive moves on the part of the pesher's original composers. In fact, the covenantal writers of this pesher may have chosen this Psalms passage for interpretation specifically *because* of its use of such amenable expressions. In any case, the pesher stays close to the scriptural passage here, going so far as to use the same words to describe the wicked, who "watches" (צפה) the righteous and "seeks to put him to death" (מ]בקש להמיתו]).

If the first half of the pesher is grounded in a reading of the Psalms text, what are we to make of the second half, with its insertion of an 'ordinance' and a 'law' that the Teacher ostensibly sent to the Wicked Priest? How did the text's original author/editor(s) understand this statement? This line provides the basis for whatever historiographical claim we might make upon the text, but it too has at least a partial literary basis. In the verse immediately prior to the one quoted above, we find the statement,

> The mouth of the righteous utters wisdom, and his tongue speaks justice. The law (התורה) of God is in his heart, his feet do not slip (Ps 37.30–31).

Like rabbinic midrash, pesher may draw on nearby verses in its interpretations, and it may be that this line (which immediately precedes the text in question, and which is regrettably fragmentary in the manuscript), is the source for the reference to the 'law' of the Teacher. From this passage, we have a source for the reference to

---

[80] See, for example, Maurya Horgan, *Pesharim: Qumran Interpretations of Biblical Books* (Washington: Catholic Biblical Association of America, 1979); George Brooke, 'Qumran Pesher: Towards the Redefinition of a Genre,' *RevQ* 10 (1981): 483–503. See also the earlier understanding of pesher as an attempt to 'unriddle' scriptural texts, in Lou Silberman, 'Unriddling the Riddle: A Study in the Structure and Language of the Habakkuk Pesher,' *RevQ* 3 (1961): 323–64.

[81] See especially the commentary on Habakkuk (1QpHab), where each prophetic passage is leveraged to refer to the community, its leader, or one of a few key opponents.

Torah in the pesher, and possibly also for the reference to an ordinance or precept, by a multiplication or duplication of terms. However, this does not explain the reference to the 'sending' of this message.

Why might the writer(s) of this pesher believe that the Teacher *sent* a Torah-text to his opponent? One possibility is that the Teacher really did send such a letter, and that the pesher-writer(s) know this fact, but this is not the only possible explanation. It is equally likely, especially if the pesharim are compositions that date from a late period in the community's development,[82] that this text reflects a communally-held tradition or belief that the Teacher engaged in such a conflict with the Wicked Priest. The pesher writers in this context may understand MMT from a believing historical perspective: it is no mere record of communal ideology, but is, instead, a copy of the actual letter written by the Teacher and designed to offer advice to a potentially misguided outside leader, to keep him from becoming what he ultimately did become, a Wicked Priest.

For the writers of this pesher, then, traditional knowledge or beliefs about the past may have shaped the composition of the text.[83] Knowing the text of MMT, the writers are able to 'remember' an occasion on which the Teacher sent a letter to the Wicked Priest. And what did the Wicked Priest do in response to the letter? The answer to that question is found *in the text of Psalms*, which is the source of the pesher writer's answer: he spied on the Teacher and

---

[82] Scholars tend to view the pesharim as relatively late compositions in the community's history, and the pesher manuscript witnesses are among the later scrolls texts. Paleographically, the pesher manuscripts tend to be dated to the second half of the first century BCE (50 BCE to 1 BCE); see Wise, *The First Messiah*, 331–32 n. 34 for a chart of dates. Several of the pesharim also have been subject to radiocarbon testing, with mixed results. Recent tests date the manuscript of the Habakkuk commentary (1QpHab) to the first century BCE (88–2 BCE with one-sigma, or 68 percent, confidence) and the Psalms commentary (4Q171) to the first century CE (29–81 CE, again with 68 percent confidence). The late dating of the Psalms pesher manuscript has been surprising to scholars and has generated some controversy. For a discussion of the issue, with attention to the specifics of radiocarbon dating technology and an explanation of terminology, see Doudna, 'Dating the Scrolls,' 430–71 (esp. the chart on 468–71), as well as the updated discussions on the Orion discussion list.

[83] Brooke makes a similar argument in a slightly different context, noting that "the pesharim may... be better understood as an attempt to rewrite the actual history of the Qumran community in terms of the fulfillment of prophetic texts read from within the tradition represented by such texts as the *Damascus Document*." See George Brooke, 'The Messiah of Aaron in the Damascus Document,' *RevQ* 15 (1991): 229.

sought to put him to death. In this way, traditions of conflict with outsiders, combined with an ideology that foregrounds boundaries and boundary-making, can be mobilized for the construction of a historical narrative that 'remembers' an incident of conflict and provides an explanation for it. The pesher writers can blame the clash between the righteous and the wicked on the Torah that the Teacher sent to the Priest, because *they have seen that Torah*. It is the text of MMT. That this scenario might be grounded in ideological 'memory' rather than historical fact would be a point of little interest for the writers of the pesher text.

For covenantal readers of this text, a constellation of other evidence provides authority and support for specific historical claims. That is, for a covenanter who knows these three texts—MMT, the Community Rule, and the Psalms pesher—and who understands each of them as an authoritative record of history and proper praxis, there is no question of the story they tell. The Psalms pesher records a description of the community's founding moments, while MMT provides an artifact of one such founding conflict. The Community Rule, in turn, supports the construction of boundaries between the righteous covenanters—the heirs of the Righteous Teacher—and the wicked of the world, who have no option but to follow the will of Belial and the teachings of the Wicked Priest.

MMT, Torah-truth, and sectarian readings

In the later generations of the covenant community, MMT may have served any of several uses. Covenanters may have encountered it as an official historical record, offering proof of the community's foundation and early history; as an element of individual or group instruction; or as a text that was read in the context of communal religious praxis. As an instructional text, MMT may have served for initial introduction into the doctrines of the community (among new members or potential members), or as a part of regular and familiar instruction for established members of the group. In the context of the community's larger textual and scriptural tradition, the specific readings of a given covenanter would be shaped by a number of factors: the covenanter's own expectations or concerns, the state of the community at the time of a given reading, and the traditions or textual interpretations that the reader might choose to mobilize. In this context, the focus on Torah-learning and Torah-practice in

MMT might be foregrounded, to generate important interpretations of the text.

It is easy to imagine a sectarian reading of MMT that might foreground the text's attention to Torah, both as a set of practices and also as a set of texts. The entire second section of MMT is given over to a presentation of Torah-interpretations, and this theme is further (and thoroughly) examined in the exhortation that follows. Appropriate practice and appropriate understanding of Torah are what protect people—including the kings of Israel—from their troubles (4QMMT C 23–25). Attention is drawn to scripture as such, with a reference to a tripartite grouping of authoritative texts (one of the earliest in ancient Judaism). In addition to "the book of Moses, and the books of the Prophets, and (the writings of) David," the text includes mention of a fourth category, "[the events of] ages past," which may be a reference to another textual source.[84] MMT is peppered with quotations and paraphrases (especially from Deuteronomy, but from other texts, as well), frequently preceded by expressions like, "and it is written" (כתוב [וא]ף) or even "and it is written in the book of Moses" (ואף כתוב בספר מושה).[85] The covenantal reader is encouraged to make a careful study, both of scripture and of the interpretations provided in MMT, in order to fully understand the claims made in the text.

The tone of this text is also a point worth foregrounding for a covenantal reader. In presenting a sense of encouragement, and a sort of reasoned assertiveness, MMT makes clear to the covenanter that the group itself is not to blame for any divisions that may have come to plague the "people of Israel." As the text makes clear, the founders of the covenant community have done no wrong (4QMMT C 8–9). Rather, it is the improper conduct of the *rest* of the nation (as reported extensively in the text's halakhic discussion) that has forced them to break away. For a covenanter with a concern to justify the actions of the community, this text's reasonable tone and reasonable claims make clear that the wrong is all on the part of outsiders. Even though 'they know' that their actions are wrong,[86]

---

[84] 4QMMT C 10–11. See Qimron and Strugnell, DJD X, 59 n. 10, 112.
[85] For "and it is written," see 4QMMT B 10, 66, 70, 76, 77 (twice); 4QMMT C 12 (twice), 17. For "and it is written in the book of Moses," see 4QMMT C 6, 11, 21; each is partially restored.
[86] For the expression "and you know" (ואתם יודעים) as a repeated motif in the text, see 4QMMT B 38, 46 (restored), 68, 80; 4QMMT C 7 (restored), 8.

these outsiders continue to behave improperly, and even when they have the chance to understand and accept "some of our statements" (מקצת דברינו), they fail to make that effort (4QMMT C 30).

The understanding of Torah in MMT is closely interwoven with a specific set of scriptural interpretations. As the text asserts, it is not enough merely to engage in Temple sacrifice or to follow the prescriptions of the Torah. Rather, one must perform these tasks in appropriate ways that match the correct interpretations of Torah. Thus, on a number of occasions, we find the text making reference to a specific דבר or מעשה (which may be translated variously as 'ruling,' 'statement,' 'deed,' or 'precept') that the audience must take into account in attempting to complete a given Torah-practice.[87] Some interpretations are presented as foregone conclusions (such as when the text reminds its readers, "and you know that..."), while others are prefaced with personal assertions ("we are of the opinion that..."), but the total outlook of MMT is fairly clear. There are proper and improper interpretations of Torah, and it is desirable for covenanters to acknowledge and accept the interpretations presented in the text.

In contrast with the neutral or 'reasonable' tone of MMT, with its presentation of a series of correct interpretations of scripture and halakhic passages, some other Dead Sea Scrolls take a significantly more exclusivist view of scripture and religious praxis. We saw that the Community Rule demonstrates a much more rigid sense of boundaries than that found in the text of MMT. Similarly, a text like the Damascus Document presents a significantly more restrictive view of Torah-knowledge than the presentation found in MMT. For this reason, it is useful to imagine a reading of MMT by a member of the Damascus covenant community, who might foreground the text's exclusivist claims while, again, backgrounding its conciliatory tone and apparent openness.[88]

The claims of MMT are to present the right and proper inter-

---

[87] The text opens and closes with such references, which also contribute to the title scholars have given to the document. See, for example, 4QMMT B 1, 2; 4QMMT C 27.

[88] Again, given the complex relationships of the Damascus Document and the Community Rule, it is best not to equate the communities associated with these texts. They may reflect the orders of a single community, at one moment or in different periods; they may also reflect the existence of several closely-related communities, of two separate communities, or of a still more complex history of social development. See n. 78, above.

pretations of scripture, and the resulting account of proper religious practices, but the text does not claim to provide the only possible interpretations of scripture. The Damascus Document, in contrast, ignores the notion of 'interpretation' and instead provides, or so it claims, 'Torah,' pure and simple. That is, the arguments in the Damascus Document, whether they reflect a direct scriptural background or an extensive interpretive frame, are presented in the text as the unitary, true, and correct understanding of scripture. There is no 'interpretation,' according to this view; there is only the willfulness, stubbornness, or ignorance of a reader who refuses to understand Torah in its true meaning. The Torah of the Damascus covenanters is a unique Torah-knowledge, and a reading of MMT by such a covenanter would highlight the exclusivist tendencies of that text as well.

An explicit picture of the Damascus Document's communal-interpretation-as-Torah claim is evident in the text's third admonition (CD 2.14–3.16). There, we find a selective presentation of the history of the world, which has been full of people who have followed their own will and stubbornly refused to follow God's commandments. The text begins with the Watchers and the children of Noah and continues through a description of the patriarchs (who, alone, actually "kept the commandments of God and did not choose [their] own will," CD 3.2–4), the people of Israel in their wilderness wanderings, and ultimately the Israelite monarchy. In each case, the failure of the people and God's anger against them are attributed to their unwillingness to follow God's commandments.[89] Finally, the text states, God raised up for himself a remnant and revealed to them

> the hidden things in which all Israel had gone astray. He unfolded before them his holy Sabbaths and his glorious feasts, the testimonies of his righteousness and the ways of his truth, and the desires of his will which a man must do in order to live (CD 3.14–15).

Note the powerful elision of terms here: the failure to follow God's commandments includes the failure to recognize the proper calendrical cycle, appropriate textual interpretation, and general way of life. In each case, that is, the claim that people have failed to follow Torah is in fact a claim that they have failed to follow *the Damascus*

---

[89] See, for example, CD 2.21, 3.8–10. Note that the same theme is expressed earlier in CD 1.21–2.1, as well.

covenanters' interpretation of Torah. The suggestion that interpretation is even a possibility is something that the writers of the Damascus Document treat with contempt: "they wallowed in the sin of man and in ways of uncleanness, and they said, 'This is our (way),'" (CD 3.17–18). As the text assumes (and does not even need to assert), there *is* no other way than the sectarian way, which is "a sure house in Israel whose like has never existed from former times till now" (CD 3.19–20). Those who suggest otherwise, or who claim that other interpretations are possible, must be either willful or deluded.

How might a Damascus covenanter have dealt with the contrasting Torah-claims in MMT and the Damascus Document? For such a covenanter, with a seriously exclusivist perspective, the conflicting tones or tendencies of these texts will be harmonized in favor of the more exclusive of the two. In foregrounding the exclusivist claims of the Damascus Document, such a covenanter might, for example, reinterpret the exhortation from MMT that its audience should heed its message, "so that you may rejoice at the end of time, finding that some of our practices are correct." In the mind of a Damascus covenanter, this expression might be understood in more extreme terms: 'you had better accept all of our practices *now*, because the endtimes are here.' A similar interpretation may befall the request that the reader:

> consider all these things and ask [God] that he strengthen your will and remove from you the plans of evil and the device of Belial (4QMMT C 28–29).

In isolation, the text of MMT seems to assume that Belial is reasonably easily defeated (at least with the help of God), and that with proper training and initiative it is easy to move away from wickedness and toward the rejoicing that will come at the end of times. But for the Damascus covenanter, the task of removing oneself from Belial is a constant challenge, especially as the endtimes draw near and only a remnant of righteous Israel continues to survive. Consequently, although MMT does not require a reading in exclusivist or predestinarian terms, for a covenanter with that perspective in mind, such claims easily can be foregrounded in a reading of the text.

It is interesting to suggest one additional reading of MMT that covenanters might have pursued.[90] This reading looks inward, rather

---

[90] See esp. Fraade, 'To Whom It May Concern,' for a reading that uses this approach to rethink the history and use of MMT in the covenant community.

than backward, taking the conciliatory tone of the text as a personal invitation, and understanding the 'you' of the text as personally directed toward the one doing the reading. For covenanters who would read MMT as an introduction to the community's halakhic norms, or as a reminder of those communal standards, the text might be taken as a strangely personal message, and not only a neutral history lesson. Framed in terms of the covenanter's own personal call to proper action, the text can take on all sorts of unexpected meanings, and messages that were formerly understood as addressed to outsiders and major leaders in the ancient Jewish community can be turned inward, toward the covenanter's own self-focus. If MMT served only as a record of communal history, the reading suggested by this approach is not especially likely. However, if the text was used in training new members of the community, or was read by covenanters as a part of personal or collective devotion, this reading is at least worth considering.

If we assume a reading of this text by a covenanter who chooses to foreground a sense of personal responsibility, much of the text can be taken in that direction. The repeated use of "and you know" (ואתם יודעים) in the main body of the text (section B) and at the beginning of the exhortation can be understood in this reading as creating a personal connection. The reader ('you') is part of a group of people who are wise enough to know what is or is not proper practice and consequently shares the views presented in the halakhic section of the text. This sense of being part of the group continues in the exhortation, with the observation, "and you all know that we have separated ourselves from the majority" (4QMMT C 7), which gives the reader reason to understand the communal separation as a response to the inappropriate behavior of the rest of populace, rather than as a poor reflection on the community *or* on the reader personally.

Such a reading might continue with an interpretation of the statement that "we have written to *you* (אליכה) so that *you* may study (שתבין) the book of Moses" (4QMMT C 10), which confirms the covenanter's own chosenness, while articulating the scope of his responsibilities. This reader knows that the endtimes are coming, the blessings and curses of Deuteronomy are already under way, the Torah is the source of all good, and the kings of Israel stand as examples for the importance of turning to the Torah. And when the text follows this description of the kings with the statement that,

> We have written to you (אליך) some precepts of the Torah that we believe [will be] good for you (לך) and for your people (ולעמך) (4QMMT C 26–27),

the reader understands that the people in question are to be identified with the 'you' of the preceding halakhic discussion: not the followers of a rival leader of Israel, but rather the covenanter's own cohort and community. He is one of a select group, and as the text indicates, he stands out even within that group (if he chooses to understand it that way).

The statement that "we have seen that you have wisdom and knowledge of the Torah" (4QMMT C 27–28) fits this same reading: it is further confirmation of the right of the covenanter to be part of this select group and to stand out within it. He deserves to be there by virtue of his attachment to Torah and his hard work in seeking the proper path. Similarly, he can understand in personal terms the exhortation to:

> Consider all these things and ask him that he strengthen your will and remove from you evil thoughts and the counsel of Belial, so that you may rejoice at the end of time, finding that some of our statements are correct (4QMMT C 28–30).

Not only some, but all of the statements of MMT are 'correct' for this reader, who knows the danger of evil thoughts and the counsel of Belial, and who works to establish his place as the endtimes come into play.

In the context of this sort of reading, the historical significance of 4QMMT is not forgotten by the covenanter, but it may be backgrounded for the moment. In place of its historic implications, this covenantal reader might focus on the ongoing and personalized significance of the text, which reflects the covenanter's own importance as an interpreter of Torah and his own place as an obedient follower of God's commandments. We might imagine a reading of this text as part of a communal gathering, in which each covenanter is reminded of his own importance to the larger community.[91] In this sort of context, the experience of an individual covenanter can be interwoven with (or perhaps mapped onto) the experience of

---

[91] Vermes suggests this possibility, which he ties to a Covenant Renewal ceremony, perhaps on Shavuot. See Vermes, *The Complete Dead Sea Scrolls*, 79–81.

the community, so that each member understands himself as an organic participant in the history of the whole group.

Contextualizing the MMT calendar

As a final point of interest, we may ask how the calendrical portion of this text (section A) fits with the larger agenda and structure of the whole. John Strugnell, in his discussion of the MMT manuscript tradition, suggests that the calendar was not a part of the original composition of the text but was appended to it in the course of its copying and transmission.[92] Whether we understand this calendrical text as early or late bears on the historical accounts that we might read in the text.

Dead Sea Scrolls scholars have noted the importance of calendar-issues in the scrolls. In addition to texts that actually lay out calendrical orders,[93] the scrolls include a number of references to the importance of maintaining proper times and seasons. According to the Damascus Document, the transgressions of the wicked include their "straying" with regard to God's "holy sabbaths [and] glorious appointed times" (CD 3.14). In contrast, the righteous Damascus covenanters are those who,

> observe the Sabbath day in its exact detail (כפרושה),[94] and the appointed times and the day of the fast, as it was found (כמצאת) by the ones who entered the new covenant in the land of Damascus.[95]

Concern for proper holiday observance, especially with regard to Yom Kippur (the likely referent for "the day of the fast" in the above passage) also is reflected in an account in the Habakkuk pesher. That text refers to a Wicked Priest who "pursued the Teacher of Righteousness to the house of his exile" on the Day of Atonement

---

[92] Strugnell argues that the majority of MMT should be understood as a polemical text, but that the calendar appears in a neutral form, as a straightforward listing of dates and holidays, with no sense of polemic or conflict. See Strugnell, DJD X, 203.

[93] See 11QT 17.1–29.9; and the texts of priestly courses, or Mishmarot (4Q320–30), which contain a calendar of the six months from Passover through Sukkot.

[94] For פרוש in the sense of 'detail,' see Baumgarten and Schwartz, 'CD,' 15 n. 16.

[95] CD 6.18–19. The theme of covenantal identity and the images of the new covenant and the land of Damascus are discussed at length in the chapters that follow.

(1QpHab 11.4–8), with the intention of causing trouble and confusion in the Teacher's community. Although the historicity of this claim is as problematic as that of any other pesher (in that it could reflect a real communal memory or the construction of such a memory),[96] the concern for proper times and seasons appears to be a central one, at least for the community or communities associated with the Damascus Document and the pesharim.

If MMT is a text that represents a less-developed sectarian tendency, it is interesting to speculate on whether it contained a presentation of the calendar in its original form, or whether that is a later addition on the part of one of the scribes who transmitted the text. If the calendar is original to the text, this presumably supports the view that calendrical issues were of major significance in the earliest history of ancient Jewish sectarian conflict. However, if Strugnell is right, and the calendrical portions are a later addition, it is possible to imagine a number of different readings of the text that might have led a later covenanter to supplement it in this direction.

We have suggested that later members of a covenant community may have looked back to the text of MMT as a source for understanding their community's history and foundations. For a covenanter with a developed sense of calendrical conflict, such as that reflected in the Damascus Document, the fact that MMT did not refer to that issue may have looked strange. We can imagine such a reader choosing to append a transcription of the community's calendar to the text of MMT in this case, in order to 'correct' what he perceived as an obviously flawed account of historical events. Later generations of readers, in turn, might have looked to the edition of MMT that contained the calendar as historical proof that calendar-issues were fundamental to the formation of the community. In this way, one generation of editors can shape the historical understanding of the next generation of readers, by reshaping a text that both view as ancient and authoritative.

---

[96] A similar dispute is recorded in the Mishnah, where Rabban Gamaliel solves a conflict over calendrical issues by requiring his opponent to come to him on what would have been his Day of Atonement, carrying his staff and his money. See m. Rosh Hash. 2.8–9. The rough similarity of these accounts (conflict over calendar; specific reference to Yom Kippur; account of one party traveling to the other's community) again raises the questions of whether and how these texts may reflect a shared tradition, some remembered communal experiences, or the invention of such experiences.

An approach to MMT that identifies a multiplicity of possible historical interpretations of the text contributes to a significant reconsideration of the way we 'do history.' As the diverse readings show, a historiographical approach to the Dead Sea Scrolls cannot uncritically follow the steps of extracting historical data from texts and using that data to generate a historical narrative. Although such an approach can produce convincing and coherent accounts of history, it is methodologically risky, for several reasons.

The first danger of such an approach is that in harmonizing the evidence from a series of similar or related texts, we may fail to recognize the singular differences between those texts, thus losing important evidence for changes in ideology or communal structures over time.[97] But a second, and less obvious, danger lies in reading a group of texts as sources for independent, confirmatory historical accounts, when in fact the texts themselves are interrelated and provide no outside confirmation for one another. This second danger contributes to the potential for writing circular historical accounts, grounded in the ideological constructions of history provided in the texts, rather than in a set of 'real' events existing outside them.

In generating a variety of different readings of a single text, we can undercut the sense of obviousness that sometimes attaches itself to harmonistic readings of history in the scrolls. And by showing that a harmonistic reading is only one of a number of possible readings of a text—either in its original setting, or at some remove from that place and time—we can demonstrate the extent to which 'the meaning' of texts is grounded in their mobilization, by audiences with agendas that may be quite removed from those of the text's original author(s) or editor(s). In addition, recognizing that texts that describe past historical events also can contribute to the later *construction* of historical knowledge, and not merely the preservation of it, allows us to recognize the extent to which our historical pursuits leave us searching not for an account of 'what really happened,' but rather for an account of the ideological constructions of history, community, and identity that are preserved in—or interpretable from within—our textual evidence.

---

[97] For Davies' critique of harmonizing historiography, see chapter one above, and Davies, *Behind the Essenes*, 15–31, esp. 25–27.

CHAPTER THREE

HISTORY AND TIME IN THE DAMASCUS DOCUMENT

History is a subject of significant interest in the Damascus Document. The text offers generalized, sweeping accounts of human experience—some extending from earliest humanity to the text's present day—as well as more limited presentations of the experiences of the people of Israel, or of the covenant community in particular. These historical accounts vary not only in their scope but also in their style of presentation. While some accounts take the form of linear narratives, others offer a more static view of human experience. A combination of these two approaches generates a third approach to history, which understands all of human experience as a cyclical repetition of the same basic actions, on the part of the people (who transgress God's will, but ultimately repent and seek to return to God) and on the part of God, as well (who punishes the sinful with exile, but ultimately permits return and redemption). Time is not simple in these narratives: an account may be at once linear and cyclical, and events from scripture may be read with the same immediacy as the community's own experiences.

The text's presentation of history has been a point of interest for scholars of the Damascus Document, as well, and not only for its literary or stylistic significance. Two passages in particular (from the first and last pages of the Admonition) provide cryptic accounts of events in the history of the covenant community and, more importantly for historians, include specific temporal references within those accounts. The first reference is to the founding of the covenant community, some 390 years after the Babylonian conquest (CD 1.5–6), and to the arrival of a Righteous Teacher, who appears on the scene after the community has wandered astray for a period of 20 years (CD 1.10). The second reference, of a rather different sort, is to the roughly 40 years that are to pass from the time of the death of the Teacher to the destruction of his chief opponents (CD 20.15).

From a modern historiographical perspective, these details are provocative. They hint at a complex history behind the text of the Damascus Document but do not lend themselves to immediate or transparent explanation. As scholarship on this text has demonstrated (both in the first half of the twentieth century and in the half-century since the discovery of the scrolls), historical readings of these details may vary widely, from those that take the claims of the text as transparently accurate to those that view them as metaphorical, scripturally-based, or entirely fabricated.

In reading these literary details for their potential historiographical usefulness, we must take seriously the multiplicity of their potential textual meaning. At the first stage of analysis (presented in this chapter), we may limit our attention to the historical claims of the text's original author/editor(s), which might—as a heuristic device—be understood as the 'original meaning' of the text, in its original setting. This sort of reading allows us to identify some of the primary concerns that appear to shape the text's historical perspective, as well as some of the textual strategies (including word-usage, repetition, and scriptural reference) that contribute to the presentation of these concerns. In addition to highlighting the ideological claims of the text, this approach allows us to ask to what extent the text, in its original setting, might have reflected a set of real historical events 'behind' it, and to what extent readers outside the text's original setting should be able to identify those events or understand the relationship of the text to the events it describes.

In the second stage of this literary-critical historiography (which follows, in the next chapter), we turn from the notion of an 'original' textual meaning to a discussion of how the text might have been read by any of a diverse range of audiences. Here, the focus is limited to the text's specific temporal references, and to the ideological claims that those references might be made to support, by a wide range of audiences. Among these audiences are some whose concerns might not correspond with those of the text's original author/editor(s) and whose social settings or intellectual assumptions might be at some distance, as well. Reading the text's temporal references in terms of audiences at some remove from the text's moment of origin highlights the potential for multiplicity of meaning in the text. It also allows us to see how the text could serve not only to reflect whatever historical events lay behind it, but also to contribute to the construction of new historical consciousness in its later covenantal audiences. With this kind of approach, scholars can attempt to sort out the historical relevance of the Damascus Document, without viewing the meaning of the text as either unitary or eternal.

A discussion of the ideological constructions of history in the Damascus Document might begin with any of several passages. The text itself takes a form that scholars have labeled a covenantal or constitutional rule.[1] It begins with a series of sermons, or admonitions, which distinguish between the righteous and the wicked, and which provide historical and theological grounding for a construction of communal identity. Following these admonitions are a series of additional discussions, in which pesher-style interpretations of scriptural passages provide a means of confirming the identity, history, and boundaries of the community of the text. Following these discussions, the text continues with a lengthy presentation of legal material, including discussions of purity, oaths and vows, Sabbath practices, dietary standards, and other matters that provide structures for community members' daily lives and ritual observances.[2]

The historical accountings presented in the narrative and sermonic portions of the Damascus Document are grounded in the text's understanding of scripture,[3] and they rely upon a complex use of scrip-

---

[1] The Community Rule is the other primary example of this textual variety. See Sarianna Metso, 'Constitutional Rules,' in Flint and VanderKam, *Dead Sea Scrolls After Fifty Years*, 1.186–210.

[2] Not all sections of the text are extant in all manuscript witnesses. The text of MS A of CD includes three admonitions and a series of scriptural interpretations and discussions (CD 1–8; scholars often label these passages collectively as 'the Admonition'), as well as a fairly substantial presentation of the community's legal norms (CD 15–16, 9–14; which does not include the penal code). The shorter text of MS B includes a version of the last portion of the Admonition (CD 19.1–34), as well as a concluding section that is not present in MS A (CD 20.1–34). The Qumran Damascus material (QD) includes fragments of all these passages (except for the variant textual passages from CD 19.1–34 in MS B), as well as certain previously-unknown material: an introduction and an admonition that precede the three admonitions found in MS A, a concluding section to the Admonition that would fall before the legal material; significant additional legal material; and the penal code mentioned above. For bibliography, see chapter 1, n. 1 and 2. The editors of the QD fragments report that these manuscripts contain a total of 689 lines, 326 of which parallel the medieval texts. In antiquity about two-thirds of the Damascus Document text would have been legal in nature; see Baumgarten and Davis, 'Cave IV, V, VI Fragments,' in Charlesworth, *Damascus Document*, 59.

[3] Campbell, *The Use of Scripture*; see also Jonathan Campbell, 'Scripture in The Damascus Document 1.1–2.1,' *JJS* 44 (1993): 83–99. Campbell provides thorough discussions of all sections of the Admonition (along with an enlightening annotation of the text, identifying scriptural quotations, paraphrases, and references). He also addresses a number of key historiographical questions: the nature of 'history' in the admonitions (50); the 'creation of history' in these narratives (87–88, 99, 102, 131); and 'creation of history' as a concept (199–200). His conclusions (175–208) are insightful, especially his discussion of the work of Davies and Knibb (194–205).

tural language, quotations, and motifs to articulate a narrative of communal history, understood in terms of the history of all Israel. In its use of scripture, the text underlines a number of key themes, which together explain the events of human history: the basic willfulness of human beings, God's selection of a remnant for salvation from among willful humanity, and the special knowledge that is given to that remnant, which allows them to stand out from the rest of humankind. Significant moments in the history of Israel receive repeated attention, so that, for example, Israel's sojourn in the wilderness after the Exodus (especially as recounted in Leviticus and Numbers) becomes a model for the experience of the Exile (often articulated in terms of expressions from Isaiah and Psalms). Together, these two periods serve as background for the foundation of a new covenant, which offers hope for God's redemption of the righteous.[4]

Of particular interest for our discussion of the text's constructions of history are the three major admonitions that open the text (roughly CD 1.1–3.16).[5] The first admonition (CD 1.1–2.1) focuses on the origins of the covenantal group and locates their history in the larger context of Israelite experience. The second admonition (CD 2.2–13) is a brief text; its view of history is centered on the experience of the divine and the place of human history in the larger context of God's reality. In contrast, the third admonition (CD 2.14–3.16) offers a comprehensive narrative account of human experiences, from the earliest generations of the world down to the text's 'present day.'[6] In discussing these three texts (with appeals to other relevant passages from CD or the QD material), we can reach a complex understanding of how time and history might be perceived to function in

---

[4] See Campbell, 'Essene-Qumran Origins,' 153, for a discussion of these themes and a listing of some relevant texts. He especially notes the centrality of Lev 26, Num 14, Deut 28ff., Isa 59, and Ps 106 in the construction of history in several sections of the Damascus Document. For a more extensive list of scriptural references, see Campbell, *The Use of Scripture*, 173.

[5] The additional admonition found in several QD manuscripts will be addressed as part of the larger discussion, but it is too fragmentary to receive specific focus of its own. See 4Q266 1–2 i; 4Q267 1; 4Q268 1; in Baumgarten, DJD XVIII, 31–36, 96–97, 119–20.

[6] The boundaries of this admonition are subject to debate, but this section is particularly relevant to the presentation of the history of Israel. In contrast, Campbell reads CD 2.14–4.12a as a coherent unit, while Davies works with CD 1.1–4.12a as a historical unit. Murphy-O'Connor presents CD 2.14–6.1 as a 'Missionary Document' that represents the earliest stratum of the text. See Campbell, *The Use of Scripture*, 67–88, esp. the annotated text on 75–76; Davies, *Damascus Covenant*, 52–53; Murphy-O'Connor, 'An Essene Missionary Document,' 201–29.

the Damascus Document. Our analysis begins with the second admonition, which provides the briefest and least 'narrative' of the major historical accounts. Discussions of the very different chronological models of history presented in the other two admonitions will build upon this initial temporal and historical foundation.

Constructions of history and the second admonition

From the perspective of the second admonition, time works simultaneously in two different ways. On the one hand, God is eternal, has always existed, and knows all that has been and will come to be.[7] God exists, that is, in a sort of permanent present tense. Humans, on the other hand, exist in a linear temporal realm, where events follow one upon another in a chronological succession from beginning to end, to form a history that is finite and bounded. It is bounded at the beginning by God's creation and at the end by the period of the endtimes,[8] but additionally it is 'bounded' on all sides by the ignorance of the majority of humanity. Most human beings have no way of escaping the inexorable day-to-day sequence of human history, and they may not even realize (or care) that their lives are constrained in this way.

According to the text, there is only one key that allows people to escape the boundaries of the human condition: knowledge. By knowing God's will and understanding how to behave (and interpret scripture) properly, certain select people are able to break down the barrier between the finite, bounded world of human experience and the infinite present of God's existence. Participation in the covenant requires taking on certain responsibilities, but in return it provides knowledge that gives the covenanters a unique perspective on the events of human history and the significance of those events, which is unavailable to 'the wicked.' Underlying this view of history and

---

[7] For a close reading that focuses on predestination in the second admonition, grounded in the text's use of wisdom language, see Armin Lange, 'Wisdom and Predestination in the Dead Sea Scrolls,' *DSD* 2 (1995): 350–52; more generally, see Lange, *Weisheit und Prädestination: Weisheitliche Urordnung und Prädestination in den Textfunden von Qumran* (New York: Brill, 1995), esp. 233–70.

[8] The endtimes is not a single moment but a period of time. For a discussion of this point and a fuller explanation of 'the endtimes,' see Annette Steudel, 'אחרית הימים in the Texts from Qumran,' *RevQ* 16 (1993): 231; John Collins, *Apocalypticism in the Dead Sea Scrolls* (New York: Routledge, 1997), 52–58.

knowledge is a fairly explicit predestinarian ideology: if God knows all that has been and will be, and if the members of God's chosen remnant have access to that special knowledge, then it follows that only the wicked are left in the dark and that they are doomed and destined to complete the course that God already knows they will take, before they even begin it.

In articulating this understanding of cosmic history and temporal order, the second admonition makes use of a number of important textual strategies. Images of the divine appear static and descriptive, rather than intensely active. When God does act, it tends to be in response to something that humans have done, while human actions themselves are constrained by the bounds of their knowledge (thus, the wicked can act only within the range of their ignorance, while God's chosen have a more enlightened path of action). In addition, knowledge is connected with notions of creation, wisdom, and existence, to highlight moments of origin and a sense of imminent conclusions in the text.

A more specific discussion will help to sort out some of this complex imagery and demonstrate its ideological payoff. The admonition begins with a discussion of the nature and ways of God, noting that although wisdom and knowledge and forgiveness are with God, so too are might, power, and wrath, which he directs toward the wicked who turn away from him (CD 2.2–7). A second portion of the text lays out God's relationship with the wicked, whose transgressions were known primordially and whose fates are predetermined (CD 2.7–10). A final passage reveals the presence of the remnant, "those called by name," who are chosen by God to fill the world (CD 2.11–13).

A central theme in this picture of cosmic history is the eternity of God, which is at times contrasted with the temporal actions of humans. The first five lines of the admonition present a God who is unbounded by time; the description is dominated by stative or non-verbal grammatical forms. No temporal boundaries are put here on God's nature, and with only a single exception, the descriptions in this passage are of general states of being, rather than specific divine acts. God "loves knowledge" (אהב דעת, CD 2.3) and "has set up" wisdom (הציב, CD 2.3); "long forbearance (is) with him and manifold forgiveness" (ארך אפים עמו ורוב סליחות, CD 2.4).[9] The single

---

[9] Following Baumgarten and Schwartz, 'CD,' 15.

statement that suggests intensive action on the part of God comes in the assertion that God is prepared "to atone" for those who are repentant (לכפר, CD 2.5), but even this statement is put in the infinitive form, which generalizes the temporal setting of the action, rather than presenting it as a single momentary act.[10]

As a foil to this eternal God, humans are somewhat more active figures, but their actions fit the admonition's general model of history. The actions are specific and stimulate specific responses from the divine, but they are not grounded in specific temporal moments or locations as such. Rather, like the admonition as a whole, they hover in a generalized temporal setting without being localized in a particular moment. God's atonement is undertaken "for those who turn from sin" (בעד שבי פשע, CD 2.5) while the wrath of the angels awaits "those who stray from the way and despise the statute" (על סררי דרך ומתעבי חק, CD 2.6), but there is no indication of *when* the repentance or sinful departures might take place, or have taken place. Rather, the use of participial forms allows for a range of temporal and contextual interpretation, further dislocating the action from a single specific context.[11]

This notion, that grammatical strategies can convey ideological agendas, has been explored by several scholars. Carol Newsom, in her article on 'Apocalyptic and the Discourse of the Qumran Community,' notes that the Community Rule demonstrates a careful use of grammar in articulating a set of primary concerns about obedience to God, God's special knowledge, and the necessary willingness to follow an appropriate path.[12] In its opening lines, the Community Rule encapsulates these responsibilities in a series of infinitive verbs: a covenanter has the responsibility, "to seek God... to do what is good... to love... to hate... to keep away... to cling... to con-

---

[10] See Lange, *Weisheit und Prädestination*, 263. For a discussion of the use of the infinitive in Dead Sea Scrolls Hebrew, see Elisha Qimron, *The Hebrew of the Dead Sea Scrolls* (Atlanta: Scholars Press, 1986), 70–72. He notes that the infinitive construct is "very common in DSS Hebrew (almost 1000 instances)," while the infinitive absolute is quite rare; see page 47. Thorion-Vardi observes that the infinitive (in construct form) is used with remarkable frequency in CD. See Talia Thorion-Vardi, 'The Use of the Tenses in the Zadokite Documents,' *RevQ* 12 (1985): 65–88, esp. 77ff.

[11] See Chaim Rabin, *The Zadokite Documents* (2nd ed., Oxford: Clarendon Press, 1958), 6 n. 2.3, as well as my discussion below.

[12] Newsom, 'Apocalyptic and Discourse,' 135–44.

duct oneself...," all in the manner that is appropriate to God's chosen way.[13] The verbal forms here are similar to those that we find in the Damascus Document, and in neither case is this an accidental use of language. Rather, as Newsom notes, in the Community Rule,

> the choice of infinitives exploits a nuance in the grammar. Where finite verbs include information on subject, aspect, and mood, the infinitive represses all of that and highlights only purpose.[14]

Similarly, in the Damascus Document, the use of infinitives and participles represses specific historical detail in favor of a focus on the covenanter's relationship with God. Temporal specificity is reduced in favor of a discussion of history that is generalized, ungrounded, and 'eternalized.' The events in this admonition might have occurred at any time, whether long in the past or in a given reader's present circumstance. In a similar discussion, John Collins notes that "the phrase 'a time of refining which co[mes...]' in the Florilegium can mean, grammatically, either that the time has come or that it is coming."[15]

This tendency toward generalized presentations of time has been noted and highlighted, too, by a number of the translators of the Damascus Document. Rabin, for example, observes that the admonition's introductory reference to "the ones entering the covenant" (באי ברית, CD 2.2) "refers to a state, not an action."[16] Schwartz, similarly, is aware of this temporal ambiguity and is careful to reflect it in his translation, as for example in his presentation of היוצאים מארץ יהודה as the ones "who depart(ed) from the land of Judah."[17] Other participial forms contribute to this same temporal perspective,[18] in which human actions are generalized and ungrounded, except within the larger eternal existence of God. In this admonition, it consequently

---

[13] 1QS 1.1–5; after Newsom, 'Apocalyptic and Discourse,' 138.
[14] Newsom, 'Apocalyptic and Discourse,' 138.
[15] Collins, *Apocalypticism*, 60–1; his discussion is in reference to 4Q174 2.1.
[16] Rabin, *Zadokite Documents*, 6 n. 2.3. Rabin cites other passages (CD 5.1, 6.19, 8.1, 9.2, 13.4, and 14.10) that use this verb in the same way; he also notes a parallel usage in the rabbinic text of b. Shabbat 22b.
[17] CD 4.3; see Baumgarten and Schwartz, 'CD,' 18–19.
[18] Note, for example, references to "those called by name" (קריאי שם, CD 2.11); in reference to the wicked, "the years of their standing" (שני מעמד, CD 2.9); and "the existence of eternity" (הוי עולמים, CD 2.10). These temporal expressions are discussed further, below.

appears that the *action* of having entered the covenant—and not the timing or historical location of that action—is what defines the covenanters' relationships with one another and with God.

In the next portion of the admonition, scriptural language and motifs contribute to a construction of human experience that is not only finite but entirely predestined. This theme is especially clear in the text's description of the wicked, who are rejected by God and have no share in the reality that lies beyond the end of human history, and whose fate has been predestined from before they even begin to act. As the admonition states, God "did not choose them [the wicked] primordially" (לא בחר אל בהם מקדם עולם),[19] and this is the reason both for their actions and for their state as 'wicked ones' in the first place.

The claim that the wicked were rejected "primordially" (מקדם עולם) is the first of a number of temporal expressions in this admonition that deserve closer scrutiny. These expressions (including references to eternity, the time of the wicked, and the completion of human time) reflect a significant, complicated interest in existence and time. Some of these expressions can be understood in terms of both specific and general implications, and at times even the distinctions between past, present, and future are obscured in them. More explicit, and at times underlined, is an appeal to common themes of wisdom, understanding, and the differential fates of the chosen and the wicked. The use of scriptural language in these passages (or of language for which we have interesting scriptural parallels) further underscores the interrelation of creation, existence, and endtimes, as they overlap and intermesh with the eternally-present periods before creation and after the end of human history. As a result, these often-multivalent expressions serve to underscore the basic temporal (and atemporal) themes articulated in this admonition.

The expression מקדם עולם, with its reference to the 'primordial' rejection of the wicked, can be understood in two slightly different ways,[20] depending on whether we read מקדם in the sense of 'from

---

[19] CD 2.7, after Baumgarten and Schwartz, 'CD,' 15. Rabin instead focuses on the connection to Mic 5.1 (מקדם מימי עולם), translating the passage as, "God has not chosen them 'from of old, <from the days of> eternity.'" See Rabin, *Zadokite Documents*, 6–7.

[20] In Biblical Hebrew, the word קדם can have any of several meanings, including 'ancient' (Deut 33.15, 33.27; Isa 19.11); 'of old' or 'long ago' (Ps 55.20, 74.2, 78.2, 119.152; Job 29.2; Jer 30.20; Lam 5.21); 'forward' (Job 23.8); 'in front' (Ps

before' the creation of the universe,²¹ or in the sense of 'from of old,' from the time of the creation of the universe.²² Although the difference in meaning of these two readings is slight, the shift in emphasis is an interesting one. Understanding the term as a reference to the time 'before creation,' or 'before the universe began,' highlights what we might think of as the period of 'sacred time,' outside the human realm and equated with the eternal existence of God. In contrast, if we read this expression as a reference to a decision by God 'from the beginning of' the world, the focus shifts to the time of creation and the period immediately following, when humans were establishing themselves (and, presumably, the fate of the wicked was being decided). Both of these readings are predestinarian, but they suggest a different focus on when the destiny of humankind was established. A third possibility is that the text can be read as pivoting through a variety of temporal periods (before, during, and immediately after creation), perhaps referring to several simultaneously. Whether this expression reflects one foundational period or several, the effect of the passage is to direct attention to the time of creation, while also creating the first of several linkages between the atemporal realm of God and the temporal narrative of human history.

A similar pattern occurs in the next line of the admonition, which provides a poetic parallel for the expression מקדם עולם. The text asserts, with regard to the wicked, that "before they were established, he [God] knew their deeds" (בטרם נוסדו ידע את מעשיהם, CD 2.7–8). Again, this line may reflect a simple reference to predestination, in the sense that God always knows what the wicked will do, even before they do it. But it too may be read in terms of a more sweeping temporal claim, that even before the wicked are born, and perhaps even before history itself is well under way, God already knows all that will follow, up to and including the final act.

139.5); and 'east' (Gen 10.30, 25.6, 29.1; Num 23.7; Judg 6.3, 6.33, 7.12; 8.10; 1 Kgs 5.10; Isa 11.14; Jer 49.28; Ezek 25.4, 25.10; Job 1.3). See BDB, 869.
²¹ See the examples in the note above. For rabbinic usage of קודם or קודם ל- to mean 'before,' see M. H. Segal, *A Grammar of Mishnaic Hebrew* (Oxford: Clarendon Press, 1980; first ed. 1927), 141, 146; see also Marcus Jastrow, *A Dictionary of the Targumim, the Talmud Babli and Yerushalmi, and the Midrashic Literature* (New York: The Judaica Press, Inc., 1989; first ed. 1903), 1316.
²² The expression מקדם, in the sense of "from of old," tends to occur in the prophetic and later biblical texts; see BDB, 869. In rabbinic Hebrew, קדם also can take the meaning "olden time." See Jastrow, *Dictionary*, 1316.

Scriptural parallels for primordial language

The language of 'primordial time' is ideologically powerful in its own right, highlighting the relationship between an eternal God and a temporal humanity, but it is further strengthened by a connection to themes of creation, history, endtimes, and especially wisdom. A number of scriptural passages provide intertextual support for a reading of the second admonition that focuses on these themes.[23] At its simplest, the scriptural use of expressions like מקדם can refer to a time 'long ago,' or 'of ancient days,'[24] but even in these cases, attention frequently focuses on God's actions in history, as in Psalm 143.5: "I remember days of old, I think about all your deeds" (זכרתי ימים מקדם הגיתי בכל פעלך).[25] God's salvation of the people of Israel is another common theme that uses this primordial language, either in generalized references ("and God, my King, is from of old (מקדם), working salvation in the midst of the earth," Ps 74.12),[26] or in more event-specific accounts, like the reference to the redemption of "the children of Jacob and Joseph," freed by "the hand of Moses and Aaron," as part of "the deeds of the Lord, ... [God's] wonders of old."[27] Notions of salvation also can be future-oriented, even when they use this past-looking language: "from you shall come forth for me one who is to rule in Israel, whose origin is from of old (מקדם), from ancient days (מימי עולם)."[28]

Explicit descriptions of creation also are common in the scriptural passages that use this language of primordial times, and it is interesting to note how frequently images of creation are mapped onto

---

[23] For an intertextual reading of this language in CD and 1QS, see Lange, *Weisheit und Prädestination*, 241–43.

[24] For example, see Neh 12.46, where a reference to events "in the days of David and Asaph long ago" (בימי דויד ואסף מקדם) carries with it only a simple temporal meaning.

[25] The expression מימי קדם ("from days of old") also occurs at times in a simple temporal sense; see Isa 23.7, 51.9; Jer 46.26; Lam 1.7; and Ps 44.2. These references also tend to bear witness to God's actions in the world.

[26] See also Hab 1.12, which highlights God's primordial and eternal presence: "Are you not from of old, O Lord my God, my holy one? You [M: We] shall not die" (הלוא אתה מקדם יהוה אלהי קדשי לא נמות (M: נמות)). Note that the variant reading (presented here as the primary text) focuses on God's immortality, while the Masoretic reading understands the passage as referring to the immortality of Israel.

[27] Ps 77.12–21. See also Mic 7.20, for a reference to salvation in terms of God's relationship with the patriarchs; the Hebrew expression in this case is מימי קדם.

[28] Mic 5.1. Rabin connects this passage directly with CD 2.7; see note 19 above, as well as Rabin, *Zadokite Documents*, 6–7.

or framed in terms of descriptions of God's salvific powers. At times the creation imagery is subtle, as in the references to "primordial chaos" (תהו) in a prophetic passage otherwise focused on God's monotheistic presence and the return of idolaters to praising God.[29] Similarly, the reference to God's salvation of "the children of Jacob and Joseph," mentioned above, contains an overlay of specific historical references, pleas to God for salvation, and a description of the waters and the Deep (תהמות) that may reflect an image of God as creator.[30] Other texts suggest more explicit connections between God's creative and salvific actions. In the passage identifying God as "King . . . from of old, working salvation in the midst of the earth" (Ps 74.12, also discussed above), the text begins by asking how long God will permit the enemies of Israel to desecrate the Temple, but it continues with a description of the creation, in lengthy and specific terms.[31] This picture of creation concentrates on the earliest stages in the formation of the universe—the arrangement of the waters, the death of the sea-monster (Leviathan), the establishment of the luminaries—in a way that underlines the connections between God's salvation of Israel in historic time and the creation of the universe in the time before human history.[32]

The use of primordial language lends itself to a number of ideological claims, especially with regard to predestination. God knows

---

[29] The passage begins at Isa 45.18, with the assertion that God did not create the world as chaos, but rather to be inhabited. The temporal expression occurs in Isa 45.21: "who told this long ago? Who declared it of old?" (מי השמיע זאת מקדם מאז הגידה).

[30] Following references to present-time suffering (Ps 77.1-10) and God's redemption of Israel (Ps 77.11-15), the text presents a description of the waters and the deep (תהמות), which fear God, and the lightning and thunder that accompany the crossing of the sea (Ps 77.16-20). The passage seems to be making use of both creation and Exodus imagery.

[31] The psalm asks God to remember the people of Israel (Ps 74.1-3), describes the enemy's attacks and asks how long retribution will have to wait (Ps 74.4-11), and then presents an account of God's creation of the world (Ps 74.12-17) and a further reminder to God to "have regard for the covenant" (Ps 74.18-23, esp. 74.20). In Ps 74.13-17, creation imagery includes references to the division of the sea, the crushing of Leviathan, the arrangement of the waters, the establishment of the luminary (מאור) and the sun (שמש), as well as the boundaries of the earth and the seasons.

[32] This creation account has less in common with the stories in Gen 1.1-2.25 than it does with the versions that appear in Job 3.8, 26.7-13; Isa 27.1, 51.9-10; and Ps 89.9-11; where we find multiple references to the primeval waters, as well as Leviathan and Rahab.

in advance about the events that are to occur in human time, whether those events ultimately favor Israel (the chastisement of Assyria) or punish the people's transgressions (the downfall of Judah).³³ This theme is developed most fully in a passage from second Isaiah, where an assertion of monotheism is connected to a description of God's eternal omniscience. With a particularly predestinarian tone, the passage states:

> For I am God, and there is no other; I am God, and there is no one like me, declaring the end from the beginning and from ancient times things not yet done (כי אנכי אל ואין עוד אלהים ואפס כמוני: מגיד מראשית אחרית ומקדם אשר לא נעשו).³⁴

In using primordial and creation language (מקדם, but also מראשית), this scriptural passage articulates an ideology much like the one that is expressed in the second admonition: all of human time is encapsulated, and the entire narrative is known to God before it ever occurs. The central narrative of this passage is not God's creation of the earth, or even the story of history from creation to its conclusion. Rather than focusing on human history in any form, the attention of this passage, like that of the Damascus Document passage, is directed toward the divine (and atemporal) realm, in which the existence of God is central, God's knowledge is complete, and the narrative of human history is brief and encapsulated.

Similar themes are conveyed, with a slightly different emphasis, in a well-known Proverbs passage describing the origins of Wisdom. Created by God primordially, Wisdom is a partner in the creation of the rest of the world. As the biblical text asserts, in the voice of Wisdom,

> The Lord created me at the beginning of his course, the former of his works of old. Ages ago I was set up, at the beginning, from the foretime of the earth (יהוה קנני ראשית דרכו קדם מפעליו מאז: מעולם נסכתי מראש מקדמי ארץ, Prov 8.23).

The passage then continues with an explicit description of creation—including the heavens, the earth, the fountains of the deep, and so on—with Wisdom as God's partner in creation (Prov 8.24–31). This

---

³³ For a predestined chastisement of Assyria, see 2 Kg 19.25 and Isa 37.26; for the predicted nature of the downfall of Judah, see Lam 2.17. All three passages use the expression מימי קדם.

³⁴ Isa 46.9–10. In context, this is a discussion of God's planned salvation of Israel, which is on its way to completion.

text, which again uses both specific creation language (ראשית), as well as language similar to that in our admonition (although the passage does not include the actual expression מקדם עולם), suggests a potential means of understanding the period before creation: primordial time is the time in which only God and wisdom ordinarily exist. It is a period that exists eternally in the present tense, as a sort of 'sacred time,' before human time and inaccessible to most human beings.

As these passages demonstrate, the use of primordial language carries with it a host of scriptural connections. Expressions like מקדם עולם offer a predestinarian perspective, but they also highlight significant assumptions with regard to the primacy of wisdom, the centrality of God's presence, and the understanding of human time as a single narrative already known to God before it even begins. Any or all of these themes may have been assumed by the author/editor(s) of the second admonition, but the most significant appears to be the specific connection of an atemporal reality outside of human time and the presence of knowledge or wisdom as the key to accessing that sacred atemporality. The impact of this intertextual reading will be discussed further below.

Concluding the second admonition

The next lines of the second admonition show an interest in the predestination of the lives of the wicked, combined with a profound (and complex) interest in notions of time, chronology, and periodicity. This passage has given problems to readers and translators of the Damascus Document, but its temporal and historiographical concerns, although complex, are also consistent. Following the reference to God's predestined knowledge of all of human history, the admonition continues with a statement on God's response to the wicked:

> He despised the generations of their standing (דורות [ע]מדם) and hid his face from the land from (...) until their completion (מי עד תומם). And he knew the years they would stand (שני מעמד) and the numbers and details of their fixed times (קציהם), during all the existence of eternity (לכל הוי עולמים) and being (ונהיית) before they came to be (עד מה יבוא) in their fixed times (בקציהם) during all the years of eternity (לכל שני עולם).[35]

---

[35] CD 2.7–10, after Baumgarten and Schwartz, 'CD,' 14–15.

A somewhat remarkable array of temporal expressions and verbs-of-being make up the complex web of this passage. Several are focused on the existence of wicked humanity, expressed in finite or limited terms ("the generations of their standing," דורות [ע]מדם; "the years they would stand," שני מעמד; "their fixed times," קציהם),[36] while others take a more generalized interest in the history of the universe, during the period of its existence ("the existence of eternity," הוי עולמים; "the years of eternity," שני עולם). Notably, none of these verbal forms makes reference to specific events in human history. The scale at all times is cosmic, and whatever narratives we might imagine in this passage ("the numbers and details of their times," for example) can be understood only as a finite temporal 'moment' within the larger—and temporally ungrounded—reality of God's existence.

The use of temporal forms in this passage—one after another, with little contextualization—contributes to the difficulty of interpretation. At times this lack of clarity is the product of textual corruption,[37] as in the garbled phrase מי עד חומם, which Schwartz carefully translates, "from (. . .) until their completion."[38] Similarly, although the reference to the wicked in terms of the "generations of their standing" (דורות [ע]מדם) is probably the best emendation of דורות מדם, it is worth mentioning an alternative reading that suggests that God despised their generations מ[ק]דם, "from the beginning."[39]

---

[36] 'Generation' and 'year' are expressions with relatively fixed durations; similarly, the semantic field of the word קץ carries with it not only a sense of fixed duration but also an explicit endpoint. See BDB, 893–94.

[37] Quite speculatively, it is interesting to wonder whether the copyists of this text were confused by its ambiguity or use of unusual verbal forms, and whether some of their errors might be the product of that confusion.

[38] For CD 2.9, MS A has מיעדתומם. Schwartz notes that "something seems to have been lost at the beginning of line 9"; see Baumgarten and Schwartz, 'CD,' 15 n. 15. Baumgarten, noting Milik's emendation of מועד תומם, fills the relevant lacuna in 4Q266 with עד מועד תומם, translated as "until the time of their complete destruction;" see Baumgarten, DJD XVIII, 37–38. Rabin fills in the lacuna, translating the text with "from [their arising] (or: [from Israel]) until their being consumed," while Davies ignores the מי and translates עד חומם with "until their annihilation." See Rabin, *Zadokite Documents*, 6–7; and Davies, *Damascus Covenant*, 236–37. Note that this line can be read with either a neutral tone or an explicitly negative one.

[39] For this solution to CD 2.8, see Davies, *Damascus Covenant*, 236–37. This reading is reasonable in light of the ideology of the previous line (in which God rejects the wicked primordially, מקדם עולם), but it does not take into account the poetic parallel structure of this passage. Schwartz' reading (in which God "despised the generations of their standing" and "hid his face from the land . . . until their com-

When we look past these textual problems, however, the temporal language in this passage is no easier. Again, as in the first section of this admonition, the use of participial and infinitive forms contributes to a generalized sense of both time and existence in this passage. In addition, it is not always clear in these lines whether the text is talking about a state of being, an action, or the actor involved in that state of being.[40] The expression ונהיית, for example, is translated here as "being,"[41] but this is only the most generalized of a number of possible readings. Equally appropriate are a future-oriented understanding ('what will come to be'), or a reading with a present-tense or temporally ambiguous sense ('all that happens').[42] Similarly, although we can understand הוי עולמים as a singular participial form, with the sense of 'the existence of eternity,' this phrase also may be a reference to a plural construct-state participle referring to the 'beings in the universe,' those whose existence is part of the period of human history between the creation of the universe and its end.[43] If the

---

pletion") makes better sense of the implicit parallel structure; see Baumgarten and Schwartz, 'CD,' 14–15. Rabin presents an emendation similar to Schwartz', but with a different temporal sense: "[He] abhorred the generations when they arose, and He hid His face from the land." See Rabin, *Zadokite Documents*, 6–7.

[40] For the participle as a form somewhere between a noun and a verb, see GKC 116a; for a similar discussion of the infinitive construct, see GKC 114a–e.

[41] Several scholars read this word as ונהיות, a more familiar niphal infinitive form, which is reasonable given the regular confusion of י and ו in these manuscripts; see Broshi, *Damascus Document Reconsidered*, 13; and Baumgarten, DJD XVIII, 37–38. Baumgarten fills a lacuna in 4Q266 with the expression לכל הוי עולמים ונהיות, translated as "for all eternity, (including) what will come to be."

[42] For a future-oriented interpretation, see Rabin, *Zadokite Documents*, 6; for a present-tense reading, see Davies, *Damascus Covenant*, 237. Schwartz' choice ("being") offers a useful match for the ambiguity of the Hebrew. Note that נהיות has been understood by Baumgarten in a present-tense sense in CD 13.8, where the Examiner (מבקר) is told to relate to the people "the happenings of eternity" (נהיות עולם); see Baumgarten and Schwartz, 'CD,' 54–55. It appears also in 1QH 5.12 (formerly 1QH 13.12), in a complex description of God's eternal existence, primordial creation, and more recent transformation of old and new things. For scriptural uses of related verbal forms, see BDB, 227. A reconsideration of MS A of CD suggests that another strange verbal form found in the text, היותו, in CD 13.12, is actually a misreading of a badly smudged word that might better be understood as נחלתו, "his inheritance." See Rabin, *Zadokite Documents*, 67 n. 12.2 for a discussion of the verbal form he sees in this passage, as well as Broshi, *Damascus Document Reconsidered*, 12–13, and Baumgarten and Schwartz, 'CD,' 54–55, for the alternative reading.

[43] The first reading takes the verb as a singular participle, הוה or "being"; the second takes it as a plural construct form, הוי or "beings." Rabin understands the phrase in this second sense, as "all them that come into being in eternity." See

הוי עולמים are the beings in the universe (rather than the 'being' of it), then the reference to the 'numbers and details of their times'[44] may be directed (forward in the text) toward them, rather than (backward) toward the wicked. Either reading is reasonable, and both fit with the ideological assumption that everyone who remains outside the covenant—whether the generalized inhabitants of the universe or the specifically 'wicked'—is doomed to share the same fate.

This use of generalized grammatical forms, which can be read as references to actions, their actors, or generic states of being, delivers a double ideological payoff in this passage. First, it generalizes all actions in the human sphere, lumping them together as basically identical. At the same time, it creates a sense of division, between the finite realm of (generalized) human action, and the infinite realm of God's divine existence. From God's perspective, all of human experience is basically identical, and all of it is predestined primordially. In the context of this ideology, the expression עולם or עולמים appears to take on a meaning that is something like, 'the realm of human existence.' Whether understood temporally or spatially (and most of these examples appear to understand space and time as interchangeable concepts), this expression appears to be synonymous with the *human* realm, and not that of the divine.[45] Although this reading does not hold for every case (as the expression עד עולם, "forever," in CD 3.13 appears to demonstrate),[46] there is a generalized

---

Rabin, *Zadokite Documents*, 6; similarly, for "all beings in eternity," see Davies, *Damascus Covenant*, 237.

[44] This translation of CD 2.9, מספר ופרוש קציהם, assumes פרוש ("detail" or "details"), rather than פרוש ("extent"). See Baumgarten and Schwartz, 'CD,' 15 n. 16; and Baumgarten, DJD XVIII, 38; for a discussion of this definition, see also Albert Baumgarten, 'The Name of the Pharisees,' *JBL* 102/3 (1983): 418–22 (noted in Baumgarten and Schwartz). Rabin reads פרוש and translates this passage as "the number (or: set times) and exact epochs." See Rabin, *Zadokite Documents*, 6–7.

[45] This reading remains speculative, but the extensive use of עולם in related sectarian texts (especially 1QH, 1QS, and 1QSb) suggests that this is a question worth extending to those other texts as well.

[46] See also CD 15.5, where the covenant is called a חוק עולם. It is possible that this expression is stylized and conventional (and therefore can convey the sense of 'forever,' even though עולם by itself refers to the human realm only). Alternatively, it may be that the covenant that God established with Israel עד עולם refers only to the human temporal realm. In this regard, note CD 12.23, where the covenanters are given a set of laws that they are instructed to follow "during the time of wickedness until the arising of the messiah of Aaron" (בקץ הרשעה עד עמוד משוח [sic] אהרן).

tendency in this text to understand the human realm in terms of עולם or עולמים, and the divine realm as something that extends beyond it, outside of ordinary space and time.

In the final lines of this admonition, we learn about the key that unlocks the boundary between ordinary human time and the atemporal realm of God. This passage makes the claim that during the years of human existence, God:

> raised for himself those called by name (קריאי שם), so as to leave a remnant (למען התיר פליטה) for the land and to fill the face of the world (ולמלא פני תבל) with their seed (CD 2.11–12).

To this remnant, and through certain intermediaries, God has given knowledge (ויודעם), while "those whom he hated, he caused to stray" (CD 2.13). Again, the use of infinitives and participles ('called by name,' 'to leave,' 'to fill') continues the generalizing temporal trend of this text,[47] but it is joined by a number of finite verbal forms, as well. In particular, God "raised for himself" (הקים לו) a remnant (CD 2.11), while "he caused [the wicked] to stray" (התעה) (CD 2.13); both verbs reflect a more direct and specific action on God's part than we might otherwise expect in this generalizing text.

On second glance, however, these finite verbs make a great deal of sense. In effect, they are a summary of *all* of God's actions—or at least, all such actions as are truly significant in the human realm— with respect to knowledge, guidance, and experience. By raising up the remnant and (even more importantly) giving them access to the knowledge that allows them to break free from the constraints of the human temporal sphere, God makes room for these covenanters to gain access to everything else that they need: perspective on the dynamics that drive human experience, access to God's true desires, and a means to survive the end of human times and the transition to whatever follows. In contrast, the wicked lack this knowledge-key, and although God has complete knowledge of their lives and times and experiences (as the previous lines indicate), they have no knowledge of those things and no way of attaining that knowledge. Thus, the ultimate shape of history—and its ultimate meaning—is known only to God and to God's covenanters. All others, in consequence of their ignorance, are therefore 'caused to stray.'

---

[47] See also CD 2.12–13, for "those who view the truth" (חוזי אמת).

This same ideology appears in a fragmentary admonition found only among the text's ancient witnesses.[48] The text claims that God has ordered "a fixed time of wrath for a people that knows him not" (קץ חרון לעם לא ידעהו),[49] as well as "times of favor for those who seek his commandments" ([מועדי] רצון לדורשי מצוותו).[50] By allowing the members of his covenant to see and hear the secrets of the universe, God permits them to understand "all being," or "all that is to be" (בכול נהיות), "before it comes upon them" (עד מה יבוא במה).[51] According to this claim, the covenanters have knowledge, not only of the proper times in which events will occur, but even of exactly which events will occur in those times. In addition, they are promised a time of favor, while those outside the covenant are destined to experience 'a period of wrath.'

The construction of history and time in the second admonition suggests a number of significant ideological implications. By presenting the events of human history as entirely predestined and constrained within a sort of temporal 'bubble' floating in the eternal present-time of God's existence, this account sharpens the distinction between fallible ('wicked') humans and the perfect (eternal) God. By articulating this distinction in terms of knowledge—God's knowledge of all of human history, compared with the ignorance of the wicked—this approach to history also makes a space for a unique understanding of the covenantal community. A covenanter is someone who can step outside of human time and who has perspective on all that has been and will be. This perspective comes from God (and through the teachings of "those anointed in his holy spirit," CD 2.12), and it alone provides the key that unlocks the barrier between human experience and divine reality. Again, Carol Newsom has addressed a similar point, this time in a discussion of the Hodayot. There, she notes that from the text's perspective,

---

[48] 4Q266 2 i 1–6, 4Q267 1 8, and 4Q268 1.1–8; see Baumgarten, DJD XVIII, 34–36, 96–97, 119–20.

[49] Found in full in 4Q266 2 i 3 and in fragmentary form in 4Q268 1 5, which has "periods of wr[ath]" (קצי ח[רון]); see Baumgarten, DJD XVIII, 34–35, 119–20.

[50] Fragmentary in both manuscripts; 4Q266 2 i 4 has only "[for those who see]k his commandments" ([לדור]שי מצוותו), and 4Q268 1 6 has "favor for those who seek his commandments" (רצון לדורשי מצוותיו); there is a textual variant in מצוות[י]ו; see Baumgarten, DJD XVIII, 34–35, 119–20.

[51] 4Q268 1 8. See Baumgarten, DJD XVIII, 119–20, for the future-oriented translation of this passage.

No activity stands outside the divine plan. Everything that happens is simply the making visible of the divine plan in which everything was already known.[52]

In the text of the second admonition, knowledge of the divine plan is a special knowledge, available only to God's chosen people. It is this knowledge that allows them to break out of their linear, human perspective and understand the universe as it really is.

In her discussion of the Hodayot, Newsom goes on to add that, "indeed what marks the created world as the expression of the divine plan is its obedient and rule-ordered activity."[53] Obedience and 'rule-ordered activity' are not concepts that have been stressed in the presentation of history in this admonition. But the importance of obedience is articulated clearly in the narrative chronological accounts of history found in the other two admonitions in the Damascus Document. It is to this discussion that we now turn.

Narrative history and the first admonition

If the second admonition demonstrates a focus on God's eternal presence and pays only scant attention to events in human time, other sections of the Damascus Document take a different approach toward the events of history. Of particular interest are the narrative accounts of histories—national, sectarian, and universal—that intermix in this document, intersecting with one another in ways that are worthy of a close analysis. At first, it may appear that these narratives have been presented by writers with no sense of the niceties of temporal boundaries or narrative order, given the variety of narratives that are linked together in the text, at times with little interest in their specific chronological connections. However, there is an explanation for these temporal leaps and narrative overlays, and it relates back to the historiographic sensibilities articulated in our reading of the second admonition. In effect, the authors of this text have constructed

---

[52] Newsom, 'Case of the Blinking I,' 17. In referring to Newsom's discussion of the Hodayot here, I do not in any way mean to conflate the authorships of 1QH and CD. These texts demonstrate many differences in addition to their notable similarities. It is the similar perspective on time and predestination in the two texts that allows me to apply Newsom's observation on 1QH to my reading of CD.

[53] Newsom, 'Case of the Blinking I,' 17.

an image of the covenanters as the owners of a special knowledge-key, which gives them access to the realm outside of human history. From this vantage point (shared only by God and Wisdom), members of the covenant are thus able to have a unique 'outsider's' perspective on all of history, claiming knowledge of its major themes and overarching truths, which are not visible from a vantage point within it. From this outside perspective, covenanters also have the flexibility to shift focus from one historical narrative to another, or to link several narratives at once, by making connections based on the overarching thematic truths to which they have access.

The Damascus Document's first admonition (CD 1.1–2.1) offers an excellent example of how a unique perspective on history allows for engagement in three projects at once: identifying the primary themes of human experience, while narrating an account of recent historical events, and ultimately mapping that narrative onto the larger national narrative of Israelite history, as well. The localized narrative described in the text begins with the fall of Jerusalem to the Babylonians but quickly focuses in on the story of a repentant remnant, a covenantal group standing in opposition to a rebellious group of apostates.[54] Interwoven with this specific story of communal development, we find traces of a more generalized narrative, whose focus is national or universal. According to this narrative, God is angry with *all* humanity ("all flesh," כל בשר, CD 1.2), on account of the people's rejection and transgression of the ancient "covenant with the first ones" (ברית ראשנים) of Israel. The text interweaves the sectarian and national/universal histories, shifting from one to the other through the interplay of keywords like covenant (ברית), Israel (ישראל), righteousness (צדק), and the first and last generations (ראשנים and אהרונים). The presence of these often-multivalent expressions allows for seamless shifts between narratives, as well as occasional overlays of one narrative upon another.

The keywords in this narrative underscore a number of primary themes in the text. The first, and most consistent, running theme in

---

[54] The language of 'apostasy' is utilized in this section in a sociological sense, to refer not merely to former members of a group, but more specifically to members who leave the group by making a radical break from it, or who are perceived in those terms by the group members they have left behind. This expression is also lexically appropriate: 'apostasy' as a 'turning away' meshes nicely with the Damascus Document's construction of transgressive behavior as 'straying' (סרה) or 'turning' (שוב) away from a proper path.

this admonition is that of righteousness (צדק). Words with this root occur regularly in this rather short passage (six times in 20 lines), and they contribute to what some scholars have viewed as a fundamentally 'Zadokite' quality in the text.⁵⁵ But the use of Zadokite language is neither regular nor consistent if we extend our reading from this admonition to the Damascus Document as a whole. Rather, although words with the root צדק are common in the text (about 25 uses, an average of more than once per page of text), they appear in clusters and are entirely absent in some places where we might expect to find them. The second admonition, for example, easily could have been peppered with this righteousness-language, and yet it contains not even one use of such an expression. Meanwhile, the text of CD 20.1–34 (admittedly a somewhat longer section) contains eight such references.⁵⁶ It is notable, too, that the most significant clusters of צדק-language occur in close proximity to discussions of the Teacher of Righteousness and his relationship with the covenant community.⁵⁷ This suggests, at minimum, that although concerns about proper action may permeate the entire text of the Damascus Document, only in certain passages are those concerns expressed in terms of explicit references to righteousness, a Righteous Teacher, or a historical figure called Zadok.

A similar pattern unfolds when we consider the other themes that are central in this first admonition. The text includes five mentions of Israel and four references to God's covenant in the course of its narrative account, and these themes are framed (twice) in reference to the "first ones" (ראשנים) and (again twice) in reference to the "last" or "latter" generations (אחרון or אחרונים).⁵⁸ Again, a comparison with

---

⁵⁵ Schechter and Schiffman, in particular, understand this text in terms of its 'Zadokite' qualities. See Schiffman, *Reclaiming*; and Schechter's arguments in Fitzmyer, *Documents*. I discuss the issue of 'Zadokite identity' at some length in chapter five below.

⁵⁶ In addition to the six references in CD 1.1–20 and the eight in CD 20.1–34, we also find a total of six uses of צדק-language in CD 3.1–4.21, as well as single references (once each) in CD 5.5, 6.11, 8.14, and 19.27. Only a single reference is found in the legal material; see CD 11.21.

⁵⁷ For mention of the Teacher, see CD 1.11 and 20.32 (also 20.1, although the term צדק is not used there). In CD 6.11, we also find a reference to an endtimes teacher of righteousness (יורה הצדק באחרית הימים).

⁵⁸ The references to Israel all occur in the first 14 lines of the admonition (CD 1.3, 1.5, 1.7, and twice in 1.14), while the other expressions are more scattered. See CD 1.4 for ראשונים בירת; CD 1.12 for both אחרון and אחרונים; CD 1.16 for

the second admonition demonstrates the fundamental difference of expression in the themes of these two texts. In the second admonition we find only one reference to covenant,[59] another potential (but oblique) reference to Israel (in the form of "the land," ארץ, CD 2.11), and *no* references to the generational groups, the first and the last. These observations suggest that for all that these two admonitions are compatible and may be read as supportive of one another, their historiographical agendas are articulated in terms of very different forms and emphases.

A close reading of the two histories interwoven in the first admonition—the national or universal narrative and the narrative of covenantal or communal development—highlights specific textual strategies that allow these narratives to be merged, with a significant ideological payoff, into one. The text opens with the standard expression "and now, hearken" (ועתה שמעו), which occurs in some form in each extant admonition,[60] but here it is directed specifically toward "all who know righteousness" (כל יודעי צדק, CD 1.1). The narrative at this point is universal in tone (God has a grievance with all flesh and will make judgment on all those who scoff at him, CD 1.2).[61] The next line of the text shrinks its field of reference from all humanity down to the range of all Israel, whose rejection of God was the direct cause of the destruction of the Temple at the hands of the Babylonians (CD 1.3–4), and the line after that introduces our covenantal remnant (CD 1.4–5), bringing us into the specific sectarian history that dominates the rest of the admonition.

ראשנים again; and CD 1.17, 1.18, and 1.20 for three separate references to covenant (ברית).

[59] However, the third admonition contains several covenant references. See CD 3.4 for the patriarchs as בעלי ברית; CD 3.10 for באי הברית הראשנים; CD 3.11 for ברית אל; and CD 3.13 for בריתו.

[60] The parallel passage in 4Q268 1 9 has the variant reading, "and now, hearken to me" (ועתה שמעו לי); see Baumgarten, DJD XVIII, 119–20. The other admonitions begin "and now, hearken unto me" (ועתה שמעו עלי), CD 2.1; and "and now, children, hearken to me" (ועתה בנים שמעו לי), CD 2.14. Two additional examples are extant only in the ancient witnesses: the admonition in 4Q266 1 a-b 5 includes, "[and now, hearken] to me, and I will make known to you" ([ועתה שמען] לי ואודיעה לכם); and the introduction to a section of legal material in 4Q270 2 ii 19 includes, "and now hearken to me, all who know righteousness" (ועתה שמעו לי כל יודעי צדק). See Baumgarten, DJD XVIII, 31–32, 145.

[61] For a discussion of God's "grievance" (ריב) with Israel, in light of its form-critical significance, see Davies, *Damascus Covenant*, 57–60. He discusses Hartman's reading of CD 1–2 in light of this literary pattern. See Lars Hartman, *Asking for a Meaning: A Study of 1 Enoch 1–5* (Lund: CWK Gleerup, 1979).

In making the shift from a national/universal perspective to a specific focus on the righteous remnant at the center of the text, familiar thematic language provides a transitional bridge. The text explains that God saved a remnant of Israel from destruction at the time of the Exile for a specific reason; this was done because of God's "remembering the covenant of the first ones" (בזכרו ברית ראשנים, CD 1.4). The valence here is a positive one; the virtue of these 'first ones' is what leads to the salvation of the later remnant. Quite likely, the patriarchs are the subjects of this reference to 'first ones,'[62] and God's covenants—with Abraham, Isaac, and Jacob, and perhaps with Noah,[63] as well—provide the source of the remnant's salvation.

Interestingly, the 'covenant of the first ones' is not always a reference to the patriarchs, nor is it always positive in valence. Several examples from elsewhere in the Damascus Document illustrate the multiplicity of meanings that may be associated with this expression. In the third admonition (which is discussed at greater length below), we find a reference to the 'first ones' that is both negative and dismissive. In this passage, which follows on a historical account of the transgressions of the world (from the antediluvian period through the time of the Exile, with only a few brief mentions of figures who managed to avoid transgressing God's commandments), we learn that:

> The first ones who entered the covenant (באי הברית הראשנים) became guilty ... and they were given up to the sword, having departed from God's covenant and chosen their own will.[64]

Instead of reflecting a group whose loyalty to the covenant is the salvation of their descendants, these 'first ones who entered the covenant' are the transgressive Israelites, whose willfulness has led to their own destruction. The term may refer specifically to the first

---

[62] Schwartz suggests that "first ones," in this specific passage, "refers to Israel's ancestors. Elsewhere it refers to the members of the first covenant (3.10) or to the first members of the New Covenant (4.8–10)." See Baumgarten and Schwartz, 'CD,' 13 n. 3.

[63] An argument in favor of his inclusion among the ראשנים is that God did, in fact, establish a covenant with him. Although Noah is not mentioned positively here or in the lengthier third admonition, it is also the case that he is not mentioned negatively in that account, which is otherwise universally negative toward all but the patriarchs and the members of the new covenant.

[64] CD 3.10–11; following Baumgarten and Schwartz, 'CD,' 16–17.

generation of Israelite covenanters (those who were present at Sinai), but by extension this reference appears to include all the generations of Israel up to the Exile, whose transgressions were its cause.⁶⁵

According to this passage, God's covenant no longer belongs to these 'first ones.' Instead, it has been taken from them and given over to the remnant of Israel who remain loyal to Torah, who will receive a covenant of their own, including an array of hidden knowledge about God's will and their own responsibilities to it (CD 3.13–16). This secret knowledge includes an accounting of all the sacred practices that they must fulfill, and all the "hidden things in which all Israel has strayed" (נסתרות אשר תעו בם כל ישראל, 3.14). In describing this new covenant, the text makes a remarkable assertion: the covenant with the remnant is, itself, the covenant that God has established *with Israel* forever (הקים אל את בריתו לישראל עד עולם, CD 3.13). This new covenant, in other words, entails replacing the old Israel—who could not or would not fulfill their responsibilities in the way that God required of them—with a new Israel, in the form of the remnant itself. And unlike the old Israel, who were singularly unable to accept responsibility (from the time of Sinai until their very exile from the land), this Israel has access to the knowledge that will permit them to follow God properly and allow them to stay in his good graces.

An expansion of this same theme occurs slightly later in the text, when a similar expression—'first ones of the covenant'—is used to refer not to figures in the mythic past (the patriarchs or the Sinai generation), but rather to the founding members of the new covenant itself. In this context (CD 4.7–10), a reference to "the covenant that God established for the first ones" (ברית אשר הקים אל לראשנים, CD 4.9) refers to the first ones of the *new* covenant, who serve as the replacements for (and are described in much the same terms as) the founding generations of Israel itself.

These passages are important both for their articulation of familiar themes and also for the way that they clarify or change them: although there are major divisions between covenanters and non-covenanters ('the righteous' and 'the wicked'), it *is* possible to change one's status. Just as a covenanter can become an apostate and cease

---

⁶⁵ For a discussion of this view in light of Lev 26.45, see Murphy-O'Connor, 'An Essene Missionary Document,' 206.

to be viewed as one of the righteous, so can an outsider join the covenant and be permitted access to private covenantal knowledge, receiving an education in "the precise meaning of Torah, which was taught to the first ones" (פרוש התורה אשר התוסרו בו הראשנים, CD 4.8). In addition, both the founding members and the later additions to the new covenant (those who join before the time of joining is past)[66] are promised forgiveness for their transgressions if they hold fast to God's commandments. In this series of passages, the keywords 'first ones of the covenant' take on a dynamic and flexible meaning, shifting from ancient to contemporary significance and from positive to negative (and back to positive) valence. Whether positive or negative, ancient or contemporary, however, these keywords underscore the importance of the special knowledge and righteous practices that are accessible only to covenant members.

With this digression as a complicating subtext, let us return to our reading of the first admonition. We have seen how the text moves in just a few lines from a universal history (God's dispute with all flesh) to a focus on Israel (whose rejection of God leads to their own destruction) and then to a view of the remnant of Israel, who are preserved only because God remembers his covenant with the first ones.[67] Again, we know that the 'first ones' here may be understood as the patriarchs of Israel, whose acceptance of God's covenant protects their descendants from destruction. But we know now, from elsewhere in the text, that the term 'first ones' is multivalent. In this passage it is a reference to the patriarchs, but it has potential to be read as a referent for 'all the rest of the people of Israel' (whose rejection of covenantal norms is the cause of their own downfall) *and* as a reference to 'the founders of the new covenant' (whose willingness to accept responsibility allows them access to special and secret knowledge). This reference to the 'first ones' of the covenant leads into the first of a series of temporal 'loops,' linking a temporally-specific passage (here, the patriarchal period) to every other relevant passage in Israelite history (the Exodus, the Exile, the foundation

---

[66] CD 4.10. In asserting that anyone can join the covenant, as long as they join before the completion of the designated time (שלום הקץ), the text demonstrates a predestinarian sense of temporal order but not of individual human action. See Daniel Schwartz, '"To Join Oneself to the House of Judah": Damascus Document 4.11,' *RevQ* 10 (1981): 435–46.

[67] CD 1.2–5, as noted above.

of the new covenant). This multivalent language serves as a sort of 'wormhole' in the text's presentation of space and time, suggesting that members of the covenant community have access to, and may move smoothly between, all points in the history of Israel and the world.

After mentioning the establishment of the remnant of Israel, the account jumps forward in time to a period 390 years later, when God's attention returns to the people, allowing "a root of planting" (שורש מטעת) to grow out of their midst and inherit the land (CD 1.5–8). The members of this chosen group are allowed to seek their own path for 20 years, until it becomes clear to God that their search is "wholehearted" (בלב שלם, CD 1.8–10). At that time, he gives them a Teacher of Righteousness to instruct them in "the way of his heart" (דרך לבו, CD 1.11). The people learn, in the course of their education, of the punishment that will fall upon all those who reject the covenant in the "last generation" (דור אחרון), including a group of apostates who break away from the covenant and follow after a false teacher (CD 1.11–15). The last quarter of the admonition presents a lengthy diatribe against these apostates, whose actions incite God to anger and ultimately lead to the apostates' own destruction (CD 1.15–2.1).

In presenting the intersecting histories of Israel, the world, and the covenant community, this text makes use of a number of textual strategies that generate temporal 'loops' between ancient and more contemporary periods. The foundation of the covenant community, whose timing can be understood in one of several different ways, offers an example of this textual dynamic. The text first states that God established the remnant of Israel at the time of the Babylonian conquest (CD 1.4–5), but it also says that 390 years after the conquest, "he turned his attention to them (פקדם) and caused to grow out of Israel and Aaron a root of planting" (CD 1.6–7). These passages might be read as reflecting a series of sequential actions: God first chose a remnant at the time of the conquest and then, 390 years later, he created a new covenantal movement (the 'root of planting') as a remnant of the remnant. In this case, the original 'remnant,' from the time of the conquest, is identical with 'Israel and Aaron.' However, a second (and equally plausible) reading might understand these two stories as parallel accounts: at the time of the conquest, God saves a remnant of the people of Israel. Then, at a later time, God does the very same thing all over again, raising up a root of planting from among the people of Israel and Aaron. Either of these two historical scenarios might lie behind the text (so that it may refer to a single continuous covenantal group, or to a series of covenantal groups that developed out of one another).[68] But for this ideological presentation of history, the focus is less on the importance of a single, specific set of events and more on the community's history as understood in terms of a complex temporal and identity-oriented overlay. The period of the Babylonian conquest blends into a period 390 years later, and the community of the covenant is understood as the remnant of Israel in its early and later stages, thanks to the temporal 'looping' effect at work in the text.

The interest in origin-moments displayed in this admonition is matched by a complex understanding of the impending 'endtimes' and the events that will occur in the "latter generations" (דורות אחרונים), when God addresses the iniquities of the apostates who have left the covenantal community.[69] The information that is provided to those 'latter generations' concerns the transgressions of the apostates (which are described at length),[70] and the judgment that will come upon them, ultimately, in 'the last generation.' This description of transgression and punishment can be understood as a generalized account, but the reference in this passage also acknowledges a specific event, in which a leader of the group ("the man of mockery," איש הלצון) broke off from the covenantal community and took a group of its members with him (CD 1.14–15). Once more, the use of a complex network of temporal and scriptural connections

---

[68] On the question of whether the scrolls movement developed in a two-stage process or a one-stage process, see the discussion in John Collins, 'The Origins of the Qumran Community: A Review of the Evidence,' in *To Touch the Text: Biblical and Related Studies in Honor of Joseph A. Fitzmyer* (ed. Maurya Horgan and Paul Kobelski; New York: Crossroad, 1989), 168–69. For a representative account of the two-stage theory of the development of the covenant community, see García Martínez, 'Qumran Origins and Early History'; and García Martínez and van der Woude, 'A "Groningen" Hypothesis.' The founding of the group also is mentioned in terms of the remnant of Israel in a fragmentary passage found in 4Q266 5 i 11–12 and 4Q267 5 ii 4–6; see Baumgarten, DJD XVIII, 47–48, 101. This passage has no parallel in CD; editors place it after CD 20 and before the legal material in the text.

[69] A passage in the introduction to 4Q266 states that this text is intended for the period "until the completion of the time of visitation" (תום המועד פקודה) of the spirit of wickedness on the earth. This statement, which is followed by a reference to the limited lifespan of human beings, sets the tone for the rest of the admonition. See 4Q266 1 a-b 1–2, 3–7; Baumgarten, DJD XVIII, 31–32.

[70] All of CD 1.13–21 is devoted, in some way, to this subject.

allows for a complex intersection of temporal moments in the text's description of this event.

The text's description of the apostates begins with an atemporal observation: they are described as "those who stray from the way" (סרי דרך), with no indication of when their straying may occur, or may have occurred. The text does goes on, however, to fix their action with a specific reference, stating that, "this is the time of which it is written, 'As a wayward cow, so did Israel stray'" (כפרה סוררה כן סרר ישראל).[71] By locating a set of recent or contemporary events (the apostasy of a group of covenanters) in the context of scriptural 'time' (within the prophecy of Hosea), this text effectively reworks the whole notion of 'time' itself. The temporal vector now points in multiple directions at once. It looks 'back' to the time of Hosea, for an explanation of a recent apostasy, which may itself be understood as an endtimes communal schism; simultaneously, it looks 'forward' in time, from Hosea's prophecies to their fulfillment in these endtime events. Although this passage is not called a 'pesher' in the text, it is an excellent example of such a reading of scripture: the text provides an 'activation' of scripture in the world and an explanation of the true meaning of scripture in contemporary events that originally were not anticipated, even by the prophets who predicted their occurrence.[72]

In leading his followers astray, this 'man of mockery' inspires a number of other transgressions of God's will. Like the initial 'straying' of the apostates, these transgressions appear as a series of generalized actions. Infinitive verbal forms allow the text to speak of the apostates' roles in "bringing low" (להשח) the heights, "straying" (לסור) from the way, "moving" (לסיע) proper boundaries, and ultimately "surrendering" (להסגיר) to covenantal punishment (CD 1.15–17). Uncontextualized as these actions may be in temporal terms, they are nevertheless contextualized by a familiar set of keywords. The path from which the apostates depart is the *righteous* one, and the proper boundaries that they move were originally established by *the first ones* (CD 1.16). Their punishment comes because they transgress the *covenant*, and it is a punishment articulated in covenantal terms (CD 1.17). Again, these keywords permit a complex intersection of

---

[71] CD 1.13–14, quoting Hos. 4.16.
[72] For more extensive discussions of pesher as a genre, see Horgan, *Pesharim*; and the other sources noted in chapter two, n. 80.

temporal or historical moments. The text refers to specific transgressions of the new covenant, but this transgressive apostasy might just as well be read in terms of an attack on the *first* 'first ones' (the patriarchs) or as reflective of the transgressions of the second set of 'first ones' (the people of Israel, who never really managed to keep their part of the covenant, in any case).

In the lines that conclude this admonition, we find a whole series of finite verbal forms, which appear to reflect a series of completed actions. These actions are presented in sequence, one after the other, with a triphammer rhythm that pounds home the enormity of the iniquity they describe. Four lines of text—and nearly a dozen separate actions—follow one upon the other in a description of the transgressive deeds of the covenantal apostates. Again, the transgressions appear without a temporal frame but are articulated in terms of familiar keywords. Among their violations of proper behavior, the apostates "justified the evil" (יצדיקו רשע) and "condemned the righteous" (ירשיעו צדיק), they caused the covenant to be transgressed (יעבירו ברית), and they "ganged up on those of righteous soul" (ינודו על נפש צדיק).[73] It is for this reason—and on account of these stereotyped, stylized and eternally relevant, transgressions—that God views these people with disfavor and ultimately, in the last generation, permits their utter destruction (CD 1.21–2.1).

Just as the covenantal community is equated at times with Israel and at times with its righteous remnant, so is the 'wicked' opposition presented in metaphorical terms at times in this text. The scriptural passage that describes the wicked states that, "as a wayward cow, so did Israel stray" (Hos 4.16). The admonition continues the use of this expression, noting that *Israel* is led astray by the lies of a misguided leader, and consequently it is 'Israel' that is guilty of the massive array of transgressions listed above. In other words, if the admonition allows us to understand 'the righteous remnant' and 'the root of planting' as replacements for 'Israel,' so does it also allow us to understand the rebellious apostates of the new covenant as replacements for the same national group. Thus, although one 'Israel' is righteous and obedient, the other 'Israel' is led astray—both by the mocker, and also (prophetically) in the account of Hosea. 'Israel,' then, is another multivalent term. It can stand for the righteous

---

[73] CD 1.19–20, after Baumgarten and Schwartz, 'CD,' 13.

remnant or the transgressive majority, or it can stand for the transgressive apostates who break off from the righteous remnant; it can be replaced or represented by any of those groups, as well. The ability to move from a specific group to an individual group, and from the righteous to the transgressive and back, facilitated by this use of multivalent keywords, allows a reader of the text to recognize the dynamic nature of the eternal conflicts of history, in which righteousness and wickedness are always embattled, and the fate of the people of Israel depends largely on whether they ally themselves with a righteous minority or a wicked majority population.

Narrative history in the third admonition

Our reading of the first admonition brought to light a narrative account of sectarian history that was grounded firmly in—and, in fact, largely understood in terms of—a scriptural and atemporal sense of history. Because of their special knowledge and because of their righteousness, true covenanters have access to any moment in the history of Israel, and they can understand their group's history in terms of its eternal truths and repeating themes. When we turn to the third admonition, we find a similar focus on certain major ideological points and eternal verities. However, this admonition also takes a more directed approach to narrative history. Instead of overlaying a brief account of the covenant group's development onto a complex scriptural background, this admonition offers a more directly chronological account of the history of human experience and the human relationship with God. The culmination of this narrative is the establishment of the new covenant and the confirmation of the special knowledge awarded to the members of that covenantal community.

As in the previous discussions, a number of textual strategies contribute to shaping this narrative. At times, history is presented in an 'accordion-fold' pattern, so that unimportant events (or events that contradict a primary thesis) are compressed, while central ones are expanded in the narrative. A repetition of key grammatical forms also contributes to the reiteration of the themes that this text presents as fundamental to the human experience: the stubborn willfulness of the wicked, the pious obedience of God's chosen remnant, and the constant conflict between the two.

The admonition begins with an assertion of the importance of its primary theme: the distinction between obedience and willfulness.

Covenanters are warned to avoid the desire to follow their own willfulness, instead of God's commandments, and are reminded that this temptation has been the downfall of many people in history, including "mighty warriors,... from the earliest times and until today" (גבורי חיל... מלפנים ועד הנה, CD 2.17). This theme carries through the entire narrative, which begins not with creation but with the Watchers, whose fall from heaven is a product of their disobedience,[74] and their sons, who were giant in size but lacked proper self-discipline. The text continues with an oblique reference to the flood (in which "all flesh which was on dry land fell"), before shifting to the generations that followed it ("the sons of Noah," בני נח, CD 3.1). Noah himself does not receive personal attention in the narrative (because he does not fit the paradigm?), but his children are criticized in the standard pattern; it is through their own disobedience that "they are cut off" (נכרתים).[75]

From the sons of Noah, the text jumps immediately to Abraham, who is our first positive role model ("for he kept God's ordinances and did not choose what his own spirit desired," בשמרו מצות אל ולא בחר ברצון רוחו, CD 3.2–3) and then to Isaac and Jacob, who together are recognized as parties to God's covenant (בעלי ברית, CD 3.3–4). But these are the only figures in history to be ranked as appropriately obedient 'lovers of God,' and the rest of the historical narrative is a series of accounts of disobedience and disrespect. The children of Jacob are reported to have strayed from God's ways, due to their willfulness (CD 3.4–5), and "their sons in Egypt" similarly are accused, each one, of "doing what was right in his own eyes" (לעשות איש הישר בעיניו, CD 3.5). The Israelites in the wilderness are unusual in our list, not for any sort of obedience, but because they are accused of specific disobedient transgressions (eating blood and refusing to accept the land, CD 3.6–7), in addition to the standard crime, a generalized disregard for God's will and God's commandments. Following upon this historical presentation, the text picks up its pace, and we learn in a single rush of description that:

---

[74] CD 2.17–19. As in 1 Enoch and other related literature, the important beginnings of civilization are centered on the experiences of the Watchers, and not those of Adam and Eve. However, as Collins notes, in CD (unlike 1 Enoch) the fall of the Watchers is "paradigmatic" but "not causative." The Watchers provide one in a series of examples, and not the primary source of wickedness on earth. See Collins, *Apocalypticism*, 36.

[75] For 'sons of Noah' as an oblique reference to the gentiles, see Baumgarten and Schwartz, 'CD,' 17 n. 21.

> they murmured in their tents, and God's anger was kindled against their congregation, and their sons perished through it, and their kings were cut off through it, and through it their heroes perished, and their land became desolate due to it (CD 3.8–10).

From this point, the narrative shifts to the new covenant, beginning with the passage discussed above, in which 'the first ones who entered the covenant' are rejected for their willfulness, and the new covenanters are awarded their special status and insider knowledge.

This narrative account is interesting for a variety of reasons. In its structure, it is quite different from the other presentations of history that we have considered. Instead of providing a temporal overlay, in which sectarian and national or universal histories are interwoven with one another or mapped onto each other, this version of history takes a largely chronological approach. A universal history (the Watchers, giants, and sons of Noah) is followed by the history of Israel, whose founders are exceptions to a general model of disobedience. When this history runs its course, all of Israel is rejected, except for that remnant who hold fast to God's commandments. Effectively, then, although this account works in linear fashion, its agenda is much the same as the other histories we have seen already: the covenantal remnant ultimately stands in for and replaces the willful people of Israel, who have been rejected by God on account of their disobedient behavior.

In addition to treating the covenantal group as the culmination of the narrative, this account structures the flow of history in an 'accordion-fold' fashion. The earliest stages of history are quite compressed: we have no mention of the cosmic creation that was so central in the second admonition, nor do we have a mention of any individual humans before the time of the flood. The Watchers and their sons, in contrast, receive a lengthy description (about four lines, CD 2.18–21), which includes a reference to their actions, their appearances, and their consistent misconduct. After a brief mention of the flood, we find another compression of time, suggesting that nothing of particular significance occurred between the transgressions of the sons of Noah and the introduction of Abraham and the other patriarchs.

The patriarchs, as I have noted already, are the only figures (other than the members of the new covenant) to receive a positive evaluation in this admonition. But their evaluation too reflects a single-minded focus on certain key themes. Abraham receives a brief description of his own, after which Isaac and Jacob are presented in a single passage, which presumably allows the text to highlight all three patriarchs without having to specify the nature of their individual pieties. Beyond the brief statements that the patriarchs were accepted as lovers of God (אוהבים לאל) and that they were active participants in his covenant (בעלי ברית), the terms used to praise them are totally generalized and stand as no more than a reversal of the transgressions attributed to the other figures in the narrative. If the sins of history are sins of disobedience, then the patriarchs stand out, befitting this general theme, simply for their obedient behavior toward God.

In addition to its tendency to compress and expand historical moments, this admonition also demonstrates a selective choice of subjects. Although the Wilderness period receives a fairly extensive description (nearly four lines), it contains no mention of Moses, Aaron, Joshua, or any other major culture-heroes. Similarly, we find no reference to any of the Judges, or the Prophets, or any specific kings, outside the brief mention of God's anger against the people, which led to the destruction of "their congregation and their sons... and their kings... and their heroes" (CD 3.9–10). In fact, very few individuals are mentioned at all in the narrative. The patriarchs receive a nod, and Noah is mentioned, although perhaps only as a place holder, but no other individual is singled out for attention, either positive or negative. This admonition's tendency to generalize is underscored by a consideration of other passages in the Damascus Document in which we do find specific references to the leaders of Israel and their actions.[76] Abraham's circumcision is discussed in one

---

[76] Similarly, the various accounts of Israelite history in other ancient Jewish texts range in their presentations from very specific to very generalized narratives, each of which highlights its own primary concerns and ideological points of consideration. See, for example, Achior's description of the history of Israel, which highlights the pre-patriarchal and patriarchal periods and emphasizes dynamics of departure or flight in that foundational period (Judith 5); the speech of Stephen (in Acts 7.1–53), which highlights the themes of disobedience and the rejection of God's prophets as a recurrent pattern in the history of Israel, and which shifts among first-person, third-person, and second-person narratives to distinguish between the speaker's position and that of his opponents, 'the Jews,' who are marked by their rejection of Jesus; and Ben Sira's account of Israel's history, framed in terms of the leadership of specific individuals, especially priests (Ben Sira 44–50). For other histories of Israel, with their own ideological claims and textual strategies, see also Ps 105, 106; 1 Enoch 85–90 (the animal apocalypse); the Sibylline Oracles (esp. book one); and the lengthier accounts of Josephus and pseudo-Philo.

passage in the Laws (CD 16.6), where his proper action is connected with the special knowledge that God has given him. Similarly, other passages in the Admonition include descriptions of Moses and Aaron (and their conflict with Jannes and his brother, CD 5.18) and of David's transgressions and forgiveness (CD 5.2–6). The tendency to generalize individual action, like the use of righteousness-language in the first admonition, is a strategy in this admonition specifically, and not simply in the text as a whole.

A similar pattern can be seen in this admonition's presentation of the sins of Israel: the text tends not to include dramatic descriptions of specific, individual transgressions. Again, this tendency to generalize is a textual strategy; elsewhere in the Damascus Document, whole sections discuss the specific sins of those who transgress the covenant. Their transgressions include a range of sexual misdeeds (CD 4.14–5.11); theft from and abuse of the weak (the poor, widows, and orphans; CD 6.16–17); and a variety of transgressions of purity standards (CD 6.15, 17–18) and calendrical norms (CD 3.14–16, 6.18–19). Other passages mention people outside the covenant who are guilty of blasphemy or arrogance, in that they reject the standards of the covenantal group and claim to have answers of their own to questions that the group already has addressed definitively.[77] In contrast with these passages, the third admonition is notable for its focus on the generalized transgressions of the masses of humanity, the origins of whose wicked actions are traced to one of a few master categories: willfulness, stubbornness, or a disobedience of God's wishes.

The admonition's distillation of history is further underscored by the regular use of the expressions "in it" (בו or בה) and "in them" (בם) in a triphammer presentation of the history of Israel's transgressions reminiscent of the repetitions found in the last few lines of the first admonition. In that passage, we saw a repetition of structure, in the form of short, declarative statements. Here, we find a

---

[77] See CD 3.17–18 for a reference to non-covenanters who claim to have their own interpretations of Torah (and who will consequently die); CD 4.17 for arrogance as a snare that is a danger to those outside the covenant; CD 5.11–17 for a long diatribe on non-covenanters with "a tongue of blasphemy," who view as false the statutes of God (i.e., the covenanters' interpretations of Torah) and against whom God has taken note. In CD 5.17–6.2, an account of rebellion against Moses is presented in parallel to this latter account of intracovenantal conflict.

repetition of simple pronoun phrases.⁷⁸ Over and over—on no fewer than 13 occasions in nineteen lines of text⁷⁹—we find that the generations of humanity are guilty of the same repeated transgressions. Whether by the "thoughts of guilty inclination and licentious eyes" ("in them," בם), through a "wantonness of heart" ("in it," בה), or because of God's anger in response to these transgressions ("in it," בו), the generations of the earth consistently manage to disappoint their God and suffer punishment for their transgressions. With this repetitive narrative structure, the text compresses the entirety of Israelite history into a brief chronology of transgression: because the people of Israel provoked God's anger, they were destroyed by it, and their kings and heroes were cut off because of it, and even their land—with its covenantal resonances—was made desolate because of it (CD 3.8–10).

These textual strategies—compressing and expanding the narrative structure, avoiding mention of specific individuals or their specific actions, and presenting a series of historical events as repetitions of one another—all contribute to an expression of this admonition's basic ideological claim. With the exception of a few notables—the patriarchs, and especially the new covenanters—all of human history is an account of a single fundamental transgression. Whether it is expressed as "straying in the thoughts of a guilty inclination and licentious eyes" (CD 2.16), "walking after the wantonness of their hearts" (CD 2.17–18), "straying" from God's chosen path (CD 3.1), or "doing what was right in their own eyes" (CD 3.6), the people of the world have been guilty of a willful refusal to follow God's wishes or to act in righteous obedience of his commands. The admonition need not mention specific actions, because any possible

---

⁷⁸ In her discussion of the second admonition, Hempel points to a similar practice of the text, involving the use of third person masculine plural suffixes to refer to groups of people. See Charlotte Hempel, 'Community Origins in the *Damascus Document* in the Light of Recent Scholarship,' in Parry and Ulrich, *Provo International Conference*, 323. See also the discussions in Murphy-O'Connor, 'An Essene Missionary Document,' 205, 207 (for possessive suffixes); and Davies, *Damascus Covenant*, 78–80 (for repetitions of keywords).

⁷⁹ For בם, see CD 2.17 (twice), 3.4, 3.14; for בה, see CD 2.18, 3.1 (twice), 3.2; for בו, see CD 3.9 (three times), 3.10 (twice). Note that CD 2.21 includes a reference to God's wrath being kindled "against them" (בם), meaning those who transgress his commandments. This latter use may have been influenced, accidentally or by design, by the repeated use of בם in this admonition.

transgression already fits into the ready-made category of 'willful disobedience of God's ordinances.'

According to this admonition, the relevant difference between the practices and understandings of the covenanters and those of outsiders is simple. The covenanters have the special knowledge that allows them to do what God really wants, while those outside the covenant, who refuse to make the least effort to learn the proper path, are guilty for their transgressions of the truths they do not know. All of human history can be boiled down to the common theme of this admonition: only those who know God's will, and who obediently seek to follow it, will be accepted into the covenant and permitted to survive the travails of the impending endtimes.

History and ideology in the Damascus Document

This brief discussion should suggest to us a two-part observation: (1) history, as it is presented in the Damascus Document, is the product of a complex dynamic, and (2) the lessons of that history are strikingly simple. On the one hand, the narrative accounts of cosmic, Israelite, and communal history in this text are wide-ranging and eclectically presented. They bounce from scriptural events to recent sectarian experience, and from ancient to contemporary issues, to articulate historical accounts that are multilayered and at times multivalent. On the other hand, the basic themes that these histories convey are remarkably consistent: God knows all, humans must remain obedient to God, human obedience is predicated upon an assumption of proper covenantal knowledge, and only members of the covenantal community have access to that salvific knowledge. The histories that can be generated from these ideological assumptions may be remarkably diverse in their presentation (we have seen both specific and general linear narratives; looping, cyclical accounts that overlay all of history upon a single set of tropes; and even static accounts of history understood in the context of an eternal present tense), but they demonstrate a fairly narrow range of interest with regard to events and experiences.

Among the events that do appear to be of interest to the author/editor(s) of this text—and we may point here to the cycles of transgression, exile, repentance, and return, as they are manifested in accounts of the patriarchal covenants, the Israelites' wandering in the Wilderness, and the experience of the Babylonian Exile—perhaps the most prominent event of all is the founding of the covenant community. We have seen already that origin-moments are of particular interest in this text, whether in terms of the cosmic origins described in the second admonition or the origins of the righteous remnant presented in the first. Additional accounts of the foundation of the new covenant are scattered throughout this text and range from simple to complex. At times, the story is brief: when the people claim that their false practices are appropriate actions, God atones for their iniquity and raises up a "sure house"—the covenant—which will grant its occupants "eternal life" (CD 3.17–20). Another account likens the establishment of the covenant community to the story of the "well," which is dug by the leaders of the people, for the sake of the covenanters (CD 6.3–11).

At other times, the account is grounded in larger historical narratives, as in the story that begins when "Belial established Jannes (יחנה) and his brother" in a plot against "Moses and Aaron [who] stood by the hand of the prince of lights" (CD 5.18–19), at the time when Belial "did evil against Israel for the first time" (בהרשע ישראל את הראשונה).[80] The text continues with the assertion that:

> At the time of the destruction of the land, the trespassers arose and led Israel astray, and the land became desolate, because they spoke deviantly (דברו סרה) against the ordinances of God (given) through the hand of Moses and also against the anointed holy ones. And they prophesied falsely, so as to cause Israel to turn away from God. And God recalled the covenant of the first ones (ברית ראשנים), and he established from Aaron men of discernment and from Israel wise men, and he allowed them to hear.[81]

---

[80] For this reading, see 4Q266 3 ii 5–7 and 4Q267 2 2–3; in Baumgarten, DJD XVIII, 41–43, 97–98. In CD 5.19 we find "when Israel first was saved" (בהושע ישראל את הראשונה), followed by a short vacat. It appears most likely that the manuscript of CD is corrupt at this point, and it is interesting to note that at least one of the Qumran manuscripts (4Q266) has a paleographical error on this same word (it appears that the scribe originally wrote ברשעה, may have corrected it to הרשעה by crossing through the ב and adding a supralinear ה, and then crossed through the whole word and rewrote something like בהרשע (although this, too, is unclear, because only the first three letters of the rewritten word remain in the manuscript).

[81] CD 5.20–6.3, after Baumgarten and Schwartz, 'CD,' 23. Schwartz translates the phrase דברו סרה as "they spoke deviantly" to convey an allusion to סרי דרך (CD 1.13), those who 'stray' or 'deviate' from God's chosen path. See his discussion on 23 n. 53.

In a now-familiar pattern, the experiences of Israel at the time of the Exodus blend, in this text, with the experiences of the new covenanters. The 'truths' of these experiences—that defiance of God's commandments leads to destruction, that obedience and knowledge are the keys to redemption—allow them to stand in for one another and to convey the most basic, and most significant, lessons of history for the author/editor(s) of this text.

As these readings demonstrate, the presentations of history in the Damascus Document reflect consistent ideological patterns and careful literary construction. What is not yet clear is the extent to which the historical narratives in the text reflect the actual experiences of the text's author/editor(s), or of the community in which the text was written and experienced. That is, although the text's constructions of history are ideological and stylized, they may nevertheless reflect—with greater or lesser clarity—a set of real historical experiences. In the next chapter, we turn to a series of readings that attempt to address this larger historical question, asking first, how and whether the text might reflect the experiences of its author/editor(s), and second, how and whether later readings of the text might have created a new understanding of the text's historical significance, and a new construction of historical experience for its later audiences.

CHAPTER FOUR

READING FOR HISTORY AND TIME IN THE DAMASCUS DOCUMENT

The discussions of the previous chapter suggested that the literary and ideological constructions of history in the Damascus Document appear in a number of distinct historical models, some linear and some cyclical, some universal and some highly specific. But, for all their stylistic variations and thematic differences, these varied models of history may be understood as complementary: linear narratives can be read in terms of their cyclical significance, while the various universal and specific histories can be interpreted for their parallel narratives of human experience. Readers of the text who attempt to make sense of its historical claims, consequently, must engage in an implicit (or explicit) interpretive practice, locating and foregrounding the details that they consider 'relevant' for their own understanding of history, while transferring to the background (or ignoring) those themes that are not relevant, or fail to support, their own picture of history.

This chapter begins with a shift of focus from the notion of historical claims and historical evidence as 'implicit in the text' to the discussion of such historical claims as elements in diverse *readings* of the text, by a wide range of readers, whose understandings of history are grounded in a diversity of interpretations of the text. By understanding the Damascus Document's historical narratives in terms of the hypothetical readings of its original audiences, as well as a variety of other audiences in the course of the lifetime of the text, such an approach allows for discussion not only of the history 'behind' the text, but also of the potential for the text to shape and contribute to an ongoing understanding of history, long after the text's original composition.

Among modern historians of the Dead Sea Scrolls, certain evidence from the Damascus Document tends to be understood as central to any discussion of the history of the community or communities associated with the text. Thus, although scholarly readings of the Damascus Document range widely in their view of its historicity and in their approach to its interpretation, these diverse readings nevertheless tend to address the same core of potential historical evidence.[1] Chief among this evidence is the claim with regard to the formation of a covenant community, that:

> In the period of wrath, three hundred and ninety years after giving them into the hand of Nebuchadnezzar, king of Babylon, [God] turned his attention to them and caused to grow out of Israel and Aaron a root of planting... and they were as blind as those who grope for a way for twenty years.... And he appointed for them a Teacher of Righteousness (CD 1.5–7, 9–10, 11).

A second passage of related significance asserts that:

> From the day the Unique Teacher was gathered in until the end of all the men of war who turned away with the Man of the Lie there will be about forty years (CD 20.13–15).[2]

Together, these historiographical statements have provided the building-blocks for a variety of modern scholarly narratives of ancient Jewish communal history, and they have taken on a centrality among modern scholars that makes them difficult to ignore.

The readings in this chapter triangulate among these three observations: that the Damascus Document presents images of history that are ideological in content; that a focus on the text as potentially meaningful in multiple ways allows for a reconsideration of its historical usefulness; and that the text's few specific temporal claims stand as central elements in scholarly discussions of history. In addressing these three points, the chapter takes the form of a series of readings, each of which considers the historical significance of the text's temporal references in terms of a different set of interpretive frames and methodological assumptions. Beginning with a simple reading of the text (as the product of a single-stage redactional process) and moving from there to a number of more complex readings (in the context of multi-stage redactions, or in social or interpretive contexts outside the text's 'original' setting), this chapter lays out a number of alternative historical narratives grounded in distinct readings of

---

[1] Summary discussions of the history of scholarship on this subject can be found in Davies, *Damascus Covenant*, 3–47; and, more recently, Collins, 'Origins,' 169–72; and Collins, *Apocalypticism*, 66–68.

[2] The distinct literary qualities of CD 20, as compared with the text of CD 1–8 and CD 19, are discussed more fully below. Evidence for CD 20 is found in 4Q266 4 i and 4Q267 3, but these fragmentary manuscripts do not contain witnesses to CD 20.13–15. See Baumgarten, DJD XVIII, 46–47, 98–99.

the Damascus Document. These discussions, in turn, provide insight into the practices of historiographical scholarship based on this text (and others like it), while also underlining the limits of such historiographical practices.

Focus on covenant formation

Among the historical themes highlighted in the previous chapter was the Damascus Document's attention to images of covenant formation, both in general Israelite terms and also in terms of the establishment of the specific community of the renewed covenant. A useful 'baseline' reading of this text—one that is fairly straightforward and may provide a foil for the interpretations that follow—begins with a consideration of this ideological point. Such a reading interprets the text's historical claims in light of the theme of covenant formation, asking how the original author/editor(s) of the text—and the original audience(s) for whom they were writing—would have understood the specific temporal references (390-plus-20-plus-40-years), given their larger interests in covenantal history and the founding of the covenant community.

This hypothetical reading begins with two critical assumptions: that the text is the product of a single redactional process, and that it was written at least in part to describe the foundation and early history of a real covenant community, whose membership includes the author/editor(s) of the text, as well as the audience to whom it is directed. These assumptions allow for a fairly straightforward approach to historiography, in that they ground the text's historical claims in the context of its larger ideologies, without calling into question a one-to-one connection between the text and a real history behind it.

For covenantal readers who chose to foreground the authenticity and history of their communal connection to God, the Damascus Document provides a remarkable array of confirmatory evidence. First is the almost atemporal claim that the founding of the covenant community can be understood in archaic and universalized tones, as God's primordial selection of the righteous, who—through all the years of human history—are to inhabit the world and walk in the truth of God's knowledge (CD 2.11–12). From this perspective, the founding of the covenant occurs in cosmic time; for as long as humans have been relevant in God's creation, the covenant community has been, at least implicitly, God's chosen remnant.

Elsewhere in the text, such a covenantal reader finds very different models for understanding the foundation of the community, grounded in much more event-oriented language, and with greater focus on human actions and the cause-and-effect relationship of transgression, punishment, and selection of the righteous. For example, in the third admonition, a lengthy discussion of human history remarks on the repeated failures of Israel's past covenants before presenting—in some detail—the account of the founding of the new covenant, and the concerns that it addresses (CD 2.16–3.16, esp. 3.12–16). From this perspective, the entire narrative of human history from creation to 'the present' culminates in God's establishment of this covenant, with its revelation of the details of sabbath and festival observance, as well as God's "righteous testimonies, his true ways, and the desires of his will," which shape the life of the covenanter (עידות צדקו ודרכי אמתו וחפצי רצונו, CD 3.14–16).

In addition to accounts of covenant formation that are cosmic or national in scope, the text also offers an array of images of the formation of specific covenants. The covenanters are the Zadokite priests of Ezekiel's vision (Ezek 44.15), who remain loyal even after the other Israelite priesthoods have fallen away, and who consequently receive the honor of offering perpetual sacrifice in God's sanctuary (CD 3.21–4.4).[3] They are the "nobles of the people," who excavate the well of God's statutes, by following the lead of his inspired representative (CD 6.2–11, esp. 6.8). They are the survivors of the split between Judah and Ephraim, which has led to the exile of God's congregation, but which also promises a triumphant future return (CD 7.11–21). And they are, in their own historical understanding, heirs of a covenant of Torah, "which Moses made with Israel" (אשר כרת משה עם ישראל, CD 15.8–9), and which Abraham sought to fulfill on the very day in which he first received it ("on the day of his knowing," ביום דעתו, CD 16.6).[4]

In comparison with these mostly-general accounts of covenant formation, the narrative of covenant formation in the first admonition

---

[3] I discuss the Damascus Document's priestly imagery more extensively in chapter five, below.

[4] For a discussion of possible textual problems (and a rejection of the need to emend this passage), see Baumgarten and Schwartz, 'CD,' 41 n. 133.

is remarkable for its specificity, although here too we find a mapping of multiple historical moments onto the single event-image of covenant-building. God preserves a remnant of Israel at the time of the Babylonian conquest (CD 1.4–5), and he returns his attention to them 390 years later (CD 1.5–6). The community that is formed in the course of this visitation thus has its roots simultaneously in its survival of the conquest and its selection by God in the later period. The foundation of the community is renewed a brief 20 years later (CD 1.10), with the arrival of the Teacher of Righteousness, whose presence confirms the validity of the covenant by providing the people with the special covenantal knowledge that guarantees the community's longterm survival (CD 1.11–12).

How might the author/editor(s) of this text, or their earliest covenantal audiences, have understood the specific temporal claims associated with covenant foundation (the 390-plus-20-years), in light of a larger interpretive focus on origin narratives and the concern for the authenticity or antiquity of the community's covenantal claims? We can imagine a number of different readings of these temporal references, depending on situation-specific as well as more general ideological issues. For example, in situations where the author/editor(s) or covenantal audiences of this text wanted to foreground the community's *eternal* bond with God and their predestined status as the 'true Israel' or the 'righteous remnant,' the temporal details of the first admonition could be backgrounded, while the more atemporal or cosmic claims of the second admonition were brought to the fore.

In contrast, in situations in which a covenantal reader faced challenges to the community's *historical* validity—for example, in the face of opponents who might question community members' authority to interpret scripture or establish religious praxis—it would be possible to foreground the very specific and very 'real world' experiences that confirmed their communal claims: surviving the Babylonian conquest, being recognized by God after a specified period of repentance, and being awarded a teacher with a direct line of wisdom from the divine realm. That these historical references can be read in line with specific visions of Ezekiel (most notably, the prophet's penance for the sins of Israel, which includes his lying on the ground for 390 days, in Ezek 4.5–6) offers further support for such authoritative claims, although again only to the extent that a covenantal reader chose to foreground that claim. In this context a reader might draw attention both to the 390 years of repentance and also to the claims to

Zadokite status (in CD 3.21–4.4, drawing upon Ezek 44.15), to show that in both general and specific ways, Ezekiel's prophecies predict the presence (and confirm the validity) of the covenant community and its historical claims.

As these readings suggest, the earliest audiences of the Damascus Document (including the text's own author/editor(s), as well as other members of their community), may well have understood the temporal claims in the text in terms of their simple meaning (390 literal years after the Exile, and 20 years after that time), but this remains only one of a number of possible readings of these temporal claims. Other readings might highlight the scriptural origins of these figures; still others might background the temporal figures altogether, while foregrounding some other primary theme or agenda. In addition, it is possible that these temporal figures represent actual calculations on the part of the author/editor(s) of the text (based on one of a number of chronological reckoning systems),[5] but such a claim is in no way required, or even highly recommended, in light of these varied reading strategies.

Sectarian schism as historical marker

Continuing with the same basic methodological assumptions—a focus on the text's original audience, including its author/editor(s), and an understanding of textual formation as the product of a single-stage redaction—we can generate a number of additional readings by altering the central thematic question of our reading. If, instead of focusing on the notion of covenant formation, a hypothetical covenantal audience were to be more concerned with issues of communal schism or intracommunal-and-extracommunal conflict, they might interpret the temporal details of this text in terms of a very different historical significance.

Reading the Damascus Document in light of its accounts of communal conflict generates, as in our first example, a remarkable array of historical narratives and vignettes. The first admonition offers a lengthy account of the transgressions of "the congregation of traitors"

---

[5] On these temporal claims in terms of ancient systems of chronology, see Steudel, 'אחרית הימים,' 236–40; and Antti Laato, 'The Chronology in the *Damascus Document* of Qumran,' *RevQ* 15 (1992): 605–7.

(עדת בוגדים, CD 1.12), who stray from the proper path like the wayward cow of Hosea's prophecy (פרה סוררה, CD 1.13, quoting Hos 4.16).[6] Their transgressions against the covenant are myriad but may be summarized in a single phrase: the exchange of righteousness for wickedness, in all actions and thought (CD 1.15–2.1). The second admonition provides a cosmic spin to this same assertion, with the dual claim that the transgressions of "those who stray from the way" (סררי דרך, CD 2.6) are determined primordially as the cause of their downfall and that it is God himself who causes the wicked to stray (CD 2.13). The accounts of human wickedness in the third admonition provide an ongoing but generalized backdrop for the text's presentation of distinctions between covenanters and those outside the fold (CD 2.14–3.12), while more explicit images of intracommunal schism are available in a reference to transgressions of the covenant at the time of the destruction of the land (CD 5.20–6.2) and an account of the divisions between Ephraim and Judah, also articulated in covenantal terms (CD 7.11–14).

An even more explicit discussion of intracommunal conflict states that punishment by the sword awaits "all those entering [God's] covenant" (כל באי בריתו) who "will not hold fast" (לא יחזיקו) to God's statutes, as understood by the covenant community (CD 8.1–2). The sins of such covenantal apostates are described in some detail in this passage (CD 8.5–9), and although they can be boiled down to the familiar crimes of willfulness and disobedience to God, they also include such specific transgressions as greed, grudge-bearing, violence, and sexual misconduct (CD 8.5–6). The transgressive apostate community is associated with a lying leader (CD 1.15, 8.13), who speaks against the Teacher of Righteousness and fails to understand the fact that punishment ultimately awaits anyone who abandons God's ordinances and turns willfully away from the authorized interpretations of scripture and practice (CD 8.14–19).

In addition to drawing upon the text's historical references to covenantal conflict, the author/editor(s) and earliest audiences of the Damascus Document may have foregrounded several legal sections that address issues of in-fighting and disloyalty to the covenant. A series of laws (in CD 9.1–10.3) governs the behavior of covenanters

---

[6] The text has פרה סורירה, but the י in סורירה is under erasure. See CD 1.13, in Baumgarten and Schwartz, 'CD,' 13.

toward one another, with explicit concern to prevent grudges, tale-telling, and unfair economic transactions within the community. Similarly, at the end of a lengthy legal discussion, the text asserts that:

> anyone who rejects these judgments, which are in accordance with all the statutes found in the Torah of Moses, will not be considered among all the sons of his truth; for his soul has despised righteous instruction. Being in rebellion let him be expelled from the presence of the many.[7]

This assertion of communal authority is followed by the description of an expulsion ceremony (and a list of penalties enforced on anyone who keeps in touch with an expelled former member); a reminder that the community will engage in an annual 'cursing ceremony' for those who have transgressed the way; and ultimately the assertion that all this is in accordance with the elaboration of the Law for the final period of wrath.[8]

For a covenantal audience that is particularly concerned about communal schism—whether because of recent events, ongoing tensions, or a fear of future conflicts—an appropriate reading of the temporal elements in the Damascus Document may require focusing on their contributions to larger questions of communal unity and disunity. From this perspective, the origin-claim that the founding of the community occurred 390 years after the Babylonian conquest can be viewed as important to the extent that it provides a point of conciliation or shared experience for covenanters attempting to work out their other conflicts. To the extent that it can be mobilized as an argument for unity ('we are all part of the new covenant; remember when God first claimed us!'), this temporal expression may serve an important ideological purpose in such a reading.

More significant, however, is the second figure, the 20 years in which the community wandered "as blind ones" (כעורים, CD 1.9), before receiving the authoritative leadership of the Teacher of Righteousness. The original author/editor(s) and earliest audiences of this text may have understood this time period—and the communal conflicts associated with it—in any number of ways, depend-

---

[7] 4Q266 11 5–8; parallels in 4Q270 7 i 19–21; see Baumgarten, DJD XVIII, 76–77, 162–64.

[8] The expulsion ceremony and penalty for contact are found in 4Q266 11 8–16; see Baumgarten, DJD XVIII, 76–77. The cursing ceremony and conclusions are in 4Q266 11 17–21, with parallels in 4Q270 7 ii 11–15; see Baumgarten, DJD XVIII, 76–77, 166–67.

ing both on their own personal experiences of the events implied in the text, and also on their interpretations of those events (and of the text itself) in the context of later discussions or communal conflicts. Again, although we do not know exactly what historical events underlie the claims of this text, we can imagine a number of very different readings of these references to covenantal loyalty, in light of several potential historical scenarios.

Consider, for example, the possibility that the Teacher of Righteousness and the Man of the Lie were opposing leaders in the covenant community, and that their conflicts over communal authority, religious praxis, or scriptural interpretation (or some combination of the three) led to a factional split among their followers. In this context, the efforts to create rigid distinctions between covenanters and apostates may reflect the ideological need to distinguish between two groups whose material differences were not so readily apparent to those outside the original conflict. For a covenanter who might otherwise wish to effect a reconciliation with his apostate brethren, a real deterrent is found in the text's rejection of the apostates (who will be judged in the endtimes and will fall by the sword, like all the other wicked of the earth, CD 3.10–11, 8.1–2). Similarly, the implicit threats in the expulsion ceremony (including a fear of one's own expulsion for those who might consider consorting with an apostate) might serve a very real purpose of erecting boundaries between former covenant partners, especially in a time after the most heated conflicts have passed.

An alternative possibility is that the covenant community experienced a *series* of conflicts and intracommunal battles, of which the references to the Teacher and the Liar are only the most spectacular. In this context, members of the covenant might read the references to communal conflict in a somewhat different way. Rather than understanding them as specific references to a single major schism, such readers might think in terms of ongoing conflicts, in which their opponents might be framed—regularly, and in familiar dualistic language—as transgressors of tradition whenever and wherever they disagreed with the mainstream of the covenant community. We should note, as well, that claims to authoritative tradition need not reflect a majority perspective. Even a covenanter with a minority view might argue that his perspective is the legitimate one, and that all other interpretations are transgressions of righteousness; after all, the text itself demonstrates that the remnant of Israel, and *not* its sinful majority, is the group with access to true knowledge of God's will. Authority, for such a covenantal reader, is grounded in proving that one's own interpretation reflects the truth of God's will and of scripture, while all other interpretations reflect willful departures from the way.

For a covenanter with ongoing concerns about communal conflict, the temporal references in the Damascus Document provide a means of establishing valuative boundaries between insiders and outsiders, *or* of drawing divided parties together. In this context, the temporal references might be mobilized as future-oriented predictions of eventual judgment and defeat of the wicked, and not only as historical references of past events.

The figure of 390 years can be mobilized as a unifying factor, and other references in the text acknowledge that some time remains for righteous outsiders to join the community (CD 4.10–11). There is also evidence that *some* people who have left the covenant, but whose transgressions are not so great, may still be judged as righteous, if only on an individual basis (CD 20.22–25). In general, though, covenanters attempting to rehabilitate a transgressive apostate would find themselves in the position of arguing for an extremely selective reading of the text, in which a wide range of anti-apostate claims would have to be backgrounded, in order for a very few conciliatory terms to be brought to the fore. In contrast, for covenanters attempting to distinguish between their own righteous deeds and the sinfulness of apostasy, the text's temporal references fit nicely in a larger discussion of the righteous remnant's longterm clash with the forces of evil, as well as their future endeavors and anticipation of an end to the time of wickedness.

Endtime expectations and textual development

Imagining an audience whose primary concern is a rapidly-impending period of endtimes provides yet another opportunity to read the Damascus Document's temporal claims in terms of their original setting and the interpretations of their original author/editor(s) and original audiences. Readers with endtimes expectations, like the other readers discussed above, have a variety of images to consider in their interpretations of the text. The first admonition hints at the fate of the apostates to the covenant, which is to occur in the "last generation"

(דור אחרון, CD 1.12), while the second admonition presents—in tone, if not in specific assertion—the view that all of human life is finite and will someday come to an end. Again, at the end of the third admonition, the reader learns that all those who enter the covenant and "hold fast to it are to have eternal life" (המחזיקים בו לחיי נצח, CD 3.20). At the completion of the appointed period of human time (שלים הקץ, CD 4.8–9, 10),[9] God will atone for these covenanters, while the wicked will be judged, and God's wrath will come upon them (CD 4.10, 5.14–16).

These passages provide generalized background for a reading in light of endtimes expectations, but others allow for a more comprehensive discussion. At this point, however, we must introduce a complicating variable into our hypothetical reading of the text. Previous readings have imagined the Damascus Document as the product of a single redaction and a single editorial imagination. However, as noted in chapter one, there is at least one major section of the text that is extant in two variant forms (CD 7.5–8.21 and CD 19.1–34a), and it is precisely in their vision of the endtimes that these texts diverge from one another. Although they contain large sections that are identical or nearly identical, their elaborations of endtimes expectations make use of very different scriptural references.[10] If the source of this variation is early (and scholars tend to view both texts as ancient in their origin, although we have scrolls witnesses only for the CD 7–8 material),[11] then we can imagine a variety

---

[9] The text reflects a slight orthographic inconsistency: CD 4.8–9 has שלים הקץ, while CD 4.10 has שלום הקץ. See Baumgarten and Schwartz, 'CD,' 18–19.

[10] Textual parallels extend through CD 7.5–8.21 and 19.1–34; the text in CD 19.34–20.34 is not paralleled in MS A. See Baumgarten and Schwartz, 'CD,' 25 n. 65, for a discussion of the parallel texts. Parallels to MS A are found in 4Q266 3 iii (CD 7.1–5, 7.17–8.3), 4Q266 3 iv (CD 8.3–9), 4Q269 5 (CD 7.17–20), and 4Q269 6 (CD 8.5–6). In addition, there are ancient witnesses for two passages from CD 20 (MS B): 4Q266 4 i (CD 20.33–34) and 4Q267 3 (CD 20.25–28). According to the recent publication of these fragments, Milik apparently understood the composition of 4Q266 to reflect the texts of CD 8.9–21, 19.34–35, and then 20.1–34. See Baumgarten, DJD XVIII, 43–47, 98–99, 128–29; for Milik's estimation, see Baumgarten, DJD XVIII, 46.

[11] For discussions of the textual variants as the result of ancient conflicts over messianism, see George Brooke, 'The Amos-Numbers Midrash (CD 7.13b–8.1a) and Messianic Expectation,' ZAW 92 (1980): 397–404; Brooke, 'The Messiah of Aaron,' 216–18, 224–27; Frederick Strickert, 'Damascus Document VII, 10–20 and Qumran Messianic Expectation,' RevQ 12 (1986): 327–49; and Geza Xeravits, 'Precisions sur le texte original et le concept messianique de CD 7:13–8:1 et 19:5–14,' RevQ 19 (1999): 47–59. For a text-critical analysis that views some variants as mechanical

of interpretations of these competing passages, grounded in their readers' varied understandings of historical events, but also in the complexities of a multi-stage redaction of the Damascus Document.[12]

The first version of this passage (CD 7.5–8.21) presents the endtimes as a period in which God will make a visitation of the land, and the wicked will be judged and punished in a scene reminiscent of earlier judgments (CD 7.9–12, citing Isa 7.17). Messianic language—including references to the booth of the king (סוכת המלך, CD 7.15–16) and the "star" and "scepter" (כוכב, שבט, CD 7.19)—contributes to a larger description of the present-day covenant community (CD 7.13–21), who protect the books of Torah and prophets that the rest of Israel has rejected (CD 7.15–18). The community anticipates—in now-familiar atemporal language, which may reflect either present or future orientation—both the "interpreter of the Torah, who comes to Damascus" (דורש התורה הבא דמשק, CD 7.18–19) and the "prince of all the congregation" (נשיא כל העדה, CD 7.20), who "in his arising, destroys (or: will destroy) all the sons of Seth" (ובעמדו וקרקר את כל בני שת, CD 7.20–21). The fate of the wicked is determined by the judgment of God (CD 8.1, 3), but it is enacted by the hand of Belial (8.2), and the cycle of judgment and destruction bears equal impact on sinful people with no connection to the covenant and on those sinful former covenanters who have strayed from the proper covenantal path (CD 8.16).

The second version of this passage differs in its presentation of endtimes events, in sometimes striking ways. Although this text shares

---

errors, rather than purposeful alterations, see Sidnie White, 'A Comparison of the "A" and "B" Manuscripts of the Damascus Document,' *RevQ* 12 (1987): 537–53. For source critical discussions of these passages, see Murphy-O'Connor, 'Original Text of CD 7.9–8.2,' 379–86; Murphy-O'Connor, 'The Critique of the Princes,' 200–16; Murphy-O'Connor, 'Literary Analysis of XIX,33–XX,34,' 544–64; and Davies, *Damascus Covenant*, 143–59.

[12] For a discussion of potential multi-stage redactions of the Damascus Document, with a general overview of the question, see Metso, 'Constitutional Rules,' in Flint and VanderKam, *Dead Sea Scrolls After Fifty Years*, 1.194–95. See also Murphy-O'Connor, 'An Essene Missionary Document,' 201–204; Davies, *Damascus Covenant*, 48–55. Davies argues that the text is the product of a complex redactional process, in which scriptural references serve as a source for the text's structure and plot. This argument is expanded in Campbell, *The Use of Scripture*. For the claim that the Laws precede the Admonition and that the two were originally separate texts, see Hartmut Stegemann, 'Das Gesetzeskorpus der "Damaskusschrift" (CD IX–XVI),' *RevQ* 14 (1990): 409–34. With regard to the legal portions of the text, recent scholarship has supported a multi-stage redaction, in which the laws were "revised and brought up to date" in the course of their transcription and transmission. See Hempel, *The Laws*, 15–23, 187–92 (quotation on 191).

the view that the wicked will be duly punished at the time of God's visitation on the land (CD 19.6), this passage contains a more complex understanding of the relationship of the community to salvation, as well as an explicit reference to a future messianic figure (or figures), who remains implicit in the parallel account. Where MS A has quotations from Numbers and Amos, this passage quotes Zechariah, highlighting the image of the shepherd and his flock. God strikes the shepherd, scattering his flock (CD 19.8, quoting Zech 13.7) and leaving only the "poor of the sheep" (עניי הצאן, CD 19.9) to preserve the true message. These preservers of the covenant will escape the final judgment, but all others will be handed over to the sword, "when the messiah of Aaron and Israel comes" (בבוא משיח אהרן וישראל, CD 19.10–11).[13] This anticipated visitation is understood in terms of Israel's experience in an earlier time (CD 19.11–12, quoting Ezek 9.4), but also in terms of the anticipated punishment of covenantal apostates, who will be punished, again, by the "hand of Belial" (ביד בליעל, CD 19.14), on account of their sinfulness. Such apostates are hated by God (CD 19.31), and they are to be erased from the covenant community for the rest of time, until the arrival of "a messiah from Aaron and from Israel" (משיח מאהרן ומישראל, CD 20.1).

With the reference to a "messiah from Aaron and from Israel," CD 20.1–34 introduces another round of endtimes imagery. A lengthy discussion of the rejection of individual apostates (CD 20.1–13) is followed by the text's third specific temporal reference: the 40 years that will pass from the time of the Teacher's death to the end of all the apostates who allied themselves with the Man of the Lie (CD 20.14–15). This passage appears in the context of a larger discussion of endtimes judgments. The text states, as well, that "salvation and righteousness" (ישע וצדקה, CD 20.20) will be revealed to those who keep the covenant faithfully, so that the distinctions between righteousness and wickedness (and, perhaps more importantly, the rewards for each) will be made clear. Ultimately, this text asserts, all those who remain loyal to the covenant, and who confess their sins and ask forgiveness for them,

> will be joyous and happy, and their hearts will take courage, and they will overpower all the sons of the earth. And God will atone for them, and they will see his salvation, for they took refuge in his holy name.[14]

---

[13] Note the use of this phrase, also, in the legal passages in CD 12.23 and 14.19. See the discussion in Collins, *Apocalypticism*, especially 'Messianic Expectation,' 71–90.

[14] CD 20.33–34; translation after Baumgarten and Schwartz, 'CD,' 37.

Ultimately, in this passage, the endtimes are presented as a time of judgment for all people, with redemption as a promise to the righteous only.

Given the complexities of this textual tradition, we can point to a number of possible models for its development, each of which suggests a different set of historical events 'behind' the text, and each of which is open to a number of different readings of the temporal data in it, even for an audience whose primary focus is the impending endtimes. The 'multiple multiples' of this discussion make it difficult to lay out every possible reading of the text, but we can suggest a few of the more likely possibilities, even while recognizing that they do not cover every possible permutation.

One possible explanation of textual development is that the text of CD 7–8 was original to the Damascus Document and that this text was revised—perhaps quite early in the history of the use of the Damascus Document—and replaced with the parallel account represented by CD 19.[15] Given this model, scholars have asked how the later text revises the ideas of the earlier text, noting that the role of CD 19 may be to introduce explicit and explicitly-future-oriented images of a messianic figure (in place of the earlier text's use of messianic imagery to describe the community itself).[16] The changes of CD 19 (and especially the messianic reference in CD 19.34–20.1) also allow for the introduction of the imagery of dual messiahs, one from Aaron and one from Israel. Incorporating the text of CD 20 into this model (as an addition to the text composed around the same time as CD 19), scholars imagine a historical background for these textual changes in the period after the death of the Teacher, when the covenanters had to come to grips with challenges from an apostate community (that of the Liar), as well as the dangers of individual apostasy and other potential challenges to the stability of the covenant community.[17]

In light of this hypothetical historical model, we can imagine a number of readings of the temporal data in this text. In the context of the Damascus Document's larger eschatological claims—which tend toward general statements about the salvation of the righteous

---

[15] See Davies, *Damascus Covenant*, 156; Murphy-O'Connor, 'The Critique of the Princes.'

[16] See Collins, *Apocalypticism*, 71–90.

[17] See Murphy-O'Connor, 'Literary Analysis of XIX,33–XX,34,' 555, for a discussion of this possibility. See also Davies, *Damascus Covenant*, 181–97.

and the judgment of the wicked—the more-specific messianic language of CD 19 and the explicit judgment statements of CD 20 may have provided authoritative grounding and a stronger argument for covenantal leaders after the death of the Teacher. In particular, the scripturally-supported claims that God himself has ordered the striking down of the shepherd and the scattering of the sheep (CD 19.7–9, quoting Zech 13.7) can serve as an ideological re-reading (in positive terms) of historical events that might otherwise have contributed to the downfall of the community. In the context of this reading, we should note that authorship, redaction, and audience interpretation are, at least from a modern vantage point, impossible to distinguish. The author/editor(s) of CD 19, who are attempting a revision of the text that actually rewrites history, can be successful in their attempts only to the extent that their audiences accept their version of the text, understand it as an authoritative rendering of historical events, and take seriously its claims for the future. An audience of covenanters who accept these claims will allow their understanding of history to be revised in terms of them. Alternatively, we can imagine a communal conflict over these parallel accounts, in which the competing texts (and their competing views of history and especially the end of human history) might require readers to choose one over the other.

This model offers a reasonably convincing account of the history 'behind' this hypothetical textual revision, but it is not the only convincing arrangement of the evidence. In fact, given that audiences are capable of harmonizing their readings of diverse ideological claims, and given that they can background and foreground the details of a text in order to support specific ideological concerns, it is equally important for us to generate a textual model that views these parallel accounts as complementary, rather than competing. We may note again Sarianna Metso's observation that the communal rule texts of the Dead Sea Scrolls may have been notations of ongoing communal norms, rather than fixed texts in their own right.[18] In this context, the presence of the parallel texts in the Damascus Document might reflect two elaborations of the same basic covenantal template. If we understand these texts as non-contradictory accounts, presented at different times and by different communal leaders, but as authoritative

---

[18] See Metso, 'Constitutional Rules,' in Flint and VanderKam, *Dead Sea Scrolls After Fifty Years*, 1.207–9.

performances of 'the same' base text, we can imagine a very different historical setting 'behind' this textual development.

In terms of this latter model, we can imagine a community whose understanding of the Damascus Document (and other central texts) involves not only the acceptance of its historical narratives and future-oriented claims, but also an understanding that the text itself (in conjunction with the authoritative voices of Israelite prophecy) can be activated to respond to ongoing challenges at a communal level. For a covenantal audience with a concern for endtimes expectations, then, either of the two parallel accounts might be mobilized to argue the same ideological points. That is, by foregrounding the legitimacy of the covenant and the righteousness of its members, a reader of these two parallel passages might understand them—for all their significant textual variation—as arguments for the same basic claim: that there is no salvation, and no messianic expectation, except through the collective power of the community, and its authoritative or messianic leaders.

Whatever the historical development of these parallel texts (and whether their covenantal audiences would have known about both versions, only one, or a number of others for which we have no record), we can imagine a context in which either or both might serve as the background for readings that would attempt to draw the covenant community together, or to split it into factions, in the face of the impending endtimes. Such a situation would have been particularly evocative if these textual additions were written in the period following the death of the Teacher, as some scholars claim. In such a context, the temporal claim of CD 20—that the final judgment of the Liar's community will come some 40 years after the Teacher's death—provides the basis for a number of potentially-important readings by later covenant-members.

In particular, this passage gives assurance that the end is near, without establishing overly-fixed constraints on its arrival. For covenanters in the years immediately following the publication of this prediction, it would provide a sense of immediacy and anticipation that might hold the community together. In later years, as those 40 years drew to a close, or even passed, we can imagine a series of re-readings and revisions of the prediction, by readers who would remind themselves first that the claim of the text is a generalized period of "about 40 years" (כשנים ארבעים, CD 20.15) and not 40 years precisely, and then, perhaps, that '40 years' itself is a highly symbolic number, whose interpretation may not be as simple as its face-value reading. Covenanters might look back to the experiences of the Israelites in the Wilderness (a favored image elsewhere in the Damascus Document), and also to the stories of figures like Noah and Elijah,[19] to re-interpret the text's temporal claims in ways that would postpone the completion of the endtimes without decreasing the authoritative power of the text. It is possible, too, that the author/editor(s) and original audience of the CD 20 temporal reference may have understood it as an implicit allusion to the 490-year endtimes prediction found in the book of Daniel (Dan 9). That is, if the career of the Teacher lasted roughly 40 years, as scholars have speculated, and if the author/editor(s) of CD 20 composed their text in the period immediately following his death, then they may have imagined the 'about 40 years' of their text as the completion of the earlier predictions of Daniel.[20] Again, this reading is in no way required by the text, but it is a possible mobilization of the text's themes and imagery.

For each of these readings, and for the many others that space does not permit discussing, a few interpretive factors are crucial. The first is that the text of the Damascus Document, in its original form, is so consistent in its ideologies but so diverse in its presentation of them that it remains open to a remarkably wide range of historical interpretations. When subject to the combined forces of audience interpretation and actual textual revision, the basic agendas of the Damascus Document—and here it is possible to foreground the concern for the impending endtimes, the judgment of the wicked, the redemption of the righteous, or any of a number of other themes— provide an authoritative framing to the later claims of the text's interpreters and re-editors. However, just as the parallel accounts of CD 7–8 and CD 19 may have lent themselves to a variety of mobilizations, and to the diverse authoritative claims of readers who may have wanted to direct 'the meaning' of the text in any of several different directions, so too do they lend themselves to modern scholarly interpretations that reconstruct a variety of potential histories 'behind' the text.

---

[19] For Noah's 40-day flood, see Gen 7.12; for Elijah's 40-day journey in the wilderness, see 1 Kg 19.8. The scriptural contexts of both the flood narrative (which intersperses a year-long deluge with the 40-day account), and the Elijah account (with its references to a journey to "the wilderness of Damascus," in 1 Kg 19.15) strike me as perfect opportunities for a covenanter to re-read the temporal claims of this text in line with scriptural references and ideological norms that already are present in the text. I have no proof that such an interpretation ever took place, but it appears eminently possible.

[20] See n. 38, below.

Textual redaction and communal foundations

The previous reading altered the analytical variables by assuming a multi-stage textual redaction and foregrounding an imagined audience's endtimes expectations. In this reading, we return to the historical narratives of the first three admonitions, asking how the constructions of community formation might be reconsidered in light of a similar multi-stage textual redaction. Here, the poetic structures of the admonitions and the content of their claims contribute to an alternative reading of the text and also of the historical events they purport to describe.[21] Literary analysis of the poetic and metrical structures in the first admonition also contributes to a discussion of whether the historical details in the text are original to it or are later additions.[22]

Murphy-O'Connor offers a reading of the Damascus Document that attempts to expose the history of the community associated with the text by distinguishing between its original form and its later redactional layers. According to his analysis, the core of the text is a "Missionary Document," which consists of the third admonition and the scripturally-based narratives that follow it (CD 2.14–6.1).[23] This text, he claims, is the product of a group with exilic origins, and was written in an effort to win support from the majority community in Judea. In later redactions, the first and second admonitions were added to this core text, to provide a historical and theological introduction to it. These passages, along with the rest of CD 6–8 and 19–20, were added at a time of communal upheaval, to provide confirmation of the identity of the covenantal group, while discounting the authority of their opponents.[24]

Davies, in a book-length study of the Damascus Document, offers a response to and expansion of Murphy-O'Connor's source critical reading of the text. Like Murphy-O'Connor, he postulates a complex history of communal development underlying the literary devel-

---

[21] Murphy-O'Connor, 'Essenes and their History,' 215–44; as well as Murphy-O'Connor, '*Damascus Document* Revisited,' 228. Other source critical discussions focusing on the 390 and 20 years can be found in Davies, *Damascus Covenant*, 61–64, 198–204; Michael Knibb, 'Exile in the Damascus Document,' *JSOT* 25 (1983): 106–7; Brooke, 'The Messiah of Aaron,' 217–18; and Hempel, 'Community Origins,' 328–29.

[22] Boyce, 'Poetry of the *Damascus Document*,' 615–28; and the previous note.

[23] Murphy-O'Connor, 'An Essene Missionary Document,' 201–29.

[24] See Murphy-O'Connor, 'Literary Analysis of VI,2–VIII,3,' 210–32; Murphy-O'Connor, 'The Critique of the Princes,' 200–16; Murphy-O'Connor, 'Literary Analysis of XIX,33–XX,34,' 544–64.

opment of this text. Of particular interest here is his discussion of the layers of redaction visible in the first admonition. In Davies' view, this first admonition was written in at least two stages: in its earliest composition, the text contained a simple message of praise for the righteous and condemnation for the wicked. At a time of conflict within the covenant community, the admonition was revised with the addition of several passages, which break up the loosely metrical structure of the text. According to Davies, a reading of the text in terms of its earlier and later redactions provides evidence for the communal schism that underlies this textual development.[25]

The claims laid out by Davies and Murphy-O'Connor provide the historical context for another hypothetical reading of the text. For a community of covenanters in the period immediately following the final redaction of this text (that is, after the grafting of certain additions onto an original base text),[26] a significant reading of the text might foreground its accounts of covenant formation and early communal history. In the context of this discussion, we can consider the first admonition in light of two different scholarly views of the text's development. In addition to Davies' reading (which extends and reworks some of the insights of Murphy-O'Connor), a rather different picture of textual development and historical background is presented in Boyce's metrical analysis of the first admonition.

Davies and Boyce are in agreement in their readings of the early portions of the text, which they view as mostly original. Their presentation of the text begins:[27]

---

[25] See Davies, *Damascus Covenant*, 61–64, for a discussion of source-critical analyses based on poetic structures. He presents and critiques the metrical analysis of G. Jeremias, *Der Lehrer der Gerichtigkeit* (Gottingen, 1963), 151–66, as well as addressing the analyses of the text in R. H. Charles, 'The Zadokite Fragments,' in *Apocrypha and Pseudepigrapha of the Old Testament* (vol. 2; Oxford, 1913), 785–834; Ginzberg, *Unknown Jewish Sect*, 110 n. 4, 259ff.; Isaac Rabinowitz, 'A Reconsideration of "Damascus" and "390 Years" in the "Damascus" ("Zadokite") Fragments,' *JBL* 73 (1954): 11–35, esp. 13; R. A. Soloff, 'Toward Uncovering Original Texts in the Zadokite Documents,' *NTS* 5 (1958/59): 62–67; and Murphy-O'Connor, 'Essenes and their History,' 224.

[26] Note that Davies views even the redaction of this later material as an early event in the history of the community, which makes it reasonable to speculate on a reading of this later material during a still-early period in the community's history. See Davies, *Damascus Covenant*, 199–201, esp. 201.

[27] CD 1.1–2.1; this passage and all the other quotations from the first admonition follow Boyce's text. Whenever possible, the poetic structure is consistent with Boyce's, although his translation is altered for consistency (unless noted). The main body of the text consists of material that both Boyce and Davies consider original;

> And now hearken all who know righteousness
> and understand the works of God;
> For he has a dispute with all flesh,
> and will make judgment on all who scoff at him
>
> For in their treachery in forsaking him,
> he hid his face from Israel [*and from his sanctuary*],
> and gave them up to the sword;
> But remembering the covenant of the first ones,
> he left a remnant to Israel,
> and did not give them up to destruction (CD 1.1–5).

This passage is largely the same in its early and late redactions. For members of the community in both settings, it offers a reminder of the situation in which the covenant was made: Israel has rejected God and drawn his wrath upon them, but a righteous remnant has been preserved. Notice that in the later edition, the text makes mention not only of the people of Israel, but also of the Temple. This addition is the first of several that call attention to priestly and Temple-related concerns.

The text continues with a description of the founding of the new covenant. Again, in this section Davies and Boyce agree in their reconstruction of the earlier and later textual forms:

> And in the period of wrath
> [*390 years after giving them into the hand of
> Nebuchadnezzar king of Babylon*]
> he turned his attention to them;
> And caused a root to grow from Israel [*and from Aaron*],
> a plantation to possess his land
> and to grow fat on the goodness of his soil.
>
> And they understood their iniquity,
> and realized that they were guilty;
> Yet they were like the blind,
> and like those who grope for a way [*for twenty years*].[28]

In its original form, this passage presents a generalized and temporally ungrounded view of the relationship between God and the remnant. The text moves from an account of God's establishing the remnant

---

the material in square brackets is understood by Boyce as secondary; the italicized material (whether or not in square brackets) is considered secondary by Davies. See Boyce, 'Poetry of the *Damascus Document*,' 617–19; Davies, *Damascus Covenant*, 232–35.

[28] CD 1.5–10; this section follows Boyce's translation, to highlight his reading of the text's poetic structure.

to their recognizing their own sinfulness and striving to find the proper path, using several infinitive forms ('to possess,' 'to grow fat') in describing God's intentions with respect to the remnant, in addition to the finite verbal descriptions of the actions of those seekers. In temporal terms, the story floats freely in a generalized 'period of wrath.'

In contrast with the ungrounded temporal setting of the text's early version, the later edition has been grounded in human time, both historical (the years after Nebuchadnezzar) and experiential (a period of 20 years, unattached to world or national events). In assigning a specific date to the period in which this new covenant was formed, the additions to the text elaborate on themes that may have been implicit in the text, or highlight a new set of themes to which the text is certainly amenable: the importance of the experience of exile as a context in which a new covenant is established; the direct connection between pre-exilic Israel and the newly-chosen remnant; and the span of time after the first generation of covenanters 'perceived their iniquity,' during which they had to 'grope for a way.' The priestly element again is underlined in this text, which highlights the presence of 'Aaron,' as well as 'Israel.' In addition, the potential allusion to Ezekiel (the 390 years) may be an attempt—as we find a few lines later in the quotation from Hosea (CD 1.13-14)—to locate sectarian experiences in the context of scriptural, and not just human, narratives. From this point, the text continues:

> And God understood their deeds—
> for with a perfect heart they sought him—
> *And he raised up for them a Teacher of Righteousness*
> *to guide them in the way of his heart* (CD 1.10-11).

In this passage, Boyce's and Davies' readings diverge for the first time, creating space for a number of conflicting historical readings of the text.

If we follow Boyce's reading and assume that this entire passage is original, it all fits into a single ideological claim. Everything at work in the text—the language of righteousness, the concern for finding the proper paths, and the distinction between those who 'scoff' at God and those who are eager to know his will—builds up to a single ideological purpose: the introduction of the Teacher of Righteousness. In the context of this scenario, the audience of the first edition may be quite similar to (or identical with) the audience of the second edition. They might understand these temporal details as appropriate expansions of the text (or, in fact, fail to recognize them as additions at all), viewing them as confirmations of the significance and authority of the community's great leader. Boyce suggests that, if this is the case, the temporal reference to 390-plus-20 years may have been added "to give an accurate timescale" to the history of the community, and in this case, "the very fact of its secondary nature may ironically prove its validity!"[29] A better suggestion may be that the secondary addition of these historical figures can be read as proof of a *belief*, on the part of the redactor of the original text, that these dates are valid and that they confirm the authenticity of the group and the authority of its leader.

In contrast, Davies' understanding of the text suggests a very different historical scenario. As he reconstructs it, the text's first edition serves as a generalized statement about righteousness and wickedness: God redeems those who seek him out, while rejecting those who reject him first. In its original setting, this generalized claim may have served to distinguish the members of a covenant community from those outside the group. The later redaction of the admonition, with its addition of references to the Teacher and his new communal order, re-reads existing communal values—appeals to righteousness, the search for the right path—in support of the authority of the new communal leader.[30]

A reading of the second half of this admonition, in line with the scholarly assertions of Davies and Boyce, again suggests two divergent reconstructions of textual development and two different understandings of underlying historical events. These readings continue:

> And he made known to the latter generations
> what he had done *with the last generation,*
> [with a congregation of traitors.
> *They are "those who depart from the way." That is the time about which was written: "like a wandering heifer so did Israel stray"*—]
> When there arose the Man of the Lie
> who spouted to Israel waters of falsehood.

---

[29] Boyce, 'Poetry of the *Damascus Document*,' 620.

[30] According to Davies, Knibb and Stegemann also understand the temporal references and the references to the teacher as late. Davies references Hartmut Stegemann, *Die Entstehung der Qumrangemeinde* (Bonn: privately published, 1971), 132–45; and Knibb, *The Qumran Community*, 17–18. See also Boyce, 'Poetry of the *Damascus Document*,' 623.

> *And he caused them to stray in a chaos without a way*
> *bringing low the eternal heights,*
> *and departing from the paths of righteousness,*
> *and removing the boundary [which the first ones set up] of their inheritance*
>
> *So as to apply to them the curses of his covenant,*
> *surrendering them to the avenging sword of the covenant's vengeance* (CD 1.11–17).

Davies' reading is the more minimalist of the two. He sees as original only the reference to God's rejection of the "congregation of traitors," which is described at length in the concluding lines of the admonition:

> For they searched for smooth things and chose delusions,
> and they watched for loopholes and chose the fair neck;
> And they justified the wicked and condemned the righteous,
> and they transgressed the covenant and violated the precept.
>
> And they ganged up on those of righteous soul
> and all those who walk perfectly their own soul(s) despised;
> And they persecuted them to the sword,
> and rejoiced at the people's strife.
>
> And the wrath of God was kindled against their congregation
> to lay waste all their multitude
> and their deeds from before him forever (CD 1.18–2.1).

According to Davies' reconstruction, the original text contains a blanket rejection of the 'congregation of traitors,' who engage in improper interpretations, pervert the standards of justice and righteousness, and generally inspire God to wrath against them. Like their transgressions, their punishment is generalized: both they and their deeds will be destroyed in the face of God's anger.

Davies' source-critical reconstruction of the text imagines a two-stage process, in which a generalized covenantal document is concentrated and refocused to refer to specific events and experiences. The generalized 'congregation of traitors,' of the first redaction is redefined in the secondary redaction, in order to be identified with a specific community of apostate covenanters who have followed after the Man of the Lie, and whose punishment will occur in the "last generation" (CD 1.12). This community—whose description is inserted into the middle of the admonition, rather than tacked onto the end—is guilty not only of generic wickedness (justifying the wicked, condemning the righteous, and the other transgressions of CD 1.18–2.1) but also of specific transgressions against the traditions of the covenant ("bringing low eternal heights," "removing the boundaries of the first ones," CD 1.15–16). Rather than engaging only in generalized sinfulness, they are guilty, as well, of specific attempts to alter or reconfigure the 'eternal' verities of the special covenant with God.

Boyce, in contrast, reads these final passages as almost wholly original, viewing only a few of the scriptural and temporal references as additions. Again, this allows him to view the additions to the text as slight alterations, intended to reconfirm an original message, but not to revise it in substantial ways. For Boyce, the apostasy of the Man of the Lie is original to the text, and both the apostates and the general community of wickedness outside the covenant are targets for God's ultimate wrath, even in the original edition of the text. The addition of a description of the transgressive apostates—pictured as the "wandering heifer" of Hosea 4.16—serves here (like the scriptural and temporal passages considered above) as a means of grounding the community's experiences in a scriptural/historical setting. This expansion, according to Boyce, helps the text's audience to contextualize the apostasy of their opponents; it also diminishes its threatening quality by reminding the covenanters that even before the apostasy occurred, God already had predicted its occurrence.

These source-critical readings offer two rather different accounts of how the first admonition developed, one that views the text as almost-unitary and another that views it as the product of a significant redactional process. The simpler model (following Boyce's text) suggests that this admonition was written and read in the context of a covenant community whose members had conflicts both with the world outside their community and also with a group that had broken off from within their midst. The text, in its original form, served as a response to—and a description of—that communal conflict, but it did not provide a strong enough argument in its original form. For this reason, some member(s) of its original audience emended the text, both to strengthen its authoritative claims and to establish a sense of its temporal boundaries. Both editions of the text were written in the period after a major communal conflict, and possibly in rapid succession, and both would have been the sole possession of a post-schism covenant community.[31]

Davies' interpretation of this textual development takes a rather different form, understanding the secondary redaction of the text as a response to covenantal conflict, in which a shared communal text

---

[31] Boyce, 'Poetry of the *Damascus Document*,' 628.

was rewritten by members of the Teacher's community, to highlight their own authoritative claims while downgrading the claims of their intra-covenantal opponents, the followers of the Man of the Lie. This redactional development, then, reflects an ideological re-reading of the text, and a mobilization of its shared authoritative claims in support of a new ideological message.[32]

A number of different historical scenarios might underlie the redaction of this text. These scenarios, in turn, allow for a number of different readings by its earliest audiences (in its original and its redacted versions), even for audiences who shared an interest in foregrounding notions of covenant formation and communal identity. If Boyce's historical model is correct, then the significance of the temporal details in the first admonition is brought into sharp relief. For a reader in this mode, the specific temporal details (along with the reference to the Temple and its priesthood) provide confirmatory anchors, designed to locate the text more firmly in a historical setting, in order to underscore (but not undercut) its more cosmic, atemporal claims, by providing them with more specific confirmation. The basic agenda of the text is the same at each redactional stage, but the addition of these details is necessary as a clarification of claims that might otherwise have been ambiguous. Because of their confirmatory nature, these additions may have received little notice from their covenantal audiences, who would have understood them as no more than explicit assertions of something already assumed to be true.

A very different picture arises if we interpret the text in terms of the more radical developmental model presented by Davies. This model understands the original edition of the Damascus Document as the property of a covenant community, whose intracommunal conflicts led to a schism of sorts. In response to this schism, one branch of the community re-interpreted the group's shared text to confirm their own covenantal claims while downgrading those of their former allies. From this perspective, the covenantal readers of the re-edited Damascus Document may have understood their new text as a natural expansion of the old version, a replacement for it, or even a new 'original.' More to the point, they may have understood

---

[32] In either case, it is possible to imagine the compilation of this text in a series of redactional layers, perhaps beginning with CD 2.14–6.1, as Murphy-O'Connor suggests, with other texts added to this base to provide additional historical and theological support. See Murphy-O'Connor, 'An Essene Missionary Document,' 225–29.

this new redaction as something of a 'pesher' of the original text. In the same way that a pesher on a scriptural prophecy or psalm exposes a meaning to the text that was always present within it but not necessarily visible to its original author, so the new audiences of the revised Damascus Document could read their own text as an explicit presentation of truths that were always, already, present in the text.

For a covenanter working with this latter perspective, the additions to the new redaction of the text would serve as the articulation of truths already implicit in its earlier forms. Thus, the original edition's mention of "righteousness" (CD 1.1, 1.19, 1.20) is understood as an implicit prediction of the arrival of the Teacher, who *is* righteousness, in much the same way that the Habakkuk pesher reads a reference to righteousness in the prophetic text (Hab 1.4c) as implicitly predicting the presence of the Teacher of Righteousness in the covenant community (1QpHab 1.12). The addition of temporally-specific references (the 390-plus-20-years) provides explicit temporal grounding for the first edition's implicit presentation of history. Similarly, the text's references to a wicked community—which are directed toward those outside the covenant, who fail to distinguish between righteousness and wickedness—are turned inward, to refer to the apostasy of the followers of the Man of the Lie. And the listing of generalized transgressions that originally closed the admonition is prefaced, in this later redaction, by an account of the more-specific transgressions of the apostates. Not only do these apostates fail to distinguish between the righteous and the wicked, but in fact they *transpose* those categories, "bringing low... the heights" and "removing the boundary" between these opposites (CD 1.15, 1.16). The punishment of the wicked, according to the revised text, will match their sins: those outside the covenant will receive the general punishment of God's anger, but the apostates who subvert the standards of the covenant will suffer the specific punishment of its own "vengeful sword" (CD 1.17).

A reading of this sort is remarkable for its ability to mobilize and lay sole claim to what was, at an earlier time, a shared source of communal authority. It is interesting to imagine the response of the followers of 'the Liar' to this re-interpretation of a text they may have understood as authoritative in its original form. It is possible that such apostates might have 'seen the error of their ways' and attempted a reconciliation in light of their reading of this text, but a more likely possibility is that they would have understood *themselves* as the followers of righteousness and their opponents as the deluded followers of a misguided leader. In this case, the final version of the Damascus Document may have served as proof of their former allies' corruption and thus as further confirmation for their own decision to leave the covenant.

As these readings demonstrate, a focus on the textual development of the Damascus Document provides the background for a historical discussion of the development of a covenant community, and its potential struggles over issues of authority and authenticity.[33] It is interesting to note, in this context, that most scholars who present a developmental model of this text understand its temporal references as part of the latest stratum of textual development. This source-critical assumption carries with it an important historical implication: if the text's temporal references are late, then they most likely reflect a re-interpretation of the text's original claims. This need not mean that the temporal references have no bearing on a historical discussion, and in fact, Boyce argues strongly for the *opposing* view, that the lateness of these expressions stands in support of their historicity. However it does suggest that the text's specific temporal claims may be secondary to its larger ideological agendas. From this perspective, the temporal references are best understood as ideological 'back-readings' of new historical claims onto an older text, whose authoritative status would provide support for them. Covenantal audiences would thus understand these temporal claims as simultaneously scripturally meaningful, experientially relevant, and historically important in a way that goes far beyond their mere chronological referentiality.

Beyond the first generations

The readings of the Damascus Document thus far have varied between approaching the text as a unified piece and as the product of a multi-stage redaction, but all have tended to focus, more or less, on the original author/editor(s) of the text, and on their earliest audiences. As a next step in the discussion of the historical significance

---

[33] A rather different set of questions arises when we discuss the historical significance of the text in light of its medieval transmission and use. See the discussion in chapter six, following.

of this text, it is useful to shift our attention to a somewhat different set of readings, asking how covenantal audiences at some remove from the text's earliest readers would have understood its temporal and historical claims. For audiences with no experience of the events described in the text, and for audiences with no personal ties to its author/editor(s), how would this text have made historical and communal sense?

The readings of later-generation covenanters would resemble those of the text's original author/editor(s) and original audiences in some ways. Later readers, much like their predecessors, might choose in any given reading to foreground a single point of concern—curiosity about the foundation of the community, questions about claims for its authenticity, worries about conflicts in the ranks, or interest in the impending endtimes—and understand the text in terms of its exposition of that one point. Again, such readers might mobilize whatever elements from the text supported their own appeals to power or authenticity, while backgrounding details that did not support their own claims.

In addition, however, readings by later covenanters would understand the text of the Damascus Document in terms of a more extensive and potentially more complex textual and interpretive tradition than that of readers of an earlier generation.[34] The complex tradition of the covenant community could have included an array of interpretations of the Damascus Document—either presented as authoritative statements, to be accepted as 'true,' or presented among a range of competing claims, requiring outside validation. This tradition also would have included a variety of other important texts, viewed as 'authoritative' or 'sacred' to the extent that they conveyed the will of God to the covenant community, and which could be read as part of a larger body of important texts for the covenanters. Such a tradition would include scriptural texts of course, but also the compositions of other communal texts, like the pesharim.

For a covenantal reader with an interest in understanding the history and origins of the community, one possible reading of the Damascus Document would frame its temporal claims in their larger scriptural context. We can imagine a reading of the 390-plus-20-years

---

[34] For a discussion of 'tradition' as a set of shared understandings that are dynamic and capable of change over time (and in the face of communal changes), see Edward Shils, *Tradition* (Chicago: University of Chicago Press, 1981).

in light of the prophecies of Ezekiel, noting that such a reading can be made to support any of several interpretive conclusions. Like the first generation audience(s) of this text, a later covenanter might read the 390 years as 'historical' in complicated ways: the text may be literally-true, confirmed by scripture, or true in some combination of the two ways. The second claim, that the Teacher arrived on the scene 20 years after the founding of the community, can be understood in a similar context, but also in light of whatever interpretive traditions had developed around that story within the covenant community. Given the historical assertions of the Ezekiel prophecy (which presents a 390-day punishment for Israel, followed by a 40-day punishment for Judah, Ezek 4.5–6), later covenanters might understand the 20 years of their text as a compression of the Ezekiel prophecy (so that the community's repentance is seen as having ended with the arrival of the Teacher), as a break in that period (with the community continuing to repent even after the Teacher's arrival), or possibly as a mere historical marker, a literal 20 years in the history of the community. In this latter case, our later covenanters may look to the Damascus Document's other temporal claim—that the judgment of the wicked will begin some 40 years after the death of the Teacher—for the completion of the cycle of repentance inspired by Ezekiel.

For covenanters with a concern about intracommunal conflicts and the hazards of apostasy, another text provides a very different sort of foil for a reading of the Damascus Document. The Habakkuk pesher, which scholars view as a later composition than the Damascus Document,[35] revisits the founding and early history of the covenant community and provides substantial information on the careers of the Teacher of Righteousness, the Liar (or Spouter of Lies), and a Wicked Priest (or series of wicked priests).[36] Together, these references provide an important description of the history of the covenant community, as well as a discussion of its major internal conflicts.

The Habakkuk pesher initially introduces the Liar and his followers in the context of a discussion of Habakkuk's order to "behold

---

[35] On the issues relevant to dating the composition of the Damascus Document, see Baumgarten and Schwartz, 'CD,' 6–7. On the dating of the Community Rule, see Metso, '*Sitz im Leben* of the *Community Rule*,' 308 n. 5. For the dating of the pesharim, see the discussion and bibliography in chapter two above (esp. n. 82); see also Collins, *Apocalypticism*, 65–66.

[36] 1QpHab 2.1–2, 5.11, 10.9.

the nations and see, marvel and be astonished; for I accomplish a deed in your days, but you will not believe it when told" (Hab 1.5), which is understood as a reference to the punishment of the wicked in the final generation. The wicked are categorized in this text into three separate classes: those who were unfaithful with the Liar and did not listen to the word of "the Teacher of Righteousness from the mouth of God," those who have been unfaithful toward the "new" covenant in other situations, and those who will be unfaithful in the endtimes (1QpHab 2.1–6). In each case, 'wickedness' is a matter of transgression of the covenant, which suggests that one focus of this text is intracommunal and that a primary concern is the development of a proper understanding of history and the endtimes.

The relationship of the Teacher and the Liar is a point of interest here. While the Damascus Document is less than clear on the specifics of their interactions, if any (CD 1.11–14, 20.13–15), the Habakkuk pesher asserts that the two are contemporaries of one another. When the Liar leads his community away, he does so by ignoring the word of the Teacher (1QpHab 2.1–2). Again, after a discussion of the Kittim, the text returns to a reference to the Liar that is framed in terms of his relationship with the Teacher. In this passage, the "House of Absalom" is chastised for failing to come to the aid of the Teacher, "against the Liar who flouted the law in the midst of their whole [congregation]" (1QpHab 5.11–12). In a third passage (this one surrounded by references to the Wicked Priest(s) of Israel), the Liar may be mentioned because of a reference to "building a town upon falsehood" in the text of Habakkuk itself (Hab 2.12–13). In that passage, he is described only as the creator of a congregation whose actions come to no good end and who will be punished, ultimately, by God's wrath (1QpHab 10.9–13).

The literary relationship of the Damascus Document and the Habakkuk pesher is not entirely clear. It is possible that the two texts draw their accounts of communal history from a shared (oral or written) tradition dating back to the events each text describes. That is, each may provide independent confirmation for the historical events 'behind' them, or for a belief that those events occurred, irrespective of their actual historicity. Alternatively, the Habakkuk pesher may be understood as an outgrowth of and response to the tradition surrounding the Damascus Document. In other words, the historical claims of the Damascus Document—whether accurate or not—may have served as the inspiration for the creativity of the pesher's author/editor(s), who chose to clarify and expand upon an account that was presented only tangentially in the earlier Damascus Document, but which was understood as important in a larger communally-shared interpretive and historical tradition.[37] In this sense, the 'history' provided in the Habakkuk pesher itself may be a creative rereading of the Damascus Document. It offers no historical information but merely attempts to narrate, retrospectively, an account of the community's origins, based on a shared communal tradition, but not an outside source of confirmatory evidence.

For the later covenantal readers of these two texts, the specifics of their literary relationship may have been of little interest. To the extent that they told a similar story, the texts could be interpreted as mutually confirmatory, and where one provided evidence that the other did not contain (as in the Habakkuk pesher's explicit linking of the Teacher and the Liar), the more-complete text could be understood as providing narrative explanations to clarify its less-complete relative. For readers with concerns about intracommunal conflict, both the Damascus Document and the Habakkuk pesher could be read as providing the historically-grounded language in which to articulate these fears, while also providing a response to their impact on the community. At the same time that the image of 'the community of the Liar' serves as a historical model of the community's past experiences, it also provides a language for dealing with present and future communal clashes, as well as an example of how to handle covenant members who refuse to stay within their proper bounds. In the language of these texts, anyone who leaves the community—whether in its present state or in the distant past—is, in fact, a follower after 'the Man of the Lie.' Understanding contemporary events in terms of such an inherited tradition thus would allow readers of these texts to make sense of their own experiences, and not only their community's historical claims.

If covenanters with concerns about their community's history or potential for communal schism could find diverse meanings in a reading of the Damascus Document in light of other texts, those covenanters with an eye to the endtimes would have found an even more remarkable potential for interpretation in their own assessments of this text's temporal claims. The visions of Daniel provide one such

---

[37] For an elaboration of this view, see the discussion in Brooke, 'The Messiah of Aaron,' 229.

context, as a number of scholars have noted, for readers who might attempt to understand the history of their community in terms of Daniel's vision of a 490-year period before history's anticipated end. According to this model, the 390 years before the community's foundation, plus 20 years of waiting for the Teacher, followed by the period of his leadership and another 40 years after his death, together might yield something like the 490 years of Daniel's vision, at least for the covenanter with such a picture already in mind.[38]

It is not clear that the members of the covenant community actually set out to calculate the years of the endtimes, based on a specific chronological scheme,[39] but we can imagine that, in the later generations of the community's history, they may have begun to wonder about the delay of the eschaton. In the context of such a delay, later covenanters might look back to the Damascus Document, with its varied predictions of endtime events, for proof that such a time was near, and for instructions on how to anticipate its arrival.[40]

For readers of a later generation, the text provides a number of images of the end. The second admonition asserts that the time of the wicked eventually will end, and that they will have dominion only "until their completion" (עד תומם, CD 2.9). The tone of this expression is somewhat ambiguous, and we might imagine a covenanter understanding it either neutrally, as a reference to the end of the time in which the wicked exist, or more intensively, as a reference to their "utter destruction."[41] Other passages make reference to the "judgment" of the wicked (משפט, CD 8.1), which leads to their being "visited unto destruction" (לפוקדם לכלה, CD 8.2) or to the time in which God will "lay waste to all their congregation" (להשם את כל המונם, CD 2.1). For readers foregrounding a concern for the endtimes, a certain tension can be read in the text: the end may

---

[38] See Dan 9.1–2, 24–27. This approach was first suggested by F. F. Bruce; for a recent articulation of this claim, see Vermes, *The Complete Dead Sea Scrolls*, 58.

[39] See Steudel, 'אחרית הימים,' 238–40, 245–46, for examples of endtimes calculations based on interpretations of the Damascus Document references and several different chronological systems. For discussions of ancient calculations of the end of the world, see Lester Grabbe, 'The End of the World in Early Jewish and Christian Calculations,' *RevQ* 11 (1982): 106–8; and Roger Beckwith, *Calendar and Chronology, Jewish and Christian: Biblical, Intertestamental and Patristic Studies* (New York: Brill, 1996).

[40] John Collins provides an extensive and insightful discussion of the endtimes expectations articulated in the Dead Sea Scrolls in Collins, *Apocalypticism*; see especially chapter 4, 'The Periods of History and the Expectation of the End,' 52–70.

[41] See BDB, 1070.

come with a fairly simple conclusion to the reign of wickedness, but it brings with it, too, the judgment of the wicked and the destruction of their communities.

In addition to looking back to the Damascus Document, such covenantal readers might interpret the eschatological claims of this text in light of other textual sources. The Habakkuk pesher, again, is of interest here, especially for its explicit references to the impending endtimes, and its assertions that the covenanter must wait patiently, even in the face of unexpected delay. Most of a column of text (1QpHab 7) is given over to a discussion of the prolonging of the final age and the responsibility of the members of the covenant to hold fast, until the times of the world should reach their appointed end. Together, these two texts convey a powerful message: time *will* certainly end, as God has planned from the beginning, but we must realize that God's own primordial constructions of human history may have included built-in delays in the arrival of the end. Knowing that the general tendency of human history is to disobey God's will, and to walk stubbornly in one's own chosen path (as in the third admonition), a later-generation covenanter might read these two texts together as a reminder to wait patiently and resist the urge to look for an alternate path to salvation.

As an alternative to 'standing fast'—which can, itself, be understood as a revision of earlier endtimes expectations—members of the covenant community also might attempt, in more explicit ways, to reconfigure the eschatological traditions that they have received. Given the complex textual parallels of CD 7–8 and CD 19, we might ask how these parallel accounts would be understood by later covenanters with a concern for the delay of God's judgment of Israel. Two very different readings suggest themselves, depending on how we imagine the history of this textual development.

In the earlier discussion, we suggested that these parallel accounts of messianic expectations may have been part of a complex dynamic of textual production, in which a single 'base text' of the Damascus Document was expanded in different interpretive readings with different scriptural passages, and a number of these different 'expansions' were preserved as shared traditions of a single community. In this case, later covenanters might receive these varied versions of the text, and they might understand them as diverse versions of a truthful account. In this context, the endtimes expectations of the later covenanters might include a complex eschatological perspective, in which the community and its leaders are presented in messianic terms (CD 7.14–21), even while less-positive images of a scattered or suffering community are entertained (CD 19.7–9, 11–13).

An alternative history of textual development looks to this very period—in the later generations of the ancient covenant community—for the composition of one of these two parallel accounts. It is notable that the prophetic passages of CD 19 tend to make reference to events or images that are painful in tone: the striking down of the shepherd and the scattering of the sheep (CD 19.7–9); and the groans of the suffering, who are marked by God (CD 19.11–13). In contrast, the parallel accounts of CD 7–8 refer to the "interpreter of the Torah who comes to Damascus" (דורש התורה הבא דמשק, CD 7.18–19) and to the future arrival of a "prince of all the congregation" (נשיא כל העדה, CD 7.20), who will destroy the wicked when he arrives. Scholars have noted that although a hypothetical textual development from CD 19 to CD 7–8 is unlikely, the reverse possibility—that an earlier text might point optimistically to a future messianic era, while a later text attempts to provide support in the face of disappointment—looks altogether more likely.

If, in fact, it is in this later covenantal generation that CD 19 was composed, we may have before us 'textual proof' of the covenanters' response to the delay of the endtimes. Rather than merely 'standing fast,' as the Habakkuk pesher recommends (or, by standing fast but in a proactive way) a later audience of this text may have taken on the role of author/editor(s) themselves, by producing a revised text that acknowledged the trials of the covenant community while encouraging a renewed commitment to its ideals, historical claims, and interpretations of scripture.

Reading for history

An audience-oriented reading of the temporal references in the Damascus Document sheds interesting light on how they may have been understood at different times during the early history of the text's usage. Whether we discuss the original author/editor(s) of the text or the successive heirs of their tradition, this approach reveals the potential for covenanters to understand these temporal references—the 390 years before the foundation of the group, the 20 years before the arising of the Teacher, and another 40 years after his death before the completion of the endtimes—as 'true.' However, the understanding of 'truth' that undergirds this observation is one that need not be based in literal facticity or a reflection of specific historical events. Rather, the distinctions between 'literally true,' 'scripturally confirmed,' and 'personally experienced' can be shaded in interesting ways: scriptural confirmation might 'prove' the literal truth of an experience or a statement, while personal experience might be understood in terms of the 'literal truth' found in scripture.

For the author/editor(s) of the Damascus Document, the narrative of history is complex, but its secrets and true meanings are accessible to anyone with the right covenantal knowledge. The various histories in the text—cosmic, national, sectarian—could all be understood by a given covenanter as reflections of his own—personal—history; his own history, in turn, could be read in terms of these larger narratives. From within this ideological construction of history, with its scriptural basis and its theological claims, a communal audience could understand not only all of time, but also its specific historical manifestations, as part of God's cosmic plan.

By reading the chronological details in the Damascus Document in light of the text's larger ideological constructions of history—and by understanding the potential readings of those details as fundamentally multiple, rather than unitary—we can 'make sense of' these historical claims without being forced to read them either at face value or as entirely useless for historical scholarship. In the process, we find that the historical narratives that we construct based upon the text are always contingent upon the reading strategies that we bring to it and the concerns that we foreground in those readings.

CHAPTER FIVE

READING FOR IDENTITY IN THE DAMASCUS DOCUMENT

For the covenanters who wrote and read the Damascus Document—whether in its original setting, or in periods of later redaction and interpretation—communal identity was an issue of primary concern. Distinguishing themselves from the wicked outside the community—including some apostates who may have looked deceptively similar to the current covenanters—required assigning descriptions and identities both to their own group and to the world outside it.[1] To construct those distinctions, the text goes beyond simplistic arguments (covenanters, good; everyone else, bad), employing scriptural themes and multivalent language to articulate a sense of communal identity that is at once open to new converts and also protective of the loyalty of existing members. The use of a variety of models of covenantal identity—as the true Israel, the righteous priesthood, an exilic community—opens this text to a wide range of interpretations. In this chapter, a discussion of the text's constructions of communal identity, and of the potential interpretations of those constructions of identity, contributes further to our understanding of the text's historical claims, as well as the potential uses of those claims by the text's diverse audiences.

Constructions of identity are multiple in the Damascus Document, in that the text utilizes a variety of models and also that these models can be read in a variety of ways, depending on the expectations and agendas of any given audience. One of the most evident constructions of identity in the text has been considered in previous readings: the construction of the community as a remnant of (and potentially a replacement for) the entire people of Israel. Descriptions of the community capture a sense of this claim by using some of

---

[1] For discussions of the construction of communal identity in the scrolls, see Newsom, 'Apocalyptic and Discourse'; Newsom, 'Case of the Blinking I'; Devorah Dimant, 'Men as Angels: The Self-Image of the Qumran Community,' in *Religion and Politics in the Ancient Near East* (ed. Adele Berlin; Bethesda, Md.: University Press of Maryland, 1996), 93–103; and Vermes, 'The Religious Ideas of the Community,' in *The Complete Dead Sea Scrolls*, 67–90.

the standard divisions of the Israelite nation: the community is mustered with "the priests first, the Levites second, the sons of Israel third, and the proselyte(s) fourth;"[2] their collective ordering is "by thousands, hundreds, fifties, and tens;"[3] and communal judges are selected from each branch of the people, "from the tribe of Levi and Aaron, and from Israel."[4] Similarly, the origins of the community are described in terms of both Aaron and Israel,[5] as are the community's endtimes expectations (including references to a "messiah of Aaron and Israel," משיח אהרן וישראל).[6]

In addition to presenting the community as a structural equivalent of the nation of Israel, the text goes a step further, by providing images of the covenant community as Israel's full-scale replacement. Not only does the remnant come to stand in for the whole, but the laws of the community and the covenant of the community also can be understood as the laws and covenant for 'all Israel.' According to the text, God's new covenant with the community is a "covenant with Israel forever" (CD 3.13), a claim that is repeated in the text on several occasions, and sometimes in subtle ways. A description of the entry of a new member into the community, for example, requires that the other members:

> muster him with the oath of the covenant that Moses made with Israel, the cove[na]nt to re[turn t]o the Torah of Moses with all heart [and with all] soul (יפקדוהו בשבועת הברית אשר כרת משה עם ישראל את הבר[י]ת לש[ו]ב א[ל] תורת משה בכל לב [ובכל] נפש, CD 15.8–10).

The awkward syntax of this passage allows for an overlay of two covenants upon one another. The first is the covenant at Sinai, which the people of Israel swore to uphold.[7] The second (which is intro-

---

[2] CD 14.3–4, 5–6; see also 4Q267 9 v 8, which parallels CD 14.3–4 but omits 'proselytes.' In 4Q267 9 v 10 (which parallels CD 14.5–6), proselytes are included. The 4QD passages can be found in Baumgarten, DJD XVIII, 109–10.
[3] CD 13.1–2; see Baumgarten and Schwartz, 'CD,' 53 n. 193.
[4] CD 10.5; four judges are chosen from the priests and Levites, and six from Israel.
[5] CD 1.7, 6.2–3.
[6] CD 19.10–11, 12.23–13.1, 14.19. CD 12.23 has משוח in place of משיח. CD 20.1 refers to "a messiah from Aaron and from Israel" (משיח מאהרן ומישראל). Scholars disagree on whether this latter passage is a reference to one messianic figure or two. For recent discussion, with bibliography, see Collins, *Apocalypticism*; and Brooke, 'The Messiah of Aaron,' 215–30.
[7] See, for example, Exod 19.8; 24.3, 7. For God's oath to give Israel the land, see Deut 31.21; for the fulfillment of that oath, see Josh 21.42. The covenant is renewed in Josh 24.24–25, but the people's acceptance in that passage is not called an 'oath.'

duced in a predicate clause preceded by את) is the covenant of the community, which causes people to engage in proper Torah practices.[8] This covenant of return is described in language that suggests that it is, at once, the special possession of the community described in the text and also fundamentally tied to the Sinai experience of the people of Israel. The statutes of the community, according to this passage, reflect a return to the *real* Torah, which was preserved by the righteous Israel (the community), although lost or rejected by the transgressors who no longer deserve to be called by that name.[9] This construction of the community's norms and interpretations as a 'return to Torah' (as opposed to a simple continuation of an inherited tradition) reflects the larger ideology of the text: that most of the people of Israel have gone astray, and that only those who have true knowledge of God's will can be expected to maintain God's covenant in its proper, authentic, and original form.

Although the text argues for a clear (and primordial) distinction between the righteous and the wicked, this distinction need not imply that the community's boundaries are closed. As the passage above demonstrates, it is still possible for righteous people outside the covenant to join its ranks and gain access to its true Torah (CD 4.10–11), just as it is possible for members of the community to transgress the covenant in irreparable ways and be forced to leave.[10] The potential permeability of the community's boundaries is highlighted by the multivalent significance of the word Israel. Although 'Israel' is defined in the text as the covenant community, it can be understood also as the whole nation to whom Moses' message originally was directed.[11] In claiming that the 'covenant of return' is a

---

[8] For "the covenant to return to the Torah of Moses" (הברית לשוב אל תורת משה), see also CD 15.12; 16.1–2, 4–5.

[9] This claim to an unbroken line of covenantal authority dating back to Sinai is not unique. See, by way of comparison, m. Avot 1.1–18, in which rabbinic tradition is understood in terms of a similar construction of tradition. Interestingly, the text of m. Avot 2.9–10 slightly undercuts the rabbinic assertion of a single linear connection, by introducing an alternative presentation of the later portion of the chain, beginning with Hillel and Shammai.

[10] CD 8.1–5, 18–19 (with parallels in CD 19.16–19, 32–33). See also CD 20.8–13, 25–27. Expulsion seems to be the punishment for slandering or complaining against the community. For examples of expulsion-worthy transgressions, and an account of the communal expulsion ceremony, see 4Q266 11 5–16; 4Q270 7 i 6–7, 11, 13–14; in Baumgarten, DJD XVIII, 76–78, 162–66.

[11] Similarly, 'Judah' can be a designation for the community itself (the "house of Judah," בית יהודה, CD 4.11), or a description of those outside it (since the covenanters depart from the sinfulness embodied in the "land of Judah," ארץ יהודה, CD 4.3, 6.5).

"covenant for all of Israel" (ברית לכל ישראל),[12] then, the text can be understood as directing itself exclusively toward the members of the community, but also more generally, toward anyone who will choose to join before that opportunity is closed. The text also recognizes distinctions among members of the covenant (depending on whether they are part of "the towns of Israel" or "the camps" of the community)[13] and even among some borderline apostates whose fate is not irrevocably tied to that of the wicked.

This latter category is particularly interesting for the way that it nuances the distinctions between 'insiders' and 'outsiders.' The passage in question appears at the end of the narrative portion of the Damascus Document, in a series of descriptions of judgments (upon covenantal apostates, as well as those who never joined the covenant in the first place).[14] Quoting a scriptural passage that extols God's long-standing mercy, the text makes specific mention of a group of covenanters (the "house of Peleg")[15] who "went out from the holy city . . . and returned to the way of the people in some few things" (יצאו מעיר הקדש . . . וישבו עוד אל דרך העם בדברים מעטים).[16] The text notes, favorably, that this community has continued to rely upon God "during the fixed time of Israel's trespass" (בקץ מעל ישראל, CD 20.23), while permitting some divergences in its members' actions or decisions. What appears to make these former covenanters different from ordinary apostates, in addition to their reliance on God, is that they continue to understand the sanctuary as impure (טמאו את המקדש, CD 20.23). Unlike ordinary apostates, who will be judged and rejected in the endtime accounting together with the rest of the wicked of

---

[12] CD 15.5; see also the claim that God has made "with you a covenant and with all Israel" (עמכם ברית ועם כל ישראל, CD 16.1).

[13] CD 15–16, 9.1–12.20, for "the rule for the settlement of the towns of Israel," סרך מושב ערי ישראל; CD 12.22–14.23, plus a series of 4QD passages, for "the rule for the settlers of [the] c[amps]," סרך מושב ה[ח]מ[חנו]ת. See Baumgarten and Schwartz, 'CD,' 53 n. 190–91. Relevant QD texts include 4Q266 10–11; 4Q267 9 vi; 4Q269 11 ii; and 4Q270 7 i-ii. See Baumgarten, DJD XVIII, 74–78, 110–11, 135, 162–67.

[14] CD 20.1–13, 21–34.

[15] This reference to the "house of Peleg" (בית פלג) may have a double significance. In the genealogies of Genesis, Peleg is the son of Eber (eponymous ancestor of the 'Hebrews'), and during his life "the earth was divided" (נפלגה הארץ, Gen 10.25). The designation 'house of Peleg' may serve, in consequence, as a genealogical expression or as a description of those who are descendants of a 'house of division.' See BDB, 811; Richard Hess, 'Peleg,' ABD 5.217–18.

[16] CD 20.22, 23–24; 'holy city,' here, appears to be a reference to the community, or one of its establishments, although it too may be a metaphorical reference to practices or beliefs, rather than geographical places.

Israel, these members of the "house of Peleg" will receive God's mercy: at the time of the distinction between "the righteous and the wicked" (בין צדיק ורשע),[17] they will be judged on their individual merits as righteous or wicked ("each one according to his spirit," איש לפי רוחו, CD 20.24), rather than in a collective act of judgment and punishment.

The 'house of Peleg' stands on the margins of the covenant, and it serves as a guide for explaining how those margins are defined. It is not the case, as the text makes clear, that covenant membership corresponds exactly with righteousness, or that outsider status corresponds with wickedness, although in the endtime such dualities will be made firm. Members of the covenant can be expelled, as the above discussion notes, which suggests that what appears to be righteousness can, on occasion, be revealed as masked wickedness. Similarly, there are righteous people who have not yet joined the covenant, and their righteousness is understood in the text as real and legitimate, even if it will not save them from being judged with the wicked should they fail to join the covenant before the endtimes judgment ("but with the completion of the time [of wickedness] ... one may no longer join the house of Judah," ובשלום הקץ ... אין עוד להשתפח לבית יהודה, CD 4.10–11).[18] The presence of the house of Peleg adds to the 'fuzziness' of the boundaries of the covenant, by acknowledging that a righteous person can stray from the statutes of the covenant 'in some few things' without losing the claim to righteousness.

If some diversity of practice is permissible, a primary concern in the text is to have a standard that distinguishes between acceptable diversity and unacceptable deviation. The author/editor(s) of the text are careful to state that although the members of the house of Peleg have returned to the ways of the people in 'some few things,' they continue to understand the sanctuary as defiled. This suggests that one possible distinction between 'insider' and 'outsider' status (along with the concern not to slander or speak against the community as a whole) may be the acceptance of a shared view of the sanctuary as defiled.

Such concern for the fate of the sanctuary hints at two themes that are highlighted in the text: priesthood and exile. Although the

---

[17] CD 20.20–21, following Mal 3.18.
[18] The scriptural references in this passage are discussed below. In addition, see Baumgarten and Schwartz, 'CD,' 19 n. 34.

community can be constructed as the remnant of and replacement for the people of Israel more generally, this is not the only significant construction of communal identity in the Damascus Document. On a number of occasions in the text, the community is presented as the righteous priesthood of Israel, who dwell in exile from their sanctuary and will do so until the time when it is cleansed of its impurities. This construction of identity is facilitated in the text by a selective presentation of priestly history, with particular attention to the foundations of the Israelite priesthood and the transitions from one priestly house to another. Attention to these transitions underscores a basic tension: the conflict between the notion of an eternal priesthood before God and that of a priesthood whose authority is conditional upon its righteousness and obedience. The language of transgression, exile, repentance, and return further contributes to the power of these descriptions. Teasing out the various thematic strands of this larger construction of identity—historical images of priesthood, thematic concerns for righteousness, and claims to exilic origins and experiences of exile—provides the basis for a variety of potential readings of the text, by audiences in diverse social settings, and for a variety of understandings and mobilizations of the text's construction of communal identity.

Priestly imagery in the Damascus Document

Just as the Damascus covenant community can be represented either as Israel in microcosm or as a priestly community, so can the Damascus Document's presentation of priesthood take either of two very different forms. In places where the community is presented as 'the remnant of Israel,' the priesthood appears as an important minority in the community, the leaders who provide judgment, instruction, and support for the covenantal population at large. In addition, a second model of priesthood understands the entire community, and each of its members, as part of the Israelite priesthood itself.

Where the covenant community is understood as a microcosm of Israel, the Damascus Document presents the priests of the community in a role that fits that understanding: they are a minority of the population, but they are among the community's authority figures, which also include an Examiner (מבקר) and a panel of judges. Priests receive the vows of the community's Israelites, as well as their tithes and firstfruits,[19] and they take possession of lost items (CD 9.13–15). In addition, they are responsible for the community's purity, in the sense that "the priests have the judgment" on matters such as the evaluation of skin disease, even if the Examiner must lead a less-knowledgeable priest through the steps of the evaluation process in order to complete it.[20] Priests make up a significant minority on any panel of judges (four out of ten),[21] and no quorum of ten covenanters is to be without a priest "versed in the book of Hagi" (מבונן בספר ההגי), although a qualified Levite can take his place if no qualified priest is present (CD 13.2–4). Priests also oversee the communal meeting and the communal expulsion ceremony, and they must be qualified for that responsibility, as well.[22]

The second sense of priesthood in the Damascus Document can be understood as the product of a double metaphor. The covenant community is the new Israel, and Israel itself can be viewed as a "nation of priests."[23] It follows, then, that the covenant community, too, can be imagined as a community of priests, who are heirs to a priestly covenant with God. The text underscores this possibility by citing or referring to narratives of priestly experiences from many stages of Israelite history, often blending the stories together or mapping them onto one another to reveal their shared truths. The imagery

---

[19] For vows, see CD 16.14; for tithes and firstfruits, see 4Q270 2 ii 5–9, in Baumgarten, DJD XVIII, 144–46. According to 4Q271 2 4–5, no covenanter can eat any produce before the priest has blessed it all; see Baumgarten, DJD XVIII, 173–75.

[20] CD 13.5–7; discussions of skin disease also are found in 4Q266 6 i 1–13; 4Q269 7; 4Q272 1 i, 1 ii; 4Q273 4 ii; see Baumgarten, DJD XVIII, 52–54, 129–30, 188–91, 196–97. Note that priests who have been captive among the gentiles, or who have betrayed the covenant in any of several ways, are no longer considered eligible to engage in religious service; see 4Q266 5 ii 5–13, in Baumgarten, DJD XVIII, 49–52. See below for a discussion of the possible exilic origins of the covenant community.

[21] CD 10.5. Anyone being disciplined is required to go to a priest and accept his judgment, according to 4Q270 7 i 16, in Baumgarten, DJD XVIII, 162–66.

[22] Such a priest must be between the ages of 30 and 60 and well-versed in the community's authoritative texts; see CD 14.6–8. He must have a clear speaking voice; see 4Q266 5 ii 1–4; 4Q267 5 iii; 4Q273 2, 4 i; in Baumgarten, DJD XVIII, 49–52, 102, 195–96. For the priest as the overseer of the expulsion ceremony, see 4Q266 11 8, in Baumgarten, DJD XVIII, 76–78.

[23] As in Exod 19.6, "and you shall be to me a kingdom of priests and a holy nation," or Isa 61.6, "you shall be called the priests of the Lord." Neither of these passages is mentioned explicitly in the Damascus Document, but both Exodus and Isaiah are quoted extensively in the text. See the discussion in Campbell, *The Use of Scripture*, as well as his chart of scriptural quotation, citation, and paraphrase in the text, 179–81.

of the priesthood—whether Levitical, Aaronite, or Zadokite—provides confirmation of the community's inherited relationship with God, which has been in effect since the beginning of human experience, but which has been transgressed by the wicked for nearly as long.

The earliest and most inclusive of the Israelite priesthoods referenced in the Damascus Document[24] is associated with the figure of Levi.[25] He appears in this text in the context of a discussion on Isaiah's warning that "fear and a pit and a snare" await the sinful of Israel (Isa 24.17). These three traps are explained in terms of a statement attributed to Levi, that Belial has three nets in which to trap Israel, and that these nets are particularly dangerous because he "makes them seem as if they were three types of righteousness" (ויתנם פניהם לשלושת מיני הצדק).[26] The discussion of these traps includes reference to diverse historical moments—creation (CD 4.21), the flood (CD 5.1), and the Israelite monarchy under David (CD 5.2–3)—which can be read as a compression of history or as an overlay of distinct historical moments that reflect common themes.[27] This interplay of historical periods allows for a 'back-reading' of the community's Torah onto the earliest stages of Israelite priesthood: it is not merely that the covenanters are heirs to the Levitical priesthood (although this, too, is true), but in fact that Levi himself was party to their covenant and shares in their Torah.

---

[24] The tradition of an earlier priesthood of Melchizedek, which is significant in some ancient Jewish and early Christian traditions, appears to be absent from this text. See Gen 14.17–21 for Melchizedek's blessing of Abram, and Ps 110.4 for the promise of a priesthood on the order of Melchizedek. The text of 'the Heavenly Prince Melchizedek' (11Q13) reflects a concern for this figure among the scrolls. An extensive discussion of his priesthood (understood as superior to that of Levi) appears in Heb 5.1–7.28.

[25] A scriptural basis for the focus on Levitical priestly authority comes from Gen 34, Exod 32.25–29, Num 25.6–13, and Deut 33.8–11, which may together be the basis for the presentation in Mal 2.4–7, according to Robert Kugler, *From Patriarch to Priest: The Levi-Priestly Tradition from Aramaic Levi to Testament of Levi* (Atlanta: Scholars Press, 1996), 7. Kugler addresses the development of this tradition in such extant texts as the Aramaic Levi document, Jub. 30.1–32.9, and the Testament of Levi; see esp. 1–8, for introduction and bibliography. See also James Kugel, 'Levi's Elevation to the Priesthood in Second Temple Writings,' *HTR* 86 (1993): 1–64; and Cana Werman, 'Levi and Levites in the Second Temple Period,' *DSD* 4 (1997): 211–25.

[26] CD 4.16–17. This passage is not paralleled in the extant Levi material, but Greenfield has noted that a passage from the Aramaic Levi Document may be its source. See Baumgarten and Schwartz, 'CD,' 19 n. 38; Jonas Greenfield, 'The Words of Levi Son of Jacob in Damascus Document IV, 15–19,' *RevQ* 13 (1988): 321.

[27] See chapter three for discussions of the compression of history and the overlay of similarly-themed historical accounts.

The interplay of these diverse historical moments thus contributes to the text's larger authoritative claims. At the time of Isaiah, God sends messages against the priests and laypeople who have transgressed the covenant (Isa 24.2, 5), but these messages are only fully understood by the later Damascus covenanters. We should note that the Damascus covenanters' explanations of Isaiah's prophecy (and their other exegeses and expansions of scriptural passages) are not to be taken as 'new' interpretations. Rather, they reflect the revelation of an eternal knowledge that previously had been accessible only to a select few. That is, according to the claims presented in the Damascus Document, the truths of this text were known as early as the patriarchal period, when Levi recognized the threats of Belial and his false claims to righteousness, but they were known only to a select few. Levi's understanding of righteousness is articulated in terms of a response to the prophecy of Isaiah, but his statement actually confirms (at least according to the ideology articulated in the Damascus Document) the antiquity and authority of the covenanters' own arguments with regard to unchastity, arrogance, and the defiling of the sanctuary (CD 4.17–18). In this text, Levi also serves as a source for the claim that all of human history is a period of wickedness, dominated by Belial and those who are sympathetic to, or innocent victims of, his false standards of practice and behavior.

The next significant moments in the Damascus Document's presentation of the history of the Israelite priesthood come after the Exodus, when the people of Israel receive their covenant with God, and the priesthood of Aaron is established. Scriptural sources offer a range of descriptions and explanations of the origins of this priesthood. Some are unequivocally positive, pointing to the divine authority behind the appointment of Aaron and his sons as priests,[28] and to the confirmation of that appointment in the priests' own righteous actions,[29] as well as in the failure of opponents to challenge

---

[28] Scriptural support for the authenticity of the Aaronite priesthood can be found in Num 3, where the sons of Levi are assigned tasks: the Gershonites tend to the tabernacle (Num 3.21–26); the Merarites are responsible for its frames (Num 3.33–37); and the Kohathites (including the family of Amram, father of Moses and Aaron) are responsible for the sacrificial paraphernalia (Num 3.27–32). According to this chapter, the descendants of Aaron are responsible for 'the rites within the sanctuary' (Num 3.38), while the rest of the Levites serve as their assistants; Eleazar is designated chief priest (Num 3.32).

[29] Scriptural support for the authenticity of the house of Eleazar includes the story of the zeal of Phineas, which ensures to the descendants of Eleazar "a covenant

their authority.³⁰ Other texts reject this specifically Aaronite priesthood, arguing instead for a more inclusive priestly structure, perhaps akin to the Levitical priesthood.³¹

In the Damascus Document, the interest in this period of Israelite history is underscored by the use of familiar language from Exodus, Numbers, and Deuteronomy.³² Priestly authority is associated with the Aaronites, in that the community leaders who collect tithes and judge purity are, on several occasions, labeled "sons of Aaron."³³ In addition, an explicit valorization of Aaron is presented in the text, in the fragmentary account of a clash with Jannes and Jambres, at the time of the Exodus.³⁴ This brief discussion pits Moses, Aaron, and the Prince of Lights against the forces of Belial, manifested in the two magicians. Again, a familiar set of battle-lines appears in this narrative: the righteous priesthood lines up together, in opposition to a wicked opponent aligned with Belial.

Although the priesthood of Aaron is of interest mostly in diffuse ways in the Damascus Document, the next 'moment' in the history of the Israelite priesthood receives specific and directed attention in the text. The Deuteronomistic tradition reports on a transition of priestly power at the time of the United Monarchy, when the authority of the house of Eli gives way to the authority of a Zadokite priestly line. In this transition, the "sons of Eli," who are the priests of Shiloh, are presented as "sons of Belial" (בני בליעל, 1 Sam 2.12), an expression that is usually translated in this context as 'worthless men.' Their priesthood is rejected by God early in 1 Samuel. That rejection finally reaches completion after Solomon takes the throne,

---

of peace... the covenant of a perpetual priesthood" (Num 25.12–13). Genealogies in Num 25.7 and Exod 6.16–25 further support this claim.

³⁰ For example, see the failed revolt of the Levites under Korah (Num 16.1–35) and the subsequent confirmation of Aaron's authority over the other tribes (Num 17.1–28).

³¹ The account of the Golden Calf (Ex 32) is the quintessential example of an anti-Aaronite narrative. The zeal of the "sons of Levi" in their response to this incident (Ex 32.25–29) offers support for a non-Aaronite Levitical priesthood.

³² Again, see Campbell, *The Use of Scripture*, 179.

³³ See 4Q266 5 ii 5, 8–10; 4Q266 6 i 13; 4Q270 2 ii 6; 4Q272 1 ii 2; in Baumgarten, DJD XVIII, 52–54, 144–46, 189–91.

³⁴ Named here as "Johne and his brother" (יחנה [ו] אחיהו, CD 5.18–19). These figures traditionally are identified with the Egyptian magicians who opposed Moses and Aaron at the time of the Exodus (Ex 7.11–12, 22); see Albert Pietersma, 'Jannes and Jambres,' *ABD* 3.638. The Jannes and Jambres tradition is described in Albert Pietersma and R. T. Lutz, 'Jannes and Jambres,' *OTP* 2.427–36. Pietersma and Lutz note that this textual tradition "virtually never" mentions Aaron by name, which makes his mention here additionally significant; see Pietersma and Lutz, 427.

when he confirms the authority of Zadok as priest of Israel, while simultaneously banishing Abiathar from the royal court.[35]

This priestly transition from the house of Eli to the house of Zadok, which is predicted long before it is fulfilled, is a point of particular interest in the Damascus Document. Here, again, the text includes passages in which a number of historical and covenantal moments converge. In one cryptic passage, the text states that David's marital transgressions—which would have been problematic under the covenant community's Torah[36]—were not held against him, because the content of that Torah was not known at the time he became king. The "sealed book of the Torah" (ספר התורה החתום, CD 5.2) was not opened from the death of Eleazar and Joshua (CD 5.3–4) until the time of Zadok's arising (עד עמוד צדוק, CD 5.5), which explains why Israel was so generally wicked during that whole time and also why David's actions do not conform to the covenanters' understanding of Torah. The explanation of this scriptural problem is clear: it is not that the covenanters' Torah is late (in fact, the Damascus Document demonstrates that this Torah is authentic and early), but rather that it was hidden away until the arrival of a truly righteous priest (Zadok) who was not of the 'worthless' priesthood of Eli ('the sons of Belial').[37]

---

[35] In 1 Sam 2.27–36, a man of God tells Eli that the priesthood will be removed from his sons because of their greed. After Solomon comes to power, he follows David's order to anoint Zadok as priest of the Lord, and he banishes Abiathar from that position, "thus fulfilling the word of the Lord that he had spoken concerning the house of Eli in Shiloh." See 1 Kg 1.32–40 for David's orders to Zadok, Nathan, and Benaiah; see 1 Kg 2.26–27 for the banishing of Abiathar and 1 Kg 2.35 for the appointment of Zadok.

[36] CD 4.20–21 forbids "taking two wives in their lifetimes," which is a reference to either polygyny or serial monogamy (remarriage after divorce). For bibliography on this topic, see Rabin, *Zadokite Documents*, 17; Murphy-O'Connor, 'An Essene Missionary Document,' 220; and Wacholder, *The Dawn of Qumran*, 125 and 261 n. 106.

[37] Scholars debate whether this 'Zadok' refers to the priest of David, a descendant of his, or another (real or idealized) historical figure. See the discussion and bibliography in James VanderKam, 'Zadok and the SPR HTWRH HHTWM in Dam. Doc. V, 2–5,' *RevQ* 11 (1984): 561–70. See also Wacholder, *Dawn of Qumran*, esp. 'Who is Zadok? 11QTorah and the Teacher of Righteousness,' 99–140, for the claim that this Zadok is actually the Teacher of Righteousness or master of the community; VanderKam disputes this claim. For another response to Wacholder, see Herbert Basser, 'The Rabbinic Citations in Wacholder's *The Dawn of Qumran*,' *RevQ* 11 (1984): 549–60. For the claim that Zadok should be understood only in a general sense, as 'a righteous one' (צדיק), see Preben Wernberg-Moller, 'צדק, צדיק and צדוק in the Zadokite Fragments (CDC), the Manual of Discipline (DSD) and the Habakkuk-Commentary (DSH),' *VT* 3 (1953): 315. VanderKam rejects Wernberg-Moller's argument, which requires emending the text from צדוק to צדיק; see VanderKam, 'Zadok and the SPR HTWRH HHTWM,' 570 n. 30.

The rejection of the house of Eli (in 1 Sam 2.35–36) provides a source of language for the Damascus Document's discussion of the establishment of the covenant community, as Daniel Schwartz has demonstrated.[38] Two related passages in the text allude to these verses from 1 Samuel. The first describes the covenant community as a "sure house in Israel" (בית נאמן בישראל, CD 3.19), an expression that recalls God's promise to appoint a faithful priest in place of the wicked house of Eli; "and I will build for him a sure house" (ובניתי לו בית נאמן).[39] Later in the text, a second passage asserts that only a limited amount of time remains in which new members will be permitted "to join the house of Judah" (להשתפח לבית יהודה, CD 4.11). As Schwartz notes, this expression may be a reference to the next verse in 1 Samuel, in which the fate of the sons of Eli is predicted: having been rejected by God, they will resort to begging for bread and a place of refuge within the new priesthood ("and he will say, 'attach me, pray, to one of the priestly positions,'" ואמר ספחני נא אל אחת הכהנות).[40]

In between these two possible allusions to the rejection of the sons of Eli, the Damascus Document introduces and interprets a passage from Ezekiel. This passage is grounded temporally in the period of the Exile, in which Ezekiel awaits the establishment of a new sanctuary, run by a righteous priesthood who have not transgressed God's covenant in the way that the ordinary Levitical priesthood has done. Ezekiel's idealized priesthood is made up of "the Levitical priests, the sons of Zadok" (הכהנים הלוים בני צדוק), who are described at length in his prophetic account.[41] As excerpted in the Damascus Document, however, this passage becomes a reference to the covenant community itself. A slight alteration of the passage (the addition of the conjunction 'and' (ו) on two occasions) allows for a reformulation

---

[38] Daniel Schwartz, '"To Join Oneself,"' 437. Schwartz focuses on CD 3.18b–4.12a in his discussion of priestly imagery. See also Baumgarten and Schwartz, 'CD,' 17 n. 26, 19 n. 34.

[39] 1 Sam 2.35. See, more generally, the narrative in 1 Sam 2.27–36. Although God promised Eli "that your house and the house of your father should go in and out before me forever," that promise is abrogated by their transgressive practices; see 1 Sam 2.30.

[40] 1 Sam 2.36. For exchanges of ש and ס (ספחני in 1 Sam 2.36, but להשתפח in CD 4.11), see Schwartz, '"To Join Oneself,"' 441. The possibility of translating אחת הכהנות with "one of the priesthoods" further underscores the potential for multiple views of priestly identity.

[41] Ezek 44.10–16; other descriptions of these Zadokites are found in Ezek 40.46, 43.18ff., and 48.11.

of its meaning, to refer to three groups, rather than just one.[42] As quoted in the text, Ezekiel's prophecy asserts that:

> The priests and the Levites and the sons of Zadok who kept the watch of my sanctuary when the children of Israel strayed from me, they will present to me fat and blood.[43]

According to the interpretation that follows,

> "The priests" are the turning-ones of Israel (שבי ישראל), the ones departing from the land of Judah, and ["the Levites" are] the ones accompanying them (והנלוים עמהם), and "the sons of Zadok" are the chosen ones of Israel, those called by name, who stand in the end of days.[44]

Again, as in the above examples, this discussion of priesthood plays with historical periods in significant ways. The idealized priesthood of Ezekiel is imagined in the moment and experience of exile, but that exilic moment is understood by the covenanters as a present-time—and an endtimes—experience. The covenant community as a whole is presented in this passage as the priests and Levites of the present-day Israel, and also as the "sons of Zadok" of endtime expectation.

As the Damascus Document presents the evidence, the Zadokite priesthood that replaces the house of Eli during the United Monarchy has much in common with the idealized Zadokite priesthood of Ezekiel's vision. Both Zadokite priesthoods are new, and both replace corrupt or problematic priestly houses. Both are understood as righteous and each is associated with special knowledge (the opening of the "sealed Torah," in CD 5.4–5; the "precise meaning of the Torah" that is taught to the new covenanters, in CD 4.8). Together, they carry the reader back and forth across time: from the establishment of the Israelite monarchy to the establishment of the covenant com-

---

[42] The quotation of the text also drops out a few words from the scriptural passage, although they are assumed in the interpretation that follows. With regard to the addition of the conjunctions, Rabin notes that this variant is "not in MT or, as far as I have ascertained, in any version"; see Rabin, *Zadokite Documents*, 13 n. 21.3. Six Ezekiel manuscripts (1Q9, 3Q1, 4Q73–75, 11Q4) were found at Qumran, as well as one at Masada, but none contains this passage. For an accounting of these manuscripts, with information on their publication and photographs, see Stephen A. Reed, et al., eds., *The Dead Sea Scrolls Catalogue: Documents, Photographs and Museum Inventory Numbers* (Atlanta: Scholars Press, 1994), 17, 38, 57, 161, 185. Similar notations with descriptions of some manuscripts can be found in Florentino García Martínez, 'List of the Manuscripts from Qumran,' *The Dead Sea Scrolls Translated* (New York: Brill, 1994), 467, 472, 478, 511.

[43] Ezek 44.15, as modified in CD 3.21–4.2.

[44] CD 4.2–4; following Baumgarten and Schwartz, 'CD,' 17–19.

munity, and from the period of the Exile to the anticipated arrival of the new Zadokite priesthood. Schwartz notes that if the references to a 'sure house' and the desire to 'be joined' to the covenant are, in fact, allusions to 1 Samuel, then this passage in the Damascus Document includes the juxtaposition of "the only two passages in the Hebrew Bible which refer to God's replacement of one priestly line by another."[45] The parallel righteous priesthoods share an 'outsider' status; in each case, the righteous must wait patiently to take power until the wicked reach their own end.[46]

With the Babylonian conquest of Judah (and the anticipated return from exile), we reach the final stage of the development of the priesthood, at least as far as the evidence of the Damascus Document suggests. While the accounts in Chronicles and the Ezra/Nehemiah tradition describe the experiences of exile and the post-exilic construction of the Second Temple (in which a post-exilic priesthood plays a major role), the Damascus Document appears to ignore these experiences. The text recognizes the Babylonian conquest of Judah (CD 1.6) but passes from there to the establishment of a remnant and their inheritance of the land (CD 1.7–8), with no mention of a new (or renewed) post-exilic priesthood. In addition, no mention is made in this text of the destruction and reconstruction of the Jerusalem Temple, although the issue of the purity of the sanctuary is a significant one.

In fact, the state of the sanctuary is problematic in this text. On the one hand, we find descriptions of proper sacrificial practices, especially for Sabbath offerings,[47] which suggest that the covenanters understood themselves as people who should (and did?) offer sacrifices to God. However, we also find the important conditional statement that the members of the covenant are not to engage in sacrifice, if it is improperly conducted (CD 6.14). Rather, just as God hid "his face from Israel and from his sanctuary" at the time of the Babylonian conquest (CD 1.3), so are the covenanters instructed "not to enter the sanctuary to light his altar in vain" (לבלתי בוא אל המקדש להאיר

---

[45] Schwartz, "'To Join Oneself,'" 438.
[46] Schwartz, "'To Join Oneself,'" 439–40.
[47] CD 11.17–21 includes a discussion of the Sabbath offering that assumes the covenanters bring an offering "to the altar" (למזבח) and provides instructions on the details of this practice. The presence of these practical statements with regard to offering sacrifice suggests that the ideology of 'closing the door' does not necessarily extend to a rejection of sacrificial practice. Some scholars have understood this text as permitting sacrifice in the Jerusalem Temple; for example, see Vermes, *The Complete Dead Sea Scrolls*, 82–83.

מזבחו חנם, CD 6.12). Although the standing priests may profane the sanctuary with improper sacrifices, the covenanters are the "closers of the door" (מסגירי הדלת),[48] who follow God's wishes by preventing the offering of inappropriate or second-rate sacrifices, or any sacrifices presented in an improper manner. The Damascus Document's selective presentation of priesthood and Temple—which ignores the construction of the Second Temple while understanding Israel's existing sanctuary as problematic—provides a foil for the appearance of the new priestly order, the Zadokite Levitical priests who are identified with the covenant community itself. In this way, the text supports a view of the community as a group of exiled priests, whose sanctuary has been desecrated but soon will be redeemed.

The Damascus Document's constructions of priestly identity draw upon the full range of Israelite history in the process of making important ideological claims. The origin-moments of the priestly traditions are highlighted in this text and molded together in a way that produces a narrative of eternal priesthood, in which the authority of the covenant community is maintained across temporal (and scriptural) bounds. The wisdom of Levi, the leadership of Aaron, the authority of Zadok, and the righteousness of Ezekiel's imagined priesthood, each—alone and in connection with one another—reflects a shared covenantal understanding of God's will and also of human responsibility.[49] For this text, it is a given that Levi and Zadok both had access to the true understanding of Torah, a knowledge of Torah that has been preserved in Israel only by the covenant community. In no way is this a new Torah, or even a new interpretation of it. Rather, it is the same Torah that Moses received at Sinai, which the people of Israel swore (and then failed) to uphold throughout their history, and which the members of the new covenant now pledge to uphold, with a greater sense of obedience to God's chosen path and a greater sense of covenantal righteousness.

---

[48] CD 6.12–13, following Mal 1.10; more generally, see Mal 1.1–2.9.

[49] Kugler addresses the issue of priesthood and power, exploring the potential for recognizing distinctions between a variety of ancient Jewish priesthoods ('Levites,' 'Aaronites,' 'Zadokites') and noting that distinctions between these varieties may be more complex than scholars realize. Ultimately, he argues that it may be best to recognize that "there were those who held power, and those who did not, and that the two kinds of groups legitimated their positions by telling their foundational stories in the names of the few priestly ancestors known to them from the Bible." See Kugler, *From Patriarch to Priest*, 226.

Exile, return, and the status of the righteous remnant

We have seen that the Damascus Document makes no mention of the Second Temple or the return from exile, other than a series of statements that the covenanters are to keep away from improper practices in an impure sanctuary. In fact, the text appears to ignore entirely such post-exilic priestly claims as those found in Ezra/Nehemiah and Chronicles, which offer genealogies and accounts of the return of the exiles in an attempt to confirm the authenticity of the post-exilic priesthood. In place of such claims, the text of the Damascus Document locates the authority of its priestly remnant in a very different sort of departure and return: the willingness of the covenanters to 'depart from' sin and also from sinful people and places, while 'returning to' righteousness, whose location is articulated in similar geographic terms.

In texts like Chronicles and the Ezra/Nehemiah traditions, the authenticity of the Second Temple priesthood is a point of significant concern. As a primary strategy in establishing priestly legitimacy, the texts lay out a series of genealogies, which draw linear connections between the authoritative founders of the Israelite priesthood and their post-exilic heirs among the returnees from exile. An introduction of Ezra, for example, lays out his credentials as a worthy priest of God—he is a scribe skilled in the law of Moses, and the hand of the Lord his God is upon him—but only after presenting the linear genealogical chain that connects him back directly to Zadok (in six generations) and from there to Aaron himself (in another eleven generations).[50] Other texts in this tradition underscore the importance of Aaronite and Zadokite origins by tracing the lineage from Aaron to Zadok[51] or from Zadok to the returnees from exile.[52] On

---

[50] Ezra 7.1–6; two other genealogies of Ezra are found in 1 Esdr 8.1–2 and 2 Esdr 1.1–3. For an extensive discussion of priestly genealogy, including a chart that organizes these texts and four other genealogical presentations, see J. R. Bartlett, 'Zadok and His Successors at Jerusalem,' *JTS* 19 (1968): 1–18.

[51] 1 Chron 6.35–37 provides the lineage from Aaron to Ahimaaz son of Zadok.

[52] Neh 11.10–11 and 1 Chron 9.10–11 include similar genealogies that trace lines from Ahitub, grandfather of Zadok, through Hilkiah to Jedaiah son of J(eh)oiarib, a returnee from exile. Other texts understand Zadok to be the son of Ahitub. For a discussion of the origins of Zadok and the textual problems that underlie the genealogical complexities, see George Ramsey, 'Zadok,' *ABD* 6.1034–36; Saul Olyan, 'Zadok's Origins and the Tribal Politics of David,' *JBL* 101 (1982): 177–93; Christian Hauer, Jr., 'Who was Zadok?' *JBL* 82 (1963): 89–94; and H. H. Rowley, 'Zadok and Nehushtan,' *JBL* 58 (1939): 113–41.

one occasion, the entire priestly genealogy is reproduced, undergirding the returnees' claims to authenticity with the weighty names of Zadok, Aaron, and even Levi himself.[53] In addition, the lists of priestly returnees from exile include occasional genealogies, which link the returnees to ancestors of just a few generations previous, whose pre-exilic priestly status may have provided their purported descendants with a further source of authority and legitimacy.[54]

The Damascus Document shares an interest in genealogical claims, but it articulates them in terms of a more direct focus on the covenanters themselves, and especially on their 'naming.' The covenanters are the ones who are "called by name" (קריאי שם, CD 2.11) to take on the responsibilities of the covenant and to be the recipients of the special knowledge of God's Torah.[55] From God's anointed leaders they receive his true teachings, which include an explication of the "details of their names" (פרוש שמותיהם).[56] A similar claim is made at greater length in a passage in which the text promises to tell these details:

> for their generations (לתולדותם) and the times of their standing, and the numbers of their troubles and the years of their residence and the details of their works (CD 4.5–6).

---

[53] 1 Chron 5.27–41 includes a genealogy that traces a line of descent from Levi through to Jehozadak, who went into exile, and includes two different figures called Zadok. See also 1 Esdr 5.5 for a reference to the priestly returnees as "sons of Phinehas son of Aaron."

[54] See 1 Chron 9.10–13 (return of Jedaiah, Jehoiarib, Jachin, Azariah, Adaiah, and Maasai; the last three with brief genealogies); Ezra 2.36 (return of the sons of Jediah of the house of Jeshua, and the sons of Immer, Passhur, and Harim); Ezra 10.18–22 (in which the men of these four families put away their foreign wives); Neh 7.39–42 (the same four families); Neh 11.10–14 (Jediah, Jachin, Seraiah, Adaiah, Amashsai, and Zabdiel; with several genealogies); and Neh 12.1–7, 12–21 (priests who returned with Zerubbabel and their heads of households). The texts of 1 and 2 Esdras duplicate many of these genealogies, with minor variations.

[55] The alternative orthography of CD 4.4 describes the covenanters as קריאי השם, rather than קריאי שם. The editors of the text translate both expressions as "those called by name"; see Baumgarten and Schwartz, 'CD,' 15, 19. It may be possible to read this expression with an inversion of the verbal form, to understand קריאי השם as "those who call upon God." For a discussion of this possibility (with specific reference to the Karaites), see Yoram Erder, 'The Negation of the Exile in the Messianic Doctrine of the Karaite Mourners of Zion,' *HUCA* 68 (1997): 109–40; see also the discussion of the medieval uses of the Damascus Document, in chapter six.

[56] CD 2.13; the passage reads פרוש שמו שמותיהם, but scholars understand the duplication as a scribal error. See Broshi, *Damascus Document Reconsidered*, 13 n. 11–11.

What follows is not an explicit generational listing, but rather a corrupt text,[57] which leaves us to wonder whether the original version contained a formal set of names and genealogies, like those in Ezra/Nehemiah or Chronicles, or whether the text originally provided only the most general of information about the covenanters and their experiences.[58]

In addition to showing an interest in naming and heritage, the Damascus Document contains references to geography and land-claims that contribute to an understanding of the origins of the covenant community and the place of the community among the larger (post-exilic) people of Israel. An interest in 'the land'—as an ideological theme in the text—is articulated in both historical and contemporary contexts. The earliest historical reference to the land comes in the narrative of the third admonition: among their other acts of willful disobedience before God, the people of Israel in the time after the Exodus refused to take possession of the land, even though God had offered it to them (CD 3.7). And even after the people took possession of the land, they were unworthy of it, and their sinfulness led to its desolation (CD 3.10, 5.21), which in turn resulted in the Babylonian conquest of it (CD 1.6). These historical assertions provide a backdrop to the text's presentation of communal claims: the land belongs to the covenanters by virtue of God's will, since he established them, his righteous remnant, specifically to inherit his land and prosper in it (CD 1.7).[59]

The assertion of a historical claim on the covenantal land is complicated by another trend that runs through the Damascus Document, the trend that has led scholars to call the text by this name. Although the community understands itself as the "house of Judah" (CD 4.11), this expression does not imply that the community is rooted in the *land* of Judah. Instead, as the text twice asserts, the founding members of the community are the ones "departing from the land of

---

[57] CD 4.6b picks up a new thought in mid-sentence. Ancient witnesses provide minimal information for this passage; see 4Q266 2 iii 24 (where the line is entirely reconstructed) and 4Q270 1 ii (fragment a has CD 4.2-3, fragment b has CD 4.7-8), in Baumgarten, DJD XVIII, 39-40, 141-42.
[58] Potential readings of this passage are discussed below.
[59] On the relationship of land and exile to notions of impurity and sin, see Jonathan Klawans, *Impurity and Sin in Ancient Judaism* (New York: Oxford University Press, 2000), 88-90.

Judah" (היוצאים מארץ יהודה, CD 4.3, 6.5), as part of establishing their covenant. Several related passages go further in grounding the covenant geographically, asserting that the covenanters "dwell in the land of Damascus" and that it is in Damascus that the new covenant was founded.[60] Additionally, a lengthy narrative that is grounded in scripture describes the migration of the covenant community "to the land of the north" (לארץ צפון, CD 7.14) at the time of the conflict between "Ephraim" and "Judah."[61] The community now lives in Damascus, armed with their Torah (CD 7.15) and "the books of the prophets whose words Israel despised" (CD 7.17–18). Their leader, the "interpreter of the Torah" is also with them in Damascus, and at the endtimes, this interpreter will be joined by "the prince of all the congregation" (CD 7.20), who will destroy all those among the wicked who survived the first confrontation (CD 7.21).

Beyond its use of geographic language, the text makes metaphorical use of the language of 'departure' and 'return,' which allows for an additional understanding of the identity of the covenanters. Not only are they the ones who have departed from the land of Judah. In addition, they are the ones who "depart from the way of the people,"[62] turning from sinfulness to righteousness, in their effort to follow the correct path of God's will.

In articulating the dynamics of covenant membership, this text relies on a variety of verbs of action: turning (שוב), departing (יצא), and straying (סור, תעה), among others,[63] which are presented in com-

---

[60] For the covenanters as those who "dwell in the land of Damascus," see CD 6.5; for "the new covenant in the land of Damascus," see CD 6.19, 8.21, 19.33–34; and for "the covenant and the oath which they had taken in the land of Damascus," see CD 20.12. "Damascus" appears as a quotation of Amos 5.27 in CD 7.15; an interpretation of that expression is found in CD 7.19.

[61] We may note that the presentation of this narrative, like many other accounts in the Damascus Document, is grounded in a generalized temporal frame; the departure from Judah may have happened (or may be happening) in any past or present historical moment. Other examples include CD 4.2b–4, which contains six participial forms but no finite verbs; and CD 6.1–14, where verbal ambiguity and a grounding in scripture contribute to a similar generalizing tendency.

[62] CD 8.16 (paralleled in 19.29).

[63] Other relevant verbs include 'dividing' (בדל), 'expulsion' or 'sending out' (שלח), and 'nearing' (קרב); the third example, in particular, offers complexity in its reference to both sacrifice and the physical act of nearing someone or something. The most important of these verbs is שוב, which appears in a variety of complex uses in the text. For a case-by-case discussion of the uses of this verb in the scrolls more generally, see Heinz-Josef Fabry, *Die Wurzel Sub in der Qumran-Literatur: Zur Semantic eines Grundbegriffes* (Koln-Bonn: Peter Hanstein Verlag GmbH, 1975). Fabry provides charts of usage on 309–15 and synonym/antonym charts on 318–28, as well as a semantic index on 329–33.

plex relationship to one another and to scripture. Such language provides ongoing subtext throughout the Damascus Document, beginning as early as the first admonition.[64] Covenanters who stray willfully from the chosen way (סור, CD 1.13, 2.6) or who are led astray by an opposition leader (סור, CD 1.15) can be understood in terms of Hosea's straying cattle (סור, CD 1.14, after Hos 4.16). Their relationship with God is reciprocal: in departing from God's will, or from the covenant (עזב, CD 1.3, 3.11), the wicked cause God to turn his face from them (הסתיר פניו, CD 1.3); in turn, either God or a human leader can cause the wicked to stray (תעה, CD 1.15, 2.13). History has demonstrated, too, that the people of Israel are quite capable of straying on their own initiative, even without external encouragement (תעה, CD 3.1, 4, 14; 4.1; 5.20), and although God would prefer that the people not turn away from him (חור, CD 2.16), they often do so anyway (חור, CD 3.11).[65] The weight of these passages (with their emphasis on Israel's and the lapsed covenanters' straying from God's way) is lightened only occasionally by statements that point to motion in a more positive direction. The covenanters depart from Judah (יצא, CD 4.3), and they turn away from sin (שוב, CD 2.5). They are presented, in the text's shorthand reference, as the "turning-ones," "turners," or "returners" of Israel (שבי ישראל, CD 4.2), who turn *away* (from sin, disobedience, and willfulness), at the same time that they turn *toward* (God's will, God's way, the covenant).[66]

The next portion of the Damascus Document, which presents the story of the "digging of the well," demonstrates a similar interest in departures and returns, while adding a new twist.[67] Here, again, we

---

[64] For the sake of simplicity, this discussion includes the admonitions in CD 1.1–3.16 and also the rest of CD 3–5. Davies has noticed a similar set of thematic connections underlying the three admonitions. See Davies, *Damascus Covenant*, 75–76, 79–80.

[65] For חור with the sense of 'turn,' see Qimron, *Hebrew of the Dead Sea Scrolls*, 97.

[66] Rabin reads שבי ישראל as an abbreviation of שבי פשע ישראל (Isa 59.20), translating with "they that turned (from impiety) of Israel," and noting also the possible influence of Isa 1.27. See Rabin, *Zadokite Documents*, 13 n. 2.3; see also CD 20.17, for a reference to the community as "turners from sin [among] Jacob" (שבי פשע יעקב). See Rabin, *Zadokite Documents*, 33 n. 4.4, for the observation that, "as in BH, the word is used in a good sense as well as of 'backsliders.'" An alternative reading understands שבי as 'captives,' coming from the root שבה. Davies supports a complex reading of this passage, understanding it in terms of both exile and captivity; see Davies, *Damascus Covenant*, 92–94.

[67] See CD 6.1–7.1, especially the first eight lines. This interpretation uses royal imagery ('princes,' 'nobles') to convey a model of the community that is structurally similar to the model in the Ezekiel text (with its 'priests,' 'Levites,' and 'Zadokites'). The two parallel accounts divide the community into two (or three) sections, which may be understood as chronological (reflecting earlier and later memberships) or

learn that the covenanters are the ones who depart from Judah (יצא, CD 6.5) and are called שבי ישראל (CD 6.5). Their leader, the "interpreter of the Torah," appears in fulfillment of a prophecy of Isaiah and "takes out" a tool for his work (יצא, hiph., CD 6.8). Because they seek God diligently, the covenanters are respected; the text asserts that their honor is not rejected by anyone (שוב, hoph., CD 6.6).[68] Their actions in this text are contrasted with those of wicked Israel, who followed false prophecies and consequently "turned away" from God (שוב, CD 6.1).

Significantly, the choice of language in this passage reflects a deliberate complication of semantic fields, or at minimum an absence of interest in distinguishing between them. Given the remarkable array of available verbs to designate transgression, repentance, and return (שוב, סור, יצא, etc.), it would be easy (at least in theory) for the text to maintain certain 'valences' for each of these expressions. That is, the text might use forms of שוב *only* in reference to repentance and a return to God, for example, while limiting uses of verbs like סור to descriptions of transgressions and other undesirable actions. But this strategy is not at work in the Damascus Document, and the remainder of the text, which makes even greater use of these expressions, shows a still more marked tendency to complicate their usage.

The text of CD 7–8 illustrates the continuing complexity of this terminology. At the time of judgment, God will repay the wicked their due (שוב, hiph., CD 7.9), and that time will be like nothing anyone has seen (again, in the words of Isaiah) "since the day Ephraim strayed from Judah" (מיום סור אפרים מעל יהודה, CD 7.12, quoting Isa 7.17). The wicked are called rebels because they failed to stray from the path of transgression (סור, CD 8.4), while the covenanters (שבי ישראל, CD 8.16) are judged as righteous for their willingness to stray from that path (סור, CD 8.16). Ultimately, a judgment of wickedness falls upon anyone who departs from God's way (עזב, CD 8.19). Note that in this passage the verb סור serves to designate both transgression (CD 7.12) and the righteous avoidance of it (CD 8.4, 16). This usage is further complicated by the presence of a double neg-

---

hierarchical (as divisions of a single communal group). See Fraade, 'Interpretive Authority,' 60, esp. n. 42, 44, for a discussion of this division as reflective of a chronological development.

[68] The text also connects the covenanters, who seek God (דרשוהו, CD 6.6) with their 'ruler,' the interpreter of the Torah (דורש התורה, CD 6.7).

ative construction: the wicked are punished not only for straying from proper action but because they *failed* to stray (לא סרו) from their wicked path (CD 8.4).

The text of CD 19, which provides a parallel to CD 7–8, includes all the 'turning'-language of that passage and introduces still more. The text asserts that the wicked will be repaid for their actions (CD 19.6, paralleling 7.9), while those who repent are rewarded for straying from the path of wickedness (CD 19.29, paralleling 8.16). The accusation against those who failed to stray from the path of wickedness (CD 19.17, paralleling 8.4) is strengthened in this text, with the addition of the claim that the misdeeds of the wicked reflect their failure to preserve the covenant of repentance (שוב, CD 19.16). Similarly, in chastising those who would depart from God's way (CD 19.33, paralleling 8.19), the text adds that anyone who apostasizes from the covenant, returning (שוב, CD 19.34) and straying from the well of living water (סור, CD 19.34) will be eliminated from the community until the coming messianic era.[69] A final addition, drawn from the prophecies of Zechariah, states that after the destruction of the shepherd, God will turn (שוב, hiph., CD 19.9, quoting Zech 13.7) his hand to the little ones. In all, a remarkable variety of uses of the verb שוב is noticeable here. In the span of fewer than 30 lines, the text makes five separate uses of this verb, with reference to subjects as diverse as the covenant (CD 19.16), its members (19.29), God's response to them (19.9), the wicked (19.34), and God's response to them, as well (19.6).

The text of CD 20 also emphasizes the themes of transgression, repentance, and return, again with somewhat remarkable reliance on forms of the verb שוב. The covenanters are called "turners from sin" (שבי פשע, CD 20.17), and the text makes repeated reference to the importance of their repentance from sinfulness (שוב, CD 20.5, 20). Complicating the use of this language, the text also refers several times to the transgressions of those who have turned *away* from the covenant, either wholly (שוב, CD 20.10, 14) or in part (שוב, CD 20.23). The covenanters are further adjured not to "reject" the statutes of the covenant (שוב, CD 20.32). Again, in only 25 lines, this composition

---

[69] In MS A, the admonition is cut off at the end of CD 8.21, which corresponds with CD 19.34a. The material in CD 19.34b–35 may have been paralleled in the lost material from MS A.

contains six expressions that use this root to present images of both transgression and repentance.[70]

The use of a core vocabulary grounded in the language of transgression, repentance, and return is an important element in the construction of communal identity in the Damascus Document.[71] As these texts demonstrate, 'return' can be both a geographic and an ethical experience, and it may be understood, as well, in terms of Israelite history and scriptural narratives. These images of return, together with the text's descriptions of priesthood and of the covenant community as a microcosm of Israel, contribute to the construction of an image of the community as the righteous remnant, heirs to a national covenant complete with a promise of land, community, and future survival. The ambiguities of this understanding of collective identity—and the hazards of mistaking wickedness for righteousness and thereby 'straying' in the wrong path, instead of turning to the right one—are underlined in this text by its use of multivalent imagery and loaded language. Only with proper knowledge and proper understanding can a covenanter 'stray' from wickedness and 'return' to God's chosen path. And only within the proper guidance of the covenant can the righteous hope to maintain the proper course and fulfill their proper roles as members of the surviving remnant of the true Israel.

---

[70] Several other uses of שוב in the Damascus Document are worth noting, as well. In the legal portions of CD, this root is used almost exclusively to refer to repentance (CD 15.7, 9, 12; 16.1, 4; 10.3) or the literal 'return' of an item from one person to another (CD 15.4; 4Q267 9 vi 3; 4Q270 7 i 12; 4Q271 3 2; see Baumgarten, DJD XVIII, 110–11, 162–66, 175–77); for guilt restitution, see CD 9.13. In the penal code, certain transgressions require that a covenanter leave the community, "and return no more" (4Q266 10 ii 1; 4Q267 9 vi 2, 5; 4Q270 7 i 7, 11, 13, 14; see Baumgarten, DJD XVIII, 74–75, 110–11, 162–66). Among the fragmentary Dead Sea Scrolls witnesses to the Damascus Document, this root is used in another mention of the שבי ישראל (4Q266 5 i 15; see Baumgarten, DJD XVIII, 47–49); a call to return to God (4Q266 11 5; 4Q270 7 i 19; see Baumgarten, DJD XVIII, 76–78, 162–66); a warning against returning to the sins of the fathers (4Q266 5 i 11; 4Q267 5 ii 3; see Baumgarten, DJD XVIII, 47–49, 101); and a remark on the return to dust (4Q266 1 a-b 22; see Baumgarten, DJD XVIII, 31–33).

[71] In addition to the examples discussed in this section, other uses of סור in the text include CD 16.5, 9; 11.7; 14.1. Other uses of יצא include CD 20.22, 27; 11.10, 11.

Reading for Zadokite identity

Given the multilayered and complex constructions of communal identity at work in the Damascus Document, we can imagine that readers in distinct social settings—or readers with different interpretive strategies and ideological concerns—might reach very different understandings of the actual, historical identity of the covenant community, its leadership, and its members. The close readings that make up the remainder of this chapter take into consideration a few possible interpretations of this text's construction of communal identity, noting the extent to which each reading provides insight into a real historical background 'behind' the text, or the extent to which each interpretation might contribute to a new construction of identity or a new understanding of the text itself. These readings, like those of preceding chapters, take into account possible understandings of identity in light of the text's original setting, its potential textual developments, and its interpretation by audiences in contexts at some remove from the text's original composition and interpretation. We will note, also, the extent to which readers' strategies—especially in terms of their ability to background and foreground selected themes—help to shape these readings and to delineate a range of potential interpretations of the text.

In the previous chapter we used the Damascus Document's specific temporal references (the 390-plus-20-year scenario) as the basis for a variety of readings of the text that contributed to a discussion of its historical usefulness. In this chapter, another passage from the Damascus Document provides a springboard for our larger discussion. In its revision and interpretation of a prophecy of Ezekiel, the Damascus Document states:

> "The priests and the Levites and the sons of Zadok who kept the watch of my sanctuary when the children of Israel strayed from me, they will present to me fat and blood."[72] "The priests" are the turning-ones of Israel (שבי ישראל), the ones departing from the land of Judah, and ["the Levites" are] the ones accompanying them (והנלוים עמהם), and "the sons of Zadok" are the chosen ones of Israel, those called by name, who stand in the end of days (CD 3.21–4.4).

---

[72] Ezek. 44.15; see above for a discussion of the details of this text and its quotation strategies.

This passage, with its interpretive reading of Ezekiel, hints at some of the major identity-issues at work in the text: the geographic origins of the community, the community's development over time, and especially the question of Zadokite priestly status as an aspect of covenant participation. Of interest are both the historicity of these claims and their potential for diverse interpretations and mobilizations by the audiences of the text.

It is useful to begin these readings with a few questions about the author/editor(s)' own conceptions of this text. How might they have understood the sense of the Ezekiel prophecy, and how did their own interpretation of the text fit with their historical understanding of covenantal identity? In particular, how might this earliest audience of the text have understood its reference to the community as the 'sons of Zadok,' the righteous priests of God's covenant? A number of scholars have commented on the 'Zadokite' nature of the text.[73] To what extent is that a useful historical designation?

For the text's original author/editor(s), the construction of communal identity in this passage begins not with an interpretation of Ezekiel, or even with the selective presentation of the prophetic text, but rather with the basic decision to make reference to this prophecy in the first place. In basing a description of the covenant community on this passage in Ezekiel, the original author/editor(s) of the text have chosen one of the few scriptural passages that stresses the significance of the Zadokite priestly claim, while downgrading any other Levitical priesthoods. Given this editorial background, a number of scholars have suggested a historical scenario that might explain the decision to quote this passage, arguing that the historical identity of the text's original author/editor(s) is that of a community of disaffected Zadokite priests, who are in exile from their sanctuary, and who anticipate a future in which they, God's elect, someday will regain their lost power.[74] With such a reading, the statement

---

[73] Discussion of the 'Zadokite' tendencies of this text began with its original publication by Schechter. Most recently, Schiffman, *Reclaiming*, has been a major proponent of the 'Zadokite' nature of this text, understanding the text as the product of a pious Sadducean community that rejected the assimilationist tendencies of the Temple priesthood. Baumgarten, too, has noted that the Zadokite label may be more appropriate than the name 'Damascus Document,' since "the meaning of 'Damascus,' whether geographical or symbolic, is still debated, while the Zadokite character of the document's laws and ideology is beyond question." See Joseph Baumgarten, 'The Laws of the Damascus Document in Current Research,' in Broshi, *Damascus Document Reconsidered*, 51 n. 1.

[74] See especially Geza Vermes, 'The Leadership of the Qumran Community:

that "the sons of Zadok are the chosen ones of Israel" (CD 4.3–4) is taken as a direct reference to the covenant community, one that can be taken at face value.[75] The driving force in this reading, then, is the content of the scriptural passage, rather than a specific interpretive mode in which it is expected to be understood.

Beyond this reading of the Ezekiel quotation, other interpretations also are possible. The mode of scriptural interpretation in this passage of the Damascus Document (and others like it)[76] is similar to that of Qumran pesher. Pesher interpretations tend to read a scriptural passage in terms of its hidden, but timeless, 'true' meaning, which may not have been known in the prophet's own day, or even by the prophet himself. From this vantage point, Ezekiel's reference to the 'sons of Zadok' is not necessarily significant for its face-value connection to a genealogical or historical category of legitimate priesthood. Rather, this reference is a placeholder, a metaphorical precursor to another and more important community, the community of the renewed covenant. Just as 'the righteous' in another pesher is understood as a coded reference to the Righteous Teacher,[77] so are the 'sons of Zadok' here to be understood as the coded reference to the 'chosen ones of Israel,' 'the ones called by name,' 'the ones who stand at the end of days,' or, in other words, to the covenant community, which understands itself as 'righteous,' or as 'sons of righteousness,' or even as the true 'sons of Zadok,' irrespective of genealogical or historical claims.[78] From this perspective, it is possible that the text's appeal to Zadokite status was viewed by

---

Sons of Zadok—Priests—Congregation,' in *Geschichte—Tradition—Reflexion: Festschrift für Martin Hengel zum 70. Geburtstag* (ed. Peter Schäfer; Tübingen: J. C. B. Mohr (Paul Siebeck), 1996), 375–84; and Vermes, 'The History of the Community,' in *The Complete Dead Sea Scrolls*, 49–66.

[75] This approach is also taken in Callaway, 'Qumran Origins,' 641. Callaway rightly understands the Ezekiel interpretation and the interpretation of the well (CD 6.3–10) as parallel accounts of community formation, but by privileging the scriptural text in his reading of the Ezekiel passage, he reaches the problematic conclusion that the community must be made up of actual priests and Levites. Later in the article, he clarifies this claim, recognizing the presence of "non-priestly Jews and *gerim*" in the community; see Callaway, 'Qumran Origins,' 645.

[76] Especially CD 6.3–11 (interpreting Numbers and Isaiah) and CD 7.12–21 (interpreting Numbers and Amos).

[77] 1QpHab 1.12–13, interpreting Hab 1.4c.

[78] The grammar of this passage lends itself to this latter interpretation, in that each reference can be read as an individual interpretation of a short quotation from scripture. Thus, for example, ובני צדוק הם בחירי ישראל (CD 4.3–4) is translated as something like, "and [with regard to] the sons of Zadok, they are the chosen ones of Israel."

its original author/editor(s) not as a claim to historical priestly status but simply as the appropriate language in which to frame an appeal to communal authority and legitimate power.

History and Zadokite priestly identity

In suggesting that the appeal to Zadokite status may be powerful regardless of its historical connection, it would be inappropriate to take the extreme opposite position and argue that the text's author/editor(s) and earliest audiences were absolutely *not* of priestly origin. In fact, the communal structure in which this text first was read may have taken any of several forms: the original audience(s) of this text may have been lay people, or a mixture of lay and priestly members, or they may have been an actual community of priests, with historical or genealogical claims to communal authority, as well as a sense of their own worth that was grounded in their special knowledge of Torah and their covenantal responsibilities. In other words, even if the Zadokite claims in this text are taken as metaphorical, this does not mean that these claims are not *also*, wholly or in part, references to historical realities. In fact, we can imagine an author/editorship for this text, and certainly an audience for it, whose claim to the legitimate priesthood actually was genealogical (whether Zadokite, or otherwise), as well as an audience whose priestly aspirations were moral and metaphorical, but not necessarily historical in kind.

If we picture the earliest audience of this text as a group of actual Zadokite priests, then the Ezekiel reference and the other priestly images in this text can be foregrounded in productive ways. From this perspective, the many references to priestly history and identity in the text serve a double purpose. They offer external historical support for the community's claims to authority, but they simultaneously assert the uniqueness of this *particular* Zadokite community. With their special covenantal knowledge and understanding of Torah, the members of this community are unique among the larger population; they even stand out from those other Zadokite priests who are not part of the community. For this special community, an understanding of collective identity is grounded in the priestly images of the text: from the Zadokite priesthood of Ezekiel (CD 4.3–4), to the Aaronites who are given certain authoritative roles in communal leadership,[79] and perhaps a more generalized Levitical priesthood, hinted at in the Levi quotation and the various references to a Levitical presence in the community.[80]

In a reading by members of this sort of community, the collection of diverse historical 'moments' sorts itself out into a single linear narrative, a genealogical chain that begins with Levi, continues through the major Israelite priesthoods, and culminates in the community, with no significant offshoots or challenges to this primary line along the way. References to key figures like Aaron and Zadok help to elaborate the picture of communal identity, by standing as major markers in the single line of priestly descent.[81] In this sort of reading, each of the generations of priesthood can be equated with any other. References to the 'sons of Zadok' are understood in the same terms as references to the 'sons of Aaron' or even the 'sons of Levi,' because all three are elements in the same Zadokite line, which has no extraneous offshoots or branches. Different names may be used in different contexts (the 'sons of Aaron' in discussions of communal administration and legal structures, for example) but each is a reference to the same group: the Zadokite priestly covenant community. Similarly, the text's references to righteousness (צדק) and the Teacher of Righteousness (מורה צדק) can be understood as oblique versions of the double claims to authority mentioned above: historically, the community comprises Zadokite priests of legitimate authority, but from the vantage point of the community's ideology, their authority is confirmed by their position as the righteous remnant who walk in God's chosen path.

Given a Zadokite priestly covenantal audience, we also can imagine a reading of this text that foregrounds its discussion of appropriate and inappropriate behavior. The Damascus Document makes reference to the various sins of the wicked (including sexual transgressions that

---

[79] Note the references to priests as "sons of Aaron" in 4Q266 5 ii 5, 8–10; 4Q266 6 i 13; 4Q270 2 ii 6; 4Q272 1 ii 2; see Baumgarten, DJD XVIII, 52–54, 144–46, 189–91.

[80] In addition to passages that have been noted already, see CD 10.5, 13.3–4 for references to Levites as judges and communal leaders.

[81] In this sort of reading, references to other priestly lines (including such unfavored offshoots as Ithamar and Abiathar) are eliminated from the picture. See Lev 10 for the priesthood of Ithamar; Num 4.16 and 25.6–13 for the primacy of Eleazar; and 1 Kg 2.26–27 for the dismissal of Abiathar.

desecrate the sanctuary, CD 5.6–7), as well as certain sins that the covenanters are to avoid (including greed for "the wealth of the sanctuary," הון המקדש, CD 6.16; and also for "wicked wealth, which is impure due to oaths and dedications," הון הרשעה הטמא בנדר ובחרם, CD 6.15). For a Zadokite community, the idea of avoiding transgressions against the sanctuary may have greater resonance than for people who have less investment in the state of the sanctuary, or who have had less opportunity to commit such transgressions. A reading of the Ezekiel interpretation supports such a claim. By understanding themselves as the "returners" or "repentant ones of Israel" (שבי ישראל), these priests underscore the importance of refraining from improper practices (thus, they "turn" from sin and "depart" from Judah, the land of the defiled sanctuary, CD 4.2–3), while maintaining the authority of their own priestly status, which will be validated once more, when they stand "in the end of days" (CD 4.4).

Our reading shifts dramatically if we think in terms of a covenant community made up of Aaronite priests with legitimate historical claims to the priesthood but no specific connection to the Zadokite line. In this case, the various historical 'moments' in the text no longer form a single narrative (from Levi, through Aaron and Zadok to the community) but instead might be understood as references to concentric circles of more- or less-inclusive Israelite priesthoods. The most inclusive priestly category falls under the Levitical designation (either as a Levitical priesthood, or merely a reference to the tribe of Levi as a historical point of origin), which is also understood as the oldest of the Israelite priestly lines. Nested within this circle, a more exclusive category (which is understood as having arisen in a later historical moment) is the Aaronite priesthood, which singles out some Levites for official authority, while positioning the rest as their assistants. More exclusive still (and thus located within the closed circle of the Aaronite priesthood) is the priesthood of Zadok, which limits itself to a single branch of the Aaronite family. If our community is made up of Aaronite priests who are not of the line of Zadok, they may consider themselves, at least genealogically, to be 'sons of Levi' and 'sons of Aaron,' but not 'sons of Zadok.'

In the previous readings, the covenanters' agenda was to underscore the direct linear connection from Levi, through the Zadokite priesthood, to the community, while also showing why this community is more legitimate than any other Zadokite community. This reading, in contrast, highlights a covenantal audience with a somewhat different agenda. This audience's claim is also twofold, but its perspective has shifted: a reading of the text for this audience must highlight the authority of the Aaronite priesthood, while simultaneously *downplaying* the importance of a specific Zadokite priestly status and lineage. In this light, the references to 'sons of Aaron' in the legal texts can be read with an ideological overtone: they argue for the view that any descendant of Aaron can have priestly authority in the community, and that special Zadokite status is not important. The use of 'righteousness' language takes on a similar ideological valence here. Frequent references to the righteousness of the community might serve as an additional reminder that it is more important that a priest be a צדיק than that he be one of the בני צדוק.

For a covenanter with an interest in foregrounding this sort of claim, the Ezekiel interpretation provides significant textual support. The fact that the text splits a single reference into three (so that Ezekiel's "Levitical priests, sons of Zadok" become the Damascus Document's "priests, Levites, and Zadokites") permits a reading that explodes the notion of Zadokite pre-eminence. The community of the text is divided into the 'priests and Levites,' who make up its founders, and the 'sons of Zadok,' who are its endtimes members. It is notable that although a textual variant is introduced in order to achieve this division, little attention is paid to the role of the Levites (whose identity is contextualized in the pun that they are those who 'accompany' the community's founders).[82] For this reason, it is possible to mobilize the text not so much to create three separate categories of members but more generally to remove the Zadokite monopoly on power, by introducing or presenting as central a non-Zadokite priestly leadership.[83] Such a reading might focus on the community's endtimes expectations with regard to their own status and identity. Although members of the community are simple priests today, in the endtimes all will be Zadokites, thanks to

---

[82] The Levites effectively disappear if we understand the Damascus Document's interpretation to refer to, "the penitents of Israel, the ones departing from the land of Judah, and the ones accompanying them (והנלוים עמהם)," CD 4.2–3. Kugler opposes this view, suggesting that the passage reflects the community's symbolic identification with the Levites, in that both groups are cut off from the sanctuary and look forward to a return to power. See Robert Kugler, 'The Priesthood at Qumran: The Evidence of References to Levi and the Levites,' in Parry and Ulrich, *The Provo International Conference*, 478–79.

[83] Again, note that the interpretation of the well, CD 6.2–11, refers to only two subgroups within the covenant.

their place in the covenant of righteousness. A reading of this sort might understand the text's general priestly references as mostly literal, but its references to the specific authority of the Zadokite priesthood as always metaphorical.

A third approach to contextualizing this text in its original setting is one in which its earliest audience(s) included a covenant community made up of lay people, or a mixture of lay people and priests. Members of this sort of group might understand themselves in terms of a collective identity that totally metaphorizes the notion of communal priestly status, including 'Zadokite' priestly status within that category. Understanding the Ezekiel passage in light of this assumption shifts the focus of the reading significantly. From this vantage point, 'the priests' of the community (and of the Ezekiel interpretation) are not priests by genealogy but by virtue of their "departing from the land of Judah" (CD 4.3) and it is that act of departure that establishes their standing in the community. Similarly, the Levites are not functionaries of a historical sanctuary, but simply are those who "accompany" the group's founders (הנלוים עמהם, CD 4.3) either in a later time or as junior members. An audience of this sort might include members who understand themselves as the 'sons of Zadok' of endtimes expectation, or they might expect a later generation to arise and fill that role.

For an audience of this sort, a number of other passages contribute to the mobilization of this construction of collective identity. The first admonition, with its regular reference to "righteousness" (צדק) is one such text. This admonition directs itself to "all who know righteousness" (כל יודעי צדק, CD 1.1) and directs punishment against those who fail to distinguish between righteousness and wickedness and those who fail to support the righteous against their wicked foes (CD 1.18–21). Elsewhere, the text stresses the importance of recognizing righteousness and wickedness for what they are, rather than being deceived by their complexities (CD 4.7). Similarly, the presence of the Teacher of Righteousness serves as a reminder of the centrality of this theme, embodied in the figure of an authoritative communal leader.[84] For a covenantal reader with an ideological—but not a genealogical—connection to the priesthood, these passages further support a reading of the Damascus Document that

---

[84] For "teacher of righteousness" (מורה צדק), see CD 1.11, 20.32. For "one who teaches righteousness" (יורה הצדק), in a future sense, see CD 6.11.

foregrounds the 'righteousness' of the covenanters while backgrounding the significance of genealogical claims.

Another narrative that might complicate the picture of communal identity for this sort of covenantal audience is found in the account of the founding of the community associated with the "digging of the well" (CD 6.2–11). According to this account, the founding of the community can be understood in terms of another scriptural passage: "the well was dug by the princes and excavated by the nobles of the people, with a ruler" (CD 6.3–4, quoting Num 21.18). The language of this reading is royal, rather than priestly, but its claims are strikingly familiar. The founding generations of the community (here, "the princes") are the "turning-ones of Israel" (שבי ישראל, CD 6.5). Where the Ezekiel text follows with two groups (one that accompanies the first, and one that stands at the end of days), the well-story follows with a single group ("the nobles"), that fills both roles: participants follow the statutes established by "the ruler," pledging to walk in them during "all the appointed time of wickedness" (כל הקץ הרשיע, CD 6.10), until the appearance of a righteous teacher, who will arise "in the end of days" (באחרית הימים, CD 6.11).

For an audience of lay or lay-and-priestly covenanters, the presence of royal imagery in this second passage provides a useful foil to the priestly imagery of the Ezekiel text. Both serve as reminders that the community represents the select and elect of Israel in every sense. The members of the community can be understood in terms of their place as the righteous priesthood of Israel, the true sons of Zadok, but they can be portrayed also as the princes and nobles of Israel (CD 6.2–11), or the last righteous remnant of the nation (CD 1.4–5, 7), or the spiritual elite of the nation as a whole ("men of discernment from Aaron and wise men from Israel," CD 6.2–3). In foregrounding one or more of these images, a covenantal audience can highlight the positive qualities of the community, using familiar imagery from scripture and tradition to do so. Similarly, such an audience might take advantage of the text's references to the community as a microcosm of the whole nation of Israel, seeing in the "priests, Levites, Israelites, and proselytes"[85] a reference to the covenantal group as a whole. Rather than taking any one of these themes literally, the members of such an audience might understand themselves

---

[85] For example, see CD 14.3–4, 5–6.

as the implied subjects of each one, irrespective of their own personal experiences or familial backgrounds.

In many ways, this third type of reading appears to make the best sense of the various motifs in the text: the theme of the community as Israel in microcosm, the use of 'righteousness' language, the metaphorization of the Zadokite priesthood, and the diverse references to an inclusive Israelite priesthood, extending all the way back to Levi. A further argument in support of this sort of reading is found in the way that communal authority appears to be structured in the text.[86] Various communal leadership roles are identified, among them the judges, only some of whom are priests;[87] the Examiner (מבקר), who orders community practices and whose status as priestly or lay is not specified;[88] and the priests and Levites themselves (including some specifically designated as 'sons of Aaron'), who are responsible for communal purities, tithes, and the like.[89] This diverse pool of leadership—whose authority is grounded in covenantal knowledge and individual righteousness, and not only in claims to a priestly genealogy—further reflects the complex identity of the covenant community articulated in this text. Although appeals to Zadokite status are a central element in that construction of communal identity, they are neither the primary claim, nor the one most usefully taken literally.[90]

Given that the original audience of this text may have been a community of disaffected Zadokite priests, a community of Aaronite priests with an interest in downgrading the authority of the Zadokites, or a mixed community of priests and laity, it is interesting to address, at least briefly, the potential for readings of this text that foreground its evidence for genealogies of members of the covenant community. We noted above that the Damascus Document makes reference to a genealogical listing, which promises to provide names, dates, and places associated with the membership of the community (CD 4.4–6). Although no manuscript witnesses provide evidence for an actual listing in the text, we can imagine a number of different readings

---

[86] See esp. Fraade, 'Interpretive Authority,' 47.

[87] Panels of judges are made up of four members "from the tribe of Levi and Aaron," as well as six "from Israel" in CD 10.4–8.

[88] CD 15.7–15, 9.16–22, 14.7–13.

[89] CD 13.2–4; for "sons of Aaron" in these capacities, see 4Q266 5 ii 5, 8–10; 4Q266 6 i 13; 4Q270 2 ii 6; 4Q272 1 ii 2; in Baumgarten, DJD XVIII, 52–54, 144–46, 189–91.

[90] For an extensive discussion of priestly authority in the context of the community, see Fraade, 'Interpretive Authority,' 53–54, 57.

of such a list, by covenanters whose attitude toward the importance of genealogy may have varied widely.

The original composition of such a genealogical list could have taken one of several forms. It is possible that the text contained a fixed list of names and families, perhaps comprising the founders of the community and the earliest audiences of the Damascus Document itself. In this context, the list might provide a material confirmation of the authenticity of the covenant community, in much the same way that the genealogies in Chronicles and Ezra/Nehemiah provide textual 'proof' of the authority of the post-exilic priesthood. In this case, a first generation reader might look to that listing—or hear it read aloud in a communal setting—and understand it as the foundation upon which the covenant community is built. Recognizing a series of familiar names (including his own?), and understanding those names in the context of accounts of the history of the community, would further permit such a covenanter to sustain the view that the community represents the true righteous remnant of Israel, with a fixed genealogical account to prove the point.[91] Alternatively, it is possible that the Damascus Document never included a formal list in this passage, but only contained a sort of 'blank,' to be 'filled in' on each occasion of communal reading with the appropriate details of genealogy and history. In this latter case, we might imagine a reading by a covenantal audience that foregrounds the actions of individual covenanters, who have stepped forward to claim their place among the righteous. Rather than focusing on genealogy, such a reading might pay more attention to the self-understanding of covenanters as the ones "called by name" (CD 2.11, 4.4). Given these potential readings, the Damascus Document's appeal to genealogy can be read as either historical (in the sense that one's ancestry does matter) or metaphorical (in the sense that membership in the covenant provides the most important 'genealogy' of all, descent from those who understand God's chosen path). It may also be both. Most importantly, however, it is not *necessarily* either one.

---

[91] The fact that the genealogies in Ezra/Nehemiah and Chronicles contain conflicting accounts of priestly lineage, similarly, suggests that it is the presence of a genealogy that is important, and not necessarily the specific listing that it contains. The conflicting genealogies of Jesus may work as a similar example in an early Christian context. See Matt 1.1–17, Luke 3.23–38.

Foregrounding exilic origins

In addition to readings that foreground the covenant community's priestly claims, we may also imagine readings that background this point and foreground another that is central to the construction of communal identity: the appeal to exilic origins. Here, again, the interpretation of Ezekiel in the Damascus Document hints at a number of important concerns. The founding generations of the covenant community, according to the text, are "the returners of Israel, the ones departing from the land of Judah" (שבי ישראל היוצאים מארץ יהודה, CD 4.2–3), along with "those accompanying them" (הנלוים עמהם, CD 4.3). The text notes that the community established itself and its covenant "in the land of Damascus" (בארץ דמשק). Again, it is useful to ask how a covenantal reader might interpret such exilic claims.

We have seen already that the language of 'turning,' 'straying,' 'repenting,' and 'returning' is a regular part of this text. Similarly, place-names like 'Judah' and 'Israel' have been seen to take on multiple meanings, depending on whether they are understood in reference to the community or its wicked opponents. In reading that the 'penitents of Israel' depart 'from the land of Judah,' for example, a covenanter may understand with absolute clarity that the righteous are the people 'of Israel,' while the wicked are those 'of Judah.' Other passages invert the sense of these expressions (referring, for example, to those who "join the house of Judah," CD 4.11; or to the straying of Israel, CD 3.14), allowing covenantal readers to understand them in the reverse light: righteousness is now on the side of the house of Judah, and the wicked are those who stray in Israel. Both Judah and Israel thus become terms that can be claimed by a reader of the text, who may embrace and mobilize them in ideologically-driven ways.[92]

If 'Judah' and 'Israel' are terms with flexible valences—in that they can be interpreted as positive or negative and can be made to refer to any of several communities—the references to Damascus tend to be a bit more consistent in this text. Almost all of these references understand 'Damascus' simply as a geographic place, in which

---

[92] For a discussion of 'Israel' in a similar light (as an identity that various communities—Jewish, Christian, or Samaritan—might attempt to claim), see Julio Trebolle Barrera, 'The Authoritative Functions of Scriptural Works at Qumran,' in Ulrich and VanderKam, *Community of the Renewed Covenant*, 101.

the covenanters live (CD 6.5); have established their covenant (CD 6.19, 8.21, 19.33–34); or have established the covenant and also taken their covenantal oath (CD 20.12). In addition to these fairly simple expressions, however, there is one rather unusual cluster of 'Damascus'-references. These references occur in the complex interpretation of Amos and Numbers (CD 7.14–21), whose powerful messianic imagery was discussed above.

The core of this reading is a pair of references to the prophecy of Amos. A brief mention of "the fallen booth of David" (סכת דויד הנפלת, Amos 9.11) serves as a foil to and a point of elaboration for the discussion of exile that it accompanies. A second reference draws from a passage of Amos that refers to the people's unjust and unrighteous actions (Amos 5.12–13) and God's rejection of their sacrifices because of their misdeeds (Amos 5.21–23). According to Amos, it is because of the sins of the people that God will send them into exile "beyond Damascus" (מהלאה לדמשק, Amos 5.27), along with the false gods that they have accumulated, "Kiyyun of your images, your star-god" and "Sikkut your king" (כיון צלמיכם כוכב אלהיכם and סכות מלככם; Amos 5.26). Again, however, in citing these prophetic passages, the author/editor(s) of the Damascus Document have made adjustments to the scriptural text. In the Damascus Document, the people are exiled not "beyond" Damascus (מהלאה), but from God's tent ("from my tent," מאהלי, CD 7.15) to Damascus (דמשק, CD 7.15),[93] in what may be a clarification of an unfamiliar expression (הלאה, "yonder," "beyond"),[94] or simply an opportunity to point the text in a more useful direction. Similarly, the false god "Sikkut your king" appears in the Damascus Document as the "booth of David" (סוכת דויד).

Beyond the textual changes to the scriptural passages, the interpretation of these passages appears to present a significant reconsideration of the prophecies themselves. While Amos speaks harshly of the sins of Israel, and pledges that, in recompense, "justice [will] roll down like waters, and righteousness like an ever-flowing stream" (Amos 5.24), in the Damascus Document this prophecy appears as a positive message for the community, who wait for God's final judgment with eager anticipation. Again, in the Damascus Document,

---

[93] CD 7.15; the text has מאהלי דמשק, which has been interpreted by modern scholars (especially in light of the Amos passage) as "from my tent (to) Damascus." See Baumgarten and Schwartz, 'CD,' 27 n. 72.
[94] For הלאה, see BDB, 229.

the references to Sikkut and Kiyyun are to be understood as the Torah and the books of the prophets respectively; that is, "Sikkut your king" is "the booth of the king" (סוכת המלך, CD 7.15–16), and the 'king' is the community, while 'the booth' is the Torah (CD 7.15–18). Thus, the people wait in Damascus, accompanied by their sacred books and also by the interpreter of the Torah, for the time when the final judgment will come (CD 7.17–21).

The complex scriptural references to exile in this text might lend themselves to a variety of readings, by covenanters in varied social settings. Again, the truth of these exilic claims need not lie in their historicity. A first-generation covenantal audience might include covenanters who see themselves in this text, each understanding his own experience as one of exile from God's sanctuary. For covenanters who understand themselves as inhabiting a waiting-period for their own return, the historical events behind this construction of identity still may vary significantly. We can imagine, for example, a community of first-generation covenanters whose experience of exile is entirely psychological: they may view themselves as exiles even as they walk the streets of Jerusalem; while bringing their proper sacrifices to the Temple, they may simultaneously see themselves as those who 'close the door' on a degraded sanctuary.

Alternatively, we can imagine a covenant community founded by people who actually have departed—physically, as well as spiritually—from the land and people they viewed as defiled. Such a community may be based in any of several places—Babylon, Damascus, Qumran itself—which the covenanters understand as the land of their 'waiting period.'[95] While waiting for the land to be cleansed and the sanctuary to be established, such covenanters still have in their possession the Torah and the books of the prophets, both of

---

[95] See especially the discussion and bibliography in Davies, 'The Birthplace of the Essenes,' 509–12. For a reading of 'Damascus' as a claim to Babylonian origins, see Davies, *Damascus Covenant*, 92–94; and Murphy-O'Connor, 'Essenes and their History,' 215–44. Iwry stresses the historicity of the 'migration to Damascus' but argues that the return to Judah is the more significant event for the covenanters, in Samuel Iwry, 'Was there a Migration to Damascus? The Problem of שבי ישראל,' *Eretz Israel* 9 (1969): 80–88. For a reading that takes 'Damascus' literally, see Callaway, 'Qumran Origins,' 644. A brief discussion that mentions both Babylon and Qumran in this light can be found in Vermes, *The Complete Dead Sea Scrolls*, 62–63. In a medieval context, too, the meaning of 'Damascus' would have been open to diverse readings, including Cairo or Fustat, among others. See chapter six for further discussion.

which are open to them in ways that they have not been for anyone before the time of the covenant (or for anyone in their own time who is not a part of the community).

A third possibility, and one that a number of scholars have suggested, is that the founding of the covenant occurred not among a community who had recently gone out from the corrupt land of Judah, but rather in a group who had departed from Judah at the time of its original punishment. In other words, the covenant itself may have been founded in exile, by Jews in Babylonia (or even Damascus), who understood themselves as the righteous survivors of exile, and who understood Judah as a land that still required cleansing. In this case, the covenantal readers of the Damascus Document may understand themselves as שבי ישראל in a double sense: they are 'turners' from sin, surely, but they are also the 'returnees' (שבי) to Judah, who have made their way back after a period of exile in Babylonia.[96]

There is little evidence to support one of these readings over the others, and in fact covenanters conceivably might have mobilized this text in support of any of these claims. However, we can point to one passage that suggests that the exilic-origins argument is less likely than some others. This passage, which appears in two of the ancient manuscript witnesses of the Damascus Document, in the context of a larger discussion of the qualifications for priestly service, makes the claim that:

> [anyone] of the sons of Aaron who was in captivity among the gentiles (ישבה לגואים) [...] to profane him (להללה) with their uncleanliness (בטמאתם). He may not approach the [holy] service.[97]

Although the text is fragmentary, it appears to make the claim that the experience of being in exile, or of being among gentiles in exile, may permanently disqualify a priest from communal service (and recall that 'sons of Aaron' in this text is a reference to the community's priestly functionaries, whatever other meanings it also may reflect). This sort of statement appears to stand in serious tension

---

[96] Davies argues for a reading of this expression with recognition of its double sense (as 'penitents' and 'returnees'); see Davies, *Damascus Covenant*, 92–94. Knibb, in contrast, sees little support for an exilic origin for this community and further argues that שבי should be understood consistently, in the religious sense of 'penitents' or 'converts' that is suggested in four of its six occurrences. See Knibb, 'Exile in the Damascus Document,' 99–117.

[97] 4Q266 5 ii 4–6; 4Q267 5 iii 8. See Baumgarten, DJD XVIII, 49–52, 102.

with the claim to exilic origins, since any priestly co-founders of the group would not be able to be leaders of its membership. In addition, a reading of this text at face value undercuts most of the authoritative claims made in texts like Ezra/Nehemiah or Chronicles, by identifying all of the post-exilic priestly leaders as unfit for service. As such, this also may be a simple statement against the leadership of the Jerusalem Temple.

Whatever the historical origins of the covenant—in the return of an exilic community from Babylonia, in the exodus of a group from Judea, or in an idealized departure with no bearing on real geography—the concern for 'departure' and 'return' is a dominant theme in this text. For later generations of covenanters, too, we can imagine that this terminology may have contributed to personalized and historically-grounded understandings of communal history and origins. Readings of this text in those later generations may have elicited stories about the group's original 'departures' and 'returns,' as well as more updated narratives (moral, geographical, or otherwise) of the community's experiences in 'Damascus,' 'Judah,' and 'Israel.' Although we have no explicit references to 'Damascus' in the later covenantal texts, we do find a reference in the Habakkuk pesher to the Teacher of Righteousness and "his house of exile" (1QpHab 11.5). In the next column of that text, we find references to both 'Jerusalem' and 'the cities of Judah,' which also may have been understood by later covenanters in terms of their historical, geographical, or metaphorical significance (1QpHab 12.7–9).

The Damascus Document accounts, as well, both for covenanters living in "settlements of the towns in Israel" (CD 12.19), and for those who are the "settlers of the camps" (CD 12.22–23). From covenanters in these living situations, we can imagine the development of similar traditions of 'departure' and 'return,' again understood in a variety of ways. Exile could be defined as wherever a covenanter was living, or wherever that covenanter found access to Torah, the writings of the prophets, and the special explanation that the covenant gave to these texts. Note the inversion of images here: if Damascus is exile, and the Torah and the covenant are in exile, then living in exile truly is more desirable than living in a defiled land. For the members of the covenant—in either its earlier or its later years—the return to Judah and its sanctuary could be effected (no matter where the covenanter was living in geographic terms) only as a result of the final judgment and God's cleansing of the land.

'Zadokite' status in later interpretations

In turning to an audience of covenanters at some remove from the text's original setting, we find that the complexities of priestly imagery in the text lend themselves to a continuing potential for diversity of interpretation. As our readings demonstrate, even in the unlikely case that this community was founded by actual Zadokite priests (wholly or in part), the force of the covenanters' claim to Zadokite status lies in the foregrounding of their righteous actions and special covenantal knowledge, and not only in their genealogies or historical associations. But later readings of this text, in the face of new developments in the community's makeup and governance, or in the context of other textual evidence, permit the interpretation and mobilization of Zadokite priestly imagery toward a variety of diverse ends.

The Damascus Document is not the only ancient Jewish text to make use of Zadokite priestly imagery in its constructions of community. A number of the Dead Sea Scrolls rule texts—especially the Community Rule (1QS), the Messianic Rule or Rule of the Congregation (1QSa), and the Blessings scroll (1QSb)—present another understanding of Zadokite participation in the community, which is markedly different from any we have seen thus far in our reading.[98] Rather than serving as another name for the community as a whole (or in its endtimes state), here the 'sons of Zadok' are a subgroup of the larger community, who serve as communal leaders in much the same capacity as the 'priests' or the 'sons of Aaron' in the Damascus Document. According to these texts, the covenant community functions under the joint authority of two groups: the "sons of Zadok, the priests who keep the covenant" (בני צדוק הכוהנים שומרי הברית, 1QS 5.2), and the ruling majority of the community itself (רוב אנשי היחד, 1QS 5.2–3). In a text that claims to describe the community in the "end of days," collective authority is assigned to "the judgment of the sons of Zadok, the priests, and the men of their covenant" (משפט בני צדוק הכוהנים ואנושי בריתם, 1QSa 1.2), who are described as having "turned" or "strayed" (סרו) from the path

---

[98] References to 'sons of Zadok' include 1QS 5.1–3, 8–10; 1QSa 1.1–3, 23–25; 2.2–3; 1QSb 3.22–25. These passages have contributed significantly to the scholarly view that "the founders of the sect who also determined its overall image were the priestly descendants of Zadok," for which, see Jacob Liver, 'The Sons of Zadok the Priests in the Dead Sea Sect,' *RevQ* 6 (1967): 30.

of the people (1QSa 1.2–3). Zadokite leaders serve as officiants at group convocations or assemblies (1QSa 1.24, 2.3), and they are praised as "the priests whom God has chosen to strengthen (לחזק) his covenant" (1 QSb 3.22–23). They are expected to instruct the people and to preserve God's statutes, walking always in his chosen path (1QSb 3.23–25).

Although this constellation of texts (1QS, 1QSa, 1QSb) imagines a role for the Zadokite priesthood that is markedly different from the authority-structure imagined in the Damascus Document,[99] the presentations of authority in these texts share a significant commonality of language and imagery. Both clusters of texts make use of the language of 'turning' (סור) and 'strengthening' (חזק), and both demonstrate a concern for a 'return' (שוב) to the Torah of Moses, which must be understood properly by the covenanter. In addition, each contains a description of its community's induction ceremony, in which new members take the oath of the covenant. According to the Damascus Document, new covenanters are required to take an oath:

> to return to the Torah of Moses, with all heart and with all soul, to that which is found to be done (אל הנמצא לעשות) during the entire fixed time of evil (בכ[ו]ל ק[ץ] הרש[ע]).[100]

Another Damascus Document passage further asserts that the new member should "return to the Torah of Moses, for in it everything is specified" (הכל מדוקדק, CD 16.2). In contrast, the oath ceremony in the Community Rule requires that each new member pledge:

> *to return to the Torah of Moses* in all that he commanded (בכול אשר צוה), *with all heart and with all soul*, according to all that was revealed of it (בכול הנגלה ממנו) to the sons of Zadok the priests, keepers of the covenant and seekers of his will, and to the multitude of the men of their covenant (לרוב אנשי בריתם), who devote themselves together (יחד) to his truth and to walking in his will (1QS 5.8–10).

The first few statements in these two passages match one another rather closely (note the italicized portion in the second quotation): both use the common reference to returning or repentance (שוב),

---

[99] In presenting 1QS, 1QSa, and 1QSb as a single unit, I mean to distinguish them from a different textual tradition preserved in 4QS MSS B and D, discussed below. The three 'cave one' texts were copied onto a single scroll and may reflect a single ideological tradition in the larger development of the Community Rule. See Metso, *Textual Development of the Community Rule*.

[100] CD 15.9–10. See CD 16.1–2, 4–5, for two references to "returning to the Torah of Moses," both of which imply a covenantal oath.

and both frame that repentance in terms of a Deuteronomic claim of complete commitment ("with all heart and with all soul," בכל לב ובכל נפש); equally, both express a concern for Torah understood specifically in terms of the community's special knowledge (which may be "found," נמצא, or "revealed" נגלה).

Moving beyond these commonalities, however, we see in the Community Rule a striking description of collective identity that is not present in the Damascus Document passage. We have noted that the Damascus Document's presentation of governance structure is not delineated in elaborate or rigid terms. It includes, at most: a panel of judges, watching over the "community" (עדה);[101] an Examiner (מבקר), who is a primary figure of authority; and the priests and Levites, who handle specific issues, like purities and tithing. In contrast, the Community Rule's presentation of the new-member-induction ceremony introduces several new administrative categories: the leadership of the 'sons of Zadok the priests' and the 'multitude of the men of their covenant.' The Zadokite priests are only a subgroup of the community, but the covenant is 'theirs,' and the other members are presented as party to this Zadokite-driven covenant. The members of the community present themselves "together" (יחד), but also "as a community" (יחד), which further underscores the two-part structure of the group: it is a community (יחד), overseen by a Zadokite minority (הכהנים בני צדוק) who are its primary authorities and the keepers of its covenant.[102] These authoritative structures too are introduced in the Community Rule and its related texts with language that resembles that found in the Damascus Document.[103] The Zadokites are identified as "keepers of the covenant" and "seekers of God's will,"[104] while the "multitude" (רוב) of covenanters share familiar concerns for "truth" and "God's will."[105]

---

[101] CD 10.4, 8. In this use of עדה, CD shares common terminology with 1QSa; see the next note. Also see CD 15.13–14 for the "multitude of the camp" (רוב המחנה).

[102] Note that 1QSa uses both עדה and יחד to designate the covenantal group. For עדה, see 1QSa 1.1, 6, 9, 12, 13, 16, 17, 19, 20, 23, 24, 25, 28; 2.5, 7, 8, 10, 12, 16. For יחד, see 1.1, 26, 27; 2.2, 11, 17, 18. Both terms are used together in 1QSa 2.21.

[103] For another similarity, see 1QSa 1.7, which has a "book of Hagi" (ספר ההגי); compare with CD 10.6 (ספר ההגו); and CD 13.2, 14.8 (ספר ההגי). See Baumgarten and Schwartz, 'CD,' 45 n. 153.

[104] For keeping God's covenant, see CD 20.17; for God as a keeper of the covenant, see CD 19.1; for keeping God's commandments, see CD 2.18, 21, 4.1; for "seekers," see especially the well interpretation, CD 6.2–11.

[105] For God's will, see the third admonition (CD 2.14–3.12); for God's truth or true ways, see CD 2.13, 3.15, 20.31.

How might a covenanter read these two sets of texts in light of one another? We can imagine a variety of situations in which a single community would have had access to, or knowledge of, both of these textual traditions. The exact relationship of these texts is a matter of scholarly debate,[106] but it is likely that they reflect the existence of similar, and possibly interrelated, communities whose social and religious structures changed over the course of their development, and whose communal texts were altered over time in a complex relationship with those changes. We can imagine a number of situations in which a covenanter would accept the ideologies and social structures articulated in one of these texts, understanding it as historically and 'covenantally' true. The assumptions of that text would then color the covenanter's reading of any other special or sacred texts, including scripture, other covenant documents, and even other editions of the covenanter's accepted rule document.

A variety of reading scenarios might be imagined. One involves an audience that takes the cave one edition of the Community Rule as their primary covenantal authority. This sort of audience might understand the Zadokite priesthood as an actual social grouping in their community and might expect those priests to take an active role in communal leadership, including positions as judges, 'examiners,' and overseers of public ceremonies. Additionally, they might understand the covenant as the legitimate possession of the Zadokites, seeing their own position in the group as a secondary one (except, of course, for those who are Zadokites themselves).

For a covenanter with this set of assumptions in mind, the text of the Damascus Document is going to take on a very different significance than it did in the first-generation readings discussed above. First, although the various references to the Israelite priesthood will be understood again as part of a single, unbroken historical narrative, that narrative will not be understood in this case as the history of the entire community. Instead, it will stand as support for the authoritative leadership of the community's Zadokite priests, who are the only legitimate priests of Israel, and whose claims

---

[106] For a discussion of the classical Essene hypothesis and its distinctions between a community associated with the Community Rule and one associated with the Damascus Document, see chapter one. Further discussion of textual similarities, overlaps, and potential conflicts can be found in Geza Vermes, 'The Community' and 'Appendix: The Essenes and the Qumran Community,' in *The Complete Dead Sea Scrolls*, 26–45, 46–48.

stretch back to Aaron, and to Levi before him. Theirs is the covenantal claim of knowledge, righteousness, and obedience to God, but it is also an explicitly historical claim to authoritative status. In this light, each of the text's references to priests—including descriptions of the 'sons of Aaron,' who conduct the community's public rituals—can be interpreted as references to the 'sons of Zadok' who are the leaders of the community. In turn, this interpretation allows the covenanter to view the texts' other priestly references (to priesthoods of the past, or priestly functions in the present or future) as references to this same Zadokite authority.[107]

A covenanter with an interest in promoting or confirming a Zadokite minority leadership structure in the community can certainly read the Damascus Document in support of that claim. The text, after all, predicts a specific series of developments in the community's authority structure: the group will be founded by a mixed population of (real or metaphorical) 'priests and Levites,' who are the ones who turn away from sin in Israel; then, in its endtimes formation (identical with the covenanter's present day) its leadership will be made up of righteous priests, who are 'sons of Zadok' both historically and morally. In this sort of reading, the authority structure of the cave one rule texts is read back onto the historical claims of the Damascus Document, so as to confirm the predestined nature of a shift in authority from non-Zadokite to Zadokite leadership.

Alternatively, such a covenantal reader might mobilize these texts to argue that the Zadokite leadership of the community is fundamental to its makeup and dates from its earliest moments. To support this sort of reading, our covenantal audience might focus on the Damascus Document's description of communal order, taking the text's reference to the 'priests and Levites' of the founding generation as a reference to a founding Zadokite priestly leadership (perhaps accompanied by a community of non-Zadokite followers). In this case, the second half of the passage, with its mention of the community in its endtimes state can even be read as an oblique promise to the non-Zadokite covenanters: in the end of days, they too will be understood as 'sons of Zadok,' on par with their historical Zadokite leadership. Although the real sons of Zadok are the

---

[107] For other mentions of the authority of the "sons of Aaron" (בני אהרון), which could be understood by readers as oblique references to the "sons of Zadok," see 1QS 5.20–21, 9.7; 1QSa 1.15–16, 23 (possibly); 2.13.

leaders of the community, in the endtimes every covenant member can hope to arise to such standing.

In light of either of these readings (but especially the second), the Damascus Document can be mobilized in support of the administrative authority of a group of actual Zadokite priests—or people who could make a claim to being 'actual Zadokite priests'—in a bid for control of the covenant community. In support of their claim, many elements in the Damascus Document can be read as a prediction of their presence and can be made to undergird their authority. The text's accounts of priestly history serve as a Zadokite subgroup's own narrative of development; the text's presentation of the community as a nation of priests suggests that they, the proper head priests, are its proper heads; and the interpretation of Ezekiel explicitly anticipates their arrival, as the ones who arise and "stand at the end of days" (העמדים באחרית הימים, CD 4.4). For audiences who assume and foreground the authoritative structures presented in the cave one rule texts, a reading of the Damascus Document provides unassailable support for the authenticity—and primordial origins—of such claims.

Of course, we can also argue that the reverse is true. If we imagine a covenanter whose primary sense of covenant is founded in the views articulated in the Damascus Document, then that covenanter will have a very different response to the authoritative claims of the cave one rule texts. These texts, after all, assign communal power specifically to the 'sons of Zadok,' and require other covenanters to follow the lead of those priests. But according to the Damascus Document, as our hypothetical covenanter well knows, *all* members of the covenant in the 'latter days' are 'sons of Zadok.' That is, although these other rule texts want to limit the leadership of the community to a small subpopulation, the Ezekiel interpretation in the Damascus Document makes room for the view that Zadokite status is available to all covenanters. Such a view, if it were argued among covenanters with an interest in laying claims to communal leadership, might seriously undercut a Zadokite minority leadership's claims to primordial and eternal authority in the community.[108] We can thus imagine a situation in which covenanters might engage in 'dueling readings' of these texts, mobilizing each in support of their own authoritative claims.

---

[108] For a recent discussion of this issue, see Albert Baumgarten, 'The Zadokite Priests at Qumran: A Reconsideration,' *DSD* 4 (1997): 137–56.

Given the potential for contradictory mobilizations of the authority-claims in these texts, it is interesting to note that the Zadokite-centered authority structure described in the cave one texts may, itself, be a secondary development of the covenant community associated with the Community Rule. Evidence from several of the cave four manuscripts of the Community Rule suggests, first, that this text underwent a complex redactional history and that multiple versions of the text may have existed throughout its lifetime, and second, that the authoritative role of the sons of Zadok may be part of the later redaction of the text and may be reflective of later communal developments.[109] In two of these texts, which were copied sometime later than 1QS but may include earlier contents, we find no reference to the claims to Zadokite authority that are articulated in the cave one manuscripts.[110] Instead of the reference to leadership by the sons of Zadok (בני צדוק) and the multitude of the men of the community (רוב אנשי היחד), these texts understand authority to fall simply with the decision of "the many" (הרבים).[111] The specific communal development that underlies this textual difference has not been established, but at minimum it appears that a literal reading of the historical claims of the cave one texts (which view the Zadokite priesthood as founders of the covenant community) is problematic and must be re-evaluated.[112]

---

[109] See Metso, *Textual Development of the Community Rule*; see also Metso, '*Sitz im Leben* of the *Community Rule*,' 306–15. The latter article is a particularly useful discussion of the potential communal authority of a text that exists in multiple recensions; see especially her discussion of oral recitation of communal texts, 313. See also Geza Vermes, 'Preliminary Remarks on Unpublished Fragments of the Community Rule from Qumran Cave 4,' *JJS* 62 (1991): 250–55.

[110] 4QS MSS B and D have been dated paleographically to the period c. 30 to 1 BCE, while 1QS is dated paleographically to c. 100 to 75 BCE. For the cave four texts, see Frank Moore Cross, 'Appendix: Paleographic Dates of the Manuscripts,' in Charlesworth, *Rule of the Community*, 57. For the paleographic dating of 1QS, see Elisha Qimron and James Charlesworth, 'Rule of the Community,' in Charlesworth, *Rule of the Community*, 2. On the dating of the content of these manuscripts, including their use of language and special communal terminology, see Baumgarten, 'The Zadokite Priests,' 138–39. Recent radiocarbon dating tests have returned mixed dates for these manuscripts, including a range from the second century BCE to the first century CE for 1QS (164–144 BCE or 116 BCE–50 CE); a second or third century CE (!) date for 4QS MS D (133–237 CE); and a first century BCE to first century CE date for a second sample of that manuscript (36 BCE–81 CE). For a discussion of these tests, with an explanation of the potential for contamination of material samples, see Doudna, 'Dating the Scrolls,' in Flint and VanderKam, *Dead Sea Scrolls After Fifty Years*.

[111] Parallels to 1QS 5.1–3 are found in 4QS MS B 5 1–3; 4QS MS D 1 i 1–3; see Qimron and Charlesworth, 1994, 60–63, 72–73.

[112] For discussions that take this perspective, see Baumgarten, 'The Zadokite

In light of these readings of the Damascus Document and the Community Rule, we may ask, as well, how later covenanters would have understood the genealogical claims articulated in the Damascus Document. Returning to the list of names, dates, and places, which the text claims to provide (CD 4–6), we can imagine a number of interpretations (or revisions!) of this textual material. In particular, if the Damascus Document did contain a genealogical listing in its earliest transcriptions, it is possible that at some point in the lifetime of the text, that listing was dropped. Schwartz notes that there are a number of reasons why such a list might be removed from the text by one of its later scribes: its dating of the endtimes may have passed, leading a scribe to remove a failed prophecy from the official record, or it may have become an inconvenience, which a scribe dropped simply because it was too long to copy.[113]

In addition to these reasons, we might suggest another: if an original genealogical listing in the text included, by name, founders of the community who were *not* of a Zadokite lineage, a later scribe may have dropped these names—and, in fact, the whole list—as contradictory to the larger claim of an eternal Zadokite leadership. Such a redactional move need not be understood as explicitly ideological in its motivation (although it may certainly be that, as well). For a scribe who assumes that founders of the covenant are Zadokite, the presence of evidence to the contrary may be read as little more than an error in the text. In this context, the decision to remove the list of names may reflect an effort to produce a text that is clear of factual errors (including the 'factual error' that the community was founded by non-Zadokite covenanters).

It is possible, too, as we suggested above, that the original version of the Damascus Document did not contain a fixed list of names and events, but only an indication of when those details were to be recited in the explication of the text. From this perspective, the later covenantal audience of this text might mobilize it toward diverse ends. The pro-Zadokite-authority reader might fill in the text with material that highlights the founding covenanters' priestly claims and priestly lineage. An anti-Zadokite faction, in contrast, might fore-

---

Priests,' 148–56; and Davies, *Behind the Essenes*. For a revision of the classical Zadokite theory in light of the new evidence, see Vermes, 'The Leadership of the Qumran Community,' 375–84; Vermes, *The Complete Dead Sea Scrolls*, 49–66.

[113] See Baumgarten and Schwartz, 'CD,' 19 n. 32.

ground whatever evidence contradicts such claims. In either case, the reader has the option of foregrounding whatever evidence, imagery, or scriptural texts support a specific claim to authority.

Reading for identity

As these audience-oriented readings demonstrate, the multiple constructions of identity in the Damascus Document can be mobilized to reflect any of a wide variety of assumptions or ideological claims. Ancient covenanters could have used this text in support of the legitimate claims of a historical Zadokite priesthood but equally as well in a rejection of those claims. Similarly, the claims to exilic origin present themselves as either historical or metaphorical, depending on a reader's interests and agendas. What is clear from this text is that the members of the covenant community understood themselves as the true 'penitents of Israel,' the righteous priests of God, who would remain in exile until the time of judgment, which was very shortly at hand.

As we found in our other audience-oriented readings, the multiple constructions of identity in this text play off one another—and off their scriptural referents, sources, and competitors—in complex and dynamic ways. To construct a history from these presentations of identity requires understanding them in terms of the larger ideological claims of the text, and not as isolated references to historical realities. In this light, a reading of the Damascus Document tells us more about what the covenant community thought of itself, or could potentially understand itself to be, than it tells us, in any objective way, about 'what really happened' in the history of this community.

CHAPTER SIX

CONCLUSIONS AND CHALLENGES

As these readings demonstrate, the construction of textual meaning is a complex and dynamic process; while 'the meaning' of a text may begin with 'an original authorial intention,' this is truly only a beginning. The ongoing interpretations and reinterpretations of a text, in a variety of contexts and by a variety of different audiences, can contribute to the construction of meanings that may be far removed from a text's original setting or its author's original goals. For a historian—and especially for a historian whose sources are as complex and allusive as the Dead Sea Scrolls—recognizing the complexities of textual meaning-construction leads to a reconsideration of some of the basic scholarly approaches to historiography.

At a most fundamental level, the insights of a literary critical approach to historiography serve as a reminder that texts are not neutral or objective in the way that they convey historical events or communal descriptions. Rather, even in their original contexts—and in terms of the meanings assigned to them by their original author(s) or editor(s)—texts like the Damascus Document reflect complex, and sometimes multivalent, constructions of history and communal identity. In the Damascus Document, the selective use of scripture, as well as a variety of other textual strategies (including the use of keywords, repetition, and the overlay of multiple narratives) contributes to the construction of historical images that are richly laden with narrative potential. For this reason, modern scholarly readings—even those that focus on the 'original meaning' of the text—must take into account the larger themes, agendas, or ideological constructions at work in it.

In arguing for readings that take ideology into account, this approach calls into question the usefulness of both atomistic and harmonistic readings. 'Atomistic' readings, those that pluck individual historical details out of a text and interpret them in isolation, are problematic because they do not take into account the constraints on interpretation provided by context (since the 'simple meaning' of a given detail may, or may not, be an appropriate interpretation of that detail in its larger context within a specific text). 'Harmonistic' readings, which begin with atomistic readings of individual texts and then combine those readings to create master narratives that explain the historical events behind the various textual witnesses, are problematic not only because they take details out of context but because they go one step further, erasing the potential differences between texts and failing to recognize the potential for development over time or diversity across a textual landscape.

The argument that historical details must be understood in their larger literary context is only a first step for the literary-critical approach outlined in this project. A more significant result of the assertion that textual meaning occurs in the process of complex reading practices is the recognition that textual meaning may change over time. This change may be mechanical and material—as when a scribe or editor reworks a text, so that its actual content has been altered—but it also may occur outside the material text itself, in the interpretations that its readers bring to it, and in the meanings that they take away. A focus on audience interpretations has allowed for the recognition that textual meanings are as much the products of a given audience's expectations, agendas, education, and social location as they are the products of the specific agendas of the text's author/editor(s).

When focus shifts away from the unitary original meaning of a text and toward the recognition of fluid and multivalent textual meaning, the historian's task shifts in significant ways, as well. Although it is still important to ask about the events that led to the composition of the literary evidence, it becomes increasingly important to ask how that literary evidence would have been *understood*—in its original setting, but also in later settings; by audiences with continuing interests in, but a potential for very different interpretations of, the historical claims presented in the text. A historical account that is understood as literal in one setting may be understood as a metaphor or a moral lesson or a prediction of future events in another. Similarly, historical accounts that are not 'originally intended' as literal might be taken—by a later reader with an interest in knowing the details of the past—in just such terms. Thus, a text like the Damascus Document might serve both to record historical events and also to 'create' those events, in the sense that later audiences might understand them to be 'factual' in ways that their original author(s) or editor(s) did not intend them to be understood.

As noted in chapter one, some of the most important questions for this discussion are the 'how' questions. The discussion thus far has been focused on how textual composition, reading, and interpretation contribute to the construction of historical narratives and images of individual or collective identity. What follows is one last set of readings, addressing the potential for textual interpretation and meaning-construction in a context at some remove from the ancient setting in which this text was first composed and transmitted. These readings, grounded in the medieval 'afterlife' of this ancient text, set the scene for a final discussion of another 'how' question: how textual meaning is constrained or expanded, and how authority is constructed, upheld, or challenged in the context of readings of foundation documents.

The challenge of the medieval manuscripts

The Damascus Document is, in some ways, the perfect test case for a discussion of changes in textual meaning over time. After all, the text has been read in diverse modern and premodern settings, including: (1) during the lifetime of the ancient Jewish community that served as the setting in which the text originated; (2) in the medieval period, during which our two most complete manuscript witnesses of the text were copied; (3) in the first half of the 20th century, after the discovery of those medieval manuscripts; and (4) in the past 50 years, since the discovery of the Dead Sea Scrolls. In each setting, interpretations of the text—and discussions of its historical content—have been shaped by whatever other knowledge its audiences have brought to their readings. It is interesting to remember, for example, that before the discovery of the scrolls, modern scholarly readers of the Damascus Document were conflicted on whether the text reflected a community of ancient origins or only a community with pretensions to claims of antiquity. That is, without the contextualizing evidence of the scrolls, either sort of reading was defensible. After the discovery of the scrolls—which confirmed the ancient origins of the text—the tendency to focus on origins led to a shift away from readings of the text in its medieval setting. In the discussion here, however, with the emphasis on the potential for later interpretations and mobilizations of earlier texts, it is actually useful to return to a reading of this text in its medieval settings. Such an approach allows for questions about how a medieval audience would understand the authoritative claims and constructions of communal identity articulated in the text.

As in previous chapters, the goal here is to address a two-fold question: how did the (medieval) readers of this text interpret its constructions of history and communal identity, and how does that interpretation shape an understanding of real historical events? However, this discussion must begin with an even more basic question, whose answer shapes the potential readings of the text: *who* were the medieval readers of the Damascus Document, and how did they gain access to the text in the first place? Did they read it from a 'sectarian' perspective, or did they understand it as the general property of a Jewish tradition in which notions of sectarian schism were irrelevant or backgrounded?

In addressing the 'who' question, scholars have noted that the worldview and halakhic framing of the Damascus Document bears striking similarities to the perspectives articulated in the Karaite texts of the period 900–1200 CE (which is also the period in which the medieval Damascus Document manuscripts were copied). The Karaite movement, which reached its height in that period, rejected the rabbinic Talmud and halakhah, arguing for an alternative interpretation of a shared Jewish tradition.[1] Early Karaite tendencies included a marked asceticism, a strict delineation of appropriate and inappropriate marriage practices, and a number of halakhic observances that differed from those of Rabbanite Judaism. Over time, the Karaite movement developed an oral tradition of its own, and scholars have noted that the differences between Karaite and Rabbanite Jews may have been overstated in the polemical texts that record their conflicts.

---

[1] For an introduction to the founding of the Karaite movement, see Salo Baron, 'Karaite Schism,' in *A Social and Religious History of the Jews* (Philadelphia: Jewish Publication Society, 1957), 5.209–85; see also Zvi Cahn, *The Rise of the Karaite Sect: A New Light on the Halakah and Origin of the Karaites* (New York: M. Tausner Publishing Co., 1937). The development of Karaite Judaism can be traced in the texts collected in Leon Nemoy, ed., *Karaite Anthology: Excerpts from the Early Literature* (New Haven: Yale University Press, 1980). In S. D. Goitein, *A Mediterranean Society: The Jewish Communities of the Arab World as Portrayed in the Documents of the Cairo Geniza* (6 vol.; Berkeley: University of California Press, 1967–1988), the practices of the Karaites are discussed and compared with those of the larger Jewish community. See especially vol. 2, *The Community* (Berkeley: University of California Press, 1971), and vol. 3, *The Family* (Berkeley: University of California Press, 1978). The relationship of Karaite and Rabbanite understandings of history is explored in Fred D. Astren, 'History, Historicization, and Historical Claims in Karaite Jewish Literature' (Ph.D. diss., University of California at Berkeley, 1993). See especially his discussion of the historiographical practice of Qirqisani, 113–31.

In fact, Karaite tradition does reflect the influence of the Talmud,[2] and, most notably, evidence suggests that marriages did take place between members of the two communities.[3]

If the medieval audience of the Damascus Document is imagined as a Karaite community, the next step in a hypothetical reading of the text is to ask how they gained access to it, since their relationship to the text also shapes the way that they would have read it. Scholars have suggested a range of possible connections between the ancient sectarian scrolls and the medieval Karaite movement, which assume varying degrees of direct or indirect contact. The most direct view argues for an explicit link between ancient and medieval Jewish sectarian movements, seeing the medieval Karaites as direct heirs to the ancient traditions reflected in the scrolls. Naphtali Wieder has taken this approach, suggesting that elements of the Dead Sea Scrolls community continued to exist into the medieval period, and that:

> some remnants of the Qumranites formed one of the dissident elements that went into the formation of the Karaite sect, and that the Qumran element was able, either through sheer spiritual and intellectual weight, or through numbers, or both, to exert a preponderant influence on the medley of heterogeneous groups and individuals that rallied to [sectarian leader] Anan [ben David]'s banner.[4]

Salo Baron goes even further, suggesting that Anan, the 8th century founder of what would later become the Karaite movement, *himself*:

> may well have taken over a good deal ... from those 'Sadducean' writings which, as we recall, were still circulating in his day, and which doubtless contained a great many modifications of the genuine teachings of ancient sectarians.[5]

---

[2] Leon Nemoy, *Karaite Anthology*, xiii–xxvi, esp. xxiii. See also Baron, *Social and Religious History*, 253.

[3] Judith Olszowy-Schlanger, *Karaite Marriage Documents from the Cairo Geniza: Legal Tradition and Community Life in Mediaeval Egypt and Palestine* (New York: Brill, 1998), 5. Olszowy-Schlanger argues that marriage documents from the Genizah demonstrate that Karaites and Rabbanites did marry one another until the early 13th century, when Maimonides rejected the practice. See Baron, *Social and Religious History*, 265–66, for the view that these marriages were occasional and infrequent; see also Baumgarten, *Flourishing of Jewish Sects*, 36, esp. n. 116. Baumgarten notes that the differences in dietary and calendrical observances were not enough to outlaw marriages between the two groups.

[4] Wieder, *Judean Scrolls and Karaism*, 254–55. See also André Paul, *Ecrits de Qumran et Sectes Juives aux Premiers Siecles de L'Islam: Recherches sur l'origine du Qaraisme* (Paris: Letouzey et Ane, 1969).

[5] Baron, *Social and Religious History*, 215.

Support for this argument lies in the similarities these scholars see between the scrolls and the early Karaite literature, as well as in external accounts of the development of the Karaite tradition.

Wieder notes, for example, that some Karaite writings demonstrate a use of language, imagery, and interpretation that is similar to that found in the scrolls, as well as a regular use of terms that are also found in the scrolls: "the perfect of way" (תמימי דרך); "those who turn from transgression" (שבי פשע, שבים); "the remnant" (שארית); and "the poor" (עניים, אביונים).⁶ Legal structures, including the prohibition of uncle-niece marriages and marriage after divorce, further suggest connections between the Karaites and the community associated with the Damascus Document in particular.⁷ According to this perspective, the accusations of Saadya Gaon—that the earliest Karaites arose "from among the remnants of the brood of Zadok and Boethus"⁸—should be taken seriously, as should Qirqisani's accounts of the history of Jewish sectarianism, which trace a path of schism from Jeroboam to the writer's present day, with significant references to Zadok and Boethus, as well as Anan.⁹ Again, in Wieder's view, the Karaites should be viewed as the direct heirs of a "heterodox [circle] which had hitherto led a more or less underground existence."¹⁰

A second approach argues for a direct link between the ancient scrolls and medieval Karaism but does not view this connection as a reflection of continuous development. According to this model, the ancient scrolls had a direct influence on medieval religious development not because they were handed down from one community to another, but because a cache of such texts was discovered in the Judean desert, in much the same way that the modern scroll discoveries took place.¹¹

---

⁶ Naphtali Wieder, 'The Qumran Sectaries and the Karaites,' *JQR* 47 (1956/57): 97–113, 269–92. Other comparative discussions include Norman Golb, 'Literary and Doctrinal Aspects of the Damascus Covenant in the Light of Karaite Literature,' *JQR* 47 (1956/57): 354–74 (which compares the Damascus Document and the letter of a 10th century Karaite, Sahl b. Masliah); and Szyszman, 'A propos du Karaïsme,' 347–48 (for a reference to the Teacher of Righteousness).

⁷ Golb, 'Literary and Doctrinal Aspects,' 362, 366.

⁸ Saadya's description of the founding of the Ananites (precursors of the Karaites) is preserved in a 12th century text by Elijah b. Abraham; see Nemoy, *Karaite Anthology*, 4. This text is quoted and discussed in Wieder, *Judean Scrolls and Karaism*, 254–55.

⁹ See Qirqisani's 'History of Jewish Sects,' in Nemoy, *Karaite Anthology*, 50.

¹⁰ Wieder, *Judean Scrolls and Karaism*, 257.

¹¹ See Paul Kahle, *The Cairo Geniza* (Oxford: Basil Blackwell, 1959), as well as the accounts of medieval manuscript discoveries in Nathan Schur, *History of the*

Paul Kahle provides a representative account of this approach, grounded in the evidence of a Syriac letter of Timotheus I (726–819 CE), the Nestorian Patriarch of Seleucia. At the turn of the ninth century (c. 800 CE), Timotheus wrote to Sergius, Metropolitan of Elam, with an account of the discovery of books some 30 years previously, in a small cave in the rocks near Jericho.[12] In his letter, Timotheus claims that he contacted certain Jews in Jerusalem, who examined the books and found that they were written in Hebrew and contained portions of the Old Testament, as well as other compositions.[13] Kahle identifies the cave near Jericho as Qumran's cave one, and he notes that by the 9th century the dominant Jewish presence in Jerusalem would have been Karaite.[14] He suggests that the Genizah fragments of the Damascus Document represent the remains of the copies that these Karaites made in their own day, and that the text itself dates back to the Zadokite priests of the time of Antiochus.[15] Thus, according to Kahle's argument, the Karaite doctrines date back to actual Saducean sources but do not reflect a generation-to-generation transmission of those sources.[16]

A third interpretation of this evidence takes a more minimalist position, arguing that the Karaite worldview and the opinions expressed in the Damascus Document look similar because both are grounded in scripture and both address common communal concerns, and not because they are linked in any direct or organic way. That is, because the composers of the Damascus Document and the early Karaites were arguing against similar claims (those of the Pharisees in the first case, and those of their Rabbanite heirs in the second), and because their halakhic and interpretive concerns were similar, the presence of commonalities of doctrine or authoritative claim should come as no surprise.

Karaites (New York: Peter Lang, 1992), 16. These include reports by Origen (c. 217) of the discovery of a Greek biblical manuscript; the letter of Timotheus (discussed in the text above); and an account by Qirqisani (c. 937), of the discovery of a cave containing manuscripts of the pre-Christian Magharians.

[12] See Kahle, *Cairo Geniza*, 15–16. For explicit support of Kahle's argument, see also Saul Lieberman, 'Light on the Cave Scrolls from Rabbinic Sources,' *Proceedings of the American Academy of Jewish Research* 20 (1951): 402.

[13] Kahle, *Cairo Geniza*, 16.

[14] Kahle, *Cairo Geniza*, 16–17. For the view that cave three was the source for such a medieval text discovery, see Stegemann, *Library of Qumran*, 69–71.

[15] Kahle, *Cairo Geniza*, 18–19.

[16] Kahle, *Cairo Geniza*, 23.

Nathan Schur provides a representative argument of this sort, taking account of the doctrinal and linguistic similarities between the scrolls and the Karaite tradition, but also noting their significant differences.[17] Among the similarities, he identifies "the implied rejection of oral tradition," an "emphasis on searching Scripture for guidance," shared terminology, especially in the names given to members, communal leaders, and their opponents, and a tendency to "regard biblical stories less as an account of historical occurrences than as prognostications of present and future events." In addition, he identifies a tendency "to search in Scripture for forecasts of the coming of the Messiah" and a "deep conviction" that they are right and everyone else is wrong.[18] At the same time, however, he notes a variety of contrasts between these two worldviews, including the lack of dualism in the Karaite worldview; a predestinarian tendency in the scrolls, as opposed to the "Karaite belief in free will and choice"; dissimilarities in religious praxis; and a lack of monastic tendencies among the Karaites.[19] He also points to a geographic disjunction, locating the early roots of Karaism in Persia, and not in a region in which the scrolls were first discovered.[20] Although he recognizes the potential for medieval discoveries of ancient manuscripts, he ultimately argues that the similarities between the texts "are common to the mainstream of Judaistic sectarianism" and that the scrolls and the Karaite literature reflect "separate—but not interdependent and consecutive—links in the long chain of Jewish schism."[21]

This third approach does not actually explain the existence of medieval manuscripts of the Damascus Document. However, in suggesting that a sectarian tendency is a regular element in the Jewish tradition, it hints at one possibility: Jewish scribes may have copied and transmitted this text in the intervening period, simply for its historical, halakhic, or interpretive interest. Such scribes may not have viewed the text as authoritative to their own lives but rather, in a sort of 'antiquarian' sense, as an important account of the development

---

[17] Similarly, Baumgarten warns against the tendency to find "a secret underground connection" or "a direct line of inspiration" between the movements of these different periods. See Baumgarten, *Flourishing of Jewish Sects*, 36.

[18] Nathan Schur, *History of the Karaites* (New York: Peter Lang, 1992), 15–16. See also Schur, 'Dead Sea Scrolls,' in *The Karaite Encyclopedia*, 84–86.

[19] Schur, *History of the Karaites*, 16–17.

[20] Schur, *History of the Karaites*, 17.

[21] Schur, *History of the Karaites*, 17.

of the Jewish covenant with God, in its many permutations. This interpretation does not explain why this *particular* text was copied and transmitted, but it does highlight the possibility that Jewish scribes might have transmitted texts—and understood them as important documents in Jewish history—without viewing them as specifically authoritative over themselves or their own community.

Each of these speculative accounts provides a slightly different context in which medieval readings of the Damascus Document may have taken place. In the first, readers might foreground the text's 'sectarian' claims, given the longterm connection to an earlier community and an older, established covenant. In the second scenario, we can imagine a reading of the text that foregrounds its call to 'return' and 'repentance,' with readers imagining themselves as a newly-discovered remnant among the wicked of Israel. Most interestingly, the third scenario suggests a reading of the text that foregrounds neither of these approaches. According to this model, a medieval Jewish reader—whether Karaite or not—might read this text as an important historical account, without making claims to a historical connection with earlier covenant communities. In any of these cases, and in the case of a number of other scenarios that we might suggest, the text's multivalent presentations of history and communal identity allow for unique readings of this text—and unique constructions of historical consciousness and historical narratives based upon it—at far remove from those imagined by the text's original composer(s) and/or its ancient users.

Of the many medieval readings of this text that can be imagined, a few stand out as particularly relevant to the larger discussions of this project. It will be useful, for this reason, to deal briefly with a number of 'sample' readings: of the text's account of the founding of the covenant community; of the appeals to Zadokite status; and of the text's messianic claims. Although these readings are necessarily brief, each hints at a number of important questions for future discussions.

History, origins, and covenant-formation

In earlier readings, we explored a number of the historical themes at work in the Damascus Document, including references to 'covenant' (ברית) and 'first ones' (ראשנים), appeals to exilic status, and an understanding of the covenant community as the true heirs, or remnant, of the people of Israel. Our readings showed that these images could be equally potent for the author(s) and editor(s) of the text and for later generations of ancient covenanters, because in each generation the value-laden language of the text could be read as personally-directed toward that generation. The presence of multiple historical models (some linear, some cyclical) and the use of covenantal language in historical descriptions together contribute to the dynamic quality of the text, which permits readers in a variety of settings to understand themselves as the text's obvious, intended audiences.

Consider, for example, the statement found at the end of one of the text's lengthy accounts of Israelite history, that:

> The first ones who entered the covenant became guilty... and they were given up to the sword, having departed from God's covenant and chosen their own will, straying after the wantonness of their heart, each doing his own will. But out of those who held fast to God's ordinances, who remained of them, God established his covenant with Israel forever (CD 3.10–13).

This passage appears, we will recall, in the context of a historical account of all humankind, from the Watchers to the Patriarchs, to the people of Israel in their Wilderness wandering and after their entry into the land. The text makes repeated references to the waywardness and stubbornness of the people, who follow their own interests and their own interpretations, rather than looking to the will of God as a guide to appropriate behavior. It ends with the assertion that only the members of the covenant community are party to God's true wishes, and only they will survive in the impending endtimes.

How might a medieval reader have understood this text? We have suggested that the ancient covenanters who were this text's earliest readers were able to insert themselves into the narrative, as the 'first ones' of the New Covenant, whose own experiences could be mapped onto those of the people of Israel. Unlike the willful Israelites who would go their own way or follow their own interpretations, the members of the covenant could see themselves as eager seekers of God's will and followers of his chosen path. For a medieval reader whose own worldview was equally steeped in scripture, this text could be mobilized to support similar claims. If scholars are correct in understanding the Karaite tradition as one that was grounded in scripture in this way,[22] then it may be possible to imagine the interpretation

---

[22] Schur, *History of the Karaites*, 16–17.

that a medieval Karaite reader would take from (or bring to) this text.

Like the ancient covenanter, such a medieval Karaite might imagine all of history as a cycle of transgression and repentance, in which the proper understanding of scripture provides the key to breaking out of the cycle. Rabbanite halakhah, and the rabbinic Talmud more generally, might serve in this context as an example of the sort of 'willful' misinterpretation that leads the people of Israel astray. Like the Watchers and the sons of Noah, the Rabbanites choose to follow their own transgressive willfulness, rather than searching for God's true desires. In this sort of reading, the Damascus Document's reference to "God's ordinances" serves to signify the Karaite understanding of scripture and halakhah, while the reference to "straying after the wantonness of their hearts" can be read and understood—'obviously'—as a reference to the Rabbanite interpretations of scripture and halakhah.

In addition to the understanding of history as a cycle of transgression and repentance, the theme of 'exile' is one that our hypothetical Karaite audience might foreground in a reading of this text. Again, the theme is a primary one in the text itself: the first admonition dates the founding of the community to the period 390 years after the Babylonian conquest; the accounts of the founding of the New Covenant stress that the covenanters are "the turning ones of Israel (שבי ישראל), the ones who depart from the land of Judah and dwell in the land of Damascus." For medieval Jews in Cairo or Damascus—and no less for medieval Jews in a Jerusalem trapped under 'foreign' domination—the notions of exile would be, if anything, even more poignant than they would have been for readers of this text before the year 70 CE. Again, as in our earlier discussions, we can imagine a medieval readership of this text who would view themselves as 'exiles,' whether from a land that they personally had left behind; from a land they had never seen but understood as their covenantal birthright; or from the sanctuary that has been destroyed, in the very land they occupied. Again, the truth-claims of this text, grounded in its scriptural references and the powerful imagery of exile, lie outside the realm of historical experience and firmly in the context of ideological interpretation.

CONCLUSIONS AND CHALLENGES   221

Zadokites, Sadducees, and priestly status

In the context of a medieval reading, in which the Jerusalem sanctuary is the memory of a millennium past, the Damascus Document references to the Zadokite priesthood are as complex as its references to exile. We have seen that the Damascus Document can be read as a 'Zadokite' text in ways that are both historical and metaphorical. The text's use of 'righteousness'-language (צדק) can be foregrounded, to support a focus on the symbolic priesthood of the righteous, but the references to the 'sons of Zadok' also can be read, by an audience with such concerns, as reflective of historical or genealogical claims.

Jacob al-Qirqisani, the 10th-century Karaite scholar, includes among his writings a history of Jewish sectarianism from the time of Jeroboam, son of Nebat, to the writer's own day. In the course of his historical account, he refers to the development, in the Second Temple period, of an anti-Rabbanite movement of Sadducees, under the leadership of "Zadok and Boethus." The description of these figures (mentioned in the Talmud in a similar capacity) is a brief one, but it provides the context for another re-reading of the Damascus Document in its medieval historical perspective.[23] The writing of Qirqisani dates to the same century as the copying of the earlier medieval Damascus Document manuscript (MS A). It is interesting, consequently, to speculate on the historical understandings that a medieval audience might have taken away from readings of the two texts, in light of one another. Equally interesting is the question of whether Qirqisani knew the Damascus Document (or knew of it, or knew a related tradition) when he composed his own historical account, or whether the two texts reflect independent traditions of historical information.

For Qirqisani, as for our hypothetical medieval Damascus Document reader, the figure of 'Zadok' might be understood in terms of his actual historicity or more generally as a standard for 'righteous' leadership. His relationship to the Zadok of the Damascus Document is an equally open question. According to the Damascus Document,

---

[23] Wacholder's discussion of the identity of the Dead Sea Scrolls community and the Teacher of Righteousness is grounded in a reading of this passage and the text's other references to Zadok. See Wacholder, *Dawn of Qumran*.

the sinfulness of the people of Israel in earlier times, especially their sexual and marital transgressions, was due in part to the fact that the true Torah, with its explanations of these basic injunctions, was "sealed" from the time of Eleazar and Joshua "until Zadok arose," and all that had been hidden was revealed (CD 5.2–5). It is possible for a medieval reader of Qirqisani to understand the Damascus Document's reference to 'Zadok' as a second description of the same Second Temple historical figure. Alternatively, such a reader could take the two figures as different historical individuals—the Zadok of David's day, and the Zadok who founded the Sadducees—but understand them as parallels of one another.

If a medieval reader might accept as historical the references to Zadok (as one figure or several; as a community founder or an ancient priest; as a historical priest or only a symbol of righteousness), this is not the only range of possible interpretations. In addition to readings that would foreground Zadok as an origin figure, the text was also open—even to a medieval audience—to forward-looking readings, concerned with a rapidly-impending endtimes experience. Such a perspective might understand both the community and its leadership in Zadokite terms. For medieval readers with endtimes expectations, there would be great appeal in the anticipated return of Zadok, and in the sense that all such faithful readers might become the "sons of Zadok," who are "the chosen ones of Israel, those called by name, who stand at the end of days" (CD 4.4–6, referencing Ezek 44.15).[24]

Following the Ezekiel interpretation in the Damascus Document is a fragmentary passage that was subject to discussion in several previous readings. The text interprets the "priests and Levites and sons of Zadok" as the various members of God's covenant and then states:

> Here are the details of their names, for their generations (לתולדותם) and the times of their standing, and the numbers of their troubles and the years of their residence and the details of their works (CD 4.4–6).

Again, the most interesting aspect of this passage is what it does not accomplish. Although it claims to provide the genealogical and historical account of a covenant community, what follows is a mere

---

[24] More generally, see CD 3.21–4.4; translation after Baumgarten and Schwartz, 'CD,' 17–19.

'blank' in the text. What is the significance of this blank? It is possible, as a previous reading suggested, that this blank already existed in antiquity, and that the medieval reader of the text—receiving it in this open form—could have understood it as an opportunity to read the covenant account as a personal one.

Another possibility is that a medieval scribe actually removed an ancient listing of names, dates, and places that had been extant in the text all along. The significance of such an action is remarkable. For a medieval reader, a text that contained specific names and details could be read most transparently as a record of the historical claims of an ancient community. But when the same text exists with a 'blank' where the names used to be, then it suddenly becomes an open source of authority and authenticity, capable of being mobilized by any reader with the interpretive skills to understand it in direct and specific terms. This latter possibility—although entirely undocumentable—is of particular interest in this context, because it suggests a purposeful rewriting of history on the part of some medieval reader. In making such a purposeful textual change, the medieval scribe would have been recognizing the power of the text's truth claims (irrespective of actual historical events) and demonstrating, through minimal editing, the historical adaptability of those claims.

Endtimes expectations and messianic claims

The references to Zadok and the Zadokite priesthood could be leveraged by medieval readers in anticipation of a still-impending endtime, a millennium after their original expectation, but this is not the only endtime imagery at work in the text. In fact, it is in the matter of endtimes imagery that a medieval reading of the Damascus Document becomes particularly interesting. Given the textual variants contained in the medieval manuscripts (which provide parallel but distinct texts in CD 7.5-8.21 and CD 19.1-34), it is interesting to speculate, once more, on the development of the textual tradition and its significance for a medieval reader. There is a tendency to view both text versions as ancient in origin, although we have manuscript evidence from the ancient fragments only for the text of CD 7-8. This textual diversity consequently raises a number of other possibilities: in addition to the possibility that both texts are ancient; it is also possible that the messianic account in CD 19.1-34 is the product of a medieval alteration of the text, and thus reflects the sensibilities of readers and redactors in that later context. If the two texts do reflect a variant of medieval-origins, how might such a textual change be explained, and how might it have been understood, by its medieval readers?

The extended scriptural interpretation in CD 7.10–21 (which is not paralleled in CD 19) locates the covenant community in Damascus, where they await the arrival of the endtimes in the company of the Torah, the books of the prophets, and a community leader called the "interpreter of the Torah" (דורש התורה, CD 7.18). The community anticipates the arrival of a "prince of all the congregation" (נשיא כל העדה, CD 7.20), who will destroy the wicked when he arises. In place of this optimistic—and Damascus-centered—prophecy, the other text has only a short reference, to the striking-down of the shepherd and the scattering of the sheep (CD 19.7–9), followed a few lines later by a reference to the mark upon the forehead of "those who sigh and groan" (CD 19.12, after Ezek 9.4).

If this textual variant is medieval, rather than ancient in origin, its existence suggests a number of significant points. First, the presence of a medieval textual variant would demonstrate that the medieval scribes who copied the text understood it as a living document, whose impact upon them was relevant and immediate enough to make that sort of textual alteration worthwhile. In this sense, such a scenario supports the larger view that foundation documents take on meanings to the extent that they are read, interpreted, and re-read by the communities that preserve them (and in this example, re-reading includes re-editing and re-publication as well).

A second major point of interest here is explicitly historiographical. If this textual variation is medieval in origin, then perhaps we can understand it as the reflection of, once again, a set of actual historical events. Like the scholarly readers of the text in the first half of this century, we may return to the speculation that Damascus really meant Damascus, and that the textual variant reflects a failed messianic prophecy among the members of a medieval Jewish community in Syria. Having anticipated the arrival of the endtimes (predicted in CD 7.10–21), the Jewish community there was not only disappointed but also, through some unrecorded crisis, scattered and struck down. To mark this crisis, they re-edited the text, reflecting both the failure of their initial optimism and also their continued, but more cautious, willingness to await the messiah.

Conclusions and challenges

Readings of the Damascus Document in a medieval setting—whether from a 'believer's' perspective or from an antiquarian view—would have been possible only to the extent that the text's audience could make sense of its complex themes and scriptural references. However, for medieval readers (whether Karaite or not) who were steeped in scripture, and for whom the notions of covenant, salvation, and righteousness were of primary regard, such readings are not overly difficult to imagine. Such an audience, in fact, may have found it easy to interpret this text, mobilizing its historical narratives and constructions of identity toward whatever ends fit best with their own agendas. Like the ancient audiences considered in previous chapters, these medieval readers could foreground whatever issues were most pressing—halakhic conflicts or historical concerns; scriptural interpretations or endtimes expectations—in drawing their own conclusions from this multivalent text.

The long 'shelf-life' of the Damascus Document is a point of significant interest, both from a literary-critical perspective and also in historical terms. Especially if it was the case that the text's medieval audiences had no organic connection to the ancient covenanters who initially composed and read it, the long-term interpretability of this text is interesting. In some ways, the quality that makes this text most confounding to historians—its constant and complex use of scriptural language and scriptural references—is one of the qualities that contributes to its long-term relevance. But an additional reason for this interpretability, by communities at a millennium's remove from one another, is grounded in the qualities that led us to describe this text, in chapter one, as a 'foundation document.'

In chapter one, we determined, first, that foundation documents work cross-temporally. Such texts lay out the history of a community—often in the context of larger national or cosmic historical accounts—but they also acknowledge the importance of the community's present-time experiences and their anticipation of the future. For this reason, readers of foundation documents can locate themselves simultaneously in their own lives and in the lives of their community's founders, ancestors, and endtimes generations. For readers of the Damascus Document, the text's constructions of history also connect to an ideology that stresses the importance of 'knowledge,' and in particular, the special knowledge of God's will that helps covenanters to follow the proper path of righteousness and avoid the temptations of willfulness. As a foundation text, the Damascus Document thus opens up all aspects of the past, the present, and the future for its readership.

In addition to opening the realms of time for their readers, foundation documents provide important guidelines, boundaries, and communal norms, which allow for the construction of a unique collective identity on the part of that readership. Distinctions between insiders and outsiders are highlighted in the Damascus Document in a variety of ways. Historical accounts of communal conflict, descriptions of the deeds of the wicked, and (especially) the lengthy presentation of the community's laws and statutes all serve to distinguish between proper and improper communal behavior. In addition, more subtle strategies, such as the use of multivalent or ambiguous keywords (including 'Israel,' 'Judah,' 'covenant,' and 'first ones') and the repetition of words, themes, or grammatical forms (noted especially in the first and third admonitions) contribute to the construction of complex distinctions between the proper behavior of communal insiders and the misbehavior of their opponents.

As this discussion suggests, the question of 'how' textual meaning is constructed is interesting from a technical perspective: which themes a reader chooses to highlight; how the reader decides whether to read literally or metaphorically, in simple or complicated ways; whether the reader understands the text as clear or opaque; all of these issues are important elements in the construction of the meaning, or meanings, of a given foundation document. But a second round of 'how' questions, at the next level of interpretation, is equally important to consider: how does the construction of textual meaning, in complex and dynamic ways, contribute to the construction of authority (or authoritative voice) and the construction of authoritative historical accounts, based on basic readings of the texts?

In effect, this set of 'how' questions takes us from the textual world to the world of historical experience, in which texts are written, read, rewritten, and interpreted, and in which the process of assigning meaning to texts may have significant material importance. For the readers of a foundation document, textual interpretations are not mere hypotheticals. Rather, they have real-world implications, relating to issues of marriage and divorce, sabbath and festival observance, and whatever other practices draw the lines between 'us' ('the righteous') and 'them' ('the wicked'). To the extent that authority is vested in foundation documents—because they stem from an important communal founder or leader; because they provide the true Torah; or because they derive, ultimately, from the will of God—it follows that textual interpretation will play a major role in the dynamics of power and leadership in any community associated with them.

Given the potential for a wide range of interpretations of the Damascus Document's constructions of history and communal identity (and the readings of the previous chapters demonstrate how very wide-ranging those interpretations can be), it follows that a member or leader of a community associated with this text would have had a variety of options for mobilizing its authoritative claims. The text itself provides examples of strategies for constructing authority that a reader might have chosen to mimic: quotation of a text, with or without strategic reworkings of it (CD 3.21–4.4, with its selective reading of Ezek 44.15); claims of eternal or universal authority (God's "covenant with Israel forever" in CD 3.13); rejection of 'interpretation,' in favor of the view that there is only one true Torah, which is the Torah of the covenanters (CD 3.17, for example). For a covenantal interpreter of the Damascus Document, similar strategies might prove amenable.[25] It matters little whether a given reading of the text actually fits with its author/editor(s)' original intentions. Rather, the key for such an interpreter would be to read the text in such a way that the desired interpretation—the desired mobilization of the text—could be made to seem 'obvious' or 'natural.' That is, to the extent that a covenanter could construct *one* meaning of the text and convince other readers that this was *the* one meaning of it, that reader might effectively mobilize the authoritative claims and authoritative status of the text within the larger covenant community.

For historians of the Dead Sea Scrolls, the issues are somewhat different, but the dynamic is quite similar. Our own readings of the Damascus Document are concerned with establishing normative historical accounts, rather than normative communal religious practices,

---

[25] Alternative strategies also are possible: it is particularly interesting to consider the cases in which a textual interpretation is presented as 'novel' or 'new,' so that what is valued is a purported *break* with tradition, rather than a claim of continuity. In asserting that the members of the 'new' covenant are those who turn away from sin (שבי פשע), and who have broken with the transgressive ways of the rest of the people of Israel, the text of the Damascus Document is certainly susceptible to this alternative interpretation.

but the process of establishing scholarly authority begins in any case with interpretation. Historians construct their accounts by identifying the evidence, interpreting it, and fitting the pieces together in the form of a historical narrative, and each stage in this process is interpretive. Different scholars will have distinct perspectives on what counts as evidence, how that evidence is to be understood, and what sorts of conclusions may or may not be drawn from it. The narratives they generate are themselves mobilizations of a selected body of evidence, rather than simple explanations of historical events. That some narratives are more responsible or more convincing than others is a given; that each is a construct is equally the case.

Recognizing our own embeddedness, as scholars, in the construction of textual meaning and the consequent construction of historical narratives suggests a number of implications for future historical scholarship on the scrolls. The first is that historical accounts of a scrolls community will always be contingent, rather than conclusive. This is in no way a new observation, but it is one that bears repeating. A second, and more interesting, point stems from the observation that single texts are always susceptible to multiple interpretations, even in their original settings, even by their original author(s) and editor(s), and certainly over the course of their 'lifetimes,' whether these reflect a single generation, or a millennium (or two), of use. It follows that scholarly attention, at the stage of selecting and interpreting the evidence, must shift away from a focus on 'original meaning' and toward a dynamic discussion of the 'lifetime' of the scrolls texts, perhaps in source-critical terms, but also and especially in terms of an explicitly audience-oriented analysis. To the extent that our evidence reflects potentially multivalent constructions of past historical events, it follows that our own historical narratives must be understood as individual mobilizations of meaning, and interpretive constructions of history, based on individual readings of evidence that is always already susceptible to many more.

BIBLIOGRAPHY

Adam, A. K. M. *What is Postmodern Biblical Criticism?* Minneapolis: Fortress Press, 1995.
Aichele, George, and Gary Phillips, eds. *Intertextuality and the Bible. Semeia* 69/70 (1995).
Anderson, Janice, and Stephen D. Moore, eds. *Mark and Method: New Approaches in Biblical Studies.* Minneapolis: Fortress Press, 1992.
Astren, Fred D. 'History, Historicization, and Historical Claims in Karaite Jewish Literature.' Ph.D. diss, University of California at Berkeley, 1993.
Bainbridge, William. *The Sociology of Religious Movements.* New York: Routledge, 1997.
Baron, Salo. *High Middle Ages (500-1200) Religious Controls and Dissensions.* Volume 5 of *A Social and Religious History of the Jews.* Philadelphia: Jewish Publication Society, 1957.
Barrett, Michele. 'Words and Things: Materialism and Method in Contemporary Feminist Analysis.' Pages 201-19 in *Destabilizing Theory: Contemporary Feminist Debates.* Edited by Michele Barrett and Anne Phillips. Cambridge: Polity Press, 1992.
Barthes, Roland. 'The Death of the Author.' Pages 125-30 in *Authorship: From Plato to the Postmodern, A Reader.* Edited by Sean Burke. Edinburgh: Edinburgh University Press, 1995.
———. 'From Work to Text.' Pages 73-81 in *Textual Strategies: Perspectives in Post-Structuralist Criticism.* Edited by Josué Harari. Ithaca: Cornell University Press, 1979.
Bartlett, J. R. 'Zadok and His Successors at Jerusalem.' *JTS* 19 (1968): 1-18.
Basser, Herbert. 'The Rabbinic Citations in Wacholder's *The Dawn of Qumran.*' *RevQ* 11 (1984): 549-60.
Baumgarten, Albert. *The Flourishing of Jewish Sects in the Maccabean Era: An Interpretation.* New York: Brill, 1997.
———. 'The Name of the Pharisees.' *JBL* 102/3 (1983): 411-28.
———. 'The Perception of the Past in the Damascus Document.' Pages 1-15 in *The Damascus Document, A Centennial of Discovery: Proceedings of the Third International Symposium of the Orion Center for the Study of the Dead Sea Scrolls and Associated Literature, 4-8 February, 1998.* Edited by Joseph Baumgarten, Esther Chazon, and Avital Pinnick. Boston: Brill, 2000.
———. 'The Zadokite Priests at Qumran: A Reconsideration.' *DSD* 4 (1997): 137-56.
Baumgarten, Joseph. 'C. Miscellaneous Rules.' Pages 57-78 in *Qumran Cave 4, XXV: Halakhic Texts.* Edited by Joseph Baumgarten. DJD XXXV. Oxford: Clarendon Press, 1999.
———. 'The Cave 4 Versions of the Qumran Penal Code.' *JJS* 43 (1992): 268-76.
———. 'The Laws of the Damascus Document in Current Research.' Pages 51-62 in *The Damascus Document Reconsidered.* Edited by Magen Broshi. Jerusalem: Israel Exploration Society, 1992.
———. 'Scripture and Law in 4Q265.' Pages 25-33 in *Biblical Perspectives: Early Use and Interpretation of the Bible in Light of the Dead Sea Scrolls.* Edited by Michael Stone and Esther Chazon. Leiden: Brill, 1998.
Baumgarten, Joseph, ed. *Qumran Cave 4, XIII: The Damascus Document (4Q266-273).* DJD XVIII. Oxford: Clarendon Press, 1996.
———. *Qumran Cave 4, XXV: Halakhic Texts.* DJD XXXV. Oxford: Clarendon Press, 1999.
Baumgarten, Joseph, Esther Chazon, and Avital Pinnick, eds. *The Damascus Document, A Centennial of Discovery: Proceedings of the Third International Symposium of the Orion Center for the Study of the Dead Sea Scrolls and Associated Literature, 4-8 February, 1998.* Boston: Brill, 2000.

Baumgarten, Joseph, and Michael Davis. 'Cave IV, V, VI Fragments.' Pages 59–79 in *Damascus Document, War Scroll, and Related Documents*. Vol. 2 of *The Dead Sea Scrolls: Hebrew, Aramaic, and Greek Texts with English Translations*. Edited by James H. Charlesworth. Louisville: Westminster John Knox Press, 1995.

Baumgarten, Joseph, and Daniel Schwartz. 'Damascus Document (CD).' Pages 4–57 in *Damascus Document, War Scroll, and Related Documents*. Vol. 2 of *The Dead Sea Scrolls: Hebrew, Aramaic, and Greek Texts with English Translations*. Edited by James H. Charlesworth. Louisville: Westminster John Knox Press, 1995.

Beckwith, Roger. *Calendar and Chronology, Jewish and Christian: Biblical, Intertestamental and Patristic Studies*. New York: Brill, 1996.

Bernstein, Moshe, Florentino García Martínez, and John Kampen, eds. *Legal Texts and Legal Issues: Proceedings of the Second Meeting of the International Organization for Qumran Studies: Cambridge 1995*. New York: Brill, 1997.

Boccaccini, Gabriele. *Beyond the Essene Hypothesis: The Parting of the Ways Between Qumran and Enochic Judaism*. Grand Rapids, Mich.: Eerdmans, 1998.

Boyarin, Daniel. *Carnal Israel: Reading Sex in Talmudic Culture*. Berkeley: University of California Press, 1993.

———. *Intertextuality and the Reading of Midrash*. Bloomington: Indiana University Press, 1990.

Boyce, Mark. 'The Poetry of the *Damascus Document* and its Bearing on the Origin of the Qumran Sect.' *RevQ* 14 (1990): 615–28.

Brooke, George. 'The Amos-Numbers Midrash (CD 7.13b–8.1a) and Messianic Expectation.' *ZAW* 92 (1980): 397–404.

———. 'Book Reviews: *The Use of Scripture in the Damascus Document 1–8, 19–20*.' *DSD* 4 (1997): 112–16.

———. 'The Explicit Presentation of Scripture in 4QMMT.' Pages 67–88 in *Legal Texts and Legal Issues: Proceedings of the Second Meeting of the International Organization for Qumran Studies: Cambridge 1995*. Edited by Moshe Bernstein, Florentino García Martínez, and John Kampen. New York: Brill, 1997.

———. 'The Messiah of Aaron in the Damascus Document.' *RevQ* 15 (1991): 215–30.

———. 'Qumran Pesher: Towards the Redefinition of a Genre.' *RevQ* 10 (1981): 483–503.

———. 'Shared Intertextual Interpretations in the Dead Sea Scrolls and the New Testament.' Pages 35–57 in *Biblical Perspectives: Early Use and Interpretation of the Bible in Light of the Dead Sea Scrolls*. Edited by Michael Stone and Esther Chazon. Leiden: Brill, 1998.

Broshi, Magen, ed. *The Damascus Document Reconsidered*. Jerusalem: Israel Exploration Society, 1992.

Büchler, Adolph. 'Schechter's "Jewish Sectaries."' *JQR* 3 (1912/13): 429–85.

Burke, Sean, ed. *Authorship: From Plato to the Postmodern, A Reader*. Edinburgh: Edinburgh University Press, 1995.

Burridge, Kenelm. *New Heaven, New Earth: A Study of Millenarian Activities*. Oxford: Basil Blackwell, 1969.

Burrows, Millar. 'Concerning the Dead Sea Scrolls.' *JQR* 42 (1951): 105–32.

Butler, Judith. *Gender Trouble: Feminism and the Subversion of Identity*. New York: Routledge, 1990.

Cahn, Zvi. *The Rise of the Karaite Sect: A New Light on the Halakah and Origin of the Karaites*. New York: M. Tausner Publishing Co., 1937.

Callaway, Phillip. 'Qumran Origins: From the *Doresh* to the *Moreh*.' *RevQ* 14 (1990): 637–50.

Cameron, Averil, ed. *History as Text: The Writing of Ancient History*. London: Duckworth, 1989.

Camp, Claudia. 'Understanding a Patriarchy: Women in Second Century Jerusalem Through the Eyes of Ben Sira.' Pages 1–39 in *"Women Like This": New Perspectives*

on *Jewish Women in the Greco-Roman World*. Edited by Amy-Jill Levine. Atlanta: Scholars Press, 1991.
Campbell, Jonathan. 'Essene-Qumran Origins in the Exile: A Scriptural Basis?' *JJS* 46 (1995): 143–56.
———. 'Scripture in The Damascus Document 1.1–2.1.' *JJS* 44 (1993): 83–99.
———. *The Use of Scripture in the Damascus Document 1–8, 19–20*. New York: Walter de Gruyter, 1995.
Cansdale, Lena. *Qumran and the Essenes: A Re-evaluation of the Evidence*. Tübingen: Mohr (Siebeck), 1997.
Castelli, Elizabeth, Stephen D. Moore, Gary Phillips, Regina Schwartz, et al., eds. *The Postmodern Bible*. New Haven: Yale University Press, 1995.
Charlesworth, James H., ed. *Damascus Document, War Scroll, and Related Documents*. Vol. 2 of *The Dead Sea Scrolls: Hebrew, Aramaic, and Greek Texts with English Translations*, Louisville: Westminster John Knox Press, 1995.
———. *Rule of the Community and Related Documents*. Vol. 1 of *The Dead Sea Scrolls: Hebrew, Aramaic, and Greek Texts with English Translations*, Louisville: Westminster John Knox Press, 1994.
Chazon, Esther. 'Is *Divreh Ha-Me'orot* a Sectarian Prayer?' Pages 3–17 in *The Dead Sea Scrolls: Forty Years of Research*. Edited by Devorah Dimant and Uriel Rappaport. Leiden: Brill, 1992.
Clines, David, Stephen Fowl, and Stanley Porter, eds. *The Bible in Three Dimensions: Essays in Celebration of Forty Years of Biblical Studies in the University of Sheffield*. Sheffield: JSOT Press, 1990.
Clines, David, David Gunn, and Alan Hauser, eds. *Art and Meaning: Rhetoric in Biblical Literature*. Sheffield: JSOT Press, 1982.
Cohen, Shaye. *From the Maccabees to the Mishnah*. Philadelphia: Westminster Press, 1987.
———. 'The Significance of Yavne: Pharisees, Rabbis, and the End of Jewish Sectarianism.' *HUCA* 55 (1984): 27–53.
Collins, John. *Apocalypticism in the Dead Sea Scrolls*. New York: Routledge, 1997.
———. 'The Origins of the Qumran Community: A Review of the Evidence.' Pages 159–78 in *To Touch the Text: Biblical and Related Studies in Honor of Joseph A. Fitzmyer*. Edited by Maurya Horgan and Paul Kobelski. New York: Crossroad, 1989.
Cook, E. 'What was Qumran? A Ritual Purification Center.' *BAR* 22.6 (1996): 39, 48–51, 73–75.
Cotton, Hannah. 'Women: The Texts.' Pages 984–87 in *Encyclopedia of the Dead Sea Scrolls*. Edited by Lawrence Schiffman and James VanderKam. Oxford: Oxford University Press, 2000.
Cross, Frank Moore. 'Appendix: Paleographic Dates of the Manuscripts.' Page 57 in *Rule of the Community and Related Documents*. Vol. 1 of *The Dead Sea Scrolls: Hebrew Aramaic, and Greek Texts with English Translations*. Edited by James H. Charlesworth. Louisville: Westminster John Knox Press, 1994.
———. 'The Development of the Jewish Scripts.' Pages 133–202 in *The Bible and The Ancient Near East: Essays in Honor of William Foxwell Albright*. Edited by G. Ernest Wright. Winona Lake, Ind: Eisenbrauns, 1979.
———. 'Paleography and the Dead Sea Scrolls.' Pages 379–402 in *The Dead Sea Scrolls After Fifty Years: A Comprehensive Assessment*, vol. 1. Edited by Peter Flint and James VanderKam. Boston: Brill, 1998.
Culler, Jonathan. *On Deconstruction: Theory and Criticism after Structuralism*. Ithaca: Cornell University Press, 1982.
Davies, Philip. *Behind the Essenes: History and Ideology in the Dead Sea Scrolls*. Atlanta: Scholars Press, 1987.
———. 'The Birthplace of the Essenes: Where is "Damascus"?' *RevQ* 14 (1990): 503–19.
———. *The Damascus Covenant: An Interpretation of the "Damascus Document"*. Sheffield: JSOT Press, 1983.

———. 'Method and Madness: Some Remarks on Doing History with the Bible.' *JBL* 114 (1995): 699–705.
———. *Sects and Scrolls: Essays on Qumran and Related Topics*. Atlanta: Scholars Press, 1996.
———. 'Was there Really a Qumran Community?' *Currents in Research: Biblical Studies* 3 (1995): 9–35.
Davies, Philip, and Joan Taylor. 'On the Testimony of Women in 1QSa.' *DSD* 3 (1996): 223–35.
Derrida, Jacques. *Of Grammatology*. Translated by Gayatri Spivak. Baltimore: Johns Hopkins Press, 1974.
Detweiler, Robert, ed. *Reader Response Approaches to Biblical and Secular Texts*. Semeia 31 (1985).
Dimant, Devorah. 'Men as Angels: The Self-Image of the Qumran Community.' Pages 93–103 in *Religion and Politics in the Ancient Near East*. Edited by Adele Berlin. Bethesda, Md: University Press of Maryland, 1996.
Doudna, Greg. 'Dating the Scrolls on the Basis of Radiocarbon Analysis.' Pages 430–71 in *The Dead Sea Scrolls After Fifty Years: A Comprehensive Assessment*, vol. 1. Edited by Peter Flint and James VanderKam. Boston: Brill, 1998.
———. 'Paleography and the dating of individual Qumran texts.' Aug. 17, 1999. http://orion.mscc.huji.ac.il/orion/programs/Doudna.html.
Draisma, Sipke, ed. *Intertextuality in Biblical Writings: Essays in Honour of Bas van Iersel*. Kampen: Uitgeversmaatschappij J. H. Kok, 1989.
Duhaime, Jean. 'Relative Deprivation in New Religious Movements and the Qumran Community.' *RevQ* 16 (1993): 265–76.
Eagleton, Terry. *Literary Theory: An Introduction*. Minneapolis: University of Minnesota Press, 1983.
Eisenman, Robert. *James the Just in the Habakkuk Pesher*. Leiden: Brill, 1986.
———. *Maccabees, Zadokites, Christians and Qumran*. Leiden: Brill, 1983.
Eisenman, Robert, and James Robinson, eds. *A Facsimile Edition of the Dead Sea Scrolls*. Washington: Biblical Archaeology Society, 1991.
Elder, Linda Bennett. 'The Woman Question and Female Ascetics Among Essenes.' *BA* 57 (1994): 220–34.
Elman, Yaakov. 'Some Remarks on 4QMMT and the Rabbinic Tradition, Or, When is a Parallel Not a Parallel?' Pages 99–128 in *Reading 4QMMT: New Perspectives on Qumran Law and History*. Edited by John Kampen and Moshe Bernstein. Atlanta: Scholars Press, 1996.
Erder, Yoram. 'The Negation of the Exile in the Messianic Doctrine of the Karaite Mourners of Zion.' *HUCA* 68 (1997): 109–40.
Eshel, Hanan. '4QMMT and the History of the Hasmonean Period.' Pages 53–65 in *Reading 4QMMT: New Perspectives on Qumran Law and History*. Edited by John Kampen and Moshe Bernstein. Atlanta: Scholars Press, 1996.
Exum, Cheryl, and David Clines, eds. *The New Literary Criticism and the Hebrew Bible*. Sheffield: JSOT Press, 1993.
Fabry, Heinz-Josef. *Die Wurzel Sub in der Qumran-Literatur: Zur Semantic eines Grundbegriffes*. Koln-Bonn: Peter Hanstein Verlag GmbH, 1975.
Fewell, Danna, ed. *Reading Between Texts: Intertextuality and the Hebrew Bible*. Louisville: Westminster/John Knox Press, 1992.
Fish, Stanley. *Doing What Comes Naturally: Change, Rhetoric, and the Practice of Theory in Literary and Legal Studies*. Durham: Duke University Press, 1989.
———. *Is There a Text in This Class? The Authority of Interpretive Communities*. Cambridge: Harvard University Press, 1980.
Fitzmyer, Joseph, ed. *Documents of Jewish Sectaries*. New York: Ktav, 1970. Reprint, with 'Prolegomenon,' of Solomon Schechter, *Fragments of a Zadokite Work*. Cambridge: Cambridge University Press, 1910.
Flint, Peter, and James VanderKam, eds. *The Dead Sea Scrolls After Fifty Years: A Comprehensive Assessment*. 2 volumes. Boston: Brill, 1998–1999.

Foucault, Michel. *The Archaeology of Knowledge and The Discourse on Language*. Translated by A. M. Sheridan Smith. New York: Pantheon Books, 1972.
——. *Power/Knowledge: Selected Interviews and Other Writings 1972–1977*. New York: Pantheon Books, 1980.
——. 'What is an Author?' Pages 141–60 in *Textual Strategies: Perspectives in Post-Structuralist Criticism*. Edited by Josué Harari. Ithaca: Cornell University Press, 1979.
Fowler, Robert. 'Who is "the Reader," in Reader Response Criticism?' Pages 5–23 in *Reader Response Approaches to Biblical and Secular Texts*. Edited by Robert Detweiler. *Semeia* 31 (1985).
Fraade, Steven. 'Interpretive Authority in the Studying Community at Qumran.' *JJS* 44 (1993): 46–69.
——. 'To Whom It May Concern: 4QMMT and Its Addressee(s).' *RevQ* 19 (2000): 507–26.
Gadamer, Hans-Georg. *Truth and Method*. 2nd rev. ed. New York: Crossroad, 1989.
García Martínez, Florentino. '4QMMT in a Qumran Context.' Pages 15–27 in *Reading 4QMMT: New Perspectives on Qumran Law and History*. Edited by John Kampen and Moshe Bernstein. Atlanta: Scholars Press, 1996.
——. 'Damascus Document: A Bibliography of Studies 1970–89.' Pages 63–83 in *The Damascus Document Reconsidered*. Edited by Magen Broshi. Jerusalem: Israel Exploration Society, 1992.
——. *The Dead Sea Scrolls Translated*. New York: Brill, 1994.
——. 'Qumran Origins and Early History: A Groningen Hypothesis.' *Folia Orientalia* 25 (1988): 113–35.
García Martínez, Florentino, and Eibert J. C. Tigchelaar, eds. *The Dead Sea Scrolls Study Edition*. 2 vols. Grand Rapids, Mich.: Eerdmans, 2000.
García Martínez, Florentino, and Adam van der Woude. 'A "Groningen" Hypothesis of Qumran Origins and Early History.' *RevQ* 14 (1990): 521–41.
Geertz, Clifford. *The Interpretation of Cultures*. New York: Basic Books, 1973.
Ginzberg, Louis. *An Unknown Jewish Sect*. New York: Jewish Theological Seminary of America, 1976. Updated revision of *Eine unbekannte jüdische Sekte*. New York, 1922.
Goitein, S. D. *A Mediterranean Society: The Jewish Communities of the Arab World as Portrayed in the Documents of the Cairo Geniza*. 6 vols. Berkeley: University of California Press, 1967–1988.
Golb, Norman. 'Literary and Doctrinal Aspects of the Damascus Covenant in the Light of Karaite Literature.' *JQR* 47 (1956/57): 354–74.
——. *Who Wrote the Dead Sea Scrolls? The Search for the Secret of Qumran*. New York: Scribner, 1995.
Grabbe, Lester. '4QMMT and Second Temple Jewish Society.' Pages 89–108 in *Legal Texts and Legal Issues: Proceedings of the Second Meeting of the International Organization for Qumran Studies: Cambridge 1995*. Edited by Moshe Bernstein, Florentino García Martínez, and John Kampen. New York: Brill, 1997.
——. 'The End of the World in Early Jewish and Christian Calculations.' *RevQ* 11 (1982): 106–8.
——. *Judaism from Cyrus to Hadrian: Vol. 2, the Roman Period*. Minneapolis: Fortress Press, 1992.
Greenfield, Jonas. 'The Words of Levi Son of Jacob in Damascus Document IV, 15–19.' *RevQ* 13 (1988): 319–22.
Grossman, Maxine L. 'Reading *4QMMT*: Genre and History.' *RevQ* 20 (2001): 3–22.
Halpern, Baruch. *The First Historians: The Hebrew Bible and History*. San Francisco: Harper and Row, 1988.
Harari, Josué. 'Critical Factions/Critical Fictions.' Pages 17–72 in *Textual Strategies: Perspectives in Post-Structuralist Criticism*. Edited by Josué Harari. Ithaca: Cornell University Press, 1979.
Harari, Josué, ed. *Textual Strategies: Perspectives in Post-Structuralist Criticism*. Ithaca: Cornell University Press, 1979.

Harrington, Hannah. 'Holiness in the Laws of 4QMMT.' Pages 109–28 in *Legal Texts and Legal Issues: Proceedings of the Second Meeting of the International Organization for Qumran Studies: Cambridge 1995.* Edited by Moshe Bernstein, Florentino García Martínez, and John Kampen. New York: Brill, 1997.

Hartman, Lars. *Asking for a Meaning: A Study of 1 Enoch 1–5.* Lund: CWK Gleerup, 1979.

Hauer, Christian, Jr. 'Who was Zadok?' *JBL* 82 (1963): 89–94.

Hempel, Charlotte. 'Community Origins in the *Damascus Document* in the Light of Recent Scholarship.' Pages 316–29 in *The Provo International Conference on the Dead Sea Scrolls: Technological Innovations, New Texts, and Reformulated Issues.* Edited by Donald Parry and Eugene Ulrich. Boston: Brill, 1999.

———. 'Community Structures in the Dead Sea Scrolls: Admissions, Organization, Disciplinary Procedures.' Pages 67–92 in *The Dead Sea Scrolls After Fifty Years: A Comprehensive Assessment*, vol. 2. Edited by Peter Flint and James VanderKam. Boston: Brill, 1999.

———. *The Damascus Texts.* Sheffield: Sheffield Academic Press, 2000.

———. 'The Earthly Essene Nucleus of 1QSa.' *DSD* 3 (1996): 253–69.

———. 'The Laws of the Damascus Document and 4QMMT.' Pages 69–84 in *The Damascus Document: A Centennial of Discovery: Proceedings of the Third International Symposium of the Orion Center for the Study of the Dead Sea Scrolls and Associated Literature, 4–8 February, 1998.* Edited by Joseph Baumgarten, Esther Chazon, and Avital Pinnick. Boston: Brill, 2000.

———. *The Laws of the Damascus Document: Sources, Tradition and Redaction.* Boston: Brill, 1998.

———. 'The Penal Code Reconsidered.' Pages 337–48 in *Legal Texts and Legal Issues: Proceedings of the Second Meeting of the International Organization for Qumran Studies: Cambridge 1995.* Edited by Moshe Bernstein, Florentino García Martínez, and John Kampen. New York: Brill, 1997.

Hess, Richard. 'Peleg.' Pages 217–18 in vol. 5 of the *Anchor Bible Dictionary.* Edited by David Noel Freedman. 6 vols. New York: Doubleday, 1992.

Horgan, Maurya. *Pesharim: Qumran Interpretations of Biblical Books.* Washington: Catholic Biblical Association of America, 1979.

Iser, Wolfgang. *The Act of Reading: A Theory of Aesthetic Response.* Baltimore: Johns Hopkins University Press, 1978.

———. *The Implied Reader: Patterns of Communication in Prose Fiction from Bunyan to Beckett.* Baltimore: Johns Hopkins University Press, 1974.

Iwry, Samuel. 'Was there a Migration to Damascus? The Problem of שבי ישראל.' *Eretz Israel* 9 (1969): 80–88.

Japhet, Sara. 'The Prohibition of the Habitation of Women: The Temple Scroll's Attitude Toward Sexual Impurity and its Biblical Precedents.' *JANES* 22 (1993): 69–87.

Jastrow, Marcus. *A Dictionary of the Targumim, the Talmud Babli and Yerushalmi, and the Midrashic Literature.* New York: The Judaica Press, Inc., 1989; first ed. 1903.

Jauss, Hans Robert. 'Literary History as a Challenge to Literary Theory.' Pages 11–41 in *New Directions in Literary History.* Edited by Ralph Cohen. Baltimore: Johns Hopkins University Press, 1974.

———. *Toward an Aesthetic of Reception.* Trans. by Timothy Bahti. Minneapolis: University of Minnesota, 1982.

Jobling, David, and Stephen D. Moore, eds. *Poststructuralism as Exegesis. Semeia* 54 (1991).

Kahle, Paul. *The Cairo Geniza.* Oxford: Basil Blackwell, 1959.

Kampen, John. '4QMMT and New Testament Studies.' Pages 129–44 in *Reading 4QMMT: New Perspectives on Qumran Law and History.* Edited by John Kampen and Moshe Bernstein. Atlanta: Scholars Press, 1996.

Kampen, John, and Moshe Bernstein, eds. *Reading 4QMMT: New Perspectives on Qumran Law and History.* Atlanta: Scholars Press, 1996.

Kee, Howard. 'Membership in the Covenant People at Qumran and in the Teaching of Jesus.' Pages 104–22 in *Jesus and the Dead Sea Scrolls*. Edited by James H. Charlesworth. New York: Doubleday, 1992.
von Kellenbach, Katharina. *Anti-Judaism in Feminist Religious Writings*. Atlanta: Scholars Press, 1994.
Kister, Menahem. 'Studies in 4QMiqsat Ma'ase Ha-Torah and Related Texts: Law, Theology, Language and Calendar.' *Tarbiz* 68 (1999): 317–71.
Klawans, Jonathan. *Impurity and Sin in Ancient Judaism*. New York: Oxford University Press, 2000.
Knibb, Michael. 'Exile in the Damascus Document.' *JSOT* 25 (1983): 99–117.
———. *The Qumran Community*. New York: Cambridge University Press, 1987.
Knohl, Israel. 'Reconsidering the Dating and Recipient of MMT.' *Hebrew Studies* 37 (1996): 119–25.
Kraemer, Ross S. *Her Share of the Blessings: Women's Religions Among Pagans, Jews, and Christians in the Greco-Roman World*. New York: Oxford University Press, 1992.
———. 'Monastic Jewish Women in Greco-Roman Egypt: Philo Judaeus on the Therapeutrides.' *Signs: Journal of Women in Culture and Society* 14 (1989): 342–70.
———. 'Women's Authorship of Jewish and Christian Literature in the Greco Roman Period.' Pages 221–42 in *"Women Like This": New Perspectives on Jewish Women in the Greco-Roman World*. Edited by Amy-Jill Levine. Atlanta: Scholars Press, 1991.
Kraemer, Ross S., and Mary Rose D'Angelo, eds. *Women and Christian Origins*. New York: Oxford University Press, 1999.
Kraft, Robert A. *Barnabas and the Didache*. New York: Nelson and Sons, 1965.
Kristeva, Julia. 'Word, Dialogue, and Novel.' Pages 64–91 in *Desire in Language: A Semiotic Approach to Literature and Art*. Translated and edited by Leon Roudiez. New York: Columbia University Press, 1980.
Kugel, James. 'Levi's Elevation to the Priesthood in Second Temple Writings.' *HTR* 86 (1993): 1–64.
Kugler, Robert. *From Patriarch to Priest: The Levi-Priestly Tradition from Aramaic Levi to Testament of Levi*. Atlanta: Scholars Press, 1996.
———. 'Hearing 4Q225: A Case Study in Reconstructing the Religious Imagination of the Qumran Community.' *DSD* 9 (2002): forthcoming.
———. 'The Priesthood at Qumran: The Evidence of References to Levi and the Levites.' Pages 465–79 in *The Provo International Conference on the Dead Sea Scrolls: Technological Innovations, New Texts, and Reformulated Issues*. Edited by Donald Parry and Eugene Ulrich. Boston: Brill, 1999.
———. 'Review of John Kampen and Moshe J. Bernstein, eds., *Reading 4QMMT: New Perspectives on Qumran Law and History*.' *Ioud. Rev.* 9.001 (1999). ftp.lehigh.edu/pub/listserv/ioudaiosreview/9.1999/kampen.kugler.001.
Laato, Antti. 'The Chronology in the *Damascus Document* of Qumran.' *RevQ* 15 (1992): 605–7.
Lagrange, M.-J. 'La secte juive de la Nouvelle Alliance au pays de Damas.' *RB* 9 (1912): 213–40, 321–60.
Lange, Armin. *Weisheit und Prädestination: Weisheitliche Urordnung und Prädestination in den Textfunden von Qumran*. New York: Brill, 1995.
———. 'Wisdom and Predestination in the Dead Sea Scrolls.' *DSD* 2 (1995): 340–54.
Lategan, Bernard. 'Introduction: Coming to Grips with the Reader.' Pages 3–17 in *Reader Perspectives on the New Testament*. Edited by Edgar McKnight. *Semeia* 48 (1989).
de Lauretis, Teresa, ed. *Feminist Studies/Critical Studies*. Bloomington: Indiana University Press, 1986.
Levine, Amy-Jill, ed. *"Women Like This": New Perspectives on Jewish Women in the Greco-Roman World*. Atlanta: Scholars Press, 1991.
Lincoln, Bruce. *Authority: Construction and Corrosion*. Chicago: University of Chicago Press, 1994.

Liver, Jacob. 'The Sons of Zadok the Priests in the Dead Sea Sect.' *RevQ* 6 (1967): 3–30.
Machor, James L., and Philip Goldstein, eds. *Reception Study: From Literary Theory to Cultural Studies.* New York: Routledge, 2001.
Magness, Jodi. 'Qumran Archaeology: Past Perspectives and Future Prospects.' Pages 47–77 in *The Dead Sea Scrolls After Fifty Years: A Comprehensive Assessment*, vol. 1. Edited by Peter Flint and James VanderKam. Boston: Brill, 1998.
Malbon, Elizabeth, and Edgar McKnight, eds. *The New Literary Criticism and the New Testament.* Sheffield: JSOT Press, 1994; Valley Forge, Penn.: Trinity Press International, 1994.
McKnight, Edgar, ed. *Reader Perspectives on the New Testament. Semeia* 48 (1989).
Metso, Sarianna. 'Constitutional Rules at Qumran.' Pages 186–210 in *The Dead Sea Scrolls After Fifty Years: A Comprehensive Assessment*, vol. 1. Edited by Peter Flint and James VanderKam. Boston: Brill, 1998.
——. 'In Search of the *Sitz im Leben* of the *Community Rule.*' Pages 306–15 in *The Provo International Conference on the Dead Sea Scrolls: Technological Innovations, New Texts, and Reformulated Issues.* Edited by Donald Parry and Eugene Ulrich. Boston: Brill, 1999.
——. *The Textual Development of the Qumran Community Rule.* New York: Brill, 1997.
Meyers, Carol. *Discovering Eve: Ancient Israelite Women in Context.* New York: Oxford University Press, 1988.
Miller, Patricia Cox. '"Words With an Alien Voice": Gnostics, Scripture, and Canon.' *JAAR* 57 (1989): 459–83.
Moore, Stephen D. *Literary Criticism and the Gospels: The Theoretical Challenge.* New Haven: Yale University Press, 1989.
——. 'The "Post"-Age Stamp: Does It Stick? Biblical Studies and the Postmodern Debate.' *JAAR* 57 (1989): 543–57.
Morris, Brian. *Anthropological Studies of Religion: An Introductory Text.* New York: Cambridge University Press, 1987.
Murphy-O'Connor, Jerome. 'The Critique of the Princes of Judah (CD VIII,3–19).' *RB* 79 (1972): 200–16.
——. 'The *Damascus Document* Revisited.' *RB* 92 (1985): 223–46.
——. 'An Essene Missionary Document? CD II,14–VI,1.' *RB* 77 (1970): 201–29.
——. 'The Essenes and their History.' *RB* 81 (1974): 215–44.
——. 'A Literary Analysis of Damascus Document VI,2–VIII,3.' *RB* 78 (1971): 210–32.
——. 'A Literary Analysis of Damascus Document XIX,33–XX,34.' *RB* 79 (1972): 544–64.
——. 'The Original Text of CD 7.9–8.2 = 19.5–14.' *HTR* 64 (1971): 379–86.
Nemoy, Leon. 'Al-Qirqisani's Account of the Jewish Sects and Christianity.' *HUCA* 7 (1930): 317–97.
Nemoy, Leon, ed. *Karaite Anthology: Excerpts from the Early Literature.* New Haven: Yale University Press, 1980.
Neusner, Jacob. *Writing with Scripture: The Authority and Uses of the Hebrew Bible in the Torah of Formative Judaism.* Minneapolis: Fortress Press, 1989.
Newsom, Carol. 'Apocalyptic and the Discourse of the Qumran Community.' *JNES* 49 (1990): 135–44.
——. 'The Case of the Blinking I: Discourse of the Self at Qumran.' Pages 13–23 in *Discursive Formations, Ascetic Piety and the Interpretation of Early Christian Literature, Part 1.* Edited by Vincent Wimbush. *Semeia* 57 (1992).
——. '"Sectually Explicit" Literature from Qumran.' Pages 167–87 in *The Hebrew Bible and its Interpreters.* Edited by William Propp, Baruch Halpern, and David Noel Freedman. Winona Lake, Ind.: Eisenbrauns, 1990.
Nicholson, Linda, ed. *Feminism/Postmodernism.* New York: Routledge, 1990.
O'Day, Gail. 'Jeremiah 9.22–23 and 1 Corinthians 1.26–31: A Study in Intertextuality.' *JBL* 109 (1990): 259–67.

O'Dea, Thomas. *The Sociology of Religion.* Englewood Cliffs, N. J.: Prentice-Hall, 1966.
Olszowy-Schlanger, Judith. *Karaite Marriage Documents from the Cairo Geniza: Legal Tradition and Community Life in Mediaeval Egypt and Palestine.* New York: Brill, 1998.
Olyan, Saul. 'Zadok's Origins and the Tribal Politics of David.' *JBL* 101 (1982): 177–93.
Orion discussion list, August–December, 1999. http://orion.mscc.huji.ac.il/orion/archives.
Pardee, Dennis, et al. *Handbook of Ancient Hebrew Letters: A Study Edition.* Chico, Calif.: Scholars Press, 1982.
Parry, Donald, and Eugene Ulrich, eds. *The Provo International Conference on the Dead Sea Scrolls: Technological Innovations, New Texts, and Reformulated Issues.* Boston: Brill, 1999.
Paul, André. *Ecrits de Qumran et Sectes Juives aux Premiers Siecles de L'Islam: Recherches sur l'origine du Qaraisme.* Paris: Letouzey et Ane, 1969.
Pérez Fernández, Miguel. '4QMMT: Redactional Study,' *RevQ* 18 (1997): 191–205.
Peskowitz, Miriam. 'Engendering Jewish Religious History.' Pages 17–39 in *Judaism Since Gender.* Edited by Miriam Peskowitz and Laura Levitt. New York: Routledge, 1997.
———. *Spinning Fantasies: Rabbis, Gender, and History.* Berkeley: University of California Press, 1997.
Peterson, Sigrid. 'Caves, Documents, Women: Archives and Archivists.' Pages 761–72 in *The Dead Sea Scrolls: Fifty Years After Their Discovery; Proceedings of the Jerusalem Congress, July 20–25, 1997.* Edited by Lawrence Schiffman, Emanuel Tov, and James VanderKam. Jerusalem: Israel Exploration Society, 2000.
Phillips, Gary, ed. *Poststructural Criticism and the Bible: Text/History/Discourse. Semeia* 51 (1990).
Pietersma, Albert. 'Jannes and Jambres.' Pages 638–40 in vol. 3 of the *Anchor Bible Dictionary.* Edited by David Noel Freedman. 6 vols. New York: Doubleday, 1992.
Pietersma, Albert, and R. T. Lutz. 'Jannes and Jambres.' Pages 427–36 in *The Old Testament Pseudepigrapha.* Vol. 2. Edited by James H. Charlesworth. Garden City, N. Y.: Doubleday, 1985.
Plett, Heinrich, ed. *Intertextuality.* New York: Walter de Gruyter, 1991.
Provan, Iain. 'Ideologies, Literary and Critical: Reflections on Recent Writing on the History of Israel.' *JBL* 114 (1995): 585–606.
Qimron, Elisha. 'Appendix 2: Additional Textual Observations on 4QMMT.' Pages 201–2 in *Qumran Cave 4.V: Miqsat Ma'ase Ha-Torah.* Edited by Elisha Qimron and John Strugnell. DJD X. Oxford: Clarendon Press, 1994.
———. 'Celibacy in the Dead Sea Scrolls and the Two Kinds of Sectarians.' Pages 287–94 in *The Madrid Qumran Congress: Proceedings of the International Congress on the Dead Sea Scrolls; Madrid, 18–21 March, 1991.* Edited by Julio Barrera and Luis Montaner. New York: Brill, 1992.
———. 'The Halakha.' Pages 123–77 in *Qumran Cave 4.V: Miqsat Ma'ase Ha-Torah.* Edited by Elisha Qimron and John Strugnell. DJD X. Oxford: Clarendon Press, 1994.
———. *The Hebrew of the Dead Sea Scrolls.* Atlanta: Scholars Press, 1986.
———. 'The Nature of the Reconstructed Composite Text of 4QMMT.' Pages 9–13 in *Reading 4QMMT: New Perspectives on Qumran Law and History.* Edited by John Kampen and Moshe Bernstein. Atlanta: Scholars Press, 1996.
Qimron, Elisha, and James H. Charlesworth. 'Rule of the Community (1QS).' Pages 1–51 in *Rule of the Community and Related Documents.* Vol. 1 of *The Dead Sea Scrolls: Hebrew, Aramaic, and Greek Texts with English Translations.* Edited by James H. Charlesworth. Louisville: Westminster John Knox Press, 1994.
Qimron, Elisha, and John Strugnell. 'An Unpublished Halakhic Letter from Qumran.' Pages 400–407 in *Biblical Archaeology Today.* Jerusalem: Israel Exploration Society, 1984.
Qimron, Elisha, and John Strugnell, eds. *Qumran Cave 4.V: Miqsat Ma'ase Ha-Torah.* DJD X. Oxford: Clarendon Press, 1994.

Rabin, Chaim. *The Zadokite Documents*. 2nd. ed. Oxford: Clarendon Press, 1958.
Rabinowitz, Isaac. 'A Reconsideration of "Damascus" and "390 Years" in the "Damascus" ("Zadokite") Fragments.' *JBL* 73 (1954): 11–35.
Rainbow, Paul. 'The Last Oniad and the Teacher of Righteousness.' *JJS* 48 (1997): 30–52.
Ramsey, George. 'Zadok.' Pages 1034–36 in vol. 6 of the *Anchor Bible Dictionary*. Edited by David Noel Freedman. 6 vols. New York: Doubleday, 1992.
Reed, Stephen, et al., eds. *The Dead Sea Scrolls Catalogue: Documents, Photographs and Museum Inventory Numbers*. Atlanta: Scholars Press, 1994.
Röhrer-Ertl, Olav, Ferdinand Rohrhirsch, and Dietbert Hahn. 'Über die Gräberfelder von Khirbet Qumran, insbesondere die Funde der Campagne 1956. I: Anthropologische Datenvorlage und Erstauswertung aufgrund der Collectio Kurth.' *RevQ* 19 (1999): 3–46.
Roudiez, Leon, ed. *Desire in Language: A Semiotic Approach to Literature and Art*. New York: Columbia University Press, 1980.
Rowley, H. H. 'The 390 Years of the Zadokite Work.' Pages 341–47 in *Melanges bibliques rediges en l'honneur de Andre Robert*. Paris: Bloud and Gay, 1957.
———. 'Zadok and Nehushtan.' *JBL* 58 (1939): 113–41.
Schechter, Solomon. 'Reply to Dr. Büchler's Review of Schechter's "Jewish Sectaries."' *JQR* 4 (1913/14): 449–74.
Schiffman, Lawrence. 'The Law of Vows and Oaths (*Num*. 30, 3–16) in the *Zadokite Fragments* and the *Temple Scroll*.' *RevQ* 15 (1991): 199–214.
———. 'Laws Pertaining to Women in the *Temple Scroll*.' Pages 210–28 in *The Dead Sea Scrolls: Forty Years of Research*. Edited by Devorah Dimant and Uriel Rappaport. New York: Brill, 1992.
———. *Reclaiming the Dead Sea Scrolls: The History of Judaism, the Background of Christianity, the Lost Library of Qumran*. Philadelphia: Jewish Publication Society, 1994.
———. *Sectarian Law in the Dead Sea Scrolls: Courts, Testimony and the Penal Code*. Chico, Calif.: Scholars Press, 1983.
Schiffman, Lawrence, and James VanderKam, eds. *Encyclopedia of the Dead Sea Scrolls*. Oxford: Oxford University Press, 2000.
Schuller, Eileen. 'Women in the Dead Sea Scrolls.' Pages 117–44 in *The Dead Sea Scrolls after Fifty Years: A Comprehensive Assessment*, vol. 2. Edited by Peter Flint and James VanderKam. Boston: Brill, 1999.
———. 'Women in the Dead Sea Scrolls.' Pages 115–31 in *Methods of Investigation of the Dead Sea Scrolls and the Khirbet Qumran Site: Present Realities and Future Prospects*. Edited by Michael Wise, Norman Golb, John Collins, and Dennis Pardee. New York: The New York Academy of Sciences, 1994.
Schuller, Eileen, and Cecilia Wassen. 'Women: Daily Life.' Pages 981–84 in *Encyclopedia of the Dead Sea Scrolls*. Edited by Lawrence Schiffman and James VanderKam. Oxford: Oxford University Press, 2000.
Schur, Nathan. *History of the Karaites*. New York: Peter Lang, 1992.
———. *The Karaite Encyclopedia*. New York: Peter Lang, 1995.
Schwartz, Daniel. '"To Join Oneself to the House of Judah": Damascus Document 4.11.' *RevQ* 10 (1981): 435–46.
Schwarz, Ottilie. *Der erste Teil der Damaskusschrift und das Alte Testament*. Lichtland/Diest, 1965.
Scott, Joan. 'Deconstructing Equality-versus-Difference: Or, the Uses of Poststructuralist Theory for Feminism.' *Feminist Studies* 14 (1988): 33–50.
———. *Gender and the Politics of History*. New York: Columbia University Press, 1988.
Seeley, David. *Deconstructing the New Testament*. New York: Brill, 1994.
Segal, M. H. 'Additional Notes on "Fragments of a Zadokite Work."' *JQR* 3 (1912/13): 301–11.

———. *A Grammar of Mishnaic Hebrew.* Oxford: Clarendon Press, 1980; first ed. 1927.
Shanks, Hershel. 'Publisher's Foreword.' Pages xii–xlv in *A Facsimile Edition of the Dead Sea Scrolls.* Edited by Robert Eisenman and James Robinson. Washington: Biblical Archaeology Society, 1991.
Sharp, Carolyn. 'Phinehan Zeal and Rhetorical Strategy in 4QMMT.' *RevQ* 18 (1997): 207–22.
Shils, Edward. *Tradition.* Chicago: University of Chicago Press, 1981.
Silberman, Lou. 'Unriddling the Riddle: A Study in the Structure and Language of the Habakkuk Pesher.' *RevQ* 3 (1961): 323–64.
Soloff, R. A. 'Toward Uncovering Original Texts in the Zadokite Documents.' *NTS* 5 (1958/59): 62–7.
Stark, Rodney, and William Bainbridge. 'Of Churches, Sects, and Cults.' *JSSR* 18 (1979): 117–33.
Starr, Raymond. 'The Circulation of Literary Texts in the Roman World.' *CQ* 37 (1987): 213–23.
Stegemann, Hartmut. 'Das Gesetzeskorpus der "Damaskusschrift" (CD IX–XVI).' *RevQ* 14 (1990): 409–34.
———. *The Library of Qumran: On the Essenes, Qumran, John the Baptist, and Jesus.* Grand Rapids, Mich.: Eerdmans, 1998.
———. 'The Qumran Essenes—Local Members of the Main Jewish Union in Late Second Temple Times.' Pages 83–166 in *The Madrid Qumran Congress: Proceedings of the International Congress on the Dead Sea Scrolls; Madrid, 18–21 March, 1991.* Edited by Julio Barrera and Luis Montaner. New York: Brill, 1992.
Steudel, Annette. 'אחרית הימים in the Texts from Qumran.' *RevQ* 16 (1993): 225–46.
Stock, Brian. *Listening for the Text: On the Uses of the Past.* Baltimore: Johns Hopkins University Press, 1990.
Strickert, Frederick. 'Damascus Document VII, 10–20 and Qumran Messianic Expectation.' *RevQ* 12 (1986): 327–49.
Strugnell, John. 'Appendix 3: Additional Observations on 4QMMT.' Pages 204–5 in *Qumran Cave 4.V: Miqsat Ma'ase Ha-Torah.* Edited by Elisha Qimron and John Strugnell. DJD X. Oxford: Clarendon Press, 1994.
———. 'MMT: Second Thoughts on a Forthcoming Edition.' Pages 57–73 in *The Community of the Renewed Covenant: The Notre Dame Symposium on the Dead Sea Scrolls.* Edited by Eugene Ulrich and James VanderKam. Notre Dame: University of Notre Dame Press, 1994.
———. 'More on Wives and Marriage in the Dead Sea Scrolls: (*4Q416* 2 ii 21 [Cf. *1 Thess* 4:4] and *4QMMT* B).' *RevQ* 17 (1996): 537–47.
Suleiman, Susan, and Inge Crosman, eds. *The Reader in the Text: Essays on Audience and Interpretation.* Princeton: Princeton University Press, 1980.
Sussman, Yaakov. 'Appendix 1: The History of the Halakha and the Dead Sea Scrolls.' Pages 179–200 in *Qumran Cave 4.V: Miqsat Ma'ase Ha-Torah.* Edited by Elisha Qimron and John Strugnell. DJD X. Oxford: Clarendon Press, 1994.
Szyszman, S. 'A propos du Karaïsme et des textes de la Mer Morte.' *VT* 2 (1952): 343–48.
Taylor, Joan. 'The Cemeteries of Khirbet Qumran and Women's Presence at the Site.' *DSD* 6 (1999): 285–323.
Taylor, Joan, and Philip Davies. 'The So-Called Therapeutae of *De Vita Contemplativa*: Identity and Character.' *HTR* 91 (1998): 3–24.
Teigas, Demetrius. *Knowledge and Hermeneutic Understanding: A Study of the Habermas-Gadamer Debate.* Lewisburg: Bucknell University Press, 1995.
Thiering, Barbara. *The Gospels and Qumran: A New Hypothesis.* Sydney: Theological Explorations, 1981.
———. *Jesus and the Riddle of the Dead Sea Scrolls.* San Francisco: HarperCollins, 1992.

Thompson, Thomas. 'A Neo-Albrightean School in History and Biblical Scholarship?' *JBL* 114 (1995): 683–98.
Thorion-Vardi, Talia. 'The Use of the Tenses in the Zadokite Documents.' *RevQ* 12 (1985): 65–88.
Tompkins, Jane, ed. *Reader-Response Criticism: From Formalism to Post-Structuralism.* Baltimore: Johns Hopkins University Press, 1980.
Trebolle Barrera, Julio. 'The Authoritative Functions of Scriptural Works at Qumran.' Pages 95–110 in *The Community of the Renewed Covenant: The Notre Dame Symposium on the Dead Sea Scrolls.* Edited by Eugene Ulrich and James VanderKam. Notre Dame: University of Notre Dame Press, 1994.
Troeltsch, Ernst. *The Social Teaching of the Christian Churches.* Translated by Olive Wyon. New York: Harper, 1960; originally published, 1911.
Van Seters, John. *The Yahwist as Historian in Genesis.* Louisville: Westminster/John Knox Press, 1992.
VanderKam, James. 'The Calendar, 4Q327, and 4Q394.' Pages 179–94 in *Legal Texts and Legal Issues: Proceedings of the Second Meeting of the International Organization for Qumran Studies: Cambridge 1995.* Edited by Moshe Bernstein, Florentino García Martínez, and John Kampen. New York: Brill, 1997.
———. *Calendars in the Dead Sea Scrolls.* New York: Routledge, 1998.
———. *The Dead Sea Scrolls Today.* Grand Rapids, Mich.: Eerdmans, 1994.
———. 'Zadok and the SPR HTWRH HHTWM in Dam. Doc. V, 2–5.' *RevQ* 11 (1984): 561–70.
de Vaux, Roland. *Archaeology and the Dead Sea Scrolls.* London: Oxford University Press, 1973.
Veeser, H. Aram, ed. *The New Historicism.* New York: Routledge, 1989.
———. *The New Historicism Reader.* New York: Routledge, 1994.
Vermes, Geza. *The Complete Dead Sea Scrolls in English.* New York: Penguin Books, 1997.
———. 'The Leadership of the Qumran Community: Sons of Zadok—Priests—Congregation.' Pages 375–84 in *Geschichte—Tradition—Reflexion: Festschrift für Martin Hengel zum 70. Geburtstag.* Edited by Peter Schäfer. Tübingen: J. C. B. Mohr (Paul Siebeck), 1996.
———. 'Preliminary Remarks on Unpublished Fragments of the Community Rule from Qumran Cave 4.' *JJS* 62 (1991): 250–55.
Vermes, Geza and Martin Goodman, eds. *The Essenes According to the Classical Sources.* Sheffield: JSOT Press, 1989.
Vermes, Geza, Fergus Millar, and Matthew Black, eds. *The History of the Jewish People in the Age of Jesus Christ.* Vol 2. Revision of Emil Schürer. Edinburgh: T. and T. Clark, Ltd., 1979.
Vorster, Willem. 'The Protevangelium of James and Intertextuality.' Pages 262–75 in *Text and Testimony: Essays on New Testament and Apocryphal Literature in Honour of A. F. J. Klijn.* Edited by T. Baarda, A. Hilhorst, et al. Kampen: Uitgeversmaatschappij J. H. Kok, 1988.
Wacholder, Ben Zion. *The Dawn of Qumran: The Sectarian Torah and the Teacher of Righteousness.* Cincinnati: Hebrew Union College Press, 1983.
Weis, P. R. 'The Date of the Habakkuk Scroll.' *JQR* 41 (1950): 125–53.
Werman, Cana. 'Levi and Levites in the Second Temple Period.' *DSD* 4 (1997): 211–25.
Wernberg-Moller, Preben. 'צדיק, צדיק and צדוק in the Zadokite Fragments (CDC), the Manual of Discipline (DSD) and the Habakkuk-Commentary (DSH).' *VT* 3 (1953): 310–15.
White, Hayden. *Metahistory: The Historical Imagination in Nineteenth-Century Europe.* Baltimore: Johns Hopkins University Press, 1973.
———. 'New Historicism: A Comment.' Pages 293–302 in *The New Historicism.* Edited by H. Aram Veeser. New York: Routledge, 1989.

———. *Tropics of Discourse: Essays in Cultural Criticism*. Baltimore: Johns Hopkins University Press, 1978.
White, Sidnie. 'A Comparison of the "A" and "B" Manuscripts of the Damascus Document.' *RevQ* 12 (1987): 537–53.
Wieder, Naphtali. *The Judean Scrolls and Karaism*. London: Horovitz Publishing, 1962.
———. 'The Qumran Sectarians and the Karaites.' *JQR* 47 (1956/57): 97–113, 269–92.
Wimbush, Vincent, ed. *Discursive Formations, Ascetic Piety and the Interpretation of Early Christian Literature, Part 1*. Semeia 57 (1992).
Winquist, Charles, ed. *Text and Textuality*. Semeia 40 (1987).
Wise, Michael. *The First Messiah: Investigating the Savior Before Jesus*. San Francisco: HarperSanFrancisco, 1999.
———. 'The Teacher of Righteousness and the High Priest of the Intersacerdotium.' *RevQ* 14 (1990): 587–613.
Wise, Michael, Norman Golb, John Collins, and Dennis Pardee, eds. *Methods of Investigation of the Dead Sea Scrolls and the Khirbet Qumran Site: Present Realities and Future Prospects*. New York: The New York Academy of Sciences, 1994.
van Wolde, E. J. *A Semiotic Analysis of Genesis 2–3*. Assen/Mastricht, The Netherlands: Van Gorcum, 1989.
———. 'Trendy Intertextuality?' Pages 43–49 in *Intertextuality in Biblical Writings: Essays in Honour of Bas van Iersel*. Edited by Sipke Draisma. Kampen: Uitgeversmaatschappij J. H. Kok, 1989.
Worton, Michael, and Judith Still, eds. *Intertextuality: Theories and Practices*. New York: Manchester University Press, 1990.
van der Woude, Adam. 'Fifty Years of Qumran Research.' Pages 1–45 in *The Dead Sea Scrolls After Fifty Years: A Comprehensive Assessment*, vol. 1. Edited by Peter Flint and James VanderKam. Boston: Brill, 1998.
———. 'Wicked Priest or Wicked Priests? Reflections on the Identification of the Wicked Priest in the Habakkuk Commentary.' *JJS* 33 (1982): 349–59.
Xeravits, Geza. 'Precisions sur le texte original et le concept messianique de CD 7:13–8:1 et 19:5–14.' *RevQ* 19 (1999): 47–59.
Zeitlin, Solomon. 'The Hebrew Scrolls: A Challenge to Scholarship.' *JQR* 41 (1951): 251–75.
———. 'The Hebrew Scrolls and the Status of Biblical Scholarship.' *JQR* 42 (1951): 133–92.
———. 'Introduction.' Pages 1–32 in *The Zadokite Fragments: Facsimile of the Manuscripts in the Cairo Genizah Collection in the Possession of the University Library, Cambridge, England*. Philadelphia: Dropsie College for Hebrew and Cognate Learning, 1952.
———. 'The Pharisees.' *JQR* 16 (1926): 383–94.
Zias, Joseph. 'The Cemeteries of Qumran and Celibacy: Confusion Laid to Rest?' *DSD* 7 (2000): 220–53.

MODERN AUTHORS

Adam, A. K. M.   13
Aichele, George   22
Anderson, Janice   13
Astren, Fred D.   213

Bainbridge, William   25, 26, 29, 36
Baron, Salo   213, 214
Barrett, Michele   47
Barthes, Roland   18, 19
Bartlett, J. R.   177
Basser, Herbert   172
Baumgarten, Albert   10, 25–27, 36, 44, 104, 206, 207, 214, 217
Baumgarten, Joseph   1, 2, 3, 8, 10, 16, 51, 85, 90, 91, 93, 95, 96, 101–4, 106, 110, 111, 115, 117, 119, 125, 130, 133, 134, 137, 139, 155, 163–66, 168, 169, 171, 173, 174, 178, 179, 184, 186, 189, 194, 197, 199, 203, 208, 222
Beckwith, Roger   158
Bernstein, Moshe   58, 59
Black, Matthew   9
Boccaccini, Gabriele   25, 29, 31
Boyarin, Daniel   22, 55
Boyce, Mark   15, 144–46, 148, 149
Brooke, George   10, 13, 14, 59, 76, 77, 137, 144, 157, 163
Broshi, Magen   1, 103, 178
Büchler, Adolph   7
Burke, Sean   19
Burridge, Kenelm   26
Burrows, Millar   7

Cahn, Zvi   213
Callaway, Phillip   9, 68, 187, 198
Cameron, Averil   30
Camp, Claudia   56
Campbell, Jonathan   10, 11, 13–17, 19, 22, 23, 38, 90, 91, 138, 168, 171
Cansdale, Lena   43
Castelli, Elizabeth   12, 13, 20
Charlesworth, James H.   1, 30, 69, 72, 207
Chazon, Esther   1, 10, 27
Clines, David   13
Cohen, Shaye   27, 36

Collins, John   39, 92, 95, 115, 119, 128, 139, 140, 155, 158, 163
Cook, E.   45
Cotton, Hannah   43
Crosman, Inge   20
Cross, Frank Moore   44, 45, 207
Culler, Jonathan   19

D'Angelo, Mary Rose   56
Davies, Philip   ix, 6, 8, 9, 10, 13, 15, 17, 31, 43, 44, 72, 87, 91, 102–4, 110, 123, 128, 138, 140, 144–46, 148, 181, 198, 199, 207
Davis, Michael   2, 90
Derrida, Jacques   19
Detweiler, Robert   20
Dimant, Devorah   162
Doudna, Greg   45, 77, 207
Draisma, Sipke   22
Duhaime, Jean   26

Eagleton, Terry   18, 20
Eisenman, Robert   39
Elder, Linda Bennett   43, 46
Elman, Yaakov   59
Erder, Yoram   178
Eshel, Hanan   66
Exum, Cheryl   13

Fabry, Heinz-Josef   180
Fewell, Danna   22
Fish, Stanley   20, 21
Fitzmyer, Joseph   1, 6, 109
Flint, Peter   4, 39, 43, 44
Foucault, Michel   19, 41
Fowl, Stephen   13
Fowler, Robert   71
Fraade, Steven   33, 35, 59, 70, 72, 82, 182, 194

Gadamer, Hans-Georg   18
García Martínez, Florentino   1, 2, 8, 25, 29, 31, 59, 69, 115, 174
Geertz, Clifford   35
Ginzberg, Louis   6, 145
Goitein, S. D.   213
Golb, Norman   39, 215

Goldstein, Philip 20
Goodman, Martin 8
Grabbe, Lester 9, 59, 158
Greenfield, Jonas 169
Grossman, Maxine L. 59
Gunn, David 13

Hahn, Dietbert 45
Halpern, Baruch 9
Harari, Josué 4, 19
Harrington, Hannah 59
Hartman, Lars 110
Hauer, Christian, Jr. 177
Hauser, Alan 13
Hempel, Charlotte 1, 2, 10, 27, 29, 44, 59, 123, 138, 144
Hess, Richard 165
Horgan, Maurya 76, 116

Iser, Wolfgang 20
Iwry, Samuel 198

Japhet, Sara 44
Jastrow, Marcus 97
Jauss, Hans Robert 20
Jobling, David 13

Kahle, Paul 215, 216
Kampen, John 58, 59, 63
Kee, Howard 30
von Kellenbach, Katharina 56
Kister, Menahem 59
Klawans, Jonathan 179
Knibb, Michael 9, 144, 148, 199
Knohl, Israel 59
Kraemer, Ross S. 15, 48, 56
Kraft, Robert A. 16
Kristeva, Julia 21, 22
Kugel, James 169
Kugler, Robert 13, 71, 169, 176, 191

Laato, Antti 132
Lagrange, M.-J. 6
Lange, Armin 92, 94, 98
Lategan, Bernard 71
de Lauretis, Teresa 47
Levine, Amy-Jill 15, 48, 56
Lincoln, Bruce 33
Liver, Jacob 201
Lutz, R. T. 171

Machor, James L. 20
Magness, Jodi 44, 45
Malbon, Elizabeth 13

McKnight, Edgar 13, 20
Metso, Sarianna 31, 32, 36, 73, 90, 138, 141, 155, 202, 207
Meyers, Carol 55
Millar, Fergus 9
Miller, Patricia Cox 19
Moore, Stephen D. 12, 13, 20–22
Morris, Brian 36
Murphy-O'Connor, Jerome 16, 69, 91, 112, 123, 138, 140, 144, 145, 151, 172, 198

Nemoy, Leon 7, 213–15
Neusner, Jacob 16
Newsom, Carol 10, 13, 27, 35, 94, 95, 107, 162
Nicholson, Linda 47

O'Day, Gail 22
O'Dea, Thomas 26
Olszowy-Schlanger, Judith 214
Olyan, Saul 177

Pardee, Dennis 39, 65
Parry, Donald 32, 39
Paul, André 214
Pérez Fernández, Miguel 59
Peskowitz, Miriam 47, 48, 56
Peterson, Sigrid 43
Phillips, Gary 12, 13
Pietersma, Albert 171
Pinnick, Avital 1, 10
Plett, Heinrich 21
Porter, Stanley 13
Provan, Iain 9

Qimron, Elisha 44, 57–61, 63–66, 69, 70, 72, 75, 79, 94, 181, 207

Rabin, Chaim 94–96, 98, 102–4, 172, 174, 181
Rabinowitz, Isaac 145
Rainbow, Paul 70
Ramsey, George 177
Reed, Stephen 174
Röhrer-Ertl, Olav 45
Rohrhirsch, Ferdinand 45
Roudiez, Leon 21
Rowley, H. H. 10, 177

Schechter, Solomon 1, 6, 7, 109
Schiffman, Lawrence 8, 27, 28, 43, 45, 46, 59, 109, 186
Schuller, Eileen 43, 45, 46, 48, 50, 54

Schur, Nathan 6, 215, 217, 218
Schwartz, Daniel 1, 2, 3, 10, 51, 85, 93, 95, 96, 101, 102–4, 111, 113, 117, 119, 125, 130, 133, 137, 139, 155, 163, 166, 169, 173–75, 178, 197, 203, 208, 222
Schwartz, Regina 12
Schwarz, Ottilie 10, 15
Scott, Joan 43, 47
Seeley, David 13
Segal, M. H. 7, 97
Shanks, Hershel 58
Sharp, Carolyn 59
Shils, Edward 154
Silberman, Lou 76
Soloff, R. A. 145
Stark, Rodney 25
Starr, Raymond 15
Stegemann, Hartmut 8, 28, 29, 31, 36, 45, 46, 69, 138, 148, 216
Steudel, Annette 92, 132, 158
Still, Judith 21
Stock, Brian 21
Strickert, Frederick 137
Strugnell, John 44, 57, 58, 60, 61, 63–66, 69, 70, 72, 75, 79, 85
Suleiman, Susan 20
Sussman, Yaakov 59
Szyszman, S. 7, 215

Taylor, Joan 43–45
Teigas, Demetrius 18
Thiering, Barbara 39
Thompson, Thomas 9
Thorion-Vardi, Talia 94

Tigchelaar, Eibert J. C. 1, 2
Tompkins, Jane 20
Trebolle Barrera, Julio 196
Troeltsch, Ernst 25

Ulrich, Eugene 32, 39

Van Seters, John 9
VanderKam, James 4, 9, 31, 39, 43, 44, 59, 61, 172
Veeser, H. Aram 40
Vermes, Geza 8, 9, 30, 33, 44, 45, 69, 70, 72, 84, 158, 162, 175, 186, 187, 198, 204, 207
Vorster, Willem 22

Wacholder, Ben Zion 7, 172, 221
Wassen, Cecilia 43
Weis, P. R. 7
Werman, Cana 169
Wernberg-Moller, Preben 172
White, Hayden 40
White, Sidnie 138
Wieder, Naphtali 7, 214, 215
Wimbush, Vincent 13
Winquist, Charles 13
Wise, Michael 39, 43, 45, 69, 77
van Wolde, E. J. 20, 22
Worton, Michael 21
van der Woude, Adam 4, 25, 29, 31, 69

Xeravits, Geza 137

Zeitlin, Solomon 7
Zias, Joseph 45

INDEX OF ANCIENT SOURCES

Hebrew Title

Genesis
1:1–2:25   99
7:12   143
10:25   165
10:30   97
14:17–21   169
25:6   97
29:1   97
34   169

Exodus
6:16–25   171
7:11–12   171
7:22   171
19:6   168
19:8   163
24:3–7   163
32   171
32:25–29   169, 171

Leviticus
10   189
18:13   51
26   91
26:45   112

Numbers
3   170
3:21–38   170
4:16   189
14   91
16:1–35   171
17:1–28   171
21:18   193
23:7   97
25:6–13   169, 189
25:7   171
25:12–13   171

Deuteronomy
17:17   51
28   91
31:21   163
33:8–11   169
33:15   96
33:27   96

Joshua
21:42   163
24:24–25   163

Judges
6:3   97
6:33   97
7:12   97
8:10   97

1 Samuel
2:12   171
2:27–36   172, 173

2 Samuel
6:19   53

1 Kings
1:32–40   172
2:26–27   172, 189
2:35   172
5:10   97
19:8   143
19:15   143

2 Kings
19:25   100

Isaiah
1:27   181
7:17   138, 182
11:14   97
19:11   96
23:7   98
24:2   170
24:5   170
24:17   169
27:1   99
37:26   100
45:18–21   99
46:9–10   100
51:9   98
51:9–10   99
59   91
59:20   181
61:6   168

INDEX OF ANCIENT SOURCES

Jeremiah
30:20	96
46:26	98
49:28	97

Ezekiel
4:5–6	131, 155
9:4	224
25:4	97
25:10	97
40:46	173
43:18ff.	173
44:10–16	173
44:15	130, 132, 174, 185, 222, 227
48:11	173

Hosea
4:16	116, 117, 133, 181

Amos
5:12–13	197
5:21–26	197
5:27	180, 197
9:11	197

Micah
5:1	96, 98
7:20	98

Habakkuk
1:4c	152, 187
1:5	156
1:12	98
2:12–13	156

Zechariah
13:7	139, 141, 183

Malachi
1:1–2:9	176
1:10	176
2:4–7	169
3:18	166

Psalms
37:30–31	76
37:32–33	75
44:2	98
55:20	96
74	99
74:2	96
74:12	98, 99
77	99
77:12–21	98
78:2	96
89:9–11	99
105	121
106	91, 121
110:4	169
119:152	96
139:5	97
143:5	98

Job
1:3	97
3:8	99
23:8	96
26:7–13	99
29:2	96

Proverbs
8:23	100
8:24–31	100

Lamentations
1:7	98
2:17	100
5:21	96

Daniel
9	143
9:1–2	158
9:24–27	158

Ezra
2:36	178
7:1–6	177
10:18–22	178

Nehemiah
7:39–42	178
11:10–11	177
11:10–14	178
12:1–21	178
12:46	98

1 Chronicles
5:27–41	178
6:35–37	177
9:10–11	177
9:10–13	178

Apocrypha and Pseudepigrapha

1 Esdras		*Ben Sira*	
5:5	178	44–50	121
8:1–2	177		
		1 Enoch	
2 Esdras		85–90	121
1:1–3	177		
		Jubilees	
Judith		30:1–32:9	169
5	121		

New Testament

Gospel of Matthew		*Acts of the Apostles*	
1:1–17	195	7:1–53	121
Gospel of Luke		*Hebrews*	
3:23–38	195	5:1–7:8	169

Dead Sea Scrolls

CD (Damascus Document)		1:12–2:1	133
1–8	90, 128	1:13	125, 133
1:1	48, 152, 192	1:13–14	116, 147
1:1–5	110, 146	1:13–15	181
1:1–20	109	1:13–21	115
1:1–2:1	91, 108, 114, 145	1:14	3, 109
1:1–2:5	113	1:14–15	3, 115
1:1–3:16	91, 181	1:15	181
1:1–4:12a	91	1:15–17	116, 152
1:2	108	1:16	109
1:3	109, 175, 181	1:17–18	110
1:4	109, 111	1:18–21	192
1:4–5	193	1:18–2:1	149
1:4–6	131	1:19–20	117, 152
1:5	109	1:20	110
1:5–6	88	1:21–2:1	81, 117
1:5–7	9, 128	2:1	110, 158
1:5–10	146	2:2	48, 95
1:5–11	68	2:2–7	93
1:6	179	2:2–13	91
1:6–8	175	2:5–6	94, 181
1:7	109, 163, 179, 193	2:6–3:12	133
1:9	134	2:7	96, 98
1:9–11	128	2:7–8	97
1:10	88	2:7–10	93, 101
1:10–11	147	2:8	102
1:10–12	131	2:9	95, 102, 104, 158
1:11	3, 109, 192	2:10	95
1:11–14	156	2:11	95, 110, 178, 195
1:11–17	149	2:11–12	129
1:12	109, 137	2:11–13	93, 105

INDEX OF ANCIENT SOURCES

2:12	34, 106	4:6b–8	179
2:12–13	105	4:7	192
2:13	178, 181, 203	4:7–10	112
2:14	110	4:8	113, 174
2:14–3:12	50, 203	4:8–10	111, 137
2:14–3:16	81, 91	4:10	113
2:14–4:12a	91	4:10–11	136, 164, 166
2:14–6:1	91, 144, 151	4:11	173, 179, 196
2:16	181	4:12–5:14	50
2:16–18	123	4:14–17	57
2:16–3:16	130	4:14–5:11	122
2:17–18	123	4:16–17	169
2:17–19	119	4:17–18	50, 170
2:18	50, 203	4:19–20	3
2:18–21	120	4:20–21	50, 51, 172
2:21	81, 123, 203	4:20–5:11	50, 57
3:1	123, 181	4:21	169
3:1–7	119	5:1	51, 95
3:1–4:21	109, 181	5:1–2	51
3:2	123	5:1–3	169
3:2–4	81	5:2–5	172, 222
3:4	110, 123, 181	5:2–6	122
3:6	123	5:4–5	174
3:6–10	53	5:5	109
3:7	179	5:6–7	190
3:8–10	81, 120, 123	5:7	50
3:9–10	121	5:7–11	51
3:10	179	5:11–6:2	122
3:10–11	111, 135	5:14–16	137
3:10–13	110, 219	5:18–19	125, 171
3:11	181	5:20	181
3:13	104, 163, 227	5:20–6:3	125, 133
3:13–16	112	5:21	179
3:14	85, 123, 181, 196	6:1	182
3:14–15	81	6:1–14	180
3:14–16	122	6:1–7:1	181
3:15	203	6:2–3	163, 193
3:17	227	6:2–11	130, 191, 193, 203
3:17–18	122	6:3–11	125, 187
3:17–20	82, 125	6:5	9, 164, 180, 182, 197
3:19	173	6:6–8	182
3:20	137	6:11	68, 109, 192
3:21–4:2	174, 222	6:12–13	176
3:21–4:4	130, 132, 185, 227	6:14	175
4–6	208	6:15–16	190
4:1	181, 203	6:15–18	122
4:2	181	6:18–19	85, 122
4:2–3	179, 191, 196	6:19	95, 180, 197
4:2–4	174, 180, 190	6:20	48
4:3	9, 95, 164, 181, 192	7–8	140, 143
4:3–4	187, 188	7:1–5	137
4:4	178, 195, 206	7:4–5	48, 53
4:4–6	2, 194, 222	7:5	57
4:5–6	178	7:5–8:21	16, 137, 138, 223

7:6–7	48	20:13–17	68
7:9	182, 183	20:14	3, 183
7:10–21	224	20:15	3, 88, 142
7:11–14	133	20:17	181, 183, 203
7:11–21	130	20:20	183
7:12	182	20:20–21	166
7:12–21	187	20:21–34	165
7:14–21	160, 180, 197, 198	20:22	184
7:17–8:3	137	20:22–25	136
8:1	95	20:23	183
8:1–2	133, 135, 158	20:24	166
8:1–5	164	20:25–27	164, 184
8:3–9	137	20:25–28	137
8:4	182, 183	20:31	203
8:5–6	137	20:32	109, 183, 192
8:5–9	133	20:33–34	137, 139
8:9–21	16, 137	15–16	90, 165
8:13	3	15:4	184
8:13–19	133	15:5	104, 165
8:14	109	15:5–6	48
8:16	180, 182, 183	15:7	184
8:18	3	15:7–15	194
8:18–19	164	15:8–9	130
8:19	182, 183	15:8–10	163
8:21	180, 183, 197	15:9	184
19:1	203	15:9–10	202
19:1–34	16, 90, 128, 137, 140, 143, 223	15:12	164, 184
		15:13–14	203
19:3	48	16:1	49, 165, 184
19:6	183	16:1–2	164, 202
19:6–20:20	139	16:4–5	164, 184, 202
19:7–9	141, 160, 224	16:6	122, 130
19:9	183	16:7	49
19:10–11	163	16:9	49, 184
19:11–13	160	16:10–12	49
19:12	224	16:14	168
19:16–17	183	9–14	90
19:16–19	164	9:1–10:3	133
19:24–25	3	9:1–12:20	165
19:27	109	9:2	95
19:29	180, 183	9:13	184
19:31	3	9:13–15	168
19:32–33	164	9:16–22	194
19:33–34	180, 183, 197	10:3	184
19:34–35	16, 137, 183	10:4–8	194, 203
20	128, 137–43	10:5	163, 168, 189
20:1	3, 68, 109, 163	10:6	203
20:1–4	16	11:7	184
20:1–13	165	11:10	184
20:1–34	16, 90, 109, 137	11:11	49, 184
20:5	183	11:12	49
20:8–13	164	11:17–21	175
20:10	183	11:21	109
20:12	180, 197	12:1	49
20:13–15	128, 156	12:10–11	49

12:19	200	2:1–2	155
12:22–23	200	2:1–6	156
12:22–14:23	165	2:7–10	69
12:23	104, 139	5:11	155
12:23–13:2	163	5:11–12	156
13:2	203	7	159
13:2–4	168, 194	7:1–5	34
13:3–4	189	8:9–10	70
13:4	95	10:9	155
13:5–7	168	10:9–13	156
13:6ff.	72	11:4–8	86
13:12	103	11:5	200
13:17	49	12:7–9	200
14:1	184		
14:3–4	163, 193	*1QH (Hodayot)*	
14:5–6	163, 193	5:12	103
14:6–8	168		
14:7–13	194	*4Q171 (Psalms pesher)*	
14:8	203	2:15	69
14:10	95	3:15	69
14:19	139, 163	4:5–9	69, 75

1QS (Community Rule)

1:1–5	95	*4Q174 (Florilegium)*	
3:13ff.	72	2:1	95
3:15–4:26	73		
5:1–3	201, 207	*4Q256 (4QS^b)*	
5:8–10	201, 202	5 1–3	207
5:20–21	205		
6:12	72	*4Q258 (4QS^d)*	
9:7	205	1 i 1–3	207
9:16–17	69, 75		
9:21	72	*4Q266 (Damascus Document^a)*	
		1 a–b 1–2	115
1QSa (Rule of the Congregation)		1 a–b 3–7	115
1:1–3	201, 202	1 a–b 5	110
1:1–27	203	1 a–b 22	184
1:7	203	1–2 i	91
1:15–16	205	2 i 1–6	106
1:23	205	2 iii 24	179
1:23–25	201	3 ii 5–7	125
1:24	202	3 iii	137
2:2–3	201	3 iv	137
2:2–18	203	4 i	128, 137
2:3	202	4 i 1–13	16
2:13	205	5 i 11–12	115, 184
2:21	203	5 i 15	184
		5 ii 1–4	168
		5 ii 4–6	199
1QSb (Blessings Scroll)		5 ii 5	171, 189, 194
3:22–25	201, 202	5 ii 5–13	168
		5 ii 8–10	171, 189, 194
1QpHab (Habakkuk pesher)		6 i 1–13	168
1:12	152	6 i 13	171, 189, 194
1:12–13	187	6 ii 1–13	49

9 iii 4–5	49
10–11	165
10 ii 1	184
11 5	184
11 5–16	164
11 5–21	134
11 8	168
12	49
14 a	49

4Q267 (Damascus Document[b])

1 9	91
1 8	106
2 2–3	125
3	128, 137
3 1–7	16
5 ii 3	184
5 ii 4–6	115
5 iii	168
5 iii 8	199
9 v 8	163
9 v 10	163
9 vi	165
9 vi 2–3	184
9 vi 4–5	49
9 vi 5	184

4Q268 (Damascus Document[c])

1	91
1 1–8	106
1 9	110

4Q269 (Damascus Document[d])

5	137
6	137
7	168
9 1–2	49
9 4–8	49
11 ii	165

4Q270 (Damascus Document[e])

1 ii	179
2 i 16–19	49
2 ii 5–9	168
2 ii 6	171, 189, 194
2 ii 15–17	49
2 ii 19	110
4 1–9	49
4 13–16	49
5 17	49
7 i–ii	165
7 i 6–7	164, 184
7 i 11	164, 184
7 i 11–15	134
7 i 12	184
7 i 13–14	164, 184
7 i 13–15	46
7 i 16	168
7 i 19	184
7 i 19–21	134

4Q271 (Damascus Document[f])

2 4–5	168
3 2	184
3 11	49
3 15	49

4Q272 (Damascus Document[g])

1 i	168
1 ii	168
1 ii 1–10	49
1 ii 2	171, 189, 194

4Q273 (Damascus Document[h])

2	168
4 i	168
4 ii	168
5 4–5	49

4Q394–398 (MMT[a-f] composite text)

B	63
B 1–2	80
B 3	62
B 5–6	62
B 8	61, 62
B 10	61, 79
B 11–13	62
B 16–17	62
B 25–26	62
B 27	61, 62
B 27–34	63
B 29	61
B 36–37	61
B 38	62, 79
B 42	61
B 46	79
B 55	61
B 60–62	63
B 63–64	62
B 65	61
B 66	61, 79
B 68	62, 79
B 70	61, 62, 79
B 73	61
B 76–77	61, 79
B 79	62
B 80	62, 79
C 6	79

C 7	83	C 28–29	82
C 7–8	62	C 29–30	75
C 7–12	79	C 30	80
C 10	62, 83	C 31–32	65
C 11–26	64		
C 17	79	*4Q398 (MMT^e)*	
C 21	79	11–13	61, 64
C 23–25	79		
C 26–28	74, 84	*11QT (Temple Scroll)*	
C 26–30	62, 65	17:1–29:9	85
C 27	57, 80		

Rabbinic Writings

m. Rosh Hash.		*b. Shabbat*	
2:8–9	86	22b	95
m. Avot			
1:1–18	164		
2:9–10	164		

Classical Authors

Josephus, War		*Philo*, Every Good Man is Free	
2:119–61	8	75–91	8
2:160–61	8, 44		
		Philo, Hypoth., *second extract*	
Josephus, Ant.		8:11:1–18	8
13:171–2	8		
18:11	8	*Pliny*, Nat. Hist.	
18:18–22	8	5:73	8

SELECTED SUBJECT INDEX

Aaron 98, 114, 115, 121, 122, 125, 128, 139, 140, 146, 147, 163, 170, 171, 176–78, 189, 190, 193, 194, 205
Aaronite priesthood, sons of Aaron 169–71, 177, 188, 190, 191, 194, 198, 199, 201, 205
Abraham 49, 50, 111, 119–21, 130,
archaeology x, 39, 44, 54
audience-oriented criticism, reader-response ix, 14, 19, 20, 23
authority 5, 18, 20–22, 24, 30, 32–36, 41, 46, 55, 56, 72, 78, 131, 134–36, 144, 148, 152, 153, 167, 170–72, 176–78, 188–92, 194, 195, 201–9, 212, 223, 226–28

Babylonia, Babylonian exile/conquest 3, 9, 11, 88, 108, 110, 114, 115, 125, 128, 131, 134, 146, 175, 179, 198–200, 220
Belial 57, 65, 74, 75, 78, 82, 84, 125, 138, 139, 169–72

Cairo Genizah 1, 7, 215, 216
calendar 59, 61, 84, 85, 86, 158
canon 3
cemetery 44, 45, 53
contemporary literary criticism ix, 5, 12–14, 22, 23, 37
critical theory 12, 13

Damascus 2, 9, 11, 138, 160, 180, 196–200, 220, 224
David 50, 51, 64, 79, 122, 169, 172, 197, 222
deconstruction: see post-structuralist criticism
discourse 24, 40, 67, 68, 94

Eleazar 50, 172, 222
Elijah 143
endtimes 2, 27, 38, 44, 64, 75, 82–84, 92, 96, 98, 115, 116, 124, 135–40, 142–44, 154, 156–60, 163, 165, 166, 174, 180, 191, 192, 201, 205, 206, 208
eschatology 140, 158, 159

Essenes, Essene Hypothesis 8, 9, 25, 28, 29, 30, 31, 44
exile 2, 37, 85, 88, 91, 111–13, 124, 125, 130, 132, 144, 147, 162, 166, 16, 173–78, 186, 195–200, 209, 218, 220, 221

foundation document x, 24, 30, 31, 35, 212, 224, 225–27

gender xi, 42–57
genre 42, 60, 65–68, 73

halakhah 24, 28, 29, 34, 36, 42, 52, 58, 59, 61–65, 69–73, 79, 80, 83, 84, 213, 216, 217, 220, 225
historiography ix, x, 1, 4, 5, 11–13, 24, 25, 37, 40, 41, 52, 57, 65, 70, 73, 76, 87–89, 101, 107, 110, 128, 129, 210, 224

ideology ix–xi, 3, 9, 10, 15, 24, 26–41, 57, 87, 89, 92, 100, 110, 115, 124–26, 128, 147–48, 153, 161, 164, 208, 209, 220, 225
intertextuality 23, 22, 37
Isaac 50, 111, 119, 120

Jambres 171
Jannes 122, 125, 171
Jacob 50, 98, 99, 111, 119, 121
Joseph 98, 99

Karaites 6, 7, 213–18

Levi 50, 169, 170, 176, 177, 189, 190, 194, 205
Levitical priesthood, sons of Levi 163, 168, 169–171, 173, 189, 190
Liar, man of the lie, Spouter 3, 75, 135, 140, 142, 152, 155–57

marriage 45, 49–51, 53, 63, 213–15
Melchizedek 169
messiah, messianism 138–42, 159, 160, 163, 183, 197, 201, 217, 218, 223, 224

… SELECTED SUBJECT INDEX

Moses 50, 64, 79, 83, 98, 121, 122, 125, 130, 134, 163, 164, 171, 176

New Historicism x, 40
New Historiography x, 37–40
Noah 50, 81, 111, 119–121, 143, 220

oaths 48, 49, 90, 163, 190, 197, 202

Peleg, house of Peleg 165, 166
pesher ix, 8, 68–70, 73–78, 85, 86, 90, 116, 151, 154–157, 159, 187, 200
postmodern theory 12, 13
post-structuralist criticism, deconstruction 12, 13
predestination 82, 93, 96–101, 104, 106, 131, 217
priesthood, priests: see specific priesthoods
purity 49, 58, 63, 65, 68, 90, 122, 167–168, 171, 175, 194, 203

radiocarbon dating 45, 77, 207
reader response criticism: see audience-oriented criticism
redaction 11, 14–17, 31–32, 129, 137–41, 144–53, 207, 208, 224
righteousness 2, 28, 30, 37, 48, 50, 52, 55, 56, 65, 74, 75, 81, 82, 90–91, 108–110, 116–18, 122, 148, 165–67, 175, 181, 187–89, 191–94

Sabbath 49, 81, 85, 90, 130, 175, 226
Sadducees 6, 63, 71, 185, 214, 216, 221, 222

sanctuary, Temple 50, 62, 63, 68, 80, 99, 110, 130, 146, 151, 165–67, 170, 173–77, 185, 186, 189, 192, 198, 200, 220, 221
schism 25, 26, 28, 36, 60, 116, 132–35, 145, 151, 157, 213, 215, 217
scripture 2, 3
sectarianism 1, 6, 8, 24–36, 39, 41, 42, 59, 215, 217, 221
sociology 24–28, 30
sons of Aaron: see Aaronite priesthood
sons of Levi: see Levitical priesthood
sons of Zadok: see Zadokite priesthood
Spouter of Lies: see Liar

Teacher of Righteousness 3, 28, 33, 68–73, 75–78, 85, 88, 109, 114, 128, 131, 133–35, 147, 152, 155, 156, 187–89, 192, 193
Temple: see sanctuary
textuality 5, 11, 12–24
Torah 64, 65, 69, 74–84, 112, 113, 130, 134, 138, 163, 164, 169, 172–80, 188, 197–200, 202, 203, 222, 224, 227

vow 90, 167, 168

Watchers 50, 81, 119, 120, 219, 220
Wicked Priest 68–78, 85, 155, 156
wisdom 33, 64, 74, 76, 84, 93, 96, 98, 101, 131, 176
Wisdom (personified) 100, 108

Zadok 50, 109, 172, 176–78, 201, 215, 221–23
Zadokite priesthood, sons of Zadok 70, 130, 131, 168, 171, 173–76, 185–94, 201–9, 221–23

STUDIES ON THE TEXTS OF THE DESERT OF JUDAH

1. Wernberg Møller, P. *The Manual of Discipline*. Translated and Annotated, with an Introduction. 1957. ISBN 90 04 02195 7
2. Ploeg, J. van der. *Le rouleau de la guerre*. Traduit et annoté, avec une introduction. 1959. ISBN 90 04 02196 5
3. Mansoor, M. *The Thanksgiving Hymns*. Translated and Annotated with an Introduction. 1961. ISBN 90 04 02197 3
5. Koffmahn, E. *Die Doppelurkunden aus der Wüste Juda*. Recht und Praxis der jüdischen Papyri des 1. und 2. Jahrhunderts n. Chr. samt Übertragung der Texte und Deutscher Übersetzung. 1968. ISBN 90 04 03148 0
6. Kutscher, E.Y. *The Language and linguistic Background of the Isaiah Scroll (1 QIsa^a)*. Transl. from the first (1959) Hebrew ed. With an obituary by H.B. Rosén. 1974. ISBN 90 04 04019 6
6a. Kutscher, E.Y. *The Language and Linguistic Background of the Isaiah Scroll (1 QIsa^a)*. Indices and Corrections by E. Qimron. Introduction by S. Morag. 1979. ISBN 90 04 05974 1
7. Jongeling, B. *A Classified Bibliography of the Finds in the Desert of Judah, 1958-1969*. 1971. ISBN 90 04 02200 7
8. Merrill, E.H. *Qumran and Predestination*. A Theological Study of the Thanksgiving Hymns. 1975. ISBN 90 04 042652
9. García Martínez, F. *Qumran and Apocalyptic*. Studies on the Aramaic Texts from Qumran. 1992. ISBN 90 04 09586 1
10. Dimant, D. & U. Rappaport (eds.). *The Dead Sea Scrolls*. Forty Years of Research. 1992. ISBN 90 04 09679 5
11. Trebolle Barrera, J. & L. Vegas Montaner (eds.). *The Madrid Qumran Congress*. Proceedings of the International Congress on the Dead Sea Scrolls, Madrid 18-21 March 1991. 2 vols. 1993. ISBN 90 04 09771 6 set
12. Nitzan, B. *Qumran Prayer and Religious Poetry* 1994. ISBN 90 04 09658 2
13. Steudel, A. *Der Midrasch zur Eschatologie aus der Qumrangemeinde (4QMidrEschat$^{a.b}$)*. Materielle Rekonstruktion, Textbestand, Gattung und traditionsgeschichtliche Einordnung des durch 4Q174 („Florilegium") und 4Q177 („Catena A") repräsentierten Werkes aus den Qumranfunden. 1994. ISBN 90 04 09763 5
14. Swanson, D.D. *The Temple Scroll and the Bible*. The Methodology of 11QT. 1995. ISBN 90 04 09849 6
15. Brooke, G.J. (ed.). *New Qumran Texts and Studies*. Proceedings of the First Meeting of the International Organization for Qumran Studies, Paris 1992. With F. García Martínez. 1994. ISBN 90 04 10093 8
16. Dimant, D. & L.H. Schiffman. *Time to Prepare the Way in the Wilderness*. Papers on the Qumran Scrolls by Fellows of the Institute for Advanced Studies of the Hebrew University, Jerusalem, 1989-1990. 1995. ISBN 90 04 10225 6
17. Flint, P.W. *The Dead Sea Psalms Scrolls and the Book of Psalms*. 1997. ISBN 90 04 10341 4
18. Lange, A. *Weisheit und Prädestination*. Weisheitliche Urordnung und Prädestination in den Textfunden von Qumran. 1995. ISBN 90 04 10432 1
19. García Martínez, F. & D.W. Parry. *A Bibliography of the Finds in the Desert of Judah 1970-95*. Arranged by Author with Citation and Subject Indexes. 1996. ISBN 90 04 10588 3

20. Parry, D.W. & S.D. Ricks (eds.). *Current Research and Technological Developments on the Dead Sea Scrolls.* Conference on the Texts from the Judean Desert, Jerusalem, 30 April 1995. 1996. ISBN 90 04 10662 6
21. Metso, S. *The Textual Development of the Qumran Community Rule.* 1997. ISBN 90 04 10683 9
22. Herbert, E.D. *Reconstructing Biblical Dead Sea Scrolls.* A New Method applied to the Reconstruction of 4QSam[a]. 1997. ISBN 90 04 10684 7
23. Bernstein, M., F. García Martínez & J. Kampen (eds.). *Legal texts and Legal Issues.* Proceedings of the Second Meeting of the International Organization for Qumran Studies, Cambridge 1995. Published in honour of Joseph M. Baumgarten. 1997. ISBN 90 04 10829 7
25. Lefkovits, J.K. *The Copper Scroll – 3Q15: A Reevaluation.* A new Reading, Translation, and Commentary. ISBN 90 04 10685 5
26. Muraoka, T. & J.F. Elwolde (eds.). *The Hebrew of the Dead Sea Scrolls & Ben Sira.* Proceedings of a Symposium held at Leiden University, 11-14 December 1995. 1997. ISBN 90 04 10820 3
27. Falk, D.K. *Daily, Sabbath, and Festival Prayers in the Dead Sea Scrolls.* 1998. ISBN 90 04 10817 3
28. Stone, M.E. & E.G. Chazon (eds.). *Biblical Perspectives: Early Use and Interpretation of the Bible in Light of the Dead Sea Scrolls.* Proceedings of the First International Symposium of the Orion Center for the Study of the Dead Sea Scrolls and Associated Literature, 12-14 May, 1996. 1998. ISBN 90 04 10939 0
29. Hempel, C. *The Laws of the Damascus Document.* Sources, Tradition and Redaction. 1998. ISBN 90 04 11150 6
30. Parry, D.W. & E. Ulrich (eds.) *The Provo International Conference on the Dead Sea Scrolls.* Technological Innovations, New Texts, and Reformulated Issues. 1998. ISBN 90 04 11155 7
31. Chazon, E.G. & M. Stone (eds.) *Pseudepigraphic Perspectives.* The Apocrypha and Pseudepigrapha in Light of the Dead Sea Scrolls. Proceedings of the International Symposium of the Orion Center for the Study of the Dead Sea Scrolls and Associated Literature, 12-14 January, 1997. 1998. ISBN 90 04 11164 6
32. Parry, D.W. & E. Qimron (eds.) *The Great Isaiah Scroll (1QIsa^{a}).* A New Edition. 1998. ISBN 90 04 11277 4
33. Muraoka, T. & Elwolde, J.F. (eds.) *Sirach, Scrolls, and Sages.* Proceedings of a Second International Symposium on the Hebrew of the Dead Sea Scrolls, Ben Sira, and the Mishnah, held at Leiden University, 15-17 December 1997. 1999. ISBN 90 04 11553 6
34. Baumgarten, J.M. & E.G. Chazon & A. Punnick (eds.) *The Damascus Document: A Centennial of Discovery.* Proceedings of the Third International Symposium of the Orion Center for the Study of the Dead Sea Scrolls and Associated Literature, 4-8 February, 1998. 1999. ISBN 90 04 11462 9
35. Falk, D.K., F. García Martínez & E.M. Schuller, *Sapiential, Liturgical and Poetical Texts from Qumran.* Proceedings of the Third Meeting of the International Organization for Qumran Studies, Oslo 1998. Published in Memory of Maurice Baillet. 2000. ISBN 90 04 11684 2
36. Muraoka, T. & J.F. Elwolde (eds.), *Diggers at the Well.* Proceedings of a Third International Symposium on the Hebrew of the Dead Sea Scrolls and Ben Sira. 2000. ISBN 90 04 12002 5

37. Goodblatt, D., A. Pinnick & D.R. Schwartz (eds.), *Historical Perspectives: From the Hasmoneans to Bar Kokhba in Light of the Dead Sea Scrolls*. Proceedings of the Fourth International Symposium of the Orion Center for the Study of the Dead Sea Scrolls and Associated Literature, 27-31 January. 2001. ISBN 90 04 12007 6
38. Elgvin, T. *Wisdom and Apocalyptic in 4QInstruction*. ISBN 90 04 11424 6
(in preparation)
39. Brin, G. *The Concept of Time in the Bible and the Dead Sea Scrolls*. 2001. ISBN 90 04 12314 8
40. Murphy, C.M. *Wealth in the Dead Sea Scrolls and in the Qumran Community*. 2001. ISBN 90 0411934 5
41. Pinnick, A. *The Orion Center Bibliography of the Dead Sea Scrolls (1995-2000)*. 2001. ISBN 90 04 12366 0
42. Fletcher-Louis, C.H.T. *All the Glory of Adam*. Liturgical Anthropology in the Dead Sea Scrolls. 2001. ISBN 90 04 12326 1
43. Fincke, A. *The Samuel Scroll from Qumran*. 4QSam^a restored and compared to the Septuagint and 4QSam^c. 2001. ISBN 90 04 123709
44. Tigchelaar, E.J.C. *To Increase Learning for the Understanding Ones*. Reading and Reconstructing the Fragmentary Early Jewish Sapiential Text 4QInstruction. 2001. ISBN 90 04 11678 8
45 Grossman, M.L. *Reading for History in the Damascus Document*. A Methodological Method. 2002. ISBN 90 04 122524

www.ingramcontent.com/pod-product-compliance
Lightning Source LLC
Chambersburg PA
CBHW030338240426
43661CB00052B/1677